Terminal Services

For Microsoft Windows Server 2003

Advanced Technical Design Guide

Brian S. Madden
Ron Oglesby

BrianMadden.com Publishing
Washington DC
www.brianmadden.com

Terminal Services for Microsoft Windows Server 2003: Advanced Technical Design Guide

International Standard Book Number (ISBN): 0971151040

Library of Congress Catalog Card Number: 2003095654

Printed in the United States of America

First Printing, January 2004

BrianMadden.com Publishing offers discounts of this book when purchased in bulk. Visit www.brianmadden.com for details.

Editor
Leah B. Ogonek

Copy Editor
Holli Madden

Technical Advisors
Shane Broomhall
Gabe Knuth
G.K. Meier
Rob Zylowski

Publisher's Cataloging-in-Publication
(Provided by Quality Books, Inc.)

Madden, Brian S.
Terminal services for Microsoft Windows server 2003 : advanced technical design guide / Brian S. Madden, Ron Oglesby.
p. cm.
Includes index.
LCCN 2003095654
ISBN 0971151040

1. Microsoft Windows server. 2. Operating systems (Computers) 3. Client/server computing. I. Oglesby, Ron. II. Title.

QA76.76.O63M3335 2004 005.4'4769
QBI03-200689

Contents at a glance

Part 1. The Server Environment

Part 2. The User Environment

Part 3. The Client environment

Part 4. Operational Considerations

Appendixes & Index

How this book is structured

This book is made up of fifteen chapters divided into four parts.

Technical books such as this are not always read straight through from cover to cover. Instead, many readers immediately turn to the chapter that is most relevant to their current environment. To facilitate this, each chapter of this book has been structured and written like an independent white paper so that all of the information you need is in the chapter that you're reading. When outside information is needed, the chapter where it can be found is referenced.

If you have some experience with Terminal Server running on Windows Server 2003, Chapters 1 and 2 of this book are probably the most boring since they contain a lot of overview and introductory information. However, if you're new to Terminal Server, the chapters of this book have been structured logically so you can read them in the order that they are arranged.

Another important thing about this book is that the topics of each chapter are "solutions focused" instead of "tool focused." For example, you will not find a chapter that explains what every single option does in the Terminal Services MMC snap-in. (If you want that, read the Microsoft product documentation.) Instead, this book details where certain options can be configured only when you need to configure them as part of your design.

Lastly, this book is designed to provide a "real world" look at how Terminal Server is really used and how real environments are put together. As you can see by quickly flipping though it, this book is *not* full of screenshots. (In fact, there are only two.) In highly technical books, they are a waste of space and often used to make a book appear thicker. (No one needs to read a passage about how to install Terminal Server with a screenshot of the "Click Next to Continue" screen.) If you need screen shots, read the manual.

Part I: The Server Environment

Part II: The User Environment

Part III: The Client Environment

Part IV: Operational Considerations

Appendixes & Index

A Note from the Authors

This book is written with the reader in mind. As writers, we're always interested in hearing your thoughts about what worked, what didn't, what was good, and what wasn't. We'd love to hear any feedback or comments you might have.

Any mistakes or clarifications found in this book will be posted to www.brianmadden.com.

For anyone wondering, neither of us (or any of the technical advisors) work for Microsoft. Ron works for a consulting firm in Chicago called RapidApp, and Brian is self-employed.

We mention several companies, products, and vendors throughout this book. None of them paid us to be listed. These are simply companies whose products we've used and liked.

Thanks for reading, and we look forward to hearing from you.

Brian Madden & Ron Oglesby
January 2004
brian@brianmadden.com

Acknowledgements

From Brian…

Once again, this book wouldn't be here if my wife Holli wasn't as supportive as she was. I can't even count how many times she picked up my share of the housework so that I could write. She's super-fly.

Thanks also to Gabe and G.K. for letting me ask them countless questions at all hours. Even late at night. And weekends.

Finally, Leah did an awesome job with the editing. I'm consistently blown-away at her abilities. She's the reason this book is 500 pages instead of 600. (Trust me, that's a very good thing.)

From Ron…

I would like to say "thank you" to my wife Dina, who put up with all the weekends and evenings when I was glued to my laptop.

Thanks to Rob Zylowski at RapidApp for his feedback and encouragement, and thanks to all the guys at RapidApp for putting up with me. They are probably sick and tired of hearing about this book.

CHAPTER 1

Terminal Server Overview

This book is designed to provide you with practical, real-world information about the use and design of the Terminal Server components of Microsoft Windows Server 2003. Before addressing advanced technical details, we will first ensure that you have a good baseline understanding of Terminal Server and its features.

As you read through this book, keep in mind that each chapter was written separately and that it's okay to read them out of order. If you're new to Terminal Server, the chapter sequence will guide you through a logical progression of the components, beginning in this chapter with an overview of Windows 2003 Terminal Server.

Understanding the Terminal Server Solution

The Terminal Server component of Windows Server 2003 allows remote client devices to access and use Windows server desktops and applications. These client devices can be Windows, Macintosh, or Linux workstations, as well as wireless devices, laptops, set top boxes, network appliances, and X-Boxes. They access the server via a TCP/IP connection over the Internet, LAN, or a WAN network.

When Terminal Server is enabled on a Windows 2003 server, users can connect to virtual "desktops" on the server. A user's applications are executed on the server instead of on the client device, and the virtual desktop is transmitted across the network to the client device. Conceptually, this design is similar to remote control-type applications, such as PCAnywhere, CarbonCopy, and VNC.

However, unlike third-party remote control applications, a Windows 2003 server running Terminal Server uses a specially-modified kernel to allow many users to connect to the server simultaneously—each running his own unique virtual desktop. A single server can support dozens or even hundreds of users. Load-balancing techniques allow a group of servers to provide virtual desktops to thousands of simultaneous users.

"Remote" applications running on Windows 2003 Terminal Server virtual desktops have the ability to access and integrate with applications running locally on users' client devices. These local and remote applications can share disk drives, serial ports, printers, audio, and the Windows clipboard.

In some environments, administrators configure their users' workstations so that users access some applications locally and some remotely (from Terminal

Servers). Other administrators choose to fully centralize end-user management by configuring their users' client devices to access *all* of their applications via remote Terminal Servers. The users still see a Start Menu and a desktop on their screens—but the desktop is running on a remote Terminal Server instead of the local client device. This architecture is commonly referred to as "Server-Based Computing."

Server-Based Computing Components

In order to understand how server-based computing works, you must be familiar with the three main components that make up all server-based computing environments:

- A multi-user operating system.
- A remote presentation protocol.
- Client software and devices.

Let's examine each of these components.

Component 1. A Multi-user Operating System

Servers that power Windows server-based computing environments rely on a service (hosted by the Windows Server operating system) that allows multiple simultaneous users to connect and run applications and virtual desktops independent of each other. Whereas standard Windows servers allow multiple users to simultaneously connect to *resources* (such as files, printers, and services), only one user can be interactively logged onto the server console at a time. A multi-user operating system allows multiple users to connect and run *interactive* sessions (such as remote control sessions) on the server, independent of what any other user is doing. In the Microsoft world, this multi-user operating system is called "Terminal Server."

Back in the Windows NT 4.0 days, the Terminal Server version of the Windows operating system was separate from the rest of the Windows Server family. It required different media, service packs, and hotfixes. Beginning with Windows 2000 Server, the services and operating system components required for a multi-user Terminal Server environment have been included as part of the standard server product, allowing selection of the multi-user Terminal Server components during Windows configuration, just as any other available service. In Windows Server 2003 environments, Terminal Server capabilities are also built-in to the regular product.

In Windows Server 2003, there are "technically" two different versions of the Terminal Server components, and it's important that you don't confuse the two. The first (and the "real" Terminal Server that we care about in this book) is the Terminal Server component that is enabled via the Control Panel (Control Panel | Add or Remove Programs | Add/Remove Windows Components | Terminal Server) or via the "Manage Your Server" application (Add or remove a role | Terminal Server). This is the real Terminal Server option that you would enable to allow multiple users to remotely run sessions on your server.

The "other" Terminal Server option in Windows Server 2003 is called Remote Desktop, and is enabled or disabled via the My Computer properties screen. (Right-click My Computer | Properties | Remote Tab | Remote Desktop) Remote Desktop is a watered-down version of the real Terminal Server. It allows only a maximum of two concurrent remote user sessions. Its primary purpose is remote administration, allowing administrators to access and control servers from remote locations. (No more PCAnywhere on your servers!)

If you're familiar with Terminal Services on Windows 2000 Server, the Terminal Server component of Windows Server 2003 is the equivalent of Windows 2000 Terminal Services in application mode, and 2003's Remote Desktop is comparable to 2000's Terminal Services in administration mode.

Throughout this book, we'll use the terms "Terminal Server" and "Terminal Server 2003" interchangeably. Both expressions refer to "Microsoft Windows Server 2003 with the (real) Terminal Server component installed." They do *not* mean "Windows Server 2003 with the Remote Desktop option enabled."

Chapter 2 will provide more detail about the architecture of a Terminal Server and how the various components are installed and configured.

Component 2. A Remote Presentation Protocol

Now that we have a server that will allow multiple users to connect concurrently and execute applications, we need a way to for users to receive the virtual desktop they are running on the server and to send information back and forth between their client and the server. This is where the Remote Desktop Protocol (RDP) comes in. This RDP protocol, which runs on top of TCP/IP, acts as a conduit for transmitting this data between the client and the server. Updates from the user's session on the server (such as screen changes, sound, or print jobs) are sent from the server to the client. In turn, the client sends key strokes and mouse input from the client device to the session on the server via the RDP protocol.

Component 3. Client Devices and Client Software

In order to connect to the Terminal Server that hosts their sessions, users need client software loaded on their client devices. For Terminal Server 2003, this client software is known as the Microsoft Remote Desktop Connection Client, or simply "RDC Client."

For years, Microsoft called this an "RDP Client," not an RDC Client. If people look at you funny when you say "RDC," gently suggest they go to the Start Menu of a Windows XP system and see for themselves. Or, pretend that you're old-school and say "RDP Client."

Chapter 10 details the exact use of this client and how it operates and interacts with the server. For now, it's important to know that in order for users to access and use a Terminal Server session, they need some version of this client installed on their client device. There are several versions available from Microsoft, as well as third-party and open source versions.

What does "RDP" really mean?

When working with Terminal Servers, the term "RDP" will come up frequently. As mentioned previously, RDP is a protocol that runs on TCP/IP (much like SMTP, HTTP, etc.). However, you'll also see the term "RDP" used as a file type. RDP files have the extension .RDP, just as Word documents have .DOC extensions.

The RDP Protocol

The Remote Desktop Protocol (RDP) is the network protocol used by Terminal Service client devices for client-to-server session communication. The RDP protocol actually transmits keystrokes and mouse movements from the client to the server, and screen images from the server to the client. This protocol is also responsible for connecting client resources, such as mapping a user's clipboard, local drives, and local ports, as well as printing and encryption.

The RDP protocol is a high-level TCP/IP protocol that can run over port 3389 (although you can change this port). It is the only server-based computing protocol that Terminal Server supports out of the box, although various third-party products use their own protocols rather than RDP.

RDP Files

RDP files contain information that RDC clients use to connect to Terminal Servers. A user can simply double-click an RDP file to launch their RDC client and establish a session with the server specified in the RDP file. These files also contain settings and configuration information for the session, including screen resolution, color depth, and device options.

Terminal Server 2003 Features

In addition to the "core" Terminal Server functionality, Windows Server 2003 includes features that help you use Terminal Server in the real world. It's worth presenting an overview of these features here, although we'll study each in more depth throughout this book from a design and best practices standpoint.

If you've used previous versions of Terminal Server but are new to Windows Server 2003, you'll notice that several core features have been carried over from earlier products while others are completely new. Out of the box functionality of Terminal Server in Windows Server 2003 has come a long way since Microsoft first introduced the "Terminal Server Edition" of Windows NT Server 4.0 in 1998.

High Color Depth. In Windows Server 2003, The RDC client can now support client sessions with up to 24-bit color. This increases the system's usability with applications that require higher color depth.

Access to Client System Resources. When connected to a Terminal Server session, users can map back to their client's local disk drives, ports, printers, and clipboard, seamlessly integrating remote Terminal Server-based and local client device-based applications.

Client Time Zone Support. Terminal Server 2003 can automatically set the time zone of users' sessions based on the time zone of their client device. In special cases where the client devices do not keep track of local time zones, users can manually set their own time zones from within their server sessions. Time zone support is extremely beneficial in environments where users may be connecting to Terminal Servers from several different times zones for applications that are time sensitive, such as calendaring and email programs.

Printer Driver Management. Printing in server-based computing environments has always posed unique challenges (as you'll see in Chapter 8). One of these is in relation to print drivers. Terminal Server 2003 has several features to make managing print drivers easier.

- Print driver mapping capabilities allow you to remap client print driver names to appropriate server print driver names.
- Automatic print driver mapping has been enhanced from Windows 2000 to provide better matching in "near-miss" cases.
- When a driver match can't be made, the trusted driver path option lets you specify generic print drivers that are pre-approved for use on your Terminal Servers.

Printer Performance. In Terminal Server 2003, the print stream between the server and client is compressed, yielding better printing performance over slow links.

Windows Keys. When using Terminal Server sessions, special key sequences such as Alt-Tab or Ctrl-Esc are sent from the client to the remote session instead of being captured locally by the client. This improves users' experience by allowing them to use familiar key sequences in their sessions.

Load-Balanced Server Clusters. Multiple Terminal Servers can be logically grouped together to form a "Server Cluster." All servers in the cluster can then be used to host user sessions. An important fact about clusters in the Microsoft world is that these are not "true" clusters in the sense of service or application clustering. Rather, "clustering" has become a generic term at Microsoft that now includes Network Load Balancing. In reality, a load-balanced server cluster like this is a group of load-balanced servers using Windows Load Balancing or a third party load-balancer to route user sessions to available servers in the pool. Full Terminal Server clustering and load-balancing is discussed in Chapter 7.

Session Directory. One of the most important new Terminal Server features introduced in Windows Server 2003 is called Session Directory. This feature enables users to be automatically routed to Terminal Servers where they have disconnected sessions. In load-balanced environments with multiple servers, disconnected users can pick up where they left off, and are prevented from having multiple "orphaned" sessions on different servers. The Session Directory is not a load-balancing tool. Rather, it's a simple database that keeps track of which users have which sessions on which servers. However, third-party load-balancing products (and Microsoft's own Network Load Balancing) utilize the Session Directory to deliver a seamless experience to users. Session Directory (and load-balancing in general) is fully covered in Chapter 7.

Web-Based Client. Terminal Services 2003 supports a web-based, scriptable, Active-X Control for connection to Terminal servers. This client can allow users to access servers and server clusters simply by visiting a web page. You can even configure this client to allow administrators to connect to remote server consoles.

Remote Control. As the name implies, this feature allows certain users to remotely control other users' sessions. This capability is most often used for training and support purposes.

Single Session Policy. This Windows policy allows you to limit users to a single session on a particular server or server cluster.

Remote Desktop Users Group. This is a new Windows local group that, by default, is the only user group with the appropriate permissions to logon to the server via Terminal Server connections. As an administrator, this group gives you an easy way to limit access to your servers. In effect, it replaces the inefficient "Allow Login to Terminal Servers" user object property from previous Windows versions (although you can still use that method in Terminal Server 2003 if you prefer). The remote desktop users group allows you to specify user permissions on a server-by-server basis. Furthermore, since it's a local group, you can add global groups to it for easy control in large environments. See Chapter 12 for more information about security and group memberships.

Security Policy Editor. This administrative tool allows you to assign Terminal Server user rights individually or by group membership. You can also use it to allow users to log on to a Terminal Server without having to be a member of the Remote Desktop Users Group.

Software Restriction Policies. These restriction policies replace the annoying Application Security (AppSec) tool used in previous versions of Terminal Server. They let you restrict the applications that can be executed by specified users simplifying the tasks associated with securing a Terminal Server.

Encryption. By default, all connections to Terminal Servers are secured by a bi-directional, 128-bit RC4 encryption algorithm.

Smart Card Authentication. For users connecting from client devices configured to utilize smart cards, their Windows logon credentials can be passed to Terminal Server's when new sessions are established. Full smart card design options are covered in Chapter 12.

Improved Terminal Server Licensing. There are now two different ways to license users for Terminal Server in Windows Server 2003: per user or per device. "Per User" mode assigns a Terminal Server Client Access License (TS CAL) to a specific user account, and that user can log on from as many client devices as he wants. The "Per Device" licensing mode allows you to permanently assign a TS CAL to a specific piece of hardware, and any user may access a Terminal Server with that hardware device. This option lends flexibility in choosing a licensing mode the best fits your environment. (Or, in the case of Microsoft licensing, you can choose the least "worst fit".) Another big licensing change introduced in Windows Server 2003 is the ability to install the Terminal Server Licensing Service on any Windows 2003 server in Active Directory environments. In Windows 2000, this service had to run on a domain controller. See Chapter 4 for all the gory details of Terminal Server licensing.

Group Policy Terminal Server Management. In Windows Server 2003, administrators can configure per-server Terminal Server settings via group policies within Active Directory. This design allows large groups of servers to be managed or configured simultaneously, and helps to reduce administrative overhead for small changes that are required on every server.

Group Policy Templates. Terminal Server Group Policy Templates have been added to Windows 2003. These templates allow you to easily configure and apply server settings across multiple servers simultaneously.

Terminal Services Manager. The Terminal Services Manager tool has been improved from previous versions to allow for easier management of large groups of servers. The improved tool gives direct access to a server by name and can even store a list of "favorite" servers.

Terminal Server Licensing Manager. This tool allows you to manage, add, and activate Terminal Server Client Access Licenses in your environment. It has been completely rewritten for Windows Server 2003, and is now much easier to use.

Windows Management Interface (WMI) Provider. A full WMI provider in Windows Server 2003 allows for completely scripted configuration of Terminal Server settings. WMI aliases have been provided to allow for simple scripting of frequently used tasks.

Active Directory Service Interfaces (ADSI). An ADSI provider allows programmatic access to per-user attributes such as Terminal Service profile settings, home directory settings, and session virtual channel settings. You can now script just about anything in Terminal Server 2003.

Connect to Console Session. In Terminal Server 2003, administrators can connect to the actual server console through a remote RDP session. This is useful when you need to perform tasks that are "not supported" via Terminal Services.

Extending Terminal Server 2003

Terminal Server 2003 is a robust platform on which to deploy applications. However, as with many Microsoft products, there are situations in which you might want to extend the base capabilities. Several third party vendors offer middleware components and utilities for Terminal Server that help increase the reach of the product.

Two companies offer end-to-end server-based computing solutions: Citrix and Tarantella. Citrix MetaFrame and Tarantella New Moon Canaveral iQ are products that install on top of Terminal Server and offer advanced load-management, security, client options, and administrative tools. While this book won't go into the details of these two products, we will provide you with a solid foundation of knowledge that you can use to determine if your environment's requirements can be met with pure Terminal Services or if a third-party solution is required. A comparison of third party products and Terminal Server can be found in the appendix.)

Furthermore, there are dozens and dozens of specialty software products designed specifically for server-based computing environments. From security to printing to performance enhancement to management, these products can simplify your life as a Terminal Server administrator. Rather than focusing on all these products at once, this book mentions relevant third-party products as they are relevant, and includes a full list of third-party products and vendor websites in the appendix. (You may always refer to `www.brianmadden.com` for a current list of third party products and vendors.)

CHAPTER 2

Terminal Server Architecture

This chapter and the next can be logically grouped together as both focus on the architecture of Terminal Server environments. This chapter covers the architectural components of Terminal Server itself. Chapter 3 addresses the architecture of the Terminal Server network environment, including those factors affecting how Terminal Servers are placed on the network and linked together.

We'll first examine how Terminal Services works. Let's take a quick tour of the various pieces and subsystems of a Terminal Server running on Windows Server 2003 and then discuss the decisions that you'll have to make before installation.

How Terminal Server Works

A Terminal Server is basically the same as the regular Windows Server operating system except that in Terminal Server environments, key components have been added or modified to provide support for multiple, simultaneous users.

Microsoft Windows has always been a "multi-user" operating system in the sense that multiple users could be connected to a single server at any given time. However, these users were connected to file services or printer services on the servers. They ran their local Windows interfaces on their local computers, and the server only supported one desktop interface via the local keyboard, mouse, and monitor. The main difference with Terminal Server is that multiple users can run their own Windows desktop sessions on the server. So Terminal Server is "multi-user" in the sense that it supports multiple desktop interfaces. Some people like to think of this as a "remote control" environment, except that the Terminal Server can accommodate many users "remote controlling" it at the same time, with each user doing something completely different.

In order for Terminal Server to support multiple user sessions, some changes had to be made to it from the regular Microsoft Windows server software. There are two fundamental differences between a regular Windows Server and one with Terminal Server installed:

- When Terminal Server is installed on a Windows 2003 server, certain core components of the Windows operating system are modified to support multiple, simultaneous user interfaces. For example, the virtual memory manager and the object manager are modified to support multiple, simultaneous desktop interfaces without getting confused. These are major modifications, requiring you to reboot the system after installing Terminal Server.

- New services and components are added when Terminal Server is installed that allow the server to support multiple user sessions. The most important of these is the "Terminal Server" service. This service, running deep inside the server, is responsible for interfacing the multiple user sessions with the operating system. It's also responsible for functions such as creating sessions, receiving users, and ending sessions.

Terminal Server Components

Although it seems that the Terminal Server is basically a glorified PCAnywhere system, it's actually a complex system made up of several different components, subsystems, and interfaces. A more complete diagram of the Terminal Server components is shown in Figure 2.1. Refer to it as you read through the next few sections describing each component that makes up Windows 2003 Terminal Server.

Figure 2.1 Terminal Server 2003 components

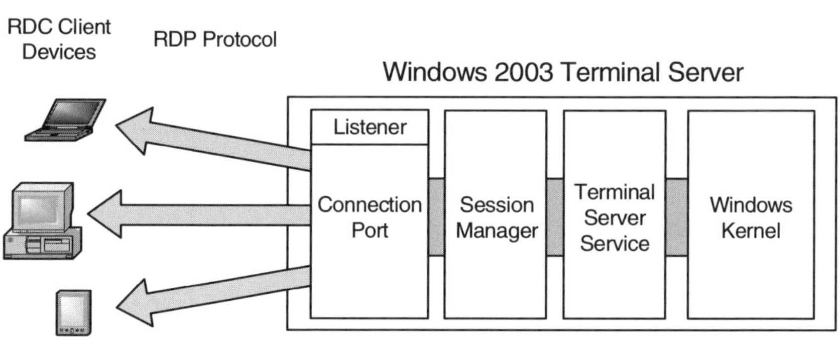

The Windows Server 2003 Kernel

You will recall that a key component of any server-based computing environment is a multi-user operating system. In Windows Server 2003, this system is controlled by the kernel.

Windows Server 2003 needs a way to distance critical operating system components from all the crazy users. To achieve this, Windows processes operate in one of two modes: user mode or kernel mode. Thinking back to your Windows NT training, you'll remember that a user mode application cannot write directly to the OS memory. Instead, it has full access to its own 4GB memory space. An operating system component called the virtual memory manager (which itself runs in kernel mode) controls all of this and writes to the system memory on behalf of the user-mode application.

In Terminal Server environments, the separation of user mode and kernel mode applications allows the system to separate and isolate the users. One users' application crash won't take down the whole system. (Of course you're thinking that an application crash *can* take down a system, however, that's usually tied to device drivers which run in kernel mode.)

In "standard" (i.e. non-Terminal Server) Windows environments where only a single user logs on interactively, all kernel-mode processes live happily together in one memory area and namespace. In multi-user environments like Terminal Server, however, this sharing won't work since requests from different users' sessions could conflict with one another. The kernel on a Terminal Server is consequently multi-session aware; it keeps each user's session separate with isolated processes and memory. Windows Server 2003 makes some changes to the kernel when the Terminal Server component is installed to accomplish this.

First, the server places some of the kernel's memory address space into virtual memory. This allows what would be conflicting requests in a single-user environment to be processed properly in the multi-user environment, and for multiple instances of kernel-mode device drivers to be loaded and used by multiple users (the reason why one user can *technically* crash the whole system).

Some system processes are not session-specific, meaning that all users in all sessions will need access to them. These processes are stored in a single (global) memory area shared by all users.

A side-effect of sharing processes like this in a Terminal Server environment is that sometimes you'll run into processes that are not "session aware." One potential (and kind of funny) result can be error messages that are displayed on the server console from applications running within a user's session. Since there's usually no one in the server room to acknowledge the message, there is the potential to prevent a user's application from continuing.

The Terminal Services Service

"The Terminal Services Service" refers to a regular Windows service (Start | Administrative Tools | Services) called "Terminal Services." In the real world, people usually refer to it as the "Terminal Service," and they use the term "Terminal Server" when referring to a Windows Server that's running the Terminal Service.

If the multi-user kernel is the foundation of server-based computing in Windows Server 2003, the Terminal Service is the cornerstone. This service (loaded via termserv.dll) is loaded right after the kernel comes online. After the server's console (keyboard, video and mouse drivers) is loaded, the Terminal Service initiates the Session Manager subsystem (smss.exe) responsible for managing and tracking all user sessions on the server.

Terminal Server Sessions

A new session is created each time a user logs onto Terminal Server. A session essentially consists of a virtual desktop from which the user can run applications and with which he can interact just as with a workstation. A server session should not be confused with the server console, since a session is not a remote control of the console but actually a new desktop separate from the console.

Each time a user connects to a Terminal Server and creates this "virtual desktop," a unique session ID number is created to differentiate the user (and therefore the user's processes) from all other sessions and users. Session IDs also enable the server to keep memory separate for each user's session. When a user logs off from a Terminal Services client, the session that was being used is deleted and the processes and memory that were launched and used by that session are removed. Each Terminal Server tracks its own Session IDs and handles the task of issuing, tracking, and removing them.

Since server sessions are "virtual" (and memory and processes are kept separate between sessions), an application crash or lockup in one session should not affect any other user sessions, even if other users are using the same application.

However, the key phrase here is "should not" affect other users. Even though user sessions are separate on a server, they still share server resources and certain segments of code. If one user invokes a process that causes the server to blue screen, this will obviously have an effect on the other users. On the other hand, simple occurrences like an application hanging on a timed out request or Microsoft Word crashing when a user opens a corrupt document will not be seen by the other users (within their own sessions) on the system.

Session States

Since a session is really a user's desktop, there are times that a session can be in various different states, much like a normal workstation. For example, if a user walks away from their workstation for a period of time, the workstation does not turn off. Rather, it is merely idle, waiting for user input. Terminal server sessions behave much the same, and can be in one of a number of different states depending on the user's activity (or inactivity), connectivity between the client and server, and session time out settings.

Figure 2.2 Each Terminal Server maintains many separate user sessions

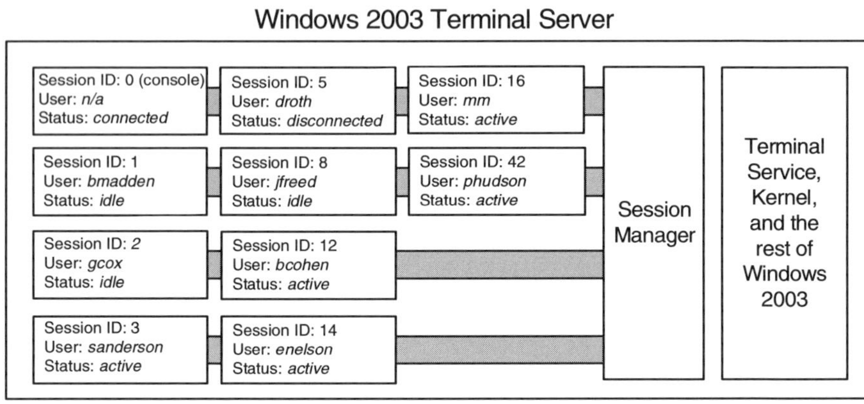

All user sessions on a Terminal Server must be in one of the following six states:

- *Active* is a live and active user. The user is interacting with the Terminal Server session and has not had a period of inactivity or a network disconnect from the server. This is the "normal" state of a session.
- *Idle* is the state a session goes into when there is no input from the user for a specified period of time.
- *Disconnected* sessions occur when the processes and programs of a "live" session are running but no RDC client is connected. (If you skipped the first chapter, "RDC Client" is the new name for the RDP Client.) The common cause is a network disconnection or when a user clicks the "X" in the upper right corner of their RDC client software. A user can reconnect to his disconnected session to bring it back to an "active" state (and to pick up with his work right where he left off). Think of a disconnected session like a locked workstation, except that the user can "unlock" his workstation from any computer in the building.
- *Connected* sessions are in a state in which a client device is connected to a server session, but no user is logged on, much like the CTRL+ALT+DEL prompt on a workstation.
- *Down* is a temporary state in which a session is being terminated and processes within the session are being killed. *Down* is the final state of a session before it ends.

- *Listen* is a state only seen on listener ports that are ready to accept inbound connections. This state does not apply to regular sessions. Rather, it applies to the processes running on the server that wait for (listen for) new session connection requests.

In most environments, administrators configure sessions with various timeouts. You can limit the amount of time that a single session can be open, or you can automatically convert an idle session to a disconnected session. Timeouts help to limit the amount of time the server spends executing processes for users that really are not working on the server. We'll cover the exact techniques and strategies for configuring these later in this book.

Connection Ports and Listeners

Every user's RDP session connects to the Terminal Server through a connection port. A connection port (commonly referred to only as a "connection") is a virtual port on the server associated with a specific network card and protocol combination.

One Terminal Server connection port is automatically created when the Terminal Server component is installed. By default, it allows any user in the "remote desktop users" group to connect to Terminal Server sessions on the server via any network card. However, even though the default connection port works with any network card with TCP/IP installed, Terminal Server connection ports are really network card-specific. You can configure a server with multiple network cards to have multiple Terminal Server connection ports—one for each card. In fact, each connection can have entirely different properties and permissions.

Figure 2.3 A Terminal Server with multiple connection ports

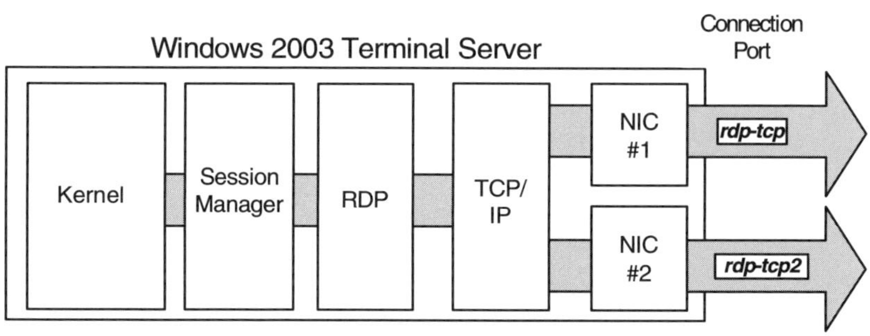

Terminal Server connections and their associated listeners can be configured in two places. The first is via the Terminal Services Configuration (TSC) MMC snap-in. You can use the TSC to configure options for RDP-based Terminal Server connections, such as settings, permissions, and over which network card a connection is valid. The second way to configure Terminal Server connections is via an Active Directory Group Policy Object (GPO) within a Windows 2003 domain. This functionality lets you assign connections for multiple servers contained with an OU in Active Directory.

Listeners

Each Terminal Server connection port has a subcomponent called a "listener." The listener component "listens" on a specific network card and protocol combination for which the connection port is configured. When a user wants to establish a new session on the server, they use their RDC client software to contact the server. The server's listener picks up the client request and forwards it on to the session manager. The listener then goes back to listening for more connection requests.

Virtual Channels

As we discussed previously, Microsoft's RDP protocol running on TCP/IP is the actual protocol that connects users to server sessions. We also mentioned that this protocol can support more than just pure virtual desktops. RDP allows remote session audio from the server to be channeled to the client device's speakers. It also allows for devices plugged into the client's serial ports to appear as if they're plugged into the server. These "extras" are available via RDP's virtual channels. A virtual channel is simply a mechanism to move data back and forth between a Terminal Server session and a client. By default, the RDP protocol on Terminal Server 2003 contains several virtual channels.

- *Audio*: Sound events generated on the server session are redirected through the RDP protocol to the RDC client device, where they are played on the client's speakers.
- *Client Drives:* Local disk drives on the client device are made available to the server, so that users can access both server drives and their local client device drives within their remote sessions.
- *Printers:* Printers available to the client device before a session is launched on a Terminal Server are made available to users from within their server sessions. Users can then print to their standard Windows printers, including printers directly attached to their client devices.
- *Serial Ports*: The serial port virtual channel allows devices plugged-in to a client device's serial port to be accessed via its remote Terminal Server sessions.
- *Windows Clipboard:* In order to integrate local applications with remote Terminal Server sessions, the Windows clipboard virtual channel

synchronizes the contents of the remote Terminal Server clipboard with the contents of the client device's clipboard. Users can seamlessly cut and paste between local and remote applications.

If default virtual channels don't meet your needs, MSDN and the Windows Server 2003 SDKs contain information on writing your own custom virtual channels. A virtual channel is a combination of two components—a client-side component and a server-side component. Both can send and receive data via the virtual channel, allowing for one- or two-way communication. Virtual channels can also be RDP independent, which means that you can customize to your environment without upgrading or changing the actual client or server software.

Why all the focus on virtual channels? Although this is not a developer's book and you'll probably never develop your own virtual channel, it's critical that you understand how they work. Just about every third-party add-on product for Terminal Server makes use of virtual channels. Understanding how virtual channels work will help you troubleshoot the third-party products that you'll undoubtedly come across in your Terminal Server career.

With that said, let's take a final look at the architecture of a virtual channel. Refer to Figure 2.4.

Figure 2.4 Terminal Server 2003's virtual channel architecture

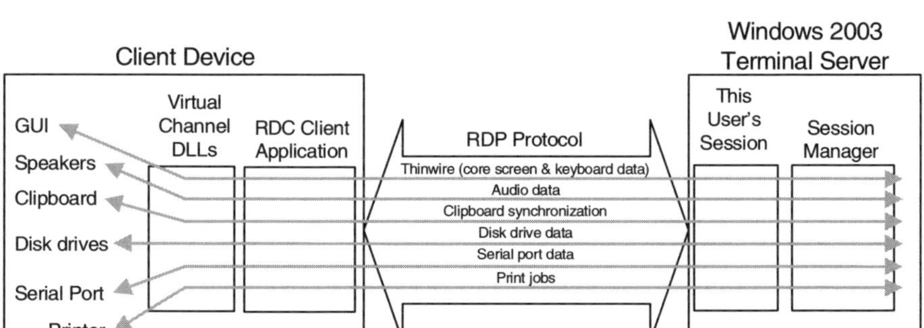

The server-side virtual channel component is usually an executable running on the Terminal Server. This component must be a user-mode component, since the server uses the session ID to determine which client-side session it should transmit to and receive data from.

The client-side virtual channel component is usually a DLL provided by Microsoft, the third-party software vendor, or custom-written by your developers. The DLL must be loaded on the client computer when the RDC client program is launched and begins the connection to the server. In most cases this is scripted or done programmatically at the client level.

How all these Components Fit Together

Now that you understand each of the various Terminal Server components, let's see how they all fit together. Follow the process that takes place as a client connection is made, referring to Figure 2.5.

Figure 2.5 A new session is established

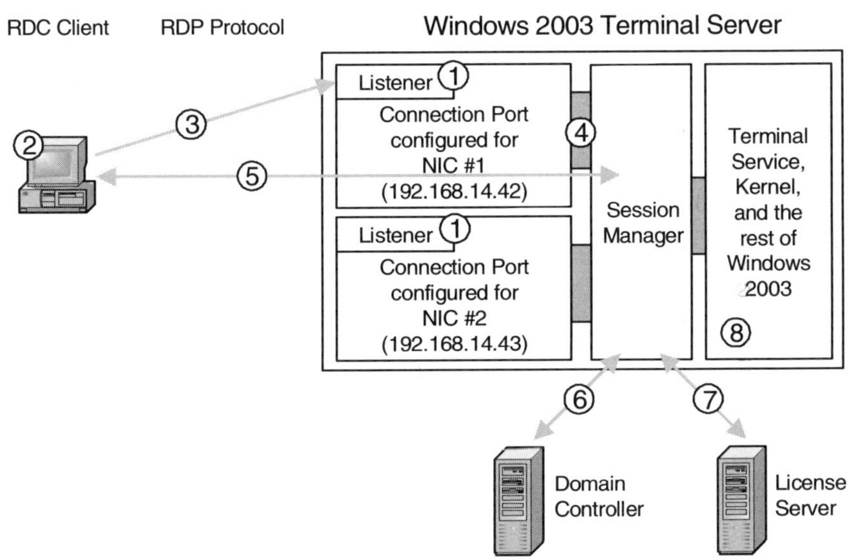

1. Before anything happens, the listeners on the Terminal Server watch certain network cards, IP address, and TCP port combinations for inbound requests to start sessions.

2. A user decides to use a remote application, so she launches her RDC client and requests a connection to "server1." Her RDC client checks to see what virtual channel DLLs are installed.

3. In this environment, the name "server1" refers to IP address 192.168.14.42 (which happens to be NIC #1 in this server). The user's RDC client sends a session connection request to 192.168.14.42.

4. The server's listener picks up the request and hands it off to the session manager. As the session manager takes over, the listener resumes listening for more sessions.
5. The server negotiates with the requesting client for its encryption level and virtual channel capabilities.
6. The user is then authenticated to the domain and her rights are checked for access to the connection.
7. The Microsoft licenses are verified. The server client access license is verified first, and then the Terminal Server client access license is verified. (Licensing is detailed in Chapter 4.)
8. At this point, the user session is ready to begin. The logon scripts run and the desktop is loaded.

In Windows Server 2003, a listener port is associated with a "connection." In fact, the two terms are almost interchangeable. You configure properties for a connection, and the connection's listener port is modified appropriately.

Now that we've covered all of the components that make up a Windows 2003 Terminal Server, turn to the requirements.

Windows Server 2003 Requirements

At this point, we're not ready to address the actual hardware requirements of the servers themselves. (That's covered fully in Chapters 5 and 13.) Instead, we're going to look at operating system requirements and configuration options that will help you make decisions environment design. First, we need to determine which flavor of Windows Server 2003 you will use.

Windows 2003 Server Versions

Right off the bat you'll be confronted with a major decision, namely, which version of Windows Server 2003 to use. Windows Server 2003 comes in 32- and 64-bit versions. 32-bit versions are segmented into Web Server, Standard Server, Enterprise Server, and Datacenter Server.

The Web Server version of Windows Server 2003 does not have the ability to host Terminal Server sessions for applications (although it does allow for that two-user limited remote desktop option). So we can toss the Web Server out of the mix right away.

There are pages and pages of small differences between the other three versions of Windows 2003, but Figure 2.6 highlights those that actually impact Terminal Server environments.

Figure 2.6 32-bit Windows Server 2003 Terminal Server features

Feature	Standard	Enterprise	Datacenter
Supports Terminal Services	•	•	•
Network Load Balancing Clusters	•	•	•
Can utilize a Session Directory		•	•
Can host a Session Directory	•	•	•
Cluster Services		•	•
Max number of processors	4	8	32
Max memory	4GB	32GB	64GB

In terms of basic Terminal Server functionality, all three versions work in the same way. The version of server you choose will ultimately be decided by your final design and the features you are required to implement.

The two most important differences are the number of processors and the amount of memory that each server supports. The version of Windows Server 2003 that you choose will depend on whether you build many little servers or a few big ones. (This decision is critical, and fully covered in Chapter 5.)

The other important difference is that the Standard Server version can't use Session Directory. If you're planning on using a third-party product such as Citrix MetaFrame, Tarantella New Moon Canaveral iQ, or RES PowerFure, then this might not matter and you can just use Standard Server. However, if you're going for a pure Terminal Server environment and want your users to be able to connect back into disconnected sessions in a multi-server environment, you'll need Session Directory, and thus at least the Enterprise Server version.

If you do plan on using a third-party product, remember that each implements different types of management and load-balancing schemes. Before deciding on a Windows Server version, look at what the product offers and requires so as to avoid wasting extra money on server licenses that are not required.

Probably in 99% of cases, the Session Directory or the processor and memory limitations are the reasons why people choose Enterprise Server over Standard Server. While it's true that Enterprise Server also supports additional functionality such as clustering, this functionality is rarely (if ever) used on the Terminal

Servers themselves, since user sessions (unlike standard services or server applications) cannot be clustered.

Server Hardware Recommendations

In addition to the underlying operating system, there are certain server hardware requirements that your Terminal Servers will have to meet in order to perform at acceptable levels. From a "bare minimum" standpoint, any computer that can run Windows Server 2003 can run Terminal Services. From a "practical" standpoint, however, there are different factors to consider relating to server hardware.

The basic idea here is that you're building a high-end workstation for your users. When designing your servers, throw the thoughts of file server out the window and start with what it would take for a high performing workstation. This generally amounts to going heavy on the processor and memory and light on the disk subsystem.

Before you buy a bunch of used IDE drives for your servers, let's expand on the phrase "light on the disk subsystem." You do not have to set up this server with five large SCSI drives configured in a RAID 5 array. A basic set of mirrored SCSI drives or *maybe* a small 3-drive RAID 5 array would suffice. Remember that since this is a workstation, no data should be stored on these servers and the amount of available drive space should not be an issue. See Chapter 5 for the full story about installing applications and needed drive space on your Terminal Servers.

Truthfully, properly sizing a Terminal Server is more of an exercise in the performance optimization of your overall Terminal Server environment than it is meeting a raw hardware requirements checklist. For this reason, the topic of Terminal Server optimization and server sizing deserves its own chapter (see Chapter 13).

Enabling Terminal Services

This book focuses on the advanced technical design of a Terminal Server environment and providing you with the knowledge to design real-world solutions. A walk-through of the service installation that takes you from screenshot to screenshot is therefore not included. (However, a Flash video of that walk-through is available at `www.brianmadden.com`.)

This section will, however, describe (from a technical standpoint) the process that takes place when you enable Terminal Services.

Unlike Windows 2000 Server, which installed with a dual-mode Terminal Services component, Windows Server 2003 separates the Remote Administration and Terminal Services functionality into separate configurable components. Remote Desktop Administration is installed by default and allows only Administrators to connect. This type of installation can cause confusion, because being able to use a Terminal Services client to connect to a server doesn't necessarily mean that Terminal Services is actually installed. If Windows 2003 is already installed you'll have to add Terminal Services manually. (Control Panel | Add or Remove Programs | Add/Remove Windows Components | Terminal Server) or (Manage Your Server tool | Add or remove a role | Terminal Server)

Let's pause here for a note on *when* to install Terminal Services. While it's true that you can technically go into the Add or Remove Programs wizard at any time to add this service, this is not recommended.

You really need to have the Terminal Server components installed *before* any applications are installed. Application installs on a Terminal Server are different from those on a normal server, and some applications do not respond well to being installed in one mode and used in another. While improvements have been made over the last couple of years it's still good practice to configure Terminal Services prior to installing any applications.

Ideally, you'll want to read through this entire book before building your production servers. If you just want to install Terminal Server as fast as possible, then you should be safe by just selecting the default options. Many people use this approach to build a test server. Then they read through this book trying the different options as they go. Finally, they complete their design and rebuild their server for "production" use.

Security Settings Installation Options

During installation of Terminal Services, you'll be asked to configure the default permissions for application compatibility. This is a bit misleading, since what you're really setting are the default permissions for your users when accessing system files and registry keys.

The first (and default) option is "Full Security," the most restrictive and obviously most secure. Choosing this option sets the default permissions on the file system and registry with what Microsoft feels applications and users will require.

In terms of NTFS permissions, the full security option configures most files and directories for Read and Execute access for regular users. The full security option also tightens the security of the registry; making most of the HKEY Local Machine hive read-only for standard users while still granting Read and Write access to most of each user's HKEY Current User hive. (See Chapter 12 for details.)

The drawback to choosing the full security option is that some older applications may not work. Assume you have an application that installs to *c:\Program Files\My App*. By default, the application directory and files inherit the directory security of settings of the *c:\Program Files* directory (which is read and execute). However, if your application requires that a temporary file be written to its program location when it's launched, an error will occur since the full security option does not allow Write access to that directory. This same example can be applied to almost any directory or registry key on the system. If the application needs to modify anything on the server, the user must have access permissions to the file or registry location being modified. There is no magic bullet workaround for basic access permissions.

The second option you can choose is "Relaxed Security." This option configures the security on the file system and critical registry keys to allow older applications to run. (This refers mainly to applications that were not designed with Terminal Server in mind.) Don't be fooled into thinking that the relaxed security option gives users full access to everything, because it doesn't. It loosens security in certain locations that older applications are known to use.

The general consensus is to always start out with Full Security. If required, you can return and manually loosen up permissions on the files or registry locations that are required without having a blanket effect on the entire system. Don't worry too much about it at this point. You can use the Terminal Services Configuration snap-in to the MMC to reset a system's security to "full" or "relaxed" at any time, as many times as you want.

CHAPTER 3

Terminal Server Network Architecture

In this chapter, we'll examine the necessary considerations for designing your Terminal Server network architecture. "Network architecture" refers to the Terminal Server environment as it relates to the network, not the specifics of individual servers.

It's crucial that your Terminal Server architecture is able to support your users over your existing network. Regardless of whether you're planning on scaling your environment to support worldwide users or you're building one server that may be the foundation for the future, you must address several aspects, including:

- Terminal Server placement (the location of your servers on the network)
- Supporting server placement

Placement of Terminal Servers

As you'll see throughout this book, quite of bit of behind-the-scenes communication takes place in Terminal Server environments. To understand where to best locate your Terminal Servers, consider the communication that takes place between physical servers on the network.

Figure 3.1 Terminal Server network communication

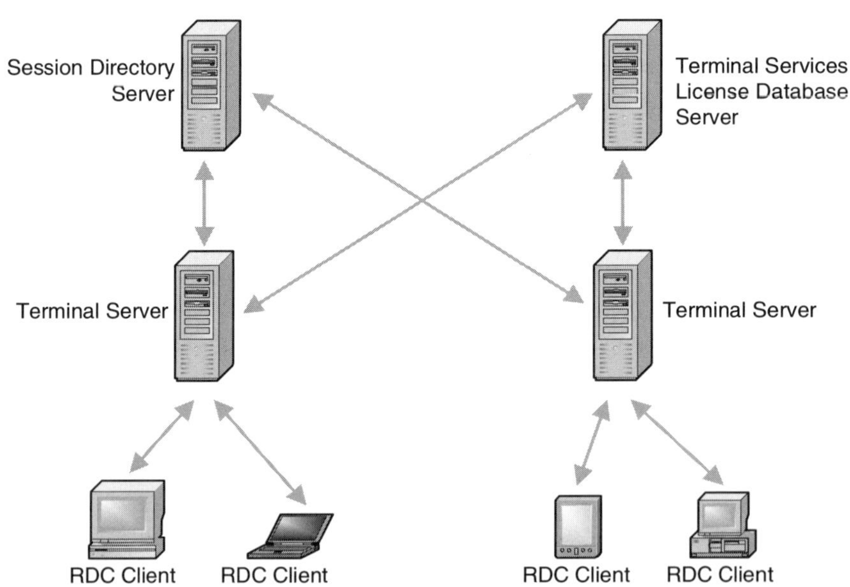

The key here is to determine where the servers should be located in relation to the data and users. Consider the environment in Figure 3.2 consisting of two office locations. Let's assume that users from both offices need to access a database-driven application housed in the main office.

Figure 3.2 Users in two offices need access to the same database application

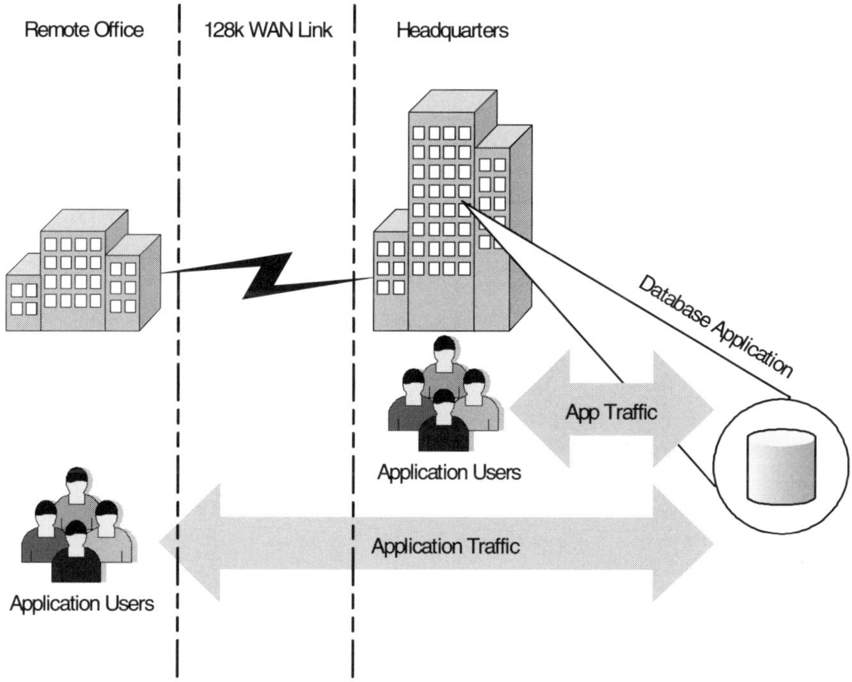

This company's IT department has decided to use Terminal Server to ease application deployment and get the best possible performance for remote users. The company is faced with two choices when it comes to the location of the Terminal Server for the remote users—they can either put the Terminal Server at the remote office with the users, or at the main office with the database.

While both choices would allow the company to manage the users' applications, putting the server near the database will yield the best performance. (See Figure 3.3 on the next page.) The network traffic between the database and the client application running on the Terminal Server is much heavier than the RDP user session traffic between the Terminal Server and the user. By placing the Terminal Server at the main office, the database client software installed on the Terminal Server is located near the database itself. Application performance is excellent due to this close proximity, and only RDP session traffic need cross the expensive, slow WAN link.

Figure 3.3 A Terminal Server at the main office

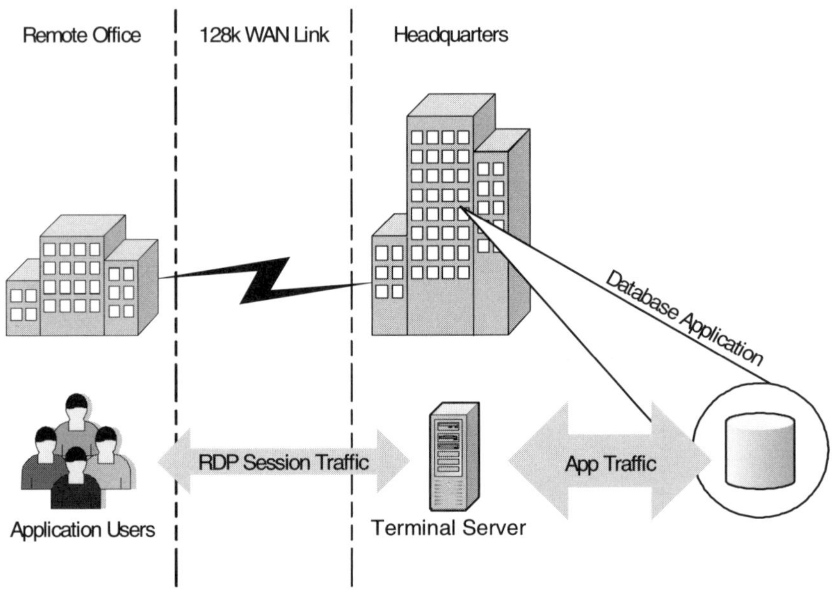

Now consider the other possible server placement option for this company. If the Terminal Server was located at the remote office (as in Figure 3.4 on the facing page), heavy database traffic would still have to cross the WAN while light, efficient RDP session traffic would be confined the remote office's local LAN, where bandwidth is plentiful. Putting the server at the remote office would not benefit application performance from an end user's point-of-view since the level of database traffic on the WAN is no different than if they weren't using Terminal Server.

As this simple example shows, it's desirable to place the Terminal Server close to the data source rather than close to the users. Microsoft's RDP protocol is designed to work over slow WAN links. Heavy application data traffic flowing between the Terminal Server and the data server remains on a local LAN.

Figure 3.4 Terminal Server placement at the remote office

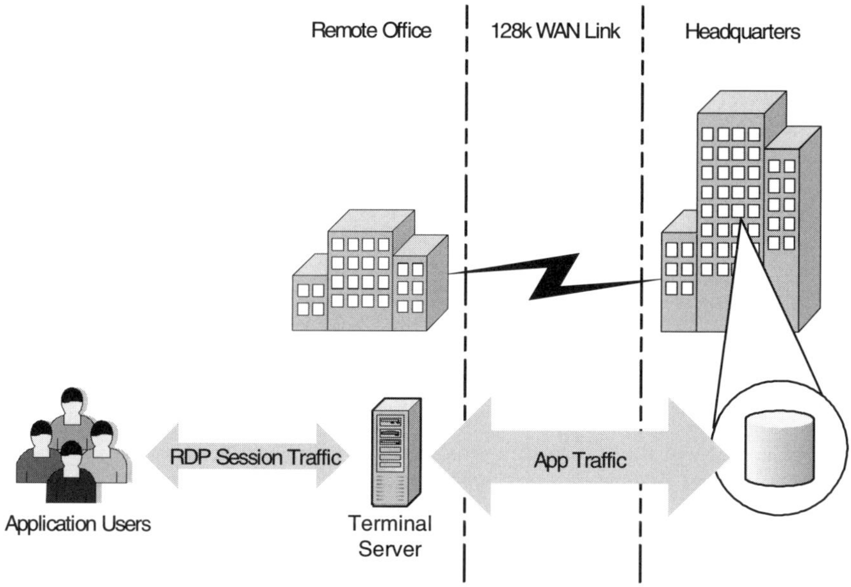

Why should you care about server placement?

As shown in the previous example, the placement of your Terminal Servers will directly impact:

- Users' session performance
- Network bandwidth usage
- Server management

Users' Session Performance

Performance of the users' sessions depends not only on the network speed between the user and the Terminal Server, but also on the speed between the Terminal Server and the data the user needs. It does no good to put a Terminal Server on the same LAN link as a user if that server must access files that are located across a 56K connection.

Performance must be balanced with the network latency between the user and the server. Users won't want to use Terminal Server applications with a two-second delay from the time they hit a key until the time the character appears on the screen.

Network Bandwidth Usage

Network bandwidth usage is directly affected by the location of the Terminal Server. Average RPD user sessions require only about 31KB per second. Many n-tier business applications (such as Baan, SAP, and PeopleSoft) require much more. If your Terminal Server is on the wrong side of the network you won't save any bandwidth by using it.

Server Management

Ultimately, someone (maybe you?) is going to need to maintain and manage the Terminal Servers. It's usually much easier for administrators to maintain them if the application servers and the Terminal Servers are both at the same physical location.

What are the server placement options?

Even after examining the complexities that arise when deciding where to put your Terminal Servers, there are really only two possible options:

- Distribute the servers throughout your environment, balancing some near each data source.
- Put all Terminal Servers in the same place, in one big datacenter.

As with all decisions, option point has distinct advantages and disadvantages that must be considered when designing the final solution.

Option 1. Terminal Servers Placed in many Locations

You may need to put multiple Terminal Servers in multiple different locations if your users need to access data that is stored in different locations. Doing so ensures that users' application sessions are close to the data they need.

In this situation, a user would simply connect to multiple Terminal Servers in order to access his data (see Figure 3.5 on the facing page). An added benefit here is that there is not one single point of failure, since losing access to one data center only affects some applications.

The downside to having Terminal Servers in multiple locations is that your overall environment becomes more complex. Servers must be managed in several physical locations. User will have to access multiple servers through different connections. It is inevitable that some data will only exist in one place, and that users will need to access it from every Terminal Server regardless of its location. (Windows roaming profiles are a good example.) Lastly, a multi-server Terminal Server environment requires that each of the servers communicate with the required backend services like Terminal Services Licensing and the

Session Directory. When all Terminal Servers are located on the same LAN, managing these services is easy since everything is centralized. However, when Terminal Servers span multiple physical locations connected by WAN links, this communication must be managed or the backend services must be deployed to the WAN sites also. (More information on planning for an enterprise deployment is found in Chapter 14.)

Figure 3.5 Multiple Terminal Servers provide fast access to data

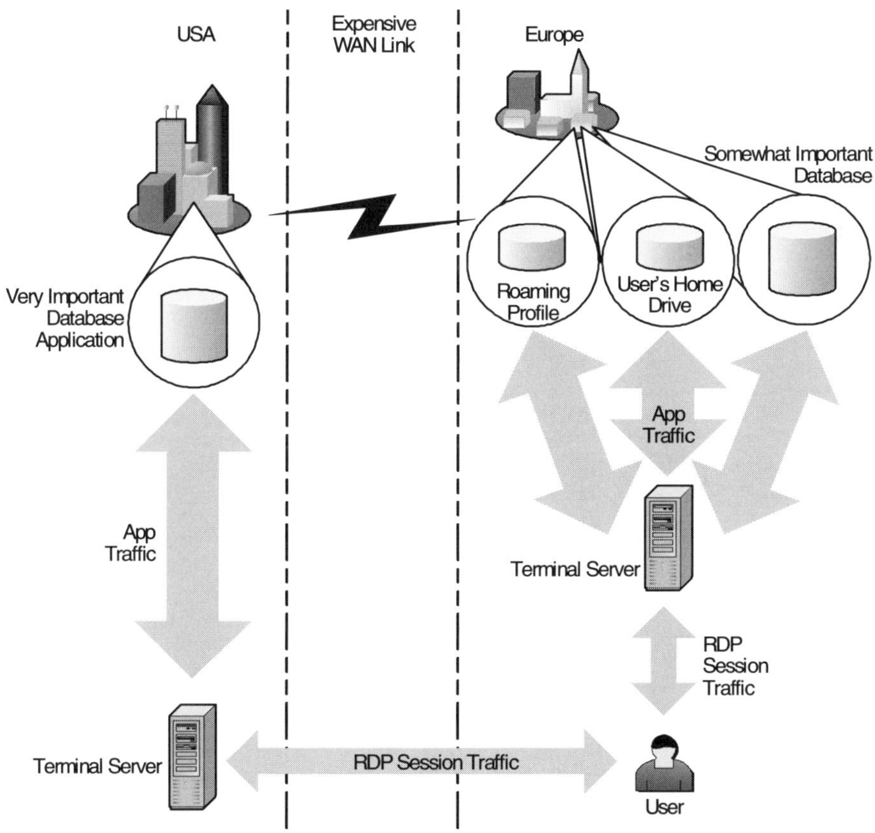

As you can see in Figure 3.5, there are several advantages and disadvantages to placing Terminal Servers in multiple locations throughout your environment.

Advantages of Placing Servers in Multiple Locations

- Users' Terminal Server sessions are always close to their data.
- Efficient use of WAN bandwidth.

- Local departments can own, control, and manage their own servers.
- Increased redundancy.

Disadvantages of Placing Servers in Multiple Locations

- More complex environment.
- Users may need to connect to multiple Terminal Servers in order to use all their applications.
- Your servers might require additional local (onsite) administrators because they are not all in the same building.

Option 2. All Terminal Servers in one Central Location

Instead of sprinkling Terminal Servers throughout your environment, you could put all of your servers in one datacenter (see Figure 3.6). After all, providing remote access to Windows applications is what Terminal Server is designed to do in the first place.

Figure 3.6 All Terminal Servers in one datacenter

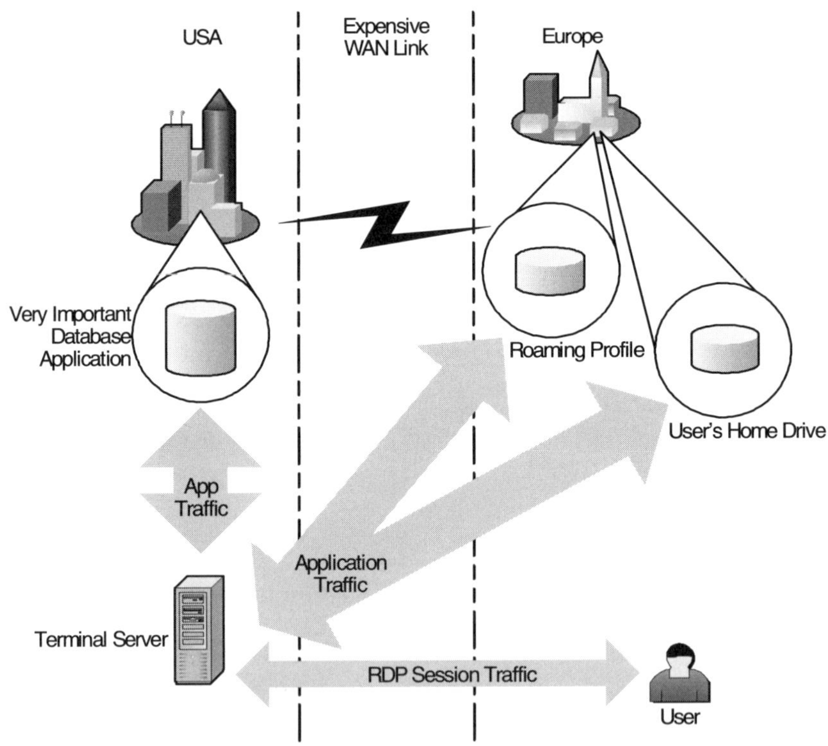

Having one central datacenter contain all of your Terminal Servers is easy to administer, but causes other issues to arise.

Any users that need to access data outside of the datacenter where the Terminal Servers are located must do it via a WAN link. While the performance of the RDP session between a user and Terminal Server won't be a problem, significant performance problems could exist within the application sessions themselves due to potential great WAN distance between the Terminal Server and the user's data.

Plus, different applications handle data latency in different ways, but your users will become frustrated if they have to wait a long time to open or save files. Additionally, WAN bandwidth might be wasted with users forced to connect to all Terminal Server applications via the WAN.

Advantages of Placing all Terminal Servers in one Location

- Simple environment to administer and support.
- Users can connect to one Terminal Server to run all of their applications.
- Terminal Servers are all in the same physical location.

Disadvantages of Placing all Terminal Servers in one Location

- Access to data may be slow if the data is located across a WAN.
- WAN bandwidth may be wasted because users would be forced to connect to a remote server for any Terminal Server application.
- No option for local Terminal Server (local control, local speed, etc.)
- Single point of failure.

As you can see, the location and placement of your Terminal Servers will directly impact many aspects of your environment. While some aspects of the design will be easy, others will require some deliberation and thorough planning (and lots of meetings).

Considerations when Choosing Server Locations

The previous example showed that the data location directly affects the placement of the Terminal Server. However, in the real world, there is more to consider, including:

- Where are the users?
- Where is the data?

- How much and what type of data is each user going to need?
- How many different applications are the users running?
- Where is the IT support for the applications?
- What does the WAN look like?

User Location

The location of users is a major factor to consider when deciding where to put the Terminal Servers. Are all of the users in one central location or are there multiple pockets of users? Is there a datacenter at every location where the users are or are the users at remote offices?

Data Sources

The data that users need to access from within their Terminal Server sessions is probably the most important consideration when deciding where to put your servers. It's important to consider all types of data that a user may need to access from a session. These include back-end application data and databases as well as files and file shares, home drives, and Microsoft Windows roaming profiles. (See Figure 3.7.)

Are the users at the same physical location as their data sources? Is all application data at the same location on the network as users' home drives and Windows roaming profiles, or will users need to pull data from multiple network locations for a single session?

Figure 3.7 Users often need to access multiple types of data from one session

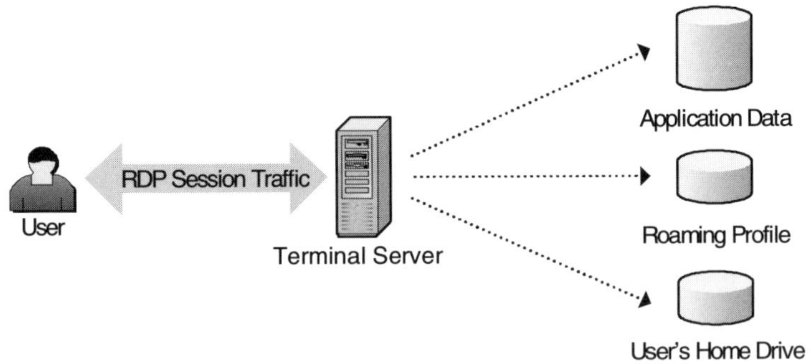

When considering the data that users need to access, think about how each data source will be used throughout the sessions. Will users need to access the data only during session startup or shutdown, or will they need constant access throughout the entire session? For each data source, will users only need to read the data, or will they need to write as well?

Finally, consider the impact of each data source on the users' sessions. What happens if the path to each data source is congested? Will users be merely inconvenienced, or will they not be able to do their jobs?

To help understand the importance of these questions, refer to Figure 3.8. This diagram details a situation that is becoming more and more common as organizations grow.

Figure 3.8 A user in Europe needs to access data throughout the world

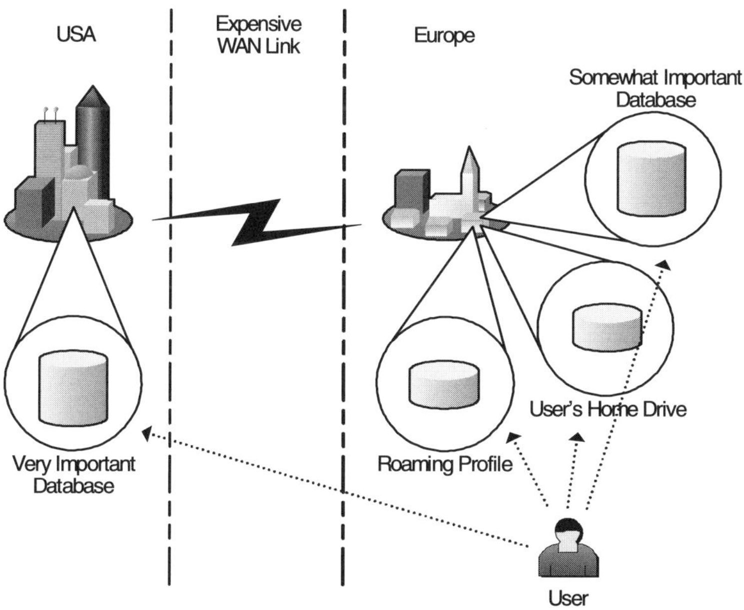

In this example, a user works for a company with a worldwide presence. Apparently this company followed the advice of consultants from the nineties, because their crucial business data has been consolidated into one single database in the US. One of the main reasons that this company chose to use Terminal Server was so that their European users have fast access to the database application. This company put a Terminal Server in the US, right next to the database server, allowing the European user to access the database through a bandwidth-efficient RDP session. Sounds great! Very simple. Unfortunately, in the real world it is not always so simple.

The European user must access applications other than that one US database. Since the user is already running applications via RDP sessions to a server in the US, he might also access other applications via that same server, right?

Let's think about this before we jump to a conclusion. Should a European user really be accessing all applications via servers in the US? Sure. If the user is already crossing the WAN to connect to the database, there is no real impact to adding more applications. But will the user always be utilizing the database? What if the user just wants to use other applications? Should the company pay for the transatlantic bandwidth so that the user can create a PowerPoint presentation? What about the user's home drive? Most likely, the user will want to save files and work with others. Should he use PowerPoint running on a US server while saving files to a file server in Europe? What about PowerPoint's auto-save feature? Will this user have the patience to wait while his file is auto-saved across the ocean WAN every ten minutes?

The point here is that users need to connect to multiple data sources, and they frequently need to access data that resides in different regions of the world. While this European example is a geographic extreme, the same ideas apply anywhere. A slow WAN is a slow WAN. The previous example also applies to users in Washington, D.C. accessing databases 30 miles away in Baltimore over a 56k frame relay.

This example illustrates a situation in which a user only needs access to a database and a home drive. Other users may need to access files and data from many different groups in many different locations. Also, don't forget about Windows roaming user profiles. If a single roaming profile is to be used for all Terminal Server sessions on servers throughout the world, then that profile needs to be accessible to the user wherever they log on. (More on roaming profiles in Chapter 6.)

If that user only needed to access data from one geographic region, the design would be simple. You would put a Terminal Server next to the data and have the user connect via an RDP session. However, with multiple geographic regions, all of which that have important data for the user, the complexity of the design increases.

Applications

The number and types of applications that you want to make available via Terminal Server also affect the decision as to where the servers should be located. The application mix needed by one user may dictate that the user must connect to multiple Terminal Servers. Some users may only need to access applications on single Terminal Server while others may need to access applications across departments via many Terminal Servers.

The mix of local applications and remote Terminal Server applications is also a factor. Will any applications be loaded locally on the users' computers or will all applications be accessed via Terminal Server? If the latter and the Terminal Servers are located across the WAN from the users and the WAN link goes down, all productivity stops. Is that an acceptable risk to the organization, or should some servers be local, though all the data may not be local?

IT Support of Applications

How does your organization's IT department support applications? If all application support is conducted from one site, it makes sense for all Terminal Servers to be located at that site. Most large organizations utilize many applications supported by different people from different locations, as shown in Figure 3.9. In these cases you may have to place Terminal Servers in multiple locations, each server placed near those that support its applications.

Figure 3.9 Application support from multiple people in multiple locations

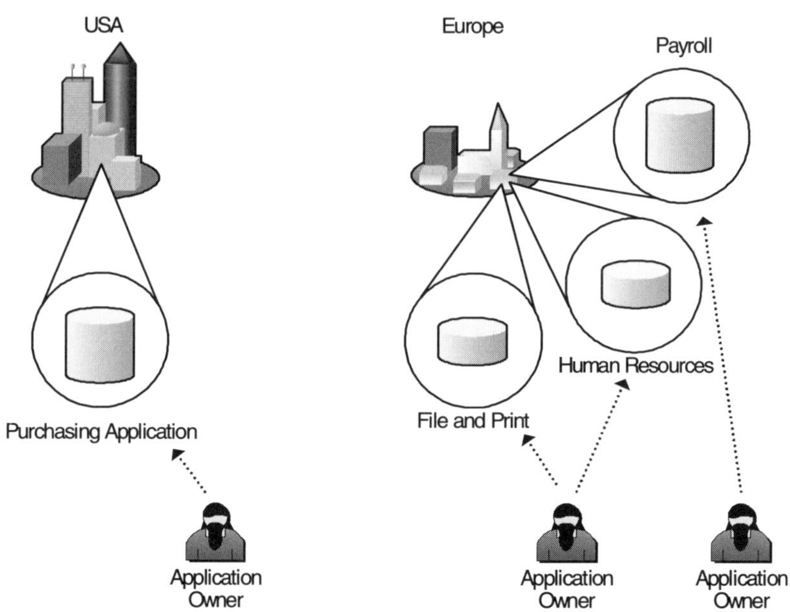

WAN Architecture

The wide area network can also affect where Terminal Servers should be located. If bandwidth is congested, Terminal Servers should be located across

WAN links because they are generally more efficient than the native applications over WAN links. (Chapter 13 has hints about what to do in bandwidth-constrained environments.)

Terminal Server's Supporting Servers

Microsoft added several new features to Windows Server 2003 to help make Terminal Server solutions more robust. While the addition of new features is always a positive, it also means that there is more for you to consider when designing your solution.

For example, two Terminal Server features—License Servers and the Session Directory—make heavy use of the network. You will need to understand how they work to design a solution adequate to your network. (And just think, these considerations are in addition to all "other" network services, like messaging, DNS, WINS (hopefully not), authentication, and printing.)

- A *Terminal Services License Server* maintains a database of Terminal Server Client Access Licenses. This database tracks issued, temporary, and existing Client Access Licenses.
- A *Session Directory* database maintains a list of the user names and session IDs connected to the servers in a load-balanced Terminal Server farm. This database routes users to the proper server when they reconnect to previously disconnected sessions.

Terminal Services Licensing

If you're familiar with the previous version of Terminal Server in Windows 2000, you know that the Terminal Services Licensing Service had to be installed and maintained on an Active Directory Domain Controller. Fortunately, Windows 2003's license service has been modified to run on any 2003 server. This service and its configuration are discussed in detail in Chapter 4. In the current chapter, we'll touch on its relevance to server location.

To appreciate the impact this sever can have on your Terminal Server availability, remember that each time a user connects to your Terminal Server, a query is submitted to the License service. As a user session is established, the license server is queried to determine if the user or device has a valid Terminal Services CAL. If either does have an existing license, access to the system is granted and the session is started. Without a license or the possibility of being issued one, the user will receive an error message and his session will be terminated. While this system seems simplistic, understand that if the Terminal Server cannot contact the license service it assumes there are no licenses available and disconnects the user's session.

Figure 3.10 is an example of how not to implement the licensing service. In it, two Terminal Server farms at two sites are connected via a WAN link. Each time a user connects to a Terminal Server at Site 1, the license server must confirm the user's license across the WAN link. If that WAN link ever breaks or becomes over-utilized, it's possible that the Terminal Server will stop accepting connections.

Figure 3.10 The wrong way to implement the licensing service.

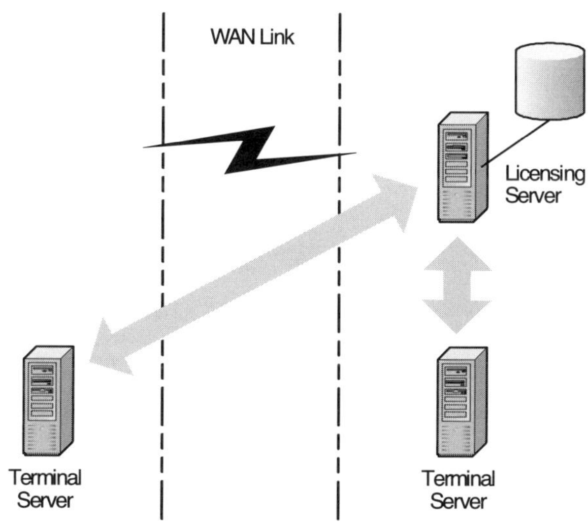

Figure 3.11 (next page) shows the same scenario, with a license server placed on each side of the WAN link. The Terminal Servers have been configured to communicate with the license Server in their locations. Doing so ensures that users connecting to Terminal Servers in either location will not be affected by a downed WAN link.

When placing a license server, redundancy should be your primary concern. The bandwidth between a license server and a Terminal Server is almost negligible—amounting to only a few packets in each direction. Licensing is covered fully in Chapter 4.

Figure 3.11 The proper way to implement the licensing service

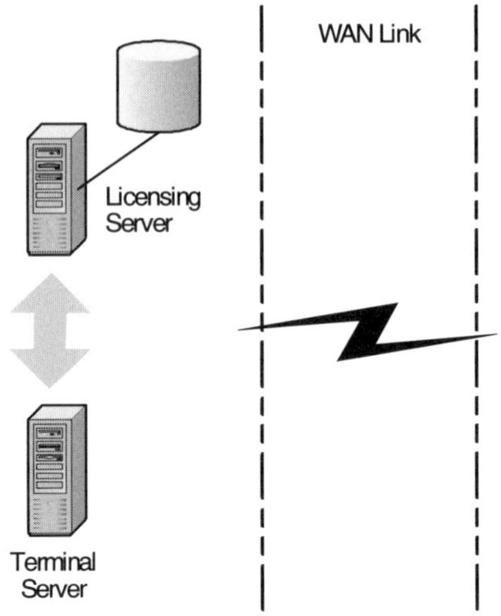

The Session Directory Service

We can examine the Session Directory Service using again the example from above. When a user connects to a load-balanced Terminal Server participating in a session directory, his username is checked against the session directory for the cluster to which he is connecting. If he has an existing disconnected session in the cluster, then he is rerouted to the Terminal Server hosting his disconnected session. This process automatically re-establishes a connection with the original session. In environments with Session Directory in use, the process repeats each time a user establishes a session.

With the Session Directory Service located on the same LAN as the Terminal Server, this query should take no longer than a second or two. However, if the query must travel across a saturated WAN link or a WAN link that has failed, then the process cannot happen at all. While lack of a connection to the Session Directory service will not keep a user from logging on, it can severely degrade the speed of the initial connection.

To prevent this scenario, your Session Directory service should be located at the same location as your Terminal Servers, much like the Terminal Server Licensing Service. Creating a highly available environment for both of these services is discussed in Chapter 7.

Domain Controllers and other Network Services

The previous examples also ring true for domain controller placement. Unfortunately, the placement of your Terminal Servers relative to the domain controllers can be a little more complicated.

Refer to Figure 3.12. The company illustrated has a single Active Directory forest with three down-level domains under a forest root domain. A user from *east.company.com* and *canada.company.com* will be accessing a Terminal Server cluster in the corporate office that resides in the *west.company.com* domain. Each location hosts a domain controller for the root domain and several domain controllers for its respective domain.

Figure 3.12 A single AD forest with three down-level domains

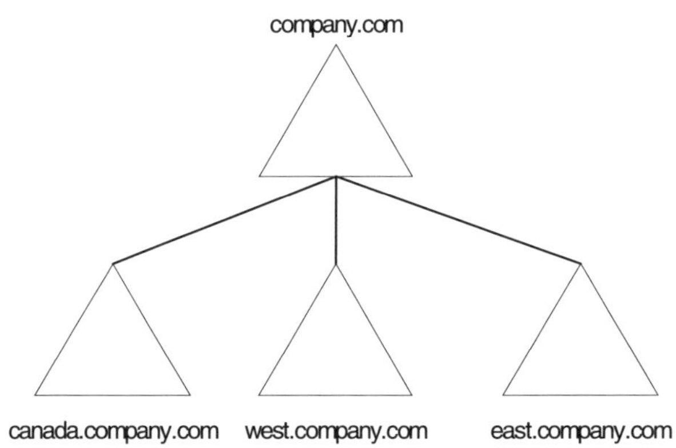

As users access Terminal Server sessions in the west domain, their user credentials will have to be passed to domain controllers within their own domains. The only problem resulting is that the down-level domain controllers for their domains are located only at their sites and not where the Terminal Servers are located. These users will most likely experience slower than necessary authentication and logon times.

If you were to place a domain controller (or multiple domain controllers) from the other domains at the site hosting the Terminal Servers, you would not only realize an increase in performance but would also be creating a solution that is more redundant.

Proper Terminal Server network design heavily relies on proper Active Directory design.

CHAPTER 4

Licensing

Licensing is probably the most dreaded component of any environment's implementation. In Terminal Server environments, you must account for both OS licenses and application licenses. Licensing is really no different from non-Terminal Server environments, except that Windows Server 2003 has technical components that force you to comply with your licenses. If you decide to skip this chapter and ignore licensing, you'll most likely revisit it in 120 days when your Terminal Servers stop functioning because they weren't licensed properly. Terminal Servers running on Windows 2000 were the first to use Microsoft's new licensing enforcement technology, and Windows 2003 builds on that.

The only thing that changes faster than technology is the licensing of technology. For that reason, it's important to note that this licensing chapter was up-to-date when this book was printed. However, it's possible that the details of Microsoft licensing have changed since then. You can find current information on the web at `www.microsoft.com/licensing` or `www.brianmadden.com`.

This chapter concludes with a look at how third-party applications are licensed in Terminal Server environments.

Terminal Server 2003 Licensing Overview

Before addressing the technical components that will make up your licensing infrastructure, let's review Microsoft's licensing policy. Microsoft licenses can be divided into two groups:

- Licenses required for each server.
- Licenses required for clients.

Terminal Server implementation will require both client and server licenses.

Licenses Required for Each Terminal Server

Microsoft requires one license for each server in a Terminal Services environment. This license, known as a "server license," is just the standard Windows Server 2003 license—you don't need anything special to run Terminal Server. It is the same license used for the base server operating system of any Windows 2003 server—whether that server is an Exchange Server, a SQL Server, or a file and print server. However, unlike some Microsoft server applications that require specific server licenses (like Exchange or SQL Server), no additional *server* licenses are required to use Terminal Server.

Some features (as described in Chapter 1) require the "Enterprise" edition of Windows Server 2003. For those you would need an Enterprise version of a Windows Server 2003 license for your server.

Microsoft Terminal Server Client Access Licenses

Before you get too excited about the fact that you don't need a special server license to run Terminal Services, remember that you'll need a client license for everyone that connects to a Windows 2003 Terminal Server.

Prior to Windows Server 2003, a Terminal Server Client Access License (TS CAL) was required for every computer device that connected to a Terminal Server. This licensing system is known as "per device" licensing. Microsoft defined one "device" as a unique piece of hardware used to access a server. If you had two computers and you accessed the same server from each of them, you had two different devices and needed a separate "per device" license for each. Such was the case even if you never used both devices at the same time. Naturally this method of licensing elicited numerous complaints.

In Windows Server 2003, Microsoft added a second TS CAL option. This "per user" client licensing option allows you to purchase one license for each user account. A user can then access a Terminal Server from multiple client devices using one license. "Per user" TS CALs are associated with user accounts, so two users cannot share a license even if they never log on at the same time. If two users share the same physical computer, then it might be preferable to employ the "per device" license option discussed in the previous paragraph.

Microsoft also offers an "external connector" Terminal Server client access license that you buy for a server and lets you connect an unlimited number of non-employees to the server.

Let's look at the three different Terminal Server client license options.

Option 1. Terminal Server "Device" Client Access License

Terminal Services licensing has traditionally been handled by the Terminal Server device Client Access License (TS Device CAL). One license is assigned to each specific client device. Each unique client device that accesses a Terminal Server requires a single TS Device CAL.

What is this license good for? If your environment has workstations that are used by a multiple users, as in round-the-clock environments such as factory floors, call centers, and nursing stations, this license is the most effective since your users could share a single TS Device CAL.

Option 2. Terminal Server "User" Client Access License

A Terminal Server user Client Access License (TS User CAL) is assigned to a user account. It then "follows" that user no matter which server he logs on to and no matter which client device he logs on from.

This license is ideal for mobile workers that roam from location to location while using Terminal Servers to access their applications. Also, if your users use multiple client devices (perhaps their work PC and home PC), this model may save your company significant licensing dollars.

Option 3. External Connector License

A challenge to using per-user and per-device CALs is the fact that they have to be assigned to a specific user account or a specific client device. While adequate for employees of the company that bought the license, what happens if a company wants to extend its Terminal Server environment to business partners where the names of users and client devices wouldn't be known? What happens if a company wants to extend an application via a Terminal Server to the Internet? Technically following the Microsoft terms, you would need to buy a license for each unique user or computer that connected to your server.

Clearly this is not feasible. To address this challenge, Microsoft introduced the External Connector License (ECL), designed to be used when systems are extended to external parties, including business partners and the public.

ECLs are available for all new Microsoft products (except products that are licensed on a per-processor basis since per-processor licenses already account for unlimited users and client devices). In Terminal Server 2003 environments, ECLs provide a simple way to buy "concurrent" user licenses for those who need to connect to your server. If you wanted to open up a server to trading partners, you would buy a Terminal Server ECL.

At this point you might be wondering why you can't just buy ECLs and forget all this per-user and per-device garbage. Microsoft has strict rules governing the use of ECLs, and users of the TS ECLs cannot be employees of the organization that bought the license.

Microsoft Windows Server Client Access Licenses

Now that you understand the difference between the three Terminal Server-specific CALs, you need to know that each client device also needs a standard Windows Server 2003 CAL. To legally access a Windows 2003 Terminal Server, each client seat requires *each* of the following licenses:

- Windows Server 2003 Client Access License.
- Windows Server 2003 Terminal Server Client Access License.

License 1. Windows Server Client Access License (Server CAL)

Any user needs this Windows Server CAL to access a Windows 2003 server. This license provides the "basic" access rights that allow users to store files, print, and be part of an Active Directory. If you have a unified Active Directory with 5000 users, then you'll have 5000 Windows Server CALs.

License 2. Windows Server 2003 Terminal Server Client Access License (TS CAL)

We discussed the TS CAL (either per-device, per-user, or External Connector License) in the previous section. It builds upon the regular Windows Server CAL, adding the legal right for users to access a "remote control" session on a Terminal Server.

If you have a 5000-user Active Directory environment with a few Terminal Servers that provide applications for 300 users, then you'll need 5000 Windows Server CALs and 300 Terminal Server CALs.

Special Licensing Scenarios

Prior to Windows Server 2003, there were special license rules for specific situations. Microsoft has changed the way these situations are handled with the introduction of Windows Server 2003.

TS CAL Requirements when Connecting to a Terminal Server from Windows XP

Prior to Windows Server 2003, client workstations that ran Windows NT, 2000, or XP Professional had the right to obtain a "free" TS CAL. The only requirement was to purchase a TS CAL for client devices that ran an operating system lower than the Terminal Server operating system. For example, Windows 2000 Professional workstations did not require purchase of a TS CAL to connect to a Windows 2000 Terminal Server since Windows 2000 client devices had the right to obtain a free Windows 2000 TS CAL. Also, since these licenses were backwards compatible, the Windows 2000 TS CAL would also apply if you were using a Windows XP Professional client to connect to a Windows 2000 Terminal Server.

Since Windows XP was released over a year before Windows Server 2003, many people bought Windows XP Professional with the assumption that it would include a "free" Windows Server 2003 TS CAL. However, with the release of Windows 2003, Microsoft removed the "free" TS CAL license that was built-in to Windows XP Professional. Unfortunately, this announcement came well after many organizations bought multiple copies of Windows XP assuming that its free TS CAL would work with Windows 2003 Terminal Servers.

Negative response to this announcement prompted Microsoft grant a free Windows 2003 TS CAL to anyone who owned a Windows XP Professional license on April 23, 2003 (the day before the release of Windows Server 2003.Does your copy of Windows XP come with a free Windows Server 2003 TS CAL? If you bought it before April 24, 2003, then it does. If you bought if after that it does not, and you'll have to buy a Windows 2003 TS CAL. (If you had TS CALs that were enrolled in Microsoft Enterprise Agreements or Software Assurance, then you automatically qualified for the Windows 2003 TS CAL upgrade.)

Interestingly, the added TS CAL costs of Terminal Server on Windows Server 2003 has upset some companies so much that they are claiming it as the sole reason that they will keep their Terminal Servers running on Windows 2000.

The Work-at-Home TS CAL

Microsoft licensing agreements also used to provide "work-at-home" licenses for Terminal Servers. These were additional, cheap TS CALs for users that used an office computer to access Terminal Servers and then went home and accessed Terminal Servers from a home PC. With the advent of Windows 2003's new *per-user* TS CAL, the work-at-home license is no longer an option.

Similar to TS CALs, any prior work-at-home licenses that are enrolled in an Enterprise Agreement or Software Assurance may be upgraded to current licenses.

Windows 2003 Terminal Server Licensing Components

Windows NT Server 4.0 Terminal Server Edition used the "honor system" for tracking licenses. While you were legally supposed to purchase the correct licenses, there was nothing technically stopping you from connecting more users than you paid for. While the honor system worked well for system administrators and thieves, it has not worked as well for Microsoft shareholders.

As alluded to in the opening sentences of this chapter, this system changed when Windows 2000 was released. In Terminal Services for Windows 2000, a Microsoft "Terminal Services Licensing Service" is required to run on one or more servers on your network. This Terminal Services licensing service is responsible for monitoring, distributing, and enforcing TS CAL usage. Microsoft implemented this licensing service as a "service to their customers" who were "deeply concerned that they might accidentally forget to pay for a license or two, every once in awhile." In Terminal Server environments running on Windows 2000 platforms, this licensing service infrastructure guarantees that there be no "accidentally forgetting" to purchase all the needed licenses.

Windows 2003 Terminal Servers also make use of licensing servers—although the exact manner depends upon for which of three licensing options a server is configured (per device, per user, or the external connector license).

In Windows 2003 environments, there are four main technical components that make up the Terminal Services licensing infrastructure:

- Terminal Services licensing servers.
- The Microsoft license clearinghouse.
- Windows 2000/2003 Terminal Servers.
- Licenses.

Figure 4.1 Microsoft licensing components

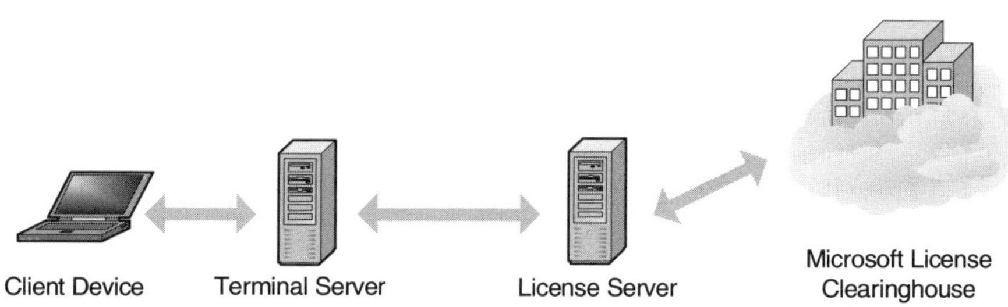

Let's take a look at the licensing–related roles of each component.

Terminal Services License Server

The Terminal Services license server is a standard Windows 2003 server with the "Terminal Server Licensing Service" installed. This license server stores digital certificates for TS CALs that are distributed to client devices. Like Windows 2000 environments, a Windows 2003 license server is responsible for issuing licenses and tracking their use.

Microsoft License Clearinghouse

TS license servers and TS client access licenses must be activated be Microsoft before they can be used. The Microsoft license clearinghouse is a large Internet-based certificate authority that authorizes and activates these licenses and servers. Microsoft does this to ensure that no TS CALs are stolen, copied, or pirated (which is why more and more Microsoft software requires activation after you input your license codes).

A TS license server will function before it's activated via the Microsoft clearinghouse, however, an unactivated license server will only pass out temporary TS CALs that expire after 90 days. In order for a license server to distribute permanent licenses, it must be activated.

Terminal Server

Windows 2003 Terminal Servers understand that client devices must be licensed. To that end, when you enable Terminal Services, the server immediately begins trying to locate a licensing server. It then communicates with the licensing server to ensure that client devices are licensed properly.

Each Terminal Server must be configured to use per-user, per-device, or external connector licenses.

Licenses

The license service that runs on a Windows 2003 server keeps track of seven different types of licenses. These include four types of licenses for Windows 2003 Terminal Servers and three types (for backward compatibility) for Windows 2000 Terminal Servers. The seven types of Windows 2003 client licenses include:

- *Windows Server 2003 TS Device CALs.* This license is the per-device CAL that is issued to unique client hardware devices. It allows the client device to access Windows 2000 and 2003 Terminal Servers.
- *Windows Server 2003 TS User CALs.* This is the per user CAL that's assigned to unique user accounts. This license allows a user to access Windows 2000 and 2003 Terminal Servers. If the client device has a valid TS Device CAL, then this TS User CAL is not needed, and vice versa.
- *Windows Server 2003 TS External Connector Licenses.* When assigned to a Terminal Server, this ECL license allows unlimited non-employee connections. When this ECL is used, TS Device CALs and TS User CALs are not needed.
- *Windows 2000 TS CALs.* These are per-device licenses for devices connecting to Terminal Servers running Windows 2000.
- *Windows 2000 TS Internet Connector Licenses.* These licenses are essentially the Windows 2000 version of the Windows 2003 TS ECL. When assigned to a Windows 2000 Terminal Server, this license al-

lows 200 simultaneous connections. These connections must be made by non-employees, across the Internet, via anonymous user accounts.

- *Windows 2000 Built-in Licenses.* These built-in licenses are used for Windows 2000 and Windows XP workstations that are connecting to Windows 2000-based Terminal Servers. Remember from the previous section that Windows 2003 Terminal Servers do not support the use of built-in licenses. (Which is why even if your Windows XP workstations qualify for "free" Windows 2003 TS CALs, you have to obtain TS Devices CALs from Microsoft—they're not automatically built in.)
- *Temporary Licenses.* If a licensing server ever runs out of activated licenses, it will issue temporary licenses to any client devices requesting per-device TS CALs (applicable to Windows 2000 or 2003-based Terminal Servers). The number of temporary TS CALs a licensing server can grant is unlimited, although the temporary CALs themselves expire after 90 days and cannot extended.

The Terminal Services Licensing Service

As you're starting to see, the Windows 2003's Terminal Server licensing environment is extremely complex. It's probably also fairly obvious that the licensing service plays a central role. In Windows 2003, this service builds on the licensing functionality that was available in Windows 2000.

TS Licensing Service Installation Considerations

The TS licensing service is separate from the actual Terminal Server components that allow users to run remote sessions.

In Windows 2003 Terminal Server environments, the TS licensing service must be installed on a Windows 2003 server. That server can be any server in your environment, and it doesn't have to be a server that's running Terminal Server. Most companies install the TS licensing service on a standard Windows 2003 file and print server.

The TS licensing service can be installed on any Windows 2003 server. It does *not* have to be installed on a domain controller. Furthermore, this installation can be done at the time of the OS installation or at any time after that via the Control Panel (Control Panel | Add Remove Programs | Windows Components | Terminal Services Licensing Service).

There is no need to build a dedicated licensing server. The TS licensing service can run on any Windows 2003 server without adversely affecting performance. It adds very little CPU or memory overhead, and its hard disk requirements are negligible. The average memory usage is less than 10MB when active, and the license database will grow in increments of only 5 MB for every 6,000 license tokens issued. The license server does not require Internet access.

TS Licensing Service Scope

As part of the licensing service setup, the installation routine asks if you want to set up the license server for your "Enterprise" or "Domain or Workgroup." The option chosen here (called the "scope") dictates how the license server communicates with your Terminal Servers and lets you control which Terminal Servers can receive licenses from your licensing server. You can configure your license server so that it provides licenses for either:

- An entire Active Directory site. (Enterprise licensing server)
- An entire domain or workgroup. (Domain/workgroup licensing server).

Enterprise Scope

If you choose the "Enterprise" installation option, your licensing server will respond to a license request from any Terminal Server in the same Active Directory site. If Terminal Servers from multiple domains exist in that Active Directory site, the license server will provide licenses for all of them.

This option requires that your Terminal Servers be part of an Active Directory domain. When the licensing service starts, it registers itself with a domain controller and creates a "TS-Licensing" object in the directory, allowing Terminal Servers from any domain to query a domain controller to locate the license server.

Domain / Workgroup Scope

Choosing the "Your domain or workgroup" option causes the license server to behave differently, depending on whether it's part of an Active Directory domain.

In AD environments, this choice causes your licensing servers to only respond to license requests from Terminal Servers in the same Active Directory domain. If an Active Directory domain crosses multiple Active Directory sites, the licensing server will fulfill requests from multiple sites. This option is useful in situations where there are multiple business units partitioned into different domains on the same network. A license server from one domain won't give licenses to clients connecting to Terminal Servers from a different domain.

In non-AD environments, choosing this option means that your license server will *not* attempt to register itself with a domain controller, and your Terminal Servers will have to find your license servers on their own. (More on this later.)

TS Licensing Server Activation

After the TS licensing service is installed on a server, it must be activated by the Microsoft clearinghouse via the Terminal Services Licensing tool. This activation gives the license server the digital certificate it will use to accept and activate TS CALs.

The license server activation is fairly straightforward (Start | Programs | Administrative Tools | Terminal Services Licensing | Right-click on server | Activate). Activation can be accomplished directly via the Internet or via a web page, fax, or telephone call. If you run the licensing tool on a computer other than the license server, the computer that you are using must have access to the Internet—not the license server.

You must install a TS licensing server within 120 days of using Terminal Services on a Windows 2003 server. (This was increased from 90 days with Windows 2000.) If a Windows 2003 Terminal Server can't find a license server after it's been used for 120 days, the Terminal Server will refuse connections to clients without valid TS CALs.

How Terminal Servers find Licensing Servers

Since you can install the licensing service on any Windows 2003 server in your environment, the real fun begins when you try to get your Terminal Servers to talk to your license server(s). Merely installing a license server on your network does not necessarily mean that your Terminal Servers will be able to find it.

License server "discovery" is the technical term for the process by which Terminal Servers locate and connect to licensing servers. As soon as the Terminal Server role is added to a Windows 2003 server, the server immediately begins the discovery process. License server discovery can happen in a number of ways, depending on which of the following environments the Terminal Server finds itself in:

- No domain (workgroup mode).
- Windows NT 4.0 domain.

- Active Directory domain, with the TS license servers operating in domain mode.
- Active Directory domain, with the TS license servers operating in enterprise mode.

Hard-Coding Preferred License Servers

Regardless of which of these four situations a Terminal Server is in, you *always* have the option of manually specifying a license server or servers that each Terminal Server should get licenses from. You can manually configure any Terminal Server to get licenses from any license server—there's no need to stay within domain, subnet, location, or site boundaries.

You can configure a Terminal Server to use a specific license server via the Terminal Server's registry. Be careful though, because this registry edit is not like most others. In this case, rather than specifying a new registry value and then entering data, you have to create a new registry key (or "folder"). To do this, browse to the following registry location:

```
HKLM\SYSTEM\ControlSet\Services\TermService\Parameters\
```

Add a new key called "*LicenseServers.*" Underneath the new *LicenseServers* key, create another key with the NetBIOS name of the license server that you want this Terminal Server to use. You don't need to add any values or data under this new key.

Add multiple keys for multiple servers if you wish, although the Terminal Server will only communicate with one license server at a time. Once you're done, reboot the server for it to take affect.

As you'll see, this manual process is needed in situations where the Terminal Servers cannot automatically "discover" the license servers. It's also useful if you want to override the default license server that a Terminal Server discovers.

Discovery in Windows NT 4 Domains or Workgroup Environments

In non-Active Directory environments, a Terminal Server first looks to the *LicenseServer* registry location to see if any license servers have been manually specified.

If the registry key is empty or if the server or servers specified there cannot be contacted, the Terminal Server performs a NetBIOS broadcast to attempt to locate a license server. (NetBIOS broadcasts are not routable, so only license servers on the same subnet as the Terminal Server making the broadcast will respond.) If multiple license servers respond, the Terminal Server remembers their names and chooses which it will use exclusively.

Once the Terminal Server picks a license server, the Terminal Server periodically verifies that it exists. (See Figure 4.2.) If the license server ever fails to respond to the verification poll from the Terminal Server, the Terminal Server attempts to connect to one of the other license servers that responded to the original NetBIOS process. If no connection can be made to a license server, the Terminal Server attempts to find a new license server by starting the entire discovery process over again.

Figure 4.2 Terminal Servers periodically verify that they can contact license servers

Licensing Mode	License server verified to exist if no activity every	In not found, discovery process occurs every
NT 4 domain or workgroup	120 min	15 min
Domain mode	120 min	15 min
Enterprise mode	60 min	60 min

Discovery in Active Directory Environments

When a Terminal Server is a member of an Active Directory domain, the license server discovery process is entirely different.

1. First, the Terminal Server attempts to contact the license server (or servers) specified in its *LicenseServers* registry key. If a license server is discovered at any point through this process, the remainder of the discovery process is aborted.
2. If that attempt fails, the server next looks for an enterprise scope licensing server by performing an LDAP query for the following object in its Active Directory site:
```
LDAP://CN=TS-Enterprise-License-Server,CN=<site-
name>,
CN=sites,CN=configuration,DC=<domainname>,DC=com
```
3. If that attempt also fails, the Terminal Server begins querying every domain controller in the site, looking for "enterprise scope" licensing servers.
4. If the Terminal Server still has not found a license server, it will query every other domain controller (outside of its site) to see if any are configured as a domain scope license server.

One thing that you might have noticed about this discovery process is that domain scope license servers must be installed on domain controllers in order for your Terminal Servers to discover them. Domain scope license servers do not register themselves with other domain controllers and Terminal Servers only query domain controllers to see if they are license servers.

There's nothing wrong with installing a domain scope license server on a non-domain controller. Just be aware than you'll need to manually configure the registries of your Terminal Servers to find those license servers. Enterprise scope license servers are not affected, since they register themselves with the domain controllers, even when not installed on a domain controller.

If a Terminal Server does not find a license server via this discovery process, the whole process is started over once every hour.

If license servers are found, the Terminal Server keeps a list of them in its registry. Enterprise licensing servers are stored in the `HKLM\Software\Microsoft\MSLicensing\Parameters\EnterpriseServerMulti` registry location, and domain licensing servers are stored in the `HKLM\Software\Microsoft\MSLicensing\Parameters\DomainLicenseServerMulti` registry location. By storing these server names in the registry, a Terminal Server is able to quickly pick a new license server if its primary choice is not available. Once a license server is found, the Terminal Server will only start the discovery process over again if it can't connect to any of the servers in the registry.

Troubleshooting License Server Discovery

You are likely to run into situations in which one of your Terminal Servers cannot find a license server and the reason is not apparent. Fortunately, the Windows Server 2003 Resource Kit includes a Terminal Server License Server viewer tool, LSVIEW.EXE. LSVIEW is a GUI-based tool that is run on a Terminal Server. It provides you with the names and types of each license server that it can discover.

Figure 4.3 Microsoft license server discovery process

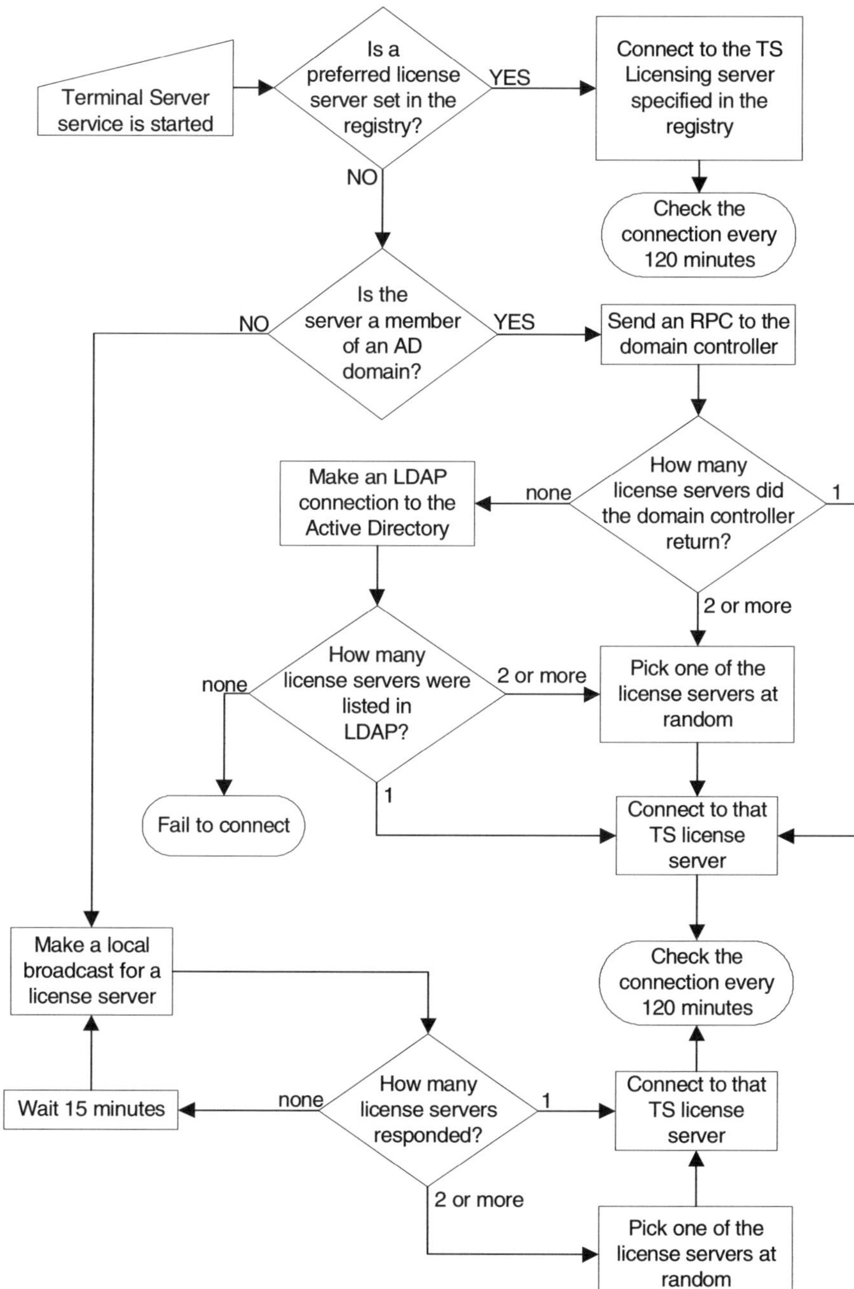

The Terminal Server 2003 Licensing Process

Let's take a look now at how the entire licensing process works. The exact process that takes place is different depending on whether the Terminal Server is configured to use device-based or user-based TS CALs.

Terminal Servers Configured for Device-Based TS CALs

When a Terminal Server is configured to use TS Device CALs (Start | Administrative Tools | Terminal Services Configuration | Server Settings | Licensing), each client device needs to have its own license.

1. Terminal Server CALs are purchased and installed into the license database on the (previously activated) TS Licensing Server.
2. The TS CALs are activated via the Microsoft License clearinghouse. The activated licenses remain on the license server, waiting for assignment to client devices.
3. A user makes an RDP connection to the Terminal Server.
4. Since the Terminal Server is in *per device* licensing mode, the Terminal Server checks for the device's TS CAL (in the form of a digital certificate).
5. If the client device does not present a valid TS CAL, the Terminal Server connects to the license server to obtain one.
6. If the license server does not have any more TS CALs, it will route the Terminal Server to another license server that does have available TS CALs (if known).
7. The license server sends the Terminal Server a digital certificate for a temporary 90-day TS CAL.
8. The Terminal Server passes this certificate down to the client.
9. The user's credentials are validated. If the user successfully authenticates, the Terminal Server contacts the license server a second time. This time around, the Terminal Server informs the license server that the TS CAL that was sent to the client should be marked as "valid." If the user did not successfully authenticate, (i.e. the connection was from an inappropriate user), the Terminal Server will not contact the license server, and the license that was sent out will not be marked "valid."
10. The next time that client device connects, it presents its 90-day temporary TS CAL to the Terminal Server.

11. The Terminal Server contacts the license server. Since the licensing server marked the CAL as valid the first time the user authenticated, the client device's temporary CAL is upgraded to a full CAL. If, for some reason, all of the license servers have depleted their inventories of TS CALs, the client device keeps its temporary 90-day TS CAL certificate. As long as the 90-day certificate has not expired, the client device can still connect, even with no available licenses on any license servers.

An unlicensed client device will always be granted a temporary 90-day TS CAL at the time of its first connection. Only after successful authentication and a second logon is the temporary TS CAL upgraded to a full TS CAL. This two–stage licensing process is used to ensure that TS CALs are only assigned to authenticated users. Previously (before hotfix 287687 or Windows 2000 Service Pack 3) any user that connected was assigned a full TS CAL, even if he did not belong on the system. The full TS CAL certificate was granted at connection time, before the logon screen even popped up. If a user thought, "Oops, I don't belong on this system!" it was too late—his client device had already received a full TS CAL certificate, even if the administrator never meant for him to access the system. This circumstance often led to license servers running out of TS CALs.

During this process, if the license server does not respond to the Terminal Server, the Terminal Server will try to connect to one of the other license servers from the list of servers it maintains in the registry that was built as a result of the license server discovery process. If it can't connect to any of them, it will start the license server discovery process again.

If a client device does not have a TS CAL and the Terminal Server cannot contact a license server, the user's session will be denied. The only exception to this is for new Terminal Servers. In Windows 2003, you have a 120-day "grace period" during which a Terminal Server will function even if it cannot contact a license server. However, 121 days after you install Terminal Services onto a Windows 2003 server, that server must be able to contact a licensing server or no new users will be able to connect. All of this action takes place a soon as the connection is made—before the user even authenticates!

TS CAL License Certificate Storage on Client Devices

As mentioned earlier, when a client device receives a TS Device CAL from a Terminal Server, it receives it in the form of a digital certificate from a license server. For this reason you must activate the license server with the Microsoft clearinghouse (which is just a certificate authority). The digital certificate is an actual certificate copied to the client device (even with Windows CE). Once a client device connects to a Terminal Server, a TS CAL digital certificate is transferred from the license server to the client device. The license server loses one of its licenses from its inventory, and the client device has the digital certificate that it can present to any Terminal Server on future connections.

The digital certificate is stored in different locations depending on the operating system. On 32-bit Windows platforms, the TS CAL digital certificate is stored in the registry at `HKLM\Software\Microsoft\MSLicensing\Store\License00x`.

Anyone who has been in the computer industry for more than five minutes can probably spot a potential flaw in this plan. Client devices tend to break. Windows-based terminals have their ROMs reflashed. Operating systems are reinstalled on workstations. PCs are reimaged. Whenever this happens, the TS CAL digital certificate stored on the client device is lost forever. The TS CAL doesn't exist on the license server after it's transferred to a client device. When that client connects back to a Terminal Server, it has no digital certificate to present. The server thinks that it has no license, and instructs the license server to issue a new TS CAL in the form of a new digital certificate. In effect, that one client device ends up consuming two TS CALs—the old one that was lost and the new one that was just issued. If the client device were reset again, a third TS CAL would be used.

In Windows 2003 (and Windows 2000 SP3), when a Terminal Server requests a TS CAL from the license server for a client device, a full TS CAL certificate is granted with an expiration date randomly selected between 52 and 89 days from the current date. The license server keeps track of the expiration date and it is also embedded into the digital certificate that represents the actual license passed down to the client device.

Every time the client device connects to a Terminal Server, it presents its TS CAL certificate to the server. The server checks not only whether the client device has a valid certificate, but also the expiration date of that certificate. If the expiration date of the certificate is within 7 days of the current date, the Terminal Server connects to the license server to renew the license for another random period of 52 to 89 days.

The license server also tracks the expiration date of TS CALs. If for some reason the client's CAL is never renewed and expires, the license server returns that TS CAL to the inventory of available unused licenses. If a client device with a TS CAL were to blow up or be rebuilt, the license server would automatically add the TS CAL back into its available license pool after it expired (a maximum of 89 days).

If the Terminal Server is not able to obtain a TS CAL renewal when the client device's TS CAL certificate expires after the 52 to 89 days, the client is denied access. A temporary 90-day certificate cannot replace a full certificate that has expired, but this shouldn't ever be a problem for you (unless you don't have enough TS CALs).

Someone at Microsoft deserves an award for the fact that the temporary TS CALs are valid for 90 days and the full TS CALs are valid for a maximum of 89 days—conveniently one day less than the temporary licenses. Consider the following scenario:

Assume that a client device successfully authenticates to a Terminal Server and is granted a full TS CAL certificate that was (worst case) randomly selected to expire at the 89 day maximum. When it passes down the certificate, the license server decrements its total TS CAL license count by one, also noting that particular certificate's expiration date. Now, assume that a catastrophic event occurs at the client, causing its local operating system to be reinstalled and its local TS CAL certificate to be lost. When that client authenticates to a Terminal Server, the Terminal Server will request a new TS CAL certificate from the license server and the license server (again) decrements its TS CAL inventory by one. At this point there have been two TS CAL licenses given out to that one client, but the first one will never be renewed because the certificate was lost when the client was rebuilt. After 89 days (the randomly selected duration of the first certificate), the first TS CAL is returned to the pool by the license server.

The administrator in this situation probably bought just enough TS CALs to cover the exact number of client devices. He did not buy extras to cover the 52 – 89 day period during which one client device had two CALs assigned. By purchasing the exact amount of TS CALs, the license server would not have any more TS CALs to give out when the client device asked for the new TS CAL certificate after the first was lost. In this case, the license server would grant a temporary 90-day TS CAL certificate to the client device because the client device appears to the server as a brand new machine.

Because the temporary TS CAL certificate is always valid at least one day longer then the full CAL certificate (90 days versus a maximum of 89 days), the old, lost full TS CAL will always be returned to the inventory on the license server at least one day before the temporary TS CAL certificate would expire. For example, after day 88, the client device's temporary TS CAL certificate will expire in 2 days, but the license server is tracking the expiration of the full TS CAL that was originally granted for 89 days. That full TS CAL only has 1 day left before it expires. The following day, when the client device's temporary TS CAL certificate has only 1 day remaining, the license server will add the original TS CAL back in its inventory pool, making it available to grant to the client as a permanent license for another random period of 52 – 89 days.

True geeks will enjoy tracing the entire licensing flow in Windows 2003 Terminal Server environments in Figure 4.4 on the facing page.

Multiple License Timeframes Explained

Throughout this license distribution and acquisition process, we have discussed two different license timeframes. While both are related to Windows 2003 Terminal Services licensing, they are actually completely different.

- A Windows 2003 Terminal Server will work without a license server for 120 days.
- If a license server runs out of TS CALs (licenses), it will issue 90-day temporary ones.

The first item relates to the presence of a license server. If a Terminal Server cannot locate a license server, it will still allow unlicensed client devices to log on. The Terminal Server itself does *not* grant 90-day temporary licenses if it cannot find a license server. Instead, if a license server cannot be located, the Terminal Server simply "looks the other way" for 120 days. After the grace period ends, unlicensed client device connections are refused. This 120-day countdown begins the first time a Terminal Services client device connects to the server.

From a legal standpoint, you must have a valid TS CAL for each client device that connects to a Terminal Server, even during the first 120 days. The 120-day threshold is not a free evaluation period. Rather, it gives you a chance to set up your Terminal Server environment and get the bugs worked out before you activate your license server.

The second item relates to the license server itself. If, over the course of business, a TS licensing server runs out of licenses, it will begin to grant 90-day temporary license certificates to client devices. Unlike Windows 2000, Windows 2003 license servers do *not* have to be activated to hand out 90-day temporary TS CALs.

Figure 4.4 The Terminal Server 2003 Device-Based TS CAL Licensing Process

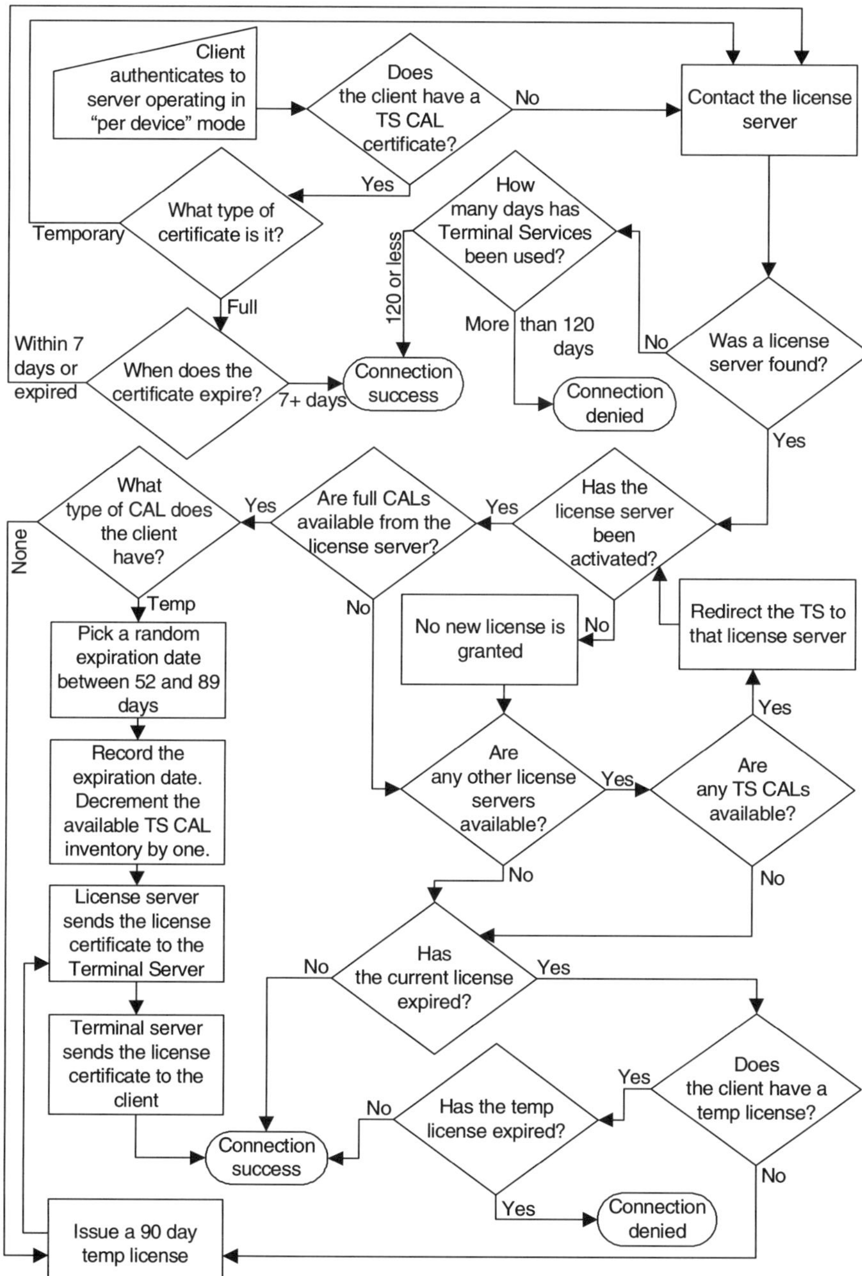

These temporary licenses can only be replaced by full TS CAL licenses—they cannot be replaced by additional temporary licenses. There is no limit to the number of temporary licenses that a license server can grant. Also, the 90-day timer for the expiration of the TS CALs is client specific, meaning that different temporary licenses can expire on different days—even if they were all granted by the same license server.

Terminal Servers configured for User-Based CALs

Everything discussed in the previous section is applicable only when Terminal Servers are configured in "per device" licensing mode. When a user connects to a Terminal Server configured in "per user" licensing mode, a different process takes place.

1. When Terminal Services is installed on a Windows 2003 server, the server verifies that it can find (via the discovery process outlined previously) a license server.
2. There is no Step Two.

That's right. All this TS CAL digital certificate, temp license, transfer mumbo-jumbo *only* applies when Terminal Servers are configured for "per device" licenses. With per user licenses, all you have to do is make sure that the Terminal Server can find a license server. (The license server doesn't even have to be activated!) Other than periodically verifying that it exists, there's no communication between a "per user" configured Terminal Server and a license server.

How did this come to be? When Windows 2003 was in beta testing, Microsoft was planning to offer a "per processor" licensing model. At the last minute (with Release Candidate 2), Microsoft changed its mind and decided to go with a "per user" option instead. This decision was a popular move on Microsoft's part. The only problem was that it was so late in the game that Microsoft didn't have time to build the "per user" technical license compliance infrastructure (although you can bet we'll see it in future versions of Windows).

Designing your Licensing Server Environment

Now that we've reviewed the details of how licensing works, let's look at some of the issues affect the design of your TS licensing servers.

- Selecting which Terminal Servers can access which license servers.
- Licensing Terminal Servers in mixed Windows 2000 and Windows 2003 environments.

Enforcing which Terminal Servers are Authorized to Receive Licenses

A new feature of Windows 2003 allows you to specify security permissions for your license servers. That is, you can specify which Terminal Servers are authorized to pass out licenses from a specific license server.

This feature is useful to organizations that manage licensing by business unit or specific users groups, since it can prevent one department from "stealing" another department's licenses.

You must first enable this security feature via a policy applied to the license server (Computer Configuration | Administrative Templates | Windows Components | Terminal Services | Licensing). Once this functionality is enabled, a local group called "Terminal Services Computers" is created on the license server. The License Server will only respond to license requests from servers (or global groups containing servers) whose computer accounts are a member of this group.

When this policy is enabled on a license server that's also a domain controller, the group that's created is a domain local group (since domain controllers don't have local groups). Therefore, if you really plan on managing your licenses by department, it's probably not the best idea to install the licensing service on a domain controller.

If you want to manage licenses by business unit, it's usually easiest to install the license server in "domain or workgroup mode" onto a server that's "owned" by that business unit. Then, activate the License Server Security via Group Policy. Once this policy is applied, add the Business Unit's Terminal Servers into the local License Server Security Group, ensuring that only authorized Terminal Servers can receive Terminal Service CALs. This is also a good way to prevent other departments or even rogue Terminal Servers from accessing your license service and using up CALs.

Licensing in Mixed Windows 2000 / 2003 Environments

If you're migrating from Windows 2000 or if you're running a 2000/2003 mixed environment, there are a few licensing issues to consider when planning your design.

Preventing TS CAL License Upgrades

Since it's possible for a single Windows 2003-based license server to distribute both Windows 2000 and Windows 2003 TS CALs, you need to give some special thought to environments where both are used.

Your Windows 2000 Terminal Servers communicates with your Windows 2003 license server and request licenses from it, and your Windows 2003 license server mimics a Windows 2000 license server.

Because Microsoft licenses are backwards-compatible, the Windows 2003 license server can technically issue either a Windows 2000 or 2003 TS CAL for clients wanting to connect to a Windows 2000 Terminal Server.

The license server will always try to provide the exact match for the version of the license. But what happens when a client device requires a TS CAL to connect to a Windows 2000 Terminal Server and the license server only had 2003 TS CALs available? Should the license server "waste" a 2003 CAL on the Windows 2000 server, or should it provide a 90-day temporary 2003 license? If the client already had a temporary CAL, should the server "upgrade" it to a 2003 permanent TS CAL, or should it deny the user's connection?

The desired outcome of this situation depends upon your business environment. You can specify which behavior you want your licensing server to follow. This functionality is controlled via the "Prevent License Upgrade" policy (Group Policy | Computer Configuration | Administrative Templates | Windows Components | Terminal Services | Licensing).

As the name implies, enabling this policy prohibits a licensing server from ever using a Windows 2003 TS CAL for a Windows 2000 environment. Chapter 6 explains how policies are used and implemented in Terminal Server environments.

Upgrading a Windows 2000 Licensing Server

If you have an existing Windows 2000 license server, it's possible to upgrade it to Windows 2003 while preserving the existing license database. During the upgrade from 2000 to 2003, the license service that was installed will be upgraded and the database content will be migrated into the new license database. After the upgrade to Windows 2003, you'll need to reactivate your license server, just as if you had installed a new license server. This can be accomplished by using the "Reactivate Server" option from the action menu in the Terminal Services Licensing Manager.

Managing your TS Licensing Servers

Once your environment grows to become a Terminal Server powerhouse serving thousands of customers with hundreds of servers, you'll need a few tools to ensure that everything is going according to plan with regards to licensing.

Managing Windows 2003 Terminal Services license servers should not take much of your time. There are only a few tasks you'll need to know about:

- Adding new licenses to the license pool.
- Administering the license server.
- Reporting on license usage.
- Troubleshooting client device license acquisition.

Adding Licenses to a TS License Server

All newly–purchased Terminal Server Client Access Licenses must be installed into a TS license server database. Since Windows Server 2003 also supports Windows 2000 licenses, you can also install your Windows 2000 TS CALs onto a 2003 server. (These licenses cannot be used for Windows 2003 Terminal Servers, but at least you'll be able to centrally manage all your licenses.)

TS CALs are purchased just like any Microsoft license. Traditionally, if you bought a Client Access License pack, that pack only contained a license agreement—nothing more than a piece of paper. Now when you buy a TS CAL license pack, it comes with a 25-character license code. This code must be entered into the TS Licensing Wizard for the TS licensing servers. If you buy licenses through a volume license agreement such as Select or an Enterprise Agreement, then you'll need to enter that agreement number into the Licensing Wizard when you add the licenses.

After the licenses have been installed, you must activate them. Licenses are activated via the same three methods you use to activate the license server (Internet, web, or phone). Once activated, the licenses are ready to be distributed to client devices. Clients that previously received the 90-day temporary licenses will be upgraded to full licenses the next time they connect.

In some situations, adding or removing licenses to a license server will cause that server to notify other license servers.

- A domain scope license server will notify other license servers within the same domain.
- An enterprise scope license server will notify other license servers in its Active Directory site.
- An enterprise scope license server will notify other license servers in its domain.

In all of these cases, adding or removing licenses to a Windows 2000 or Windows 2003 license server will cause the server to notify the appropriate Windows 2003 license servers as mentioned. A Windows 2003 license server will not notify a Windows 2000 license server.

As outlined earlier in this chapter, this notification allows the license servers to redirect client requests to other license servers should the first server run out of licenses.

Remotely Administering License Servers

The TS licensing service is mainly a "set it and forget it" kind of service. Theoretically, it only needs to be administered when new licenses are purchased or old licenses are removed.

However, there are times when it would be convenient to administer TS licensing servers remotely. For technical reasons, the TS Licensing Tool cannot be run via a remote Terminal Services session. However, this tool can be executed locally on any Windows 2003 computer and used to connect back to one or more TS license servers. To do this, copy the *licmgr.exe* and the *lrwizdll.dll* files from the *\system32* directory of the TS licensing server to the *\system32* directory of the computer you would like to use. Run licmgr.exe to use the tool.

As was mentioned previously, running the tool in this manner can be helpful when activating TS licensing servers or TS CAL packs. During the activation, the machine running the TS Licensing Tool needs access to the Internet—not the actual license server itself. This method works well in scenarios in which the Terminal Servers are not connected to the Internet but there are certain administrator workstations connected to the Internet and the internal network.

Maintaining TS license servers is simple. One TS licensing console can connect to all of the license servers in your environment, facilitating centralized administration.

Reporting on License Usage

The Terminal Server License Reporting tool, *lsreport.exe*, from the *Windows Server 2003 Resource Kit* can be used to view and analyze the data contained within the licensing server database. This tool outputs the information in the database into a tab-delimited format that allows you to create reports of who is using your licenses. Run "`lsreport /?`" from a command prompt for a list of options.

Uncovering Client Device TS CAL Details

The Terminal Server Client License Test tool, TSTCST.EXE, is a command-line client-side tool that displays information about a client device's local TS CAL. Also included in the *Windows Server 2003 Resource Kit*, it provides the following information about a license:

- Issuer
- Scope
- Issued to computer
- Issued to user
- License ID
- Type and Version
- Valid From
- Expiration date

By using the "*/A*" switch, the following additional information is displayed:

- Server certificate version
- Licensed product version
- Hardware ID
- Client platform ID
- Company name

This tool is used from the command line of a client device. It's useful when you need to locate information about the TS CAL certificate that's stored locally on that device.

Application Licensing

All this work on the Terminal Server licensing might almost make you forget that you have to properly license your applications as well. While the purpose of this book is to focus on Terminal Server, there are some common threads worth pointing out regarding application licensing.

Because there are so many different ways that applications can be licensed, it's impossible go into specifics here. However, in almost all cases, the application usage license is tied in some way to the number of users or client devices. Most application licenses are not linked to the number of times the application is installed because the application vendors don't want you to buy one copy of the application for each Terminal Server that you have and then make that application available to hundreds of users per server.

Most applications today have licensing agreements that fall into one of two categories:

- *Per Named User.* One license for each user that could execute the application.
- *Per Concurrent User.* One license for each concurrent copy of the application that is executed.

Enforcing Named User Application Licenses

Applications that are licensed "per named user" require that you have a license for each user that could access the application. If you have 100 users with access to an application but no more than 10 ever connect at the same time, you still need to purchase 100 application licenses. Most Microsoft applications are licensed this way, in addition to many expensive line-of-business applications.

The key to properly enforcing per named user application licenses is permitting or preventing users from being able to access the applications. An easy way to do this is to create a domain group with all the user accounts of the users that will need to access the application. Then, add these users to the Remote Desktop users group on the Terminal Server hosting the application so that only members of that domain group can use it. This can also be done by setting NTFS permissions on the executable if users that don't use this application connect to the same Terminal Server.

Another option is to create a Software Restriction Policy to restrict that application to only a certain group of users. This policy could be applied in the Group Policy at the OU level for a large number of Terminal Servers.

By restricting access to the application itself, you guarantee that only appropriate users will ever use the application. When it comes time to pay for your application licenses, all you have to do is count the number of users that are in your application group and buy that number of licenses.

Enforcing Concurrent User Application Licenses

Applications whose licenses are based on the number of concurrent users only require that an application license is purchased for each concurrent connection. If you have 100 users that have access to an application but no more than 10 ever connect at the same time, you only need to purchase 10 licenses. Your company's accountants will appreciate applications that are based on concurrency. You will probably not appreciate them because they are harder to enforce from a technical standpoint.

Within Terminal Server, there are two ways to enforce concurrent users:

- Limit the number of connections on the Terminal Server hosting the application. This can be done in the Terminal Server Configuration utility by editing the RDP connection properties.
- Create a batch file that writes to a flag file before an application is launched. That batch file can be configured to check the flag file to see how many other instances of the application are running. For environments in which applications are executed across more than one server, the flag file can be stored on a network drive. When users quit the application, the flag file is updated to reflect the user change. The only problem with this (other than the complexity of writing the scripts in the first place) is that the flag file is not updated if users do not exit the application properly.

Hardware Dongles in Terminal Server Environments

The only additional item worth mentioning about application licensing relates to applications that require a hardware key. If you have an application that requires a hardware key, or "dongle," it probably won't work on a Terminal Server. Microsoft has intentionally disabled this functionality because the sole purpose of a hardware key is to prevent multiple users from using an application, and Terminal Services' sole purpose is to allow multiple users to use an application.

If your hardware key vendor did not use the standard Microsoft APIs when writing the application, the hardware key may work on a Terminal Server. If this is the case for your application you must ensure that its use in a Terminal Server environment is acceptable from a licensing standpoint.

CHAPTER 5

Application Strategies and Server Sizing

Previous chapters detailed necessary considerations for designing your Terminal Server environment. Terminal Server exists for one reason—to allow users to run applications. Clearly, it's important to build your Terminal Server design around the applications that your users require and the methods by which those applications are accessed.

We begin this chapter with a study of what it takes in install applications onto a Terminal Server. We'll then examine how to design load-balanced clusters, and close with a section on Terminal Server sizing and hardware selection.

Installing Applications

When installing applications onto a Terminal Server, the installation is more complex than on standard workstations. (You probably learned this the hard way when you stuck an Office 2000 CD into a Terminal Server and were informed that you needed MSTs and transforms and text editors and…) In Terminal Server environments, you must first prepare the server for a new application installation.

All this extra work is necessary due with the fact that when Microsoft Windows was designed, only one user could be locally logged onto a computer at any given time. With Terminal Server, hundreds of users can be simultaneously logged on "locally."

As an aside, a user is said to be logged on "locally" to a Windows computer if he is viewing that computer's screen and using its keyboard and mouse. In traditional network environments, users are "locally" logged onto their own workstations, but are not locally logged onto the servers because they are only accessing server resources through the network rather than using the server's keyboard and mouse and viewing its screen.

In older versions of Terminal Server, the term "interactively" was used in place of "locally." Now these two terms can be used interchangeably. Technically, to say that a user is logged on "locally" in Windows 2003 is deceptive. Terminal Server users are said to be logged on "locally" even though they're connecting through the network and not using a console session.

Either way, installing applications in multi-user environments such as Terminal Server is more involved than installing applications on regular computers. In this section, we'll take a look at some of the decisions you'll have to make and the problems that you'll likely encounter when installing applications.

Problems with Applications in Multi-User Environments

Prior to installing applications onto your Terminal Servers, you should understand how applications function in multi-user environments. Problems can arise that don't exist in traditional single-user workstation application installs. These problems derive from:

- Application configuration files being used incorrectly.
- The Windows registry being used incorrectly.

Problem 1. Application Config Files are not Used Correctly

A lot of older applications store their configuration options in .INI files located in common folders, such as *c:\program files\old application name\appconfig.ini.* This setup is acceptable if only one user will ever use the application (as in standard workstation-based computing environments), but it doesn't suffice when multiple users need to use the application on the same computer (i.e. the Terminal server). In Terminal Server environments, any configuration options that one user changes would affect users since they are all pointing back to the same .INI configuration files.

Applications that work this way are becoming increasingly rare, although there are still enough of them out there to keep your job interesting.

Problem 2. The Windows Registry is not Used Correctly

Some Windows applications do not properly make use of the Windows registry. Such applications are usually expensive industry-specific applications written by very small vendors (and coincidentally tend to be the types of applications most used in Terminal Server environments).

To understand how applications often incorrectly use the Windows registry, we should first look at how applications correctly use the registry. The Windows registry consists of several main sections, or "hives." Applications store their configuration information in two hives: the "machine" hive and the "user" hive.

- The machine hive (*HKEY_LOCAL_MACHINE*, or simply *HKLM*) contains settings and configurations for applications that apply machine-wide (for all users that log onto that particular computer).
- The user hive (*HKEY_USERS*, or *HKU*) contains application settings and configurations that apply to each individual user, allowing different users to have different settings. If these settings ever conflict with application settings as configured in the machine hive, the user-hive settings take precedence.

The HKU hive has a subtree (a registry folder) for each locally (or "interactively") logged-on user, named by the user's Security Identifier, or SID. Remember from your basic Windows training that a SID is a unique serial number (such as *S-1-5-21-1993962763-920026266-854245398-1002*) that is used internally by Windows to keep track of each user.

Each time a user logs on to a Terminal Server, his own subtree is added to the HKU hive. If you have two users logged onto a server then you will see two SIDs listed under the HKU hive and each user's unique settings stored in the registry structure under his SID. Fifty users logged in at the same time will appear as fifty SID folders listed in the HKU hive.

Incidentally, if you look in the registry (via regedit.exe), you will notice a hive called HKEY_CURRENT_USER, or HKCU. This hive does not contain any real data; rather, it is simply a pointer (or "alias") to the current user's SID in the HKU hive. This hive exists to allow an application that's running within a user's session to be able to read and write settings for that user. (Essentially, the application only has to request data from the HKCU hive, and the system will automatically sort out which SID folder in the HKU hive it will use.)

If you view the HKCU hive from an RDP session that is logged on as "Brian," you will see one set of data. Viewing the HKCU from another session logged on as "Ron" will reveal a different set of data. You can edit a user's registry settings in either place—the HKCU hive or the user's SID subtree in the HKU hive.

For an application to be properly installed onto a multi-user server, the application must store each user's personal configuration options in his personal registry keys in the HKU hive, not in the server-wide HKLM hive. Many of today's applications store configuration information in the HKLM hive, meaning that the same settings will apply to all users. Luckily, there are ways to avoid this scenario in Terminal Services environments.

How Terminal Server Addresses These Two Problems

The main problem introduced by these two application scenarios is that certain applications do not recognize user-specific application settings. Individual users cannot customize their own applications. Another way to describe this issue is that any changes one user makes to the application are suddenly applied to all users of the application.

In traditional, non-Terminal Server environments, whenever a user exclaimed, "I didn't change anything! It just happened," you always knew he was lying.

However, with Terminal Servers, each user is essentially sharing his computer with several dozen of his closet coworkers. Suddenly the "I didn't do it" excuse seems not so ridiculous.

Windows Server 2003 includes features that can help you to alleviate these problems.

How Terminal Server 2003 Handles Application Installations

Put your Terminal Server into an application "installation mode" before attempting to install any applications. When you do this, your Terminal server captures all registry and .INI file changes during the software installation. These changes are all redirected to the *HKLM\Software\Microsoft\WindowsNT\CurrentVersion\TerminalServer\Install* registry location, which acts as a caching area for the current application installation session. This registry location contains two subkeys: *software* and *machine*. Any changes or additions made by the application's installation program to the current user's hive (HKCU) are copied to the software key. Changes or additions made to the machine hive (HKLM) are added to the machine subkey.

After the application installation is complete, take the server out of the installation mode. Subsequently, whenever a user launches an application, the server checks for the proper registry entries in the real HKLM and the user's HKCU and compares those to the entries that the system previously recorded from the software installation. If the entries to not exist in the proper HKLM and HKCU locations, the server will copy them from the install keys listed above to the proper locations in HKLM and HKCU.

Ordinarily, a Terminal Server operates in "execute mode." You can place a Terminal Server into "install mode" by installing new software via the "Add / Remove Programs" component of the Control Panel. When adding new software this way, you're given the choice as to whether you are installing the software for the current user only (causing the server to remain in execute mode) or for any user that logs on (temporarily setting the server into install mode). You can also manually set the server into install mode via the command "`change user /install`." Change it back to execute mode with the command "`change user /execute`." If you forget which mode your server is in, check it with the command "`change user /query`."

Install mode and execute mode work the same for both Terminal Services on Windows 2000 and Windows 2003. Both versions of Windows contain logic that attempts to "force" you to remember to use install mode for installing applications. If you try to run a program like *setup.exe* or *install.exe*, the system will display a pop up box asking you to click "next" once the installation is complete. When this happens, the server has basically forced the system into "install mode" just as if you have manually run *change user /install* from a command prompt. This is a nice feature, because there were many occasions with early versions of Terminal Server when people installed applications only to realize later that they forgot to place the server into "install mode." The only remedy was to uninstall the application, change the server to "install mode," and then reinstall the application.

Some applications need to wait for a reboot in order to complete certain installation. They do this by adding commands to the "*runonce*" registry key (*HKLM\Software\Microsoft\Windows\CurrentVersion\RunOnce*). Any program listed in this key is executed one time after the server is rebooted. Terminal Server is smart enough to use install mode for all entries that are listed in the "runonce" key, even after a reboot.

Dealing with configuration files introduces a whole other set of issues. Generally, 16-bit (and even some 32-bit) applications read a user's settings from some type of configuration files. The most common files are .INI files, but .CFG and .DAT are not unheard of. The problem resides not with the files themselves but with how the applications attempt to locate them.

If an application was hard-coded to look for its .INI file in the *c:\Windows* folder, multiple users logged onto the same system looking to use the same .INI file can be a problem. Most new applications avoid this difficulty by using the *%WINDIR%* system variable instead of containing the hard-coded path of *c:\windows*" In these cases, Terminal Server masks the real *%WINDIR%* from the application, instead redirecting the *%WINDIR%* path to a "*windows*" folder in the user's home folder. (Home folders are discussed in Chapter 6.)

With new applications, at worst you would have to copy the required .INI files to the user's home directory. On the other hand, if the application is absolutely 100% hard-coded to use the "*c:\Windows*" directory and each user requires a unique .INI, you may be out of luck.

Windows Server 2003 Registry Changes

Microsoft made several changes to the registry in Windows Server 2003. (Technically these changes were introduced in Windows XP.) For example, the Windows 2003 registry has no size limit and doesn't consume nearly as much memory, but those attributes are more relevant to server sizing. We'll cover them in Chapter 13.

Relevant here is the fact that Windows 2003 changes the way "classes" are managed in the registry. In the Windows registry, "classes" (and their associated "class IDs") refer the filename associations and data associated with COM objects.

In prior versions of Windows, class information was stored in the *HKLM\Software\Classes* key—a shared location. (This key is an alias to the HKEY_CLASSES_ROOT hive.) Windows 2003 extends this key by writing additional class information to a personal key for each user—the *HKCU\Software\Classes* key. (This key is an alias to the HKU\<SID>_Classes key.)

Translation? Quite simply, it means that with Terminal Server 2003, individual users can each have their own class settings. This is important for two reasons:

- Prior versions of Terminal Server (even as recent as Windows 2000) would often show DCOM errors when shared registry keys couldn't be updated or when an application accidentally registered a class to another user's SID. This doesn't happen in Windows 2003.
- In Windows 2003, you can easily customize file associations on a per-user basis (since those associations are now stored in the HKCU hive instead of the HKLM hive). You can make the default application associated with .DOC files the free Word viewer instead of having to buy a full Microsoft Word license for each user. At the same time, you can have Word installed on the server and configured for only the users who need it. Not only does this save you money, but it also saves server resources, ultimately enabling more users to fit on a server.
- As you can see, the Windows Server 2003 registry has come a long way in terms of supporting multiple users in Terminal Server environments.

Installing New or Untested Applications

Now you can begin the actual process of installing your applications. Although installing an application on a Terminal Server is similar to installing an application on any standard workstation, adhering to some best practices ensures your application is installed properly:

- Install all of the application options that you think any user would ever need. Disk drive space is so cheap and plentiful these days that it really doesn't do any good to restrict certain application features by not installing them (unless you have business reasons to prevent users from using certain application features). For example, if you're installing Microsoft Office, perform a "custom" setup and select all the options.

- Check out the application's "readme" file. Because Terminal Server deals with applications differently from regular computers, there are often little tweaks and tricks that you will need to apply to applications to get them to run correctly. Terminal Server has been around for a while now, and most applications are written to support it. More often than not, Terminal Server-specific information is included in the application's *readme* file. The THIN online community (`http://thethin.net`) gets a few requests per week from novice administrators asking how to install Microsoft Office XP on a Terminal Server, even though the exact process is described step-by-step in the Office readme file.
- Refer to an online support community such as the THIN list. (See the appendix of this book for a complete list.) Whatever application you're trying to install, there's a good chance that someone else has already installed it on a Terminal Server. Visit `http://thethin.net` and search the THIN list archive for your application's name. (This archive grows by about 2000 messages each month.) If you don't find anything in the archive, try sending a message out to the group asking about your application.

Knowing Which Application Options to Use

Many applications used in Terminal Server environments have "workstation" and "server" install modes. These applications have two components: the server component and the workstation component. Since your Terminal Servers are essentially gigantic shared workstations, you need to perform a "standard" workstation install on your servers.

If there's ever a situation in which you don't know which installation options to choose for an application when you're installing it on a Terminal Server, choose the options that you would use if you were installing the application onto a standard user's workstation.

For example, some applications have a "thin client" mode of installation. At first this might seem like the perfect installation option to use on a Terminal Server. But for a lot of applications the "thin client" mode of installation indicates that the bulk of the application's client files have been preinstalled onto a file share somewhere, and that the local workstation install only needs to contain user configuration information. Lotus Notes, Baan, SAP, and PeopleSoft are all examples of these types of applications.

If your application offers it, there's nothing wrong with using this type of "thin client" installation option on your Terminal Server, but you shouldn't automatically use it just because you're using Terminal Services. Again, the bottom line is that you should install your application with the same options as if you were performing a standard end user workstation install.

Legacy Application Compatibility

Microsoft (well, technically Citrix) had to do quite a bit of engineering and redeveloping of many Windows components to allow multiple users to be simultaneously logged on "locally" to servers in Terminal Server environments. Even with the work that was done to the OS, the vendors who create software applications don't always take Terminal Server environments into consideration when writing their applications.

When Terminal Server first came out in 1998, just about every application in existence didn't quite work right when installed on it. To combat that, Microsoft (and the other vendors) created application compatibility scripts that "fixed" applications to work on multi-user servers. These scripts were nothing more than batch files that ran to change certain application settings (file locations, registry entries, etc.).

Fortunately, much has changed in six years, and these application compatibility scripts are largely a relic of the past. Terminal Server 2003 only ships with scripts for three applications (as compared to dozens in previous versions of Windows). However, even though Microsoft has decided it doesn't need to support many legacy applications, you might not be as fortunate in your own situation.

We won't take the time here to detail exactly how Windows uses the few remaining out-of-the-box application compatibility scripts, but it is important that you have at least a basic knowledge of how they work in case you need to design your own for the occasional misbehaving application.

Most application compatibility scripts are used in pairs. The first script is typically executed by an administrator just after an application is installed. The second is run once for each user, usually as part of a logon script. Let's consider a sample application. We'll use Lotus Notes, since it is widely familiar and is (was?) typical of an application that requires the use of compatibility scripts.

Once Notes was installed on the Terminal Server, you had to run the first application compatibility script. This script made several changes to Notes .INI files, changing the default options so to be saved on a per-user instead of per-server basis.

Next, you logged on as a dummy user and perform a Lotus Notes "node" install. This install configured Notes for the user and put a whole bunch of files in his home directory, including more .INI configuration files.

Then you logged on as an administrator and copied all the Notes files from the dummy user's home directory to a network share. The final step was to add the second application compatibility script to each user's logon script. Upon logon, this script would check to see if the current user had a "Notes" folder in his home directory. If not, the script would copy the default configuration files from the network share into the home directory, thus completing the "per-user" configuration of Lotus Notes.

Remote desktops or full screen applications?

Now that you know how to get your applications installed (and where to go for help when you run into trouble), we can look at some different strategies for making these applications available to your users. You'll need to create an application strategy that answers several questions, among them:

- Will your users run full remote desktops or will they simply connect to individual applications?
- If you decide to use only applications, will you configure only one copy of each application or multiple copies with different options for different users?

First be aware of *how* Terminal Server allows users to connect to servers and applications. The basic idea behind a Terminal Server is that it allows a user to launch a remote server desktop session. Within that session, the user can run applications and interact with the server as if it were his workstation. However, Terminal Server and the RDC client allow you (or the user) to specify an application that's launched on the server instead of launching the entire desktop, called an "initial program." These settings can be configured on the client allowing it to connect to different individual applications, even if the servers all reside in the same load-balanced cluster.

Things to Consider when Creating your Strategy

In order to help you create your application strategy, consider your answers to the following:

- What type of client hardware devices will be used?
- How many different applications will each user need?
- How many applications will be on each server?
- Will different types of users need to access the same application?

Client Hardware Devices

If your users are connecting from client devices that have a local Windows desktop such as Windows 95 or Windows XP clients, there is no need for them to run a remote desktop on your Terminal Server. Running a remote desktop in addition to a local desktop could actually be confusing because users would have two Start Menus, two recycle bins, etc. Most users may not understand the concept of having a "local" desktop and a "remote" desktop anyway.

However, if your users are connecting from client devices that do not have local Windows desktops, such as Windows CE or UNIX, running a remote Terminal Server desktop could make it easier for users to run their applications.

Number of Applications per User

If your users open and close several applications throughout the day, a remote desktop shell will probably be faster and easier to use as opposed to connecting and disconnecting to several individual applications.

If users only access a couple of applications and keep those applications open all day, then the full remote desktop is not needed. However, some non-Windows client devices only allow one RDP session at a time. If you want to allow users to multitask, they will need the ability to connect to a full Windows desktop on the Terminal Server, as they would not be able to connect to more than one individual application at a time.

Number of Applications per Server

With many applications installed on each of your Terminal Servers the chances are pretty high that all of a user's applications will be located on the same server. If this is the case, you will most likely want your users to connect to a full remote desktop.

However, if a user's applications are spread across multiple Terminal Servers then it doesn't make sense to force the user to connect to a full desktop on each server. Your users would have to navigate the full desktop shell for each different server—very confusing for them.

Different User Types for the Same Application

If all users for an application have the same configuration, you can create a single connection from the client for that application. At the same time,, there may be some situations in which different groups of users need to access the same application with different parameters. In this case, you may need to create multiple copies of the connection to the application.

Often, the configuration of these applications can be set with a text file referenced via the command line when the application is launched, or you could call a specific file from the command line such as an Access database. With applications like this you can create two different configuration files, one for each group, and then create two different connections to the application. You can specify a different configuration file in the command line of each published application

Consider, for example, a sales database application called "Sales Tracker" that has a different database for each region. The first connection to the application you could be for the North region:

> Connection Name: *Sales Tracker – North*
> Initial Program: *c:\Program Files\Office10\ACCESS.EXE" "\\Server\Share\North.mdb*

You could then configure a second copy of the application for the south region:

> Connection Name: *Sales Tracker – South*
> Initial Program: *c:\Program Files\Office10\ACCESS.EXE" "\\Server\Share\South.mdb*

Furthermore, if the application was a database application that could open a specific DSN, you could also configure it as shown below. The real trick is understanding the types of input and switches your applications can use.

> Connection Name: *Sales Tracker – North*
> Command Line: *c:\SalesTrack\tracker.exe /d:north.dsn*

You could then configure a second copy of the application for the south region:

> Connection Name: *Sales Tracker – South*
> Initial Program: *C:\SalesTrack\tracker.exe /d:south.dsn*

These configurations would allow you to run the applications off of the same Terminal Servers for different groups of users. You could then use file and share permissions to control access to the data files or even the application executables.

What are the Connection Strategy Options?

Despite the myriad considerations involved in creating your connection strategy, there are really only three options available:

- Initial program connections.
- Connections to the Windows desktop.
- Use-third party tools that enable seamless windows.

Option 1. Initial Program Connections

Your first option is to create connections to specific applications for your users. When you do this, users will need to connect separately to each application. Once a connection is launched it will immediately begin the application that has been configured and not allow the user access to the server desktop. Since users are not running the entire Windows desktop from a Terminal Server, individual applications can be easier to secure. Some of the local security policies that affect access to items such as the Start menu and "My Computer" do not need to be used since the server's Start menu and "My Computer" are not available to the user when an initial program is specified. You then use GPOs to really secure the server's desktop from the end users.

Another big "win" with this option is the ability to segregate applications. If your users must run conflicting applications, then these types of connections allow them to launch both applications without having to navigate multiple remote desktops.

A drawback to having users connect directly to applications is that it can give you a false sense of security. You might feel that the users' environment is secure because they don't have a desktop. But if a user can get to a server's remote desktop there would be no security in place. One famous example comes from old versions of Microsoft Word. Even when it ran as an initial program, users could click "Help | About" from within Word. From there, they could launch the System Information utility and choose "File | Run," allowing them to run "explorer.exe," thus opening up a remote desktop shell session.

Another disadvantage to running only this type of connection is that non-Windows users would not receive the full Windows experience. They would be forced to switch between server applications with their local client devices, instead of through the clean Windows interface.

Advantages of Initial program Connections

- One user can use applications from multiple servers or multiple clusters and geographic locations.
- Can be easier to secure.
- Connection settings can be stored centrally.
- Multiple connections to the same server can each have their own RDP settings (such as color depth, resolution, mapping, etc.).

Disadvantages of Initial program Connections

- No desktop for non-Windows users.
- False sense of security.
- Multiple connections (even to the same server) will each start their own RDP sessions.

Option 2. Server Desktop Connections.

In contrast to using initial program connections only, you can choose to give users access to server applications via Terminal Server desktop. This is the default choice and is what happens when an initial program is not specified. (This is also another reason to secure the desktop via a GPO). Users connecting from non-Windows clients with this option get the full Windows experience (although only you can decide if this is actually a good thing). They will be able to quickly switch between applications because all will be running in the same window of one server session. A full desktop will also allow users to do those "little things" that they do with desktops, like adjusting printers, using calculator, and editing files with notepad.

In general, users with access to the full desktop have a fair amount of power and often spend their entire day in remote desktop sessions. Some companies use the full remote desktop and completely lock it down with policies, protecting the servers from those who would otherwise try to change important settings. Some of these locked-down desktops have no icons, only a Start menu with a few programs. (See Chapter 6 for details.)

Remote desktops are not convenient if a user needs to connect to applications on multiple servers since that would require the user to run multiple remote desktops. Also, Windows-based clients already have a local Start menu, so the duplicate Start menu presented via the remote desktop session can be confusing. With remote desktops, providing users the ability to do those "little things" is a double-edged sword. End users could potentially have access to more than you intended. When giving users access to full desktops, even with policies in place, it is crucial that security is adequately addressed. (See Chapter 12.)

Advantages of the Published Desktop

- Quick switching between applications.
- Non-Windows client devices get the full Windows experience.
- Users can more easily do "the little things."

Disadvantages of the Published Desktop

- All applications must be on one server.
- Full Windows clients receive second Start menu and a duplicate desktop environment.
- Users can more easily do "the little things."
- Security must be carefully applied.

Option 3. Seamless Windows with Third-Party Tools

If you decide to use third-party tools, you can make applications available to users via "seamless" windows. Seamless windows are useful for users who connect from traditional Windows desktops. Terminal Server applications accessed via seamless windows look and feel just like local applications to the users. Unlike specifying an initial application for a Terminal Server, seamless applications can be dynamically resized and can fully integrate with the users' desktop.

Add-on products such as Citrix MetaFrame Presentation Server, Tarantella Canaveral iQ, DAT Panther, and Jetro CockpIT all add seamless windows functionality to Terminal Server. (A full feature-by-feature comparison of these products is available in the appendix.)

Connection Strategies in the Real World

In most environments, the manner in which end users access applications depends on many factors. Rarely is the configuration identical for all users across. Many companies have task-based workers that use only three or four applications per day, all day, every day. For these users' needs, it makes sense to use Windows-based thin client terminals configured to run remote Windows desktops. Of course, these desktops only have a handful of icons and no access to configuration information. (See Chapter 9 for about a discussion on thin client devices and Chapter 6 for information on creating the locked down desktops.)

Often, these same companies will also have users with legitimate needs for full PCs. These users, however, can still access specific applications through Terminal Server sessions. They often connect to the applications directly (without first accessing a server desktop). The applications run in a remote desktop window and allow access to the client workstation's drives, printers and COM ports.

It's possible to accommodate both scenarios in the same environment. Many companies have these two environments mixed on the same servers with the same applications—some accessed directly as applications and some accessed via full desktops.

Application / Server Installation Groups

Now is the time to think about your strategy for deciding which applications to put on which servers.

In smaller environments with few applications, you'll likely put all applications on all servers. In a larger environment you might be faced with a tougher decision: what should you do if you have twenty applications and twenty servers? Do you put one application on each server? Do you put all twenty applications on all twenty servers? Most likely your solution will be to create a mixed environment, grouping some applications together on some servers and other applications on other servers.

What are the Application Location Options?

When deciding which applications to put on which servers, there are three basic options:

- Install a few related applications on each Terminal Server (or set of Terminal Servers), creating several different server configurations.
- Install all applications on all Terminal Servers, creating only one type of server configuration.
- Use a third-party application management tool that "virtualizes" all applications.

Similar to other design options we've reviewed thus far, each of these options works well in different situations.

Option 1. Put All Applications on All Servers

Your first option is to configure your Terminal Servers to be identical, meaning that you install all applications onto all servers. If there are a total of five applications in a server farm, then every server in the farm would run all five applications.

There are several other benefits to choosing this course. Users who access multiple applications only need to connect to one server. Greater economies of scale can be realized since every user can be crammed onto one of a few servers. No user has any reason not to do everything on one server. Aspects of this environment make it easier to manage, especially since all the servers are configured the same.

In this case, ease of management may come at the expense of complexity. The more applications installed on your system the better the chance of encountering application conflicts. Going with this type of arrangement also increases the amount of regression testing that will have to be done every time an application is installed or updated. And finally, poorly performing or conflicting applications would not be segregated to separate servers, limiting your scalability.

Advantages of Putting All Applications on All Servers

- Better economies of scale.
- Fewer servers.
- All servers can be 100% identical.
- Less-likely to hit Windows 2003's built-n 32-node load-balancing limit.

Disadvantages of Putting All Applications on All Servers

- Extremely complex application upgrades.
- Frequent server servicing.
- Constantly changing server environment.
- Limited scalability.
- More difficult to troubleshoot.
- Not realistic in large environments.

Option 2. Install a Few Related Applications on Each Server.

If your Terminal Server environment has to support a large number of applications, you might choose to install only a few applications on each server, even if all servers are members of the same cluster. This design essentially creates multiple groups of load-balanced servers, each containing a subset of applications. Such small groups of servers are called "load-balancing groups" or "silos."

The decision already made about the placement of your servers (as discussed in Chapter 3) should not change. The application location decision comes into play only after you've decided where the servers need to reside. Of course, the ability to load balance a set of servers is generally limited within the TCP/IP subnet, affecting your application location decisions. Consider the environment outlined in Figure 5.1.

Figure 5.1 Applications installed on various silos

Applications per Server	Number of Load-Balanced Servers in the Silo
Word Excel PowerPoint Internet Explorer Outlook	60
Data warehouse Production Line Manager	10
Research Application	15
HR Application Payroll	4

The 89 Terminal Servers depicted here are broken down into four separate silos. Each silo contains servers that are load-balanced with similar applications. With this design, an update to a payroll application will not affect servers outside of the HR silo. Additionally, application integration and testing time is reduced as there are fewer applications per server to potentially interfere with any new update.

If a user needs to access applications from multiple silos, he will need to establish RDP connections with multiple Terminal servers. Of course, if the user is using a thin-client device he will have to connect to two separate servers or establish another RDP session from within his remote desktop.

By limiting each Terminal server to a few applications, the overall environment is generally easier to support and maintain. This is true for several reasons. First, since only a few (or even only one) applications are installed on each server, the chance of applications not being compatible with each other is diminished. Also, fewer applications mean fewer application updates with hotfixes and service packs. In general, the fewer number of applications per server, the more static—and stable—the server can be.

This added stability comes at a price. Because applications are spread across many servers, servers (and applications) are not used as efficiently as they could be. Not only might more servers be needed, but those servers will most likely be underutilized. Plus, in order to use the session directory components of Windows Server 2003 (discussed in Chapter 7), you'll have to run the "Enterprise" version of Windows. This version is much more expensive than the standard version, an expense that is magnified in designs that call for many servers.

Advantages of Installing a Few Applications on Each Server

- Ease of support. There are no conflicts between applications.
- Simpler application upgrades. Application version compatibility tests are easier when there are fewer applications that could potentially interfere.
- Application silos can be split among geographic locations
- More static servers. If application hotfixes are released quarterly, six applications on one server result in new server code every other week.

Disadvantages of Installing a Few Applications on Each Server

- Higher Cost. More servers are needed.
- Thin client users may not have access to all applications within their "desktop".
- Potentially underutilized servers.

Option 3. Use a Third-Party Application Management Tool

There is a basic problem with installing many applications on a single server. The applications will conflict with each other since they must first be installed before they can be used. Often the installation process causes common or conflicting components to overwrite each other.

A unique third-party solution is contained in a product called "SoftGrid" from Softricity (`www.softricity.com`). SoftGrid is an application deployment and management solution. The basic concept behind SoftGrid is to isolate an application in its own virtual environment within the user's session. This virtual environment contains all the information (registry information, INI files, program files, etc.) that the application needs to run. When SoftGrid is used, the application is never actually installed on the Terminal Server. Instead, it's run out of a cache it receives from the SoftGrid server.

Softricity's application virtualization is a simple. Imagine that you could run an application on your desktop without ever having installed it. Unlike using Citrix or Terminal Services to connect to it from a client workstation, the application would execute locally using local resources such as the processor, memory, disk, and network card. Conceptually, this approach is similar to running applications from the network (which was popular several years ago), except that SoftGrid emulates the registry and other critical functions so that the applications think and act as if they're running locally.

In addition to avoiding application installations, SoftGrid also gives you the ability to run multiple versions of the same application on one machine. These virtualized applications are isolated from each other in their own virtual environments, each containing the files and registry settings necessary to allow the application to run without ever having to be installed on the client. The application interacts with the local computer and uses the local system as its base just as any other application, except that the virtualized application is not allowed to change the local file system or registry.

The application executes on the local machine (the Terminal Server in this case) using the local machine's resources, but is not allowed to modify the machine. Instead, it runs in a small virtual environment that contains the registry entries and files that it needs to execute. This virtual environment acts as a layer between the application and the operating system. This layer is very "light" (generally a couple of MB of memory) and loads just prior to the application loading.

While this is a high-level overview of how an application executes in a SoftGrid environment, there is obviously much more to this product. Additional benefits you will see when using Softricity's SoftGrid include:

Advantages of Softricity SoftGrid

- Ability to run conflicting applications on a single system.
- No application regression testing is needed when deploying new applications.
- You can usually reduce the overall number of Terminal Servers since you won't waste resources in as many clusters or silos.
- Instant provisioning of applications to Terminal Servers.
- Reduced cost in application management.
- Reduced costs in application troubleshooting.

Disadvantages of Softricity SoftGrid

- You have to pay for SoftGrid on top of your Microsoft and application licenses.
- It's an additional layer of software to manage.
- Overkill for small environments with only a few applications.
- It's one more thing to learn (or one more consultant to hire).

Considerations when Deciding where to Install Applications

A silver-lining to all this apparent complexity is that while there are many issues to consider, each issue on its own is relatively simple solve.

Ask the following questions about each application:

- Who owns and maintains the application?
- How often is the application updated (including new versions, service packs, and hotfixes)? How long does this take?
- Can this application be grouped with others into a logical family (such as Microsoft Word and Excel)?
- Where are the servers going to be located?
- How much server power does the application require?
- What is the total number of applications that you have?
- What type of server hardware do you have?

Application Ownership

If certain groups of applications are owned or maintained by the same groups of administrators, then it makes sense to keep them together on the same servers. That way, each department only has to deal with its own applications. However, if all applications in your environment are supported by one large group of administrators, then this is not a factor.

Application Complexity

Applications that are updated frequently should be kept away from applications that are almost never updated. Imagine that you have two applications, each hosted by two servers. *Application A* is updated every other week, and *Application B* is updated quarterly. If you publish both applications to all four servers then you will need to touch and update all four servers every other week. But if you limit each application to two servers, then you will only need to update those two servers for *Application A* every other week.

Application Groups

If you have certain groups of applications that are used by the same groups of users, it might make sense to confine them to selected servers. Many companies keep all applications specific to a department on Terminal Servers separate from those that host company–wide applications.

Server Location

If you've decided to locate the servers close to their data resulting in the spread of servers across multiple locations, you will need multiple silos due to the broadcast domain limitation of Microsoft's Network Load Balancing (discussed fully in Chapter 7). Even if this were not an issue due to a third-party load balancer, would you really want to load balance across different locations with the data in only one of them?

Server Resources Needed

If many applications require significant server power, it may not be possible (or economical) to put them on the same server as other applications with high resource requirements.

Number of Applications

The more applications you have, the more likely it is that you will need to put specific applications on specific servers. With three applications, you can efficiently put all on each server. However, with one hundred applications, there is no way that you would put all on every server.

Server Hardware

The type of server hardware you have (or plan to have) will also help you decide whether to put all applications on all servers or to divide your farm in silos. With six quad-processor servers, your application installation options would be different from having twenty single-processor servers.

Silo Design in the Real World

In most environments, your decision to create a new silo may have to take into account factors that are not listed above. These other factors are not always technical and can include internal political pressures, pressures to segregate applications that don't have to be, or the need (or imagined need) to segregate a mission critical application. Often companies will go to one extreme or the other. Some will wind up segregating every application or application suite onto different servers with an end result of having too many little environments to manage. Or they will try to install every application into one silo creating a nightmare for themselves as the environment grows and applications continue to be added.

Most designs generally begin with a primary application silo consisting of applications needed by a majority of users. These applications should all be well performing, not conflict with each other, and (of course) not change often. This reduces the amount of changes and possible problems within this silo.

Secondary silos are typically added once the primary silo is up and running. Secondary silos contain applications that conflict with the primary applications, change often, or are extremely resource-intensive. By segregating these applications from the primary silo you ensure that the applications with the largest user base are at a reduced risk for problems.

Generally, the split between these two silos follows the good old fashioned "80/20" rule, where applications that 80% of your users use will be installed in the primary silo and the remaining 20% will be installed in secondary silos. Obviously, this is not a hard and fast rule. Your environment may require a 60/40 split due to a large number of misbehaving or frequently changing applications. Your priority should be to keep it as simple as possible so as to reduce the risk of application problems.

As a final thought, remember that your silo design can have a lot to do with the way your users will be accessing the system. If you have a percentage of users that will require a Terminal Server desktop then you will most likely have a primary silo to support these connections. The opposite also applies. If you're going to host only a few applications and these will be connected to via initial program connections, then a primary silo may not be required.

Server Sizing

Now that you've figured out which applications to install on which servers, you must next address the issue of server size. At first, it may seem like this issue was already addressed in the last section. In fact, it's a very different question.

You might have determined from the last section that you want to make a load-balanced silo that hosts Microsoft Office and Adobe Acrobat Reader. What if you have 1,200 users who need access to these applications? Although you've determined which applications you'll install on which servers, you still must decide whether to build 12 servers that will each host 100 users or 3 servers that will each host 400 users. Terminal Server sizing involves:

- Understanding how server sizing works in Terminal Server environments.
- Creating your server sizing strategy.
- Testing your server sizing strategy.

The objective is simple: to build your servers large enough to support your users, yet small enough accommodate your budget. There's plenty to think about when you get ready to size your servers.

Why should you care about server sizing?

Server sizing is not about buying the fastest processors and the most memory. When it comes to server sizing, the maximum number of users a server can support is less important than the maximum number of users you *know* it can support. If you build a server planning for fifty but only get ten users you will run into problems.

A proper server sizing strategy involves creating a balance between too many small servers and too few large servers. It's possible to build a sixteen processor server with 48 gigabytes of memory. But just because you can build one gigantic server for all of your Terminal Server users—should you? There are plenty of deployed servers out there that have terrible session performance with only 50% of their processors and 30% of their memory utilized.

Server Sizing Options

By building several smaller Terminal Servers, you're able to increase the redundancy of your environment. If you build one gigantic $60,000 server and something happens to it, all of your users are down. However, if you build three $20,000 servers and you lose one, only one-third of your users are not able to access their applications. It really comes down to how many users your're willing to drop at any one time.

Your server environment will ideally balance between the two extreme options:

- Build fewer "large" servers.
- Build more "small" servers.
- Build fewer "large" servers that host more "small" servers via virtual server technology.

A similar topic was discussed previously with regard to the number of applications installed on a server. The difference here is that now we're thinking about the actual number of servers. For example, you might have decided to put only one application on each server. However, if you have 1,000 users accessing that application, you have a choice when it comes to server sizing. You can build a few gigantic servers (two servers supporting 500 users each) or many small servers (ten servers supporting 100 users each).

Option 1. Build a Few Gigantic Servers

Drive space, processors, and memory are so inexpensive these days that many people are transfixed by the idea of creating a few massive servers that can each support hundreds of Terminal Server users. (See Figure 5.2.) They like the concept of only having a few servers to manage and the fact that they can spend money on mission–critical redundant drives, processors, NICs, and power supplies.

Figure 5.2 A few gigantic servers

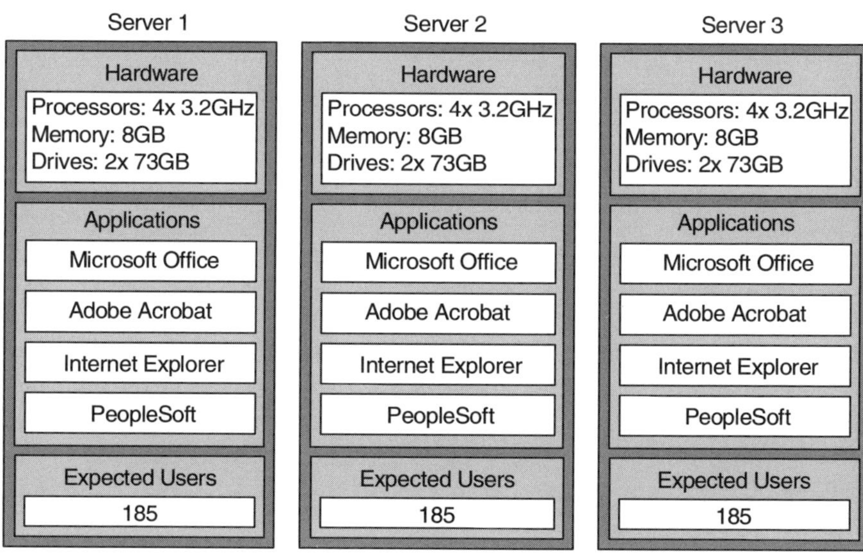

However, every server is going to have limits, and quite often user load does not scale linearly. Two dual-processor servers will commonly scale better than a single quad-processor server in Terminal Server environments.

Advantages of Building a Fewer Large Servers

- More economies of scale.
- Fewer licenses required.
- Fewer servers to manage.

- The scalability of Windows 2003 makes this a reality. (Even more so than Windows 2000.)

Disadvantages of Building a Fewer Large Servers

- Single point (or fewer points) of failure.
- If you support multiple applications, many of them will need to be installed (and therefore tested) together on the same server.

Option 2. Build Many Smaller Servers

Instead of building a few large servers, you might choose to build several smaller servers (as shown in Figure 5.3 on the facing page). This option lessens the risk that one system's failure could debilitate a significant user population.

When considering building multiple smaller servers, two advantages become apparent, most notably redundancy and scalability. Because you have multiple servers, you could lose one without the entire user population going down. (And therefore you might not get paged if this happens, allowing for a full night's sleep.) Also, you can schedule servers to be taken down for maintenance or to be rebooted without affecting everything.

Furthermore, you might be able to support more users with the same amount of money. (Or, you could look at this as being able to save money.) Many Terminal Server administrators also like the fact that building multiple smaller servers gives them more flexibility to dynamically deploy and re-deploy applications as users' needs change.

Another benefit of multiple, smaller servers is the ease with which servers are managed and provisioned today. Many companies are leveraging 1U "pizza box" servers or blade servers to build large farms of redundant servers. (Think of it as "RAIS"—Redundant Array of Inexpensive Servers.) They view Terminal Servers in much the same way as they view thin clients. If one breaks, they can replace it quickly and cheaply and get back to business.

In reality, it becomes easy to replace or increase capacity with the addition of a blade or 1U server, while additional four- or eight-way servers are an expensive way to increase overall user capacity.

Figure 5.3 Many smaller servers

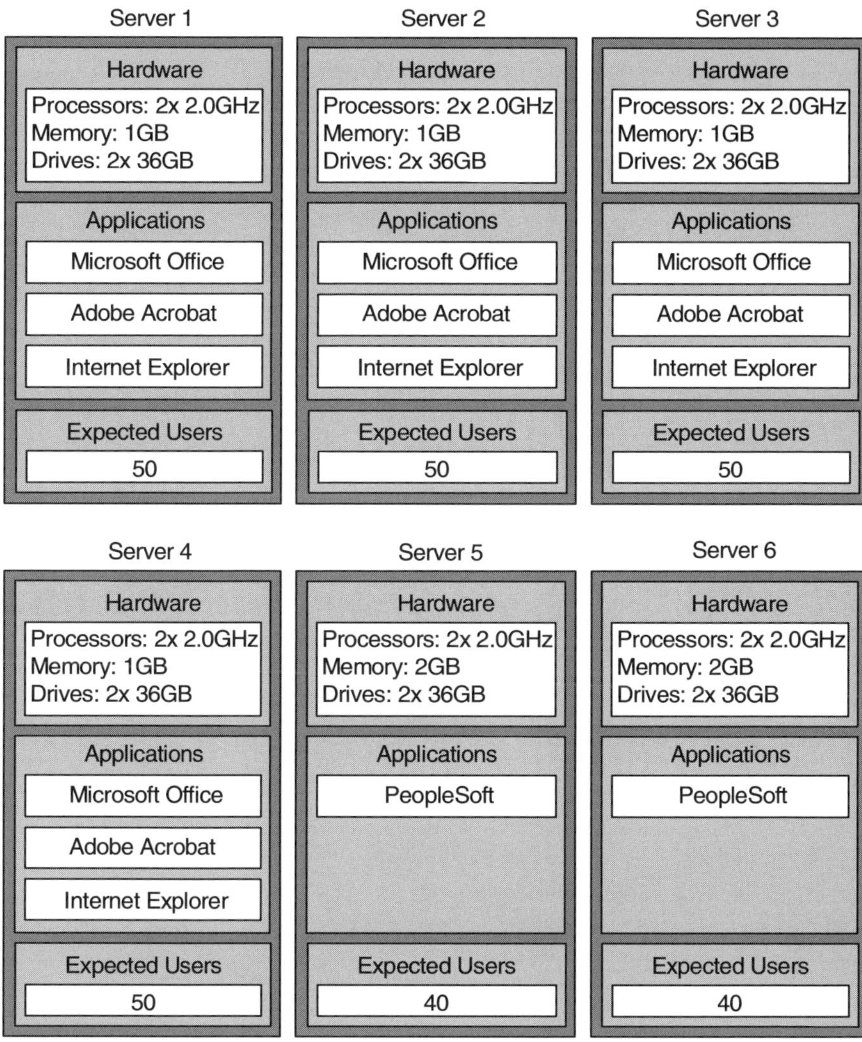

Advantages of Building Many Small Servers

- Redundancy
- Easier scalability
- Flexibility. Redeploy applications and servers and move them around as needs shift.

Disadvantages of Building Many Small Servers

- Some utilization might be wasted.

- You will need to purchase additional licenses for applications licensed on a "per server" basis (such as the Microsoft Windows operating system).
- A higher server count might not work in organizations that are pushing for "server consolidation."

Option 3. Build Large Physical Servers Hosting Several Smaller Virtual Servers

A third popular server sizing option involves building fairly large "host" servers that host multiple virtual server sessions. This is done with products such as VMWare or Microsoft's Virtual Server (which they purchased in 2003 from Connectix).

Both of these products work in the same basic way, as, they allow you to run multiple virtual instances of Windows on the same physical server. Each instance has its own IP address, server name, and virtual drives, and you can reboot a virtual server without affecting the others. In a sense, your host server becomes your "rack," and each virtual server acts as its own server.

Since virtual server technology applied in Terminal Server environments is so new, there are not many definitive best practices as of yet. Refer to the resources listed in the appendix for the most up-to-date information.

Advantages of Using Virtual Server Technology

- Allows you to host more users per physical server than would otherwise be possible.
- Efficient use of server resources (since any resources not used by one virtual server can be used by another).
- Works in environments with "server consolidation" mandates.
- Partitioning a single-server into multiple virtual servers allows you to install applications in separate servers, lessening the risk of application interference.

Disadvantages of Using Virtual Server Technology

- This concept is new, and some people have reservations about using virtual server technology in production environments.
- Server software is usually licensing per virtual server, not per physical server.

Choosing Terminal Server Hardware

The hardware that powers Microsoft Terminal Servers is usually different from that of traditional server environments. Since multiple users simultaneously access Terminal Servers, the hardware tends to be more robust

There is much to consider when picking the hardware that will run your environment. The first rule is to pick "real" server hardware. Desktop computers turned on their side do not constitute "real" hardware. Even though many of your users might have computers that are faster than your servers, they will not perform well. A 2.0GHz Walmart PC with 512MB of memory will not perform nearly as well as an HP Proliant 2.0GHz with 512MB server. Server class hardware and system architecture are what make a server a server.

This is especially true in Terminal Server environments. Terminal Servers are usually pushed to their limits due to the aggregate user processing taking place on them. Low-end PCs typically do not have the internal bus speed or internal bandwidth to support many users, even if they have fast processors and a ton of memory. For testing purposes, low-end PCs are adequate "just to see if it works," but you will not be able to extrapolate any performance numbers from low-end test PCs to real servers.

Let's look at it one more way. You can't keep from upgrading twenty-five workstations by giving them a hosted desktop on a single new workstation. However, you *can* do this if you use a single server. Use common sense and build your Terminal Server like a server. You're going to have a lot of users on this server, so it's not worth cutting corners to save a few dollars.

Now, let's explore server hardware in these environments by looking at some initial strategies for sizing your servers. Detailed performance tuning and optimization techniques are discussed in Chapter 13.

Terminal Server hardware sizing can be accomplished by adhering to one premise: "Lots of processing power, gobs of memory, nothing else matters." Admittedly oversimplified, but if this is the only thing you remember from this section then you'll be doing all right.

Memory

In the real world, memory usage in Terminal Server environments is extremely complex. Rather than explain the details of memory usage here, this section outlines the basic concept. Chapter 13 provides the (somewhat excruciating)

details about how to accurately estimate and test the amount of memory in your Windows 2003 Terminal Servers.

Microsoft recommends 256MB of memory for the Standard and Enterprise editions of Windows Server 2003. However, your Terminal Servers will need much more. Every user that runs an application on a Terminal Server will use the memory for that application just as if they were running it on a normal workstation. For example, a quick check of the task manager shows that Microsoft Word requires about 10MB of memory to run. Each user of Word will need 10MB, meaning that 20 simultaneous users will theoretically require 200MB of memory. This is on top of the overhead required for each user to run a session, which is about 4MB. Twenty users running Word require a collective 280MB of memory on the Terminal Server.

Even a small Terminal Server designed for only 20 Microsoft Office users could easily require 512MB. Large servers that support 100 users typically have 2 to 4 GB of memory.

Processors

When it comes to picking processors for your Terminal Servers, don't waste the time calculating how many megahertz or gigahertz you need to support your users. Processor speeds are dictated by Intel and the hardware vendors, and you're pretty much forced to take whatever they offer—save for some choices regarding cache (more is better for Terminal Server). The real decision when sizing processors is the number of processors. In most cases you need to figure out whether your Terminal Servers will be single, dual, quad or eight processor boxes.

In deciding how many processors you want in your servers, keep in mind that in Terminal Services environments, the multi-user kernel is based on a *cooperative* multitasking algorithm. Each user's session sends requests to the processor only as needed. If one user does not need much processor time, then more processing power is available to others. Terminal Services does not work the same as old timesharing servers with which each user was allocated his particular time whether he used it or not.

Due to cooperative multitasking and the fact that each user's session operates several threads, Terminal Servers tend to scale very well with multiple processors—even when more than two are used. (That whole "Windows doesn't use more than two processors" argument is old school and completely irrelevant in Windows 2003 Terminal Server environments.)

The downside to scaling above dual or quad systems is that you run a greater risk of creating a bottleneck in other areas. You might be able to put more physical memory and processors in the server but then you may have a disk or network bottleneck. (Chapter 13 provides a step-by-step approach to identifying and rectifying any bottlenecks you might find.)

In a perfect world, your processor utilization would constantly be 99%, indicating that you didn't waste money buying too many processors, but also that no users have to wait for processing bottlenecks.

Processors are very fast and very cheap. When sizing servers, many people buy single processor servers that are dual processor capable, allowing them to test with a single processor and then add a second if the single processor does not give the results they want.

Hard Drives

In most environments, your Terminal Servers need to only contain the operating system, the page file, your software application files, and enough free space to temporarily store user profiles and temp files. Permanent user and application data is usually stored on non-Terminal Servers or a storage area network (SAN).

Ideally, all your servers will be identical so that users can successfully load balance across them and you can easily replace individual servers without affecting the entire system.

Because of the way that hard drives are typically used in Terminal Server environments, you don't need very much storage space on individual servers. Most people buy two drives and mirror them for redundancy. It's hard to find drives smaller than 18GB anymore, and 18GB should be more than enough storage space for each server, especially if you follow the guidelines outlined in Chapter 6 to prevent users' roaming profiles from being permanently cached on your servers, and you prevent users from saving data on the servers.

Since Terminal Servers don't store much data locally, you should be able to build your servers with two drives configured to mirror each other for redundancy. Today, most Terminal Servers are the thin, 1U servers or blades with only two drives anyway. If your company standard calls for RAID 5 configurations, don't go overboard for your Terminal Servers. Buying five drives for a mirrored OS and a three-drive RAID array for data is useless if you're not storing data on the system.

Server Hardware Redundancy

Most name-brand servers now have options for redundant and hot-swappable components, including power supplies, fans, memory, network cards, and PCI cards. Many people think these types of redundant devices are needed on Terminal Servers since the Terminal Servers are so important to the business. While this is true, these devices are not always needed in Terminal Server environments.

Quite often, redundancy in Terminal Server environments is built in at the server level. Instead of spending extra money on fancy servers, many administrators spend money on an extra server that can be added into the load-balance cluster to support users if a server is lost. This has the additional benefit of increasing performance on a day-to-day basis since you have more servers than are required and will allow you to "pull" a server from the cluster for maintenance while still being able to host all of the users.

The only problem with this approach is that if a server fails, users' sessions will go down. Even if you build a well-designed load-balanced environment, all you can do is allow your users to seamlessly connect to another server. If you absolutely must do everything possible to prevent a user's session from going down, then you'll need invest in some expensive hardware redundancy for individual servers.

Server Capacity Testing

Once you finalize your strategy (or perhaps in order to help you solidify your strategy), you'll need to run performance tests on your servers to determine the number of users they can support. Though there are dozens of Internet sites and research studies that provide server-sizing benchmarks, it's impossible to get exact results given the variations between environments, including network speed, protocols, Windows profiles, and hardware and software revisions.

One mistake that many people make after performing benchmark tests is to assume that the system will scale linearly based on high-level information available in task manager. Suppose that a server with no users has 4% processor utilization and 150 MB memory utilization. With five active users, the processor utilization rises to 14% and the memory to 200 MB. A quick estimate reveals that the processor would max out at 48 users, with 630 MB memory utilization.

However, performance tests might indicate that 25 users can connect, but any more cause the system to run extremely slow, though plenty of memory and processing power is available. In these situations, the server bottleneck is not visible on the surface with task manager. The disks may be overused or the server's system bus may be full.

It is imperative that a detailed analysis be performed to determine the true system utilization. It should be no surprise that Microsoft recommends purchasing the fastest server possible. In most situations, however, this is not feasible, so you will have to test your server hardware to determine your maximum load.

There are several tools and techniques that you can use to determine the capacity and performance of your Terminal Servers. You'll need to simulate user load on your servers and record the performance of the system. From there, you'll be able to determine the system's bottlenecks and capacity limits.

It should be noted here that performance should not only be looked at from a server performance metric standpoint (like processor and memory utilization), but also from an end user response time perspective. User sessions may slow down before any server metrics seem maxed out. Some load testing tools will do this while watching server metrics and can inform you of a performance problem on either side of the test. If you are not using one of these products you should at the very least keep a connection open to the server that you can use to test responsiveness within the session.

Regardless of the exact tool or technique that you use, all capacity planning and testing follows the same basic methodology:

- Choose the application or applications that you would like to use for the load testing.
- Determine what tasks a user will do within that application.
- Determine what performance speed or response time is required (how fast the user should be able to complete a task).
- Determine how users use the application.
- Create a script or automated process that can simulate a user using the application.
- Prepare to monitor the server's performance during the test.
- Perform the test by executing the scripts.
- Analyze the results.
- Ask your boss for more money to buy a bigger server.

Results from this method of server testing should tell you two things:

- How many users the server can support.
- How the server performs when it is highly loaded. (For example, does performance lag for current sessions, or does it stop accepting new sessions?)

Let's detail each of the testing steps.

Step 1. Choose your Test Application

When testing the performance of a server, the first thing to do is identify an application or applications to test. Ideally, you'll be able to test the applications that are most important to your business.

Step 2. Determine Test Tasks

Once you've determined an application that you want to use for your testing, you need to think about what users will be doing with that application. Is it a line-of-business application where users will be entering data into forms and running reports on that data, or is it a spreadsheet application where users will be performing calculations? Maybe it's a word processing application where users write documents?

Step 3. Determine Appropriate Response Times

Identifying the appropriate application response time will allow you to determine whether a server is too busy. If your test application is Microsoft Word, you might require that a letter appear on the screen within 0.2 seconds of the user pressing the key. This would be your threshold for acceptable performance. Later on in your testing process, you may find that your server can support 130 simultaneous users before crashing, although each user has to wait 0.5 seconds for the key response delay. In this case, you may find that you can only support 80 users with the 0.2 second response time.

As another example, your users might need to pull up reports in a line of business application. You need to determine what the appropriate wait time is for them. If you decide that a user should not have to wait more than 15 seconds for a report, then it is unacceptable to put 60 users on a server if they must each wait 20 seconds for their reports.

Step 4. Determine how Users Use the Application

Once the appropriate responsiveness of your applications is identified, you need to determine how active your users are. For example, some users enter data into a screen, then rummage around through papers at their desk, then enter more data. For these users, you might discover that they can enter the data in 10 seconds, but that they only do this once per minute. On the other hand, more active users might perform the same 10-second transaction six times per minute.

Knowing your mix of users is important, because a server that can support 75 "slow" users might only be able to support 40 active users. When testing you should try to simulate the activity of the user population as closely as possible.

Step 5. Create the Application Simulation Script

Now that you've thought about the application that you would like to test and the way that users will use the application, you can begin thinking about the testing process itself. The main technique you'll use in your capacity planning is to have multiple users access your application at the same time. By watching the performance of the system during this time, you can determine how the system will scale.

Instead of cornering a bunch of users and asking them to "use the system" while you observe the performance, most people create user simulation scripts. These scripts simulate users using the system. The nice thing about creating a script is that you (as one single person) can test hundreds of users accessing the system at the same time. The other advantage of using a script instead of test users is that you can get consistent, repeatable loads and thus you'll know if any changes you make to the server actually affect performance.

An application simulation script is essentially a batch file that automates the process of a user launching and using an application. There are dozens of tools on the market that can be used to script your user sessions. The most popular are detailed in Figure 5.4.

Figure 5.4 Popular Windows application usage scripting tools

Product	URL	Cost
AutoIt	www.hiddensoft.com/AutoIt	Free
WinBatch	www.winbatch.com	US $100
WinTask	www.wintask.com	US $100

These tools offer a "recording" mode that allows you to perform some functions (such as typing a document, browsing the web, using PeopleSoft, etc). Once a script is recorded, you can play it back to simulate a user using the system.

When your application simulation script is complete, you should end up with a file or files that you can launch from the command line (such as, *"autoit.exe*

/word" or "*myappscript.cmd*"). The script should launch the application and then begin "playing back" the simulated user interaction.

Step 6. Prepare to Monitor the Performance

Before you begin testing, you need to configure your system to record the performance of your server during the testing. It's important that your testing data is logged and saved. While you're conducting the test, you will be focused on creating a good simulation. You don't want to worry about trying to view the results of the test as you're conducting it. It's much better to record the results and view them in detail at a later time.

There are two ways to measure performance in Terminal Server environments:

- Use a third-party performance monitoring tool.
- Use the Windows Performance MMC snap-in.

Most third-party tools utilize the same counters that are found within the Windows Performance MMC. These tools usually offer the advantage of logging results to a SQL database and offering more enhanced analysis capabilities.

Another advantage to using third-party tools is that some of them can track Terminal Server session response time. However, for many situations, Windows' built-in Performance tools will do just fine.

Think back to your Windows training. Do you remember how to use the Windows Performance tool to record performance counters to a log file so that you can view them later?

1. On the Windows 2003 Terminal Server that you would like to test, launch the Performance MMC (Start | Programs | Administrative Tools | Performance).
2. Expand the tree under "Performance Logs and Alerts" in the left pane. Right-click on "Counter Logs" and choose "New Log Settings...."
3. Type a name for your new log file. This should be a "friendly" name, such as "50 user test with MS Word."
4. Click the "Add..." button on the screen that pops up. This is where you choose the specific counters to record. For Windows 2003 Terminal Servers, you should monitor the following performance counters

   Process | Working Set | _Total

Memory | Pages Input/Sec
Memory | Pages Output/Sec
Memory | Available Bytes
Terminal Services | Active Sessions
Paging File | % Usage | _Total
Processor | % Processor Time | _Total
System | Processor Queue Length
Physical Disk | % Disk Time
Physical Disk | Current Disk Queue Length
Network Interface | Bytes Total/sec | Select your card
Network Interface | Output Queue Length | Select you card
Memory | Free System Page Table Entries
Memory | Paged Pool Bytes
Cache | Copy Read Hits %

5. If Terminal Server sizing and optimization is new to you, be sure to also read Chapter 13, which provides an in-depth description of how to read each of these counters and how they're relevant to Terminal Server sizing.
6. Highlight each counter and instance that you would like to record and click the "Add" button to add them to the log file. After you've selected all the counters you'd like, click the "Close" button to go back to the log file settings screen.
7. By default, the system is configured to record a sample of the data every 15 seconds. Depending on your test size and hard drive space, you might want to increase the frequency to every 5 seconds or so.
8. If you would like to change the path of the log file, you may do so by clicking the "Log Files" tab. (Note: if you wish to be able to import this data to Excel for creating charts, you can change the data type of the log file to a Comma Delimited format.)
9. You can also click on the "Schedule" tab to configure your log file to automatically start and stop at specific times, although most people don't do this when they're running specific tests.
10. Once your counter log is fully configured, it will appear in list in the Performance MMC. When it's time for your testing to begin, you can start the log by right-clicking it and selecting "Start" from the context menu. The icon next to the log will change from red to green.

Step 7. Conduct the Test

Now that you have your application simulation scripts created and are ready to monitor the performance of the server during the test, you can begin the actual testing process.

There are several ways to launch the test scripts. Most people simply launch several RDP sessions and then manually kick-off the test script from the command line. You could also automate this process by placing a shortcut to the test script in the Startup folder so that the script runs as soon as the RDP session is launched.

Microsoft provides some Terminal Server capacity planning tools in the Windows Server 2003 Deployment Kit and Windows Server 2003 Resource Kit. These tools, called Roboclient and Roboserver, help you automate the testing process. While these tools can be helpful, they have limitations. The Roboclient software only allows five concurrent RDP sessions from a single client device, even though a decently-sized client can easily support 10-15 sessions.

Regardless of the exact testing methodology that you use, you must also attend to the following:

- Add your test users in groups. Never attempt to launch 20 connections at a time. Instead, try adding groups of 5 or 10 users spaced four or five minutes apart.
- Start one session from a client device that does not run the automated test script. This session will allow you to understand how the load affects "real" user sessions throughout the testing process.
- Keep in mind that the script interpreter (or whatever mechanism you're using to run your test scripts) will require some resources. This could potentially need to be subtracted from the actual performance numbers.
- Once your server begins to near its full load, you should start adding users one at a time instead of five at a time.

Don't forget to stop your performance monitor recording log once your testing is done. You can then examine it to determine the results of your test.

Step 8. Analyze the Results

Once you've stopped your performance monitor log, view the results within the Performance MMC console. With the "System Monitor" object highlighted in the left-hand pane, click the button with the picture of the cylinder on it and browse to your log file, configuring the graph so that it pulls its data from the log file instead of from the current system activity.

Even after you configure the graph to get its data from the log file, you'll notice that the graph is still blank. You must manually add the performance counters that you want to view. Use the "+" button on the toolbar, just as you would with live data. The only difference is that when you're displaying data from a log file, the only performance counters listed will be the ones you recorded in the log file.

Chapter 13 details what you need to know to successfully analyze the results of your performance test.

As you analyze your results, keep in mind that you're looking for the bottlenecks in your system. Every system will max out at some point. If your system seems to be running out of memory then you can probably add more. Once you do that and run the tests again, you might find out that you can support 10 additional users but then your processors start to max out.

Another fact to keep in mind is the amount of resources that are used by the testing software. Some software packages can add 2-5 MB of memory per session that is tested. Also, capturing performance logs takes up system resources.

Based on the data from the log file of your test, you can probably figure out the point at which your server performance starts to fall drastically. Looking at the Active Sessions counter will tell you how many sessions there were when that performance drop occurred. Once you determine how many users your system can hold, you may want to run your tests again. For this second round of tests, ask live users to log on in addition to your test users. The live users will be able to tell you whether the system is usable or not.

You can import your performance data into Excel if you saved it as a comma delimited file. Browse to the log file and open it directly with Excel. You will notice the counter name is across the top row and the counters from the test form the columns. These columns can be highlighted and a chart can be inserted into the worksheet. When creating these charts, you will generally include a standard performance counter and the number of active sessions, allowing you to compare how a resource performed as the user load increased. Charts are an easy way to create detailed reports for management justifying why you need more hardware.

Server Sizing Tools

If your Terminal environment is important to your business, or if you work for a consulting company, there are some third-party server sizing and stress test tools that are easy to use and produce accurate results. (Of course, the downside is that they are expensive.)

The two most popular tools are StressTest by Scapa Technologies (`www.scapatech.com`) and LoadRunner by Mercury Interactive (`www.mercuryinteractive.com`). These tools are similar. In addition to being easy to use, they have the ability to test the performance of a Terminal Server from end-to-end, instead of only testing the impact of multiple user sessions and application execution as with Microsoft's RoboClient and Citrix's Citrix Server Test Kit.

The Scapa and Mercury tools can test the aggregate affects of server load, network bandwidth, compression, encryption, and virtual channel use. Also, because they work by using dedicated testing workstations to monitor session performance, the testing itself doesn't impact the results (unlike the Performance MMC which itself consumes server resources).

The process by which these third-party tools are used is the same as described earlier in the chapter. You still have to write application simulation scripts. However, the third party tools make it easier to run the tests and interpret the data.

Both the Scapa and Mercury tools are widely used, and it's up to you to determine which is more appropriate for your environment. Mercury Interactive has always positioned themselves at the top tier of testing products, and their pricing for their Terminal Server tools reflects that. (Their product is more than twice the cost of Scapa's product.) However, if you work for a consulting company, Scapa offers a "consulting" license that allows you to take their testing tools from customer to customer.

Advantages of Third-Party Testing Tools

- They test the performance of the entire system, not just the server.
- They employ outside "control" testing stations, so the act of testing does not skew the testing results.
- They provide the most accurate, end-to-end Terminal Server sizing and stress testing.

Disadvantages of Third-Party Testing Tools

- They are expensive.

CHAPTER 6

Customizing the User Environment

In this chapter, we'll look at the technical components that shape the environment of your users' Windows 2003 Terminal Server sessions. These include the elements that work together to ensure each user gets customized access to their environment and information, including:

- Active Directory user attributes.
- User profiles.
- Policies.
- Home folders.
- Logon scripts.

We'll conclude with a real world case study detailing the solution that a hospital network came up with for their users.

The key to success when creating Terminal Server environments is to create a balance between giving users total freedom to configure their environment and locking down your server in order to ensure it's stability. This chapter analyzes the many ways in which you can manage your users' environment.

Active Directory User Object Attributes

We'll look first to the very basics—configuring properties of a user's Active Directory account object.

Each of the user attributes discussed here can be found in the "Sessions" or "Environment" tab of the user account object's properties within the Active Directory User and Computers MMC snap-in.

- *Starting Program* specifies the application that should be executed whenever the user opens a Terminal Server session. This is the same as the "initial program" settings described elsewhere in this book.
- *Connect Client Drives at Logon* will map back to the user's client drives within their Terminal Server session.
- *Connect Client Printers at Logon* will connect the printers from the client device to the user's terminal session.
- *Default to Main Client Printer* will configure the default printer within the session based on the default printer configured at the client device. The *connect client printers* option must be enabled for this to have an effect.

- *End a Disconnected Session* configures the amount of time that a session remains in a disconnected state before the server terminates it.
- *Active Session Limit* specifies the maximum amount of time that a session can be active before the server takes some action. This setting is optional, and most environments don't have session limits.
- *Idle Session Limit* configures the amount of time that a connected session can be in the idle state before the server takes some action. This setting is also optional.
- *When a Session Limit is Reached or Connection is Broken* allows you to specify what action is taken when the active session limit or idle session limit is reached. This action can consist of automatically disconnecting the session or terminating a session.
- *Allow Reconnection From* configures whether a user must reconnect to a session from the original disconnecting client or any client.

The nice thing about configuring these settings on a "per user" basis as part of a user's account object is that they follow the user from server to server and apply no matter where the user logs in. (However, we'll see later in this chapter that these settings can be overridden with policies.)

Advantages of Configuring User Settings at the User Level

- Allows you to specify different settings per user.
- Simple to apply and configure.
- Settings will follow the user to any Terminal Server.

Disadvantages of Configuring User Settings at the User Level

- Each user must be configured individually.
- Management is difficult.

These settings are generally not modified at the user level but instead are done at the server level or with a Group Policy. (More on this later.)

User Profiles

Windows 2003 user profiles allow customization and configuration of your users' environment. A "profile" is a collection of settings, configurations, and personal files that are unique to each user. Profiles permit multiple users to have different environments, even if they're all connected to the same server at the same time.

Correctly implementing user profiles allows one user to set his Windows background to a picture of his kids, his mouse pointer to a dinosaur, and his menu color to purple—while another user can log on with normal settings.

There are hundreds of components that can be configured via user profiles. Some of these include:

- Windows desktop configuration and settings
- Internet connection settings
- Printers and mapped drive connections
- Temporary Internet file locations
- Application settings, such as file paths, options, and preferences

In addition to the hundreds of Windows components that can be configured with a user profile, every application loaded on a server introduces more of its own settings. (Microsoft Word has hundreds of settings, including file save locations, custom dictionary locations, grammar checking preferences, etc.) In fact, you can use a profile to customize practically any setting stored in the registry.

Before discussing how user profiles are used in Terminal Server environments, let's see how they work.

How User Profiles Work

A user that logs on to any Windows NT, 2000, XP, or 2003 computer uses some form of a Windows user profile. This user profile is made up of two parts:

- A collection of user-specific files and folders.
- Registry settings.

The files and folders that make up a Windows user profile allow each user to have his own unique environment. One user's "My Documents" folder can be different from another user's "My Documents" folder. Even though each user sees the folder as "My Documents," they are two separate destinations accessed by two separate paths.

In addition to "My Documents," user profiles also include folders such as Desktop, Temporary Internet Files, Start Menu, and Favorites. (Basically, any folder containing files specific to a user is part of the user profile.) User profiles are important in Terminal Server environments since there can be hundreds of users on the same server at the same time, and each needs access to his own custom folders.

In addition to the collection of folders, a user profile also contains Windows Registry settings that are used to maintain the user's individual application preferences and settings. These include the file save locations in Microsoft Word, the proxy settings for Internet Explorer, the mouse cursor and scroll speed of Windows, and mapped printers and network drives.

Registry settings are stored in each user's profile in a file called *ntuser.dat*. Whenever a user logs on to Windows, his preferences are read from the *ntuser.dat* file in his user profile and merged into the system registry for his session. (Remember from Chapter 5 that the HKEY_CURRENT_USER registry hive maintains the user's settings during the session.)

Because each user has his own HKCU hive (even when multiple users are logged on at the same time), each can have his own settings on a Terminal Server. This means that each user also has his own *ntuser.dat* file to permanently store his settings.

What about the few remaining applications that use .INI configuration files instead of the registry for their configuration information? How do user profiles support different .INI files for different users? Fortunately, the architecture of Terminal Server allows multiple users to each have his own copy of centralized .INI files, even if these .INI files are stored in common locations. This architecture is set up automatically when a server is placed into "install mode" for application installation. (Refer to Chapter 5 for more information on install mode.)

When an application is installed while the server is set to "install mode," any .INI configuration files usually written to common folders are instead diverted to the user profile location. For example, if an application installation procedure tries to create a file called application.ini in the c:\windows\ folder, Terminal Server will add a "Windows" folder to the user profile and put the application.ini file in that new folder. Then, whenever the application looks for its application.ini configuration file, it is redirected to the stored .INI file in the user profile, not the one in the common Windows folder. This allows each user to maintain his own unique settings for applications, even if the applications don't properly use the Windows registry.

In order to further understand user profiles, let's examine a sample. Figure 6.1 lists the files and folders that together make up the "default" user profile. In the real world, all user profiles are different, but this table lists the basics.

Figure 6.1 Elements of a user profile.

File or Folder	Description
NTUSER.DAT	Registry file containing all HKCU registry settings for that user
ntuser.dat.LOG	Transaction log file for ntuser.dat
ntuser.ini	Contains a list of directories excluded from the roaming profile and the last state of the profile upload to the network location
Application Data	User specific application configuration information
Cookies	Internet Explorer cookies
Desktop	Contents of the Windows Desktop
Favorites	Windows Favorites shortcuts
Local Settings	Contains Temp, Temporary Internet Files, and History folders for the user
My Documents	My Documents
SendTo	Shortcuts for the user's "Send To..." context menu
Start Menu	Custom shortcuts for the user's Start Menu
Windows	Any Windows folder components that are specific to that user, usually configuration and log files. This directory can also be located in the user's home folder.

It's important to note that every user who logs on to your Terminal Server has some form of user profile, even if that user only runs a single application and not a Windows desktop. This is due to the fact that running an application in an RDP session does not prevent Windows from running a server desktop in the background. Terminal Server hides this desktop from the user so that the user can use his own local desktop.

Now that we've reviewed the basics of Windows user profiles, let's take a look at the four different ways that profiles can be used in Terminal Server environments:

- Local profiles
- Roaming profiles
- Mandatory profiles
- Flex / Hybrid profiles

Every Terminal Server user profile must be one of these four types. Each type is useful for different situations, and you can mix and match different types on the same server as needed.

User Profile Type 1. Local Profiles

A "local profile" is a user profile stored locally on one computer. Local profiles contain the files, folders, and registry settings for each user as previously discussed. However, local profiles are only applied to the user environment when the user logs on to the computer where the local profile is stored. By default, local profiles are stored in the *\%systemdrive%\Documents and Settings \%username%* folder.

Because local profiles only apply when the user logs on to the particular computer where the profile is stored, they work best when users are allowed to save their settings and configurations in single-server environments.

As outlined in Figure 6.2 (next page), whenever a user with a local profile logs on to a Windows 2003 server, the system will search its local hard drive to see if the user has an existing local profile. If the user's profile is found, it is loaded into memory and its settings are applied. If the system cannot find an existing local profile for the user, a new local profile is created by making a copy of a generic profile template. This creates a local profile for the user, and any changes made to the configurations or preferences are stored in the user's new local profile. When the user logs off, the system retains the user's local profile so that the next time the user logs on to that computer his own customized environment is loaded (complete with pink backgrounds and dinosaur cursors).

Local profiles work well when users only log on to one server. The main disadvantage of local profiles is that they are always "local" to the computer where they were created. If a user has a local profile on one computer and logs on to another computer, a different local profile will be used or created. There is no way for the second computer to access the profile that the user has created on the first computer.

Obviously, local profiles can cause problems in an environment with multiple Terminal Servers since each server will contain a different local profile for each user. In an environment with five Terminal Servers, each user would have five different local user profiles. Users would get a different profile depending on which server they logged on to. Confusion would be compounded when users connected to load-balanced applications where they are automatically connected to the least busy server. One day, a user might connect to Server A. The next day, he might get Server B. From the user's standpoint, each day could bring a different profile with a different Windows background or application settings.

Figure 6.2 The user logon process with local profiles

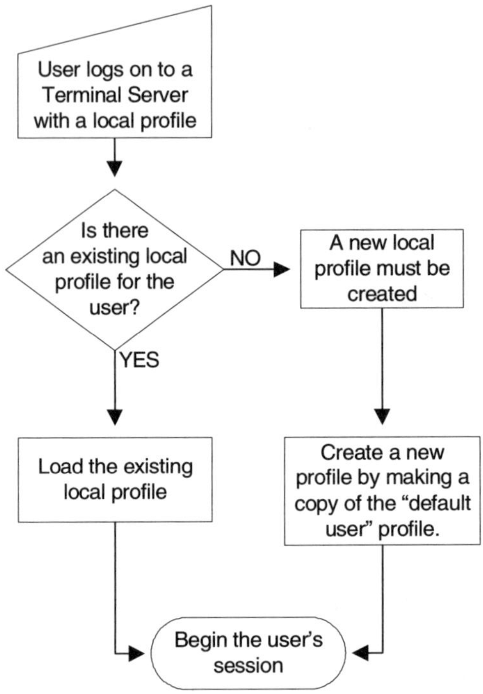

In light of this scenario, it would be helpful if there were a way to store user profiles in a centralized location, allowing the user to get his own profile no matter what Terminal Server he logged on to. Roaming profiles accomplish just that.

User Profile Type 2. Roaming Profiles

A roaming profile is a user profile stored on a network share instead of on a local computer. When the user logs on to a computer, the computer checks to see if that user is configured to use a roaming profile. If so, the computer copies the contents of the user's profile from the network share to the local computer, and the profile is loaded into its memory. In this way, each user gets her own environment no matter where she logs on. Any changes that the user makes throughout the session are saved in the profile. When the user logs off, the profile is copied back to the original network share. That way, the next time the user logs on, the environment is exactly as she left it, even if she logs on to a different computer.

Figure 6.3 The user logon process with roaming profiles

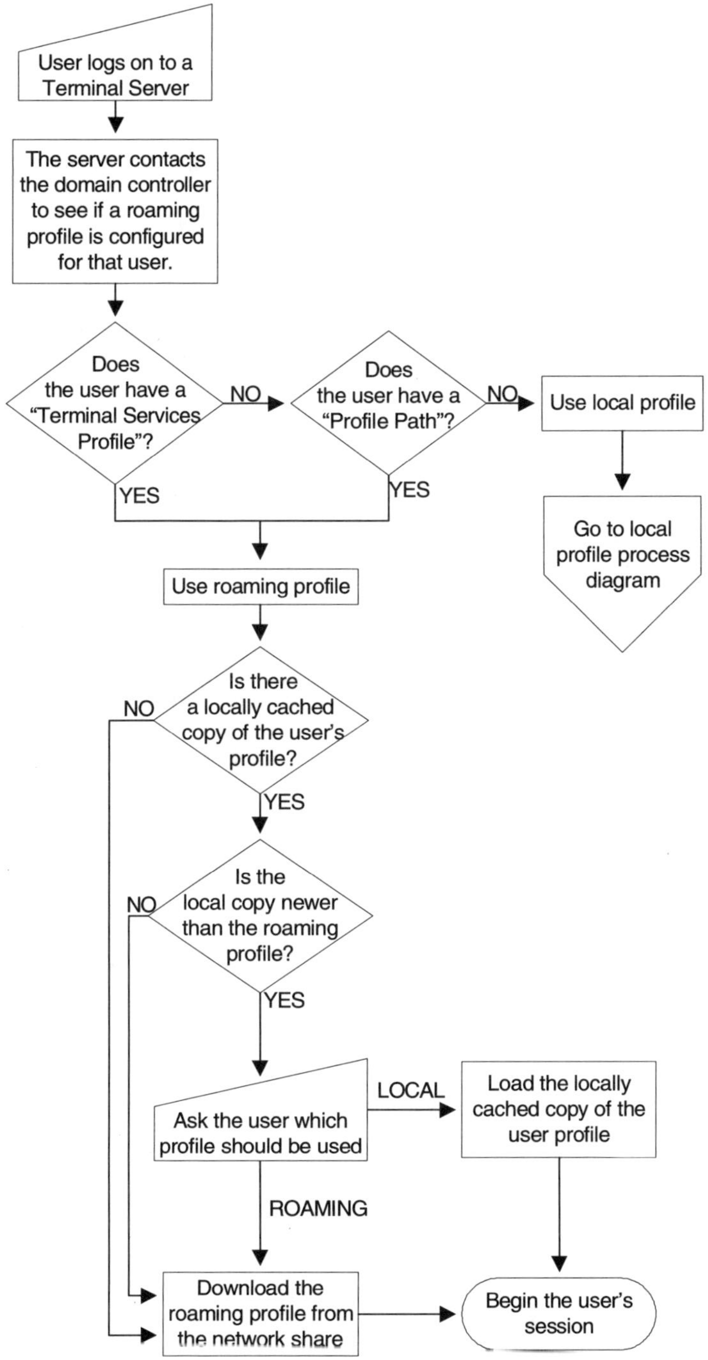

For a user to have a roaming profile, you simply specify the network path where the profile will be stored. (Do this by editing the user's attributes in Active Directory Users and Computers or be configuring a profile path via a GPO.) When configuring a user's domain account, you will see two profile fields listed in the user's properties. One is labeled "User Profile" and the other is labeled "Terminal Services Profile." Both of these fields allow you to enter the network share path where the "master" copy of the roaming profile will be stored.

These two fields are empty by default, indicating that the user is configured for a local profile. To configure a roaming profile, you must understand the differences between these fields and how they relate to each other. Let's consider what happens when a domain user logs onto a Terminal Server. You can visualize this process with Figure 6.3 (previous page).

When a domain user logs on to a Terminal Server, the server contacts a domain controller and receives the user's profile paths. It then attempts to load that user's roaming profile from the network path specified in the "Terminal Services Profile" text field property of the user's account. If that field is blank, the server will attempt to load the roaming profile from the path specified in the "Profile Path" text field. If that field is also blank, the server knows that no roaming profile has been specified, and so it creates or uses a local profile.

If a user logs onto a non-Terminal Server, the system will immediately look for the roaming profile in the "Profile Path" location, bypassing the "Terminal Services Profile" text field. This allows you to specify different profiles for users depending on whether they log on to a Terminal Server or a regular computer. This is useful because profiles on Terminal Servers tend to be different from profiles on regular workstations.

When a user with a roaming profile logs off of a computer, the roaming profile is copied from the computer back up to the roaming profile master location. As a result, the user will access the most up-to-date profile the next time he logs on, including any changes made during his last session.

Figure 6.4 The user logoff process with roaming profiles

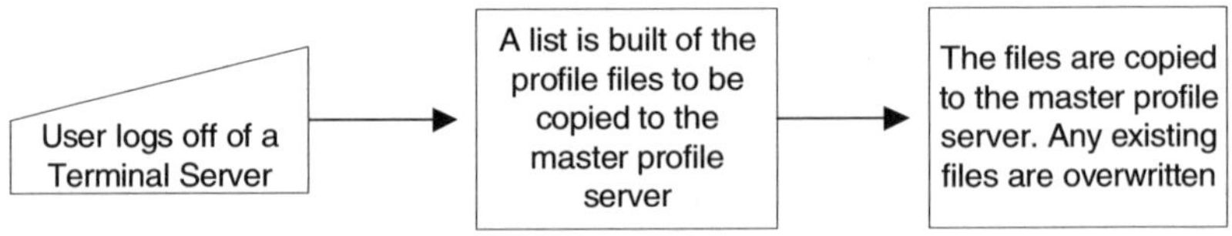

Roaming profiles contain the same components, files, and folders as local profiles. In fact, if you were to compare the two types of profiles, you would find them to be identical. The only difference is that a profile stored in the network location specified in the user's domain account properties is called a "roaming profile." If the profile is stored locally on a computer not specified in the user account, it's called a "local profile."

Roaming profiles are great for Terminal Server environments, although there are a few things that you need to be careful with. The first is that as users use their profiles, the collective size of all the files that make up the profile will start to grow. Left unchecked, user profiles can potentially grow to several (or even hundreds of) megabytes. This can severely slow down the logon and logoff process since all those files would need to be copied across the network. (This is so important, in fact, that a whole section of this chapter is dedicated to limiting the size of your roaming profiles.)

Another potential problem with roaming profiles occurs when you have multiple groups of Terminal Servers separated by WAN links. On which side of the WAN do you store the profiles for users who need to use servers on both sides? Fortunately, there are tricks you can implement via Terminal Server GPOs that override your users' Terminal Server profile paths. We'll look at user GPO settings that are specific to Terminal Server later in this chapter.

User Profile Type 3. Mandatory Roaming Profiles

If you need strict control over your users, you can implement mandatory profiles. Mandatory profiles are a form of roaming profile. They both operate in the same way, except that with mandatory profiles the user's settings are not saved when they log off. Any configurations or settings that the user changes are not retained.

Mandatory profiles allow you to create standard profiles distributed to multiple users. They prevent users from "breaking" anything, since their changes do not get copied back up to the master profile location when they log off. The next time they log on, their mandatory profile is downloaded again, exactly the same as it was the first time.

User Profile Type 4. Flex / Hybrid Profiles

The last profile type is called a "flex" or "hybrid" profile. (These terms are usually interchangeable.) A flex profile is not really a profile type as defined by Microsoft. Instead, it is process that combines the security and control advantages of mandatory profiles with some scripting to achieve the flexibility of roaming profiles. Flex profiles have the advantages of roaming and mandatory profiles without the weaknesses.

Flex profiles allow you to control the user environment while still letting the users have some leeway in what they can and cannot change. The best part about flex profiles is that you can define *which* parts and settings of the profile are retained the next time the user logs on and which are discarded.

Figure 6.5 The user logoff process with Hybrid profiles

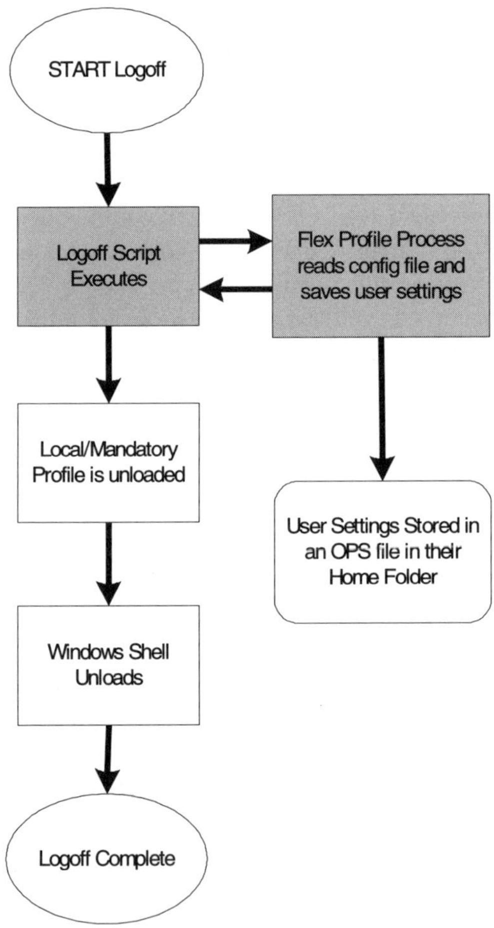

With the flex profile, you configure a mandatory profile for your user's Terminal Server session. This mandatory profile is loaded the first time a user logs on to your Terminal Server. The user works in her environment and modifies her settings as usual (most likely Office settings). When the user logs off, a script runs that calls an executable that saves the configurable settings you specified a file in the user's home folder. This file is usually between 20k and 100k.

Once the settings have been saved, the logoff process continues and the user's profile (which was based on a copy of the mandatory profile) is deleted.

The original mandatory profile is loaded the next time the user logs on. Once it's loaded, a logon script runs that "customizes" the user's environment with the settings that were saved in the home folder from the previous session.

Figure 6.6 The user logon process with Hybrid profiles

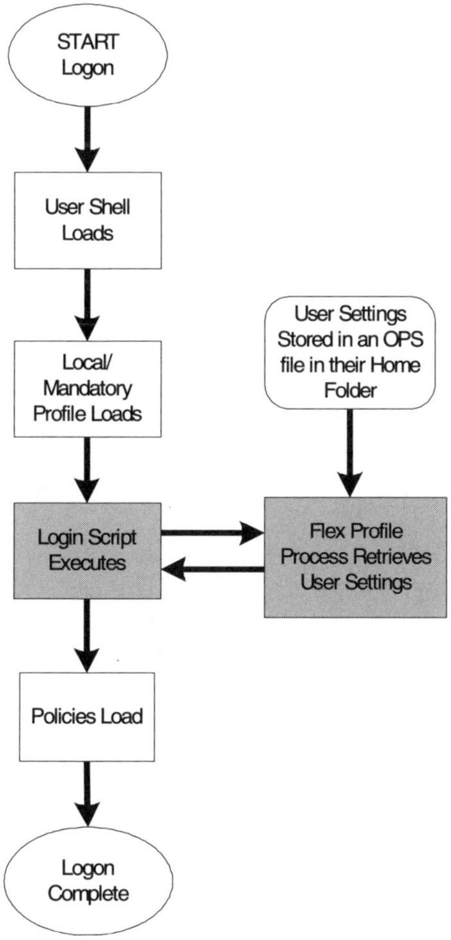

The beauty of this system is that you get the speed and stability of mandatory profiles, (not to mention the control they give you as an administrator), while still having the ability to allow users to retain certain settings within from their sessions. On top of that, flex profiles significantly reduce the chance of "profile corruption." Profile corruption usually occurs when large profiles are copied over congested networks. This is a common cause of support calls in Terminal Server environments that make heavy use of roaming profiles when the design hasn't been well-thought through.

The only drawback to flex profiles is that they are not officially supported by anyone. The idea itself has been around for quite some time, but it's implemented in different ways depending on where you find it. Support is generally only available from public web forums and communities. (See the appendix for a complete list.)

The most popular version of the flex profile is available for free. Called the "Flex Profile Kit," this tool was written by Jeroen van de Kamp of Log*in Consultants in The Netherlands. (Visit `www.logincosultants.nl` to download this kit. Work your way to the "tools" and then to the "downloads" section of the site.)

Van de Kamp's system utilizes a simple logon script that calls proflwiz.exe from the Office XP resource kit. This executable uses a simple INI configuration file to determine which registry settings or directories within the profile should be retained. When setup properly it takes no more than a second or so to run at logon and logoff, which in most cases is much faster than a standard roaming profile after users have been working on the system for awhile.

What's great about van de Kamp's script is that it can also be modified to use the *ifmember.exe* utility from the resource kit. This lets you configure settings to be retained based on a user's group membership.

Let's assume you have one group of users for whom you wish to retain Office settings and another group for whom you wish to retain only Visio settings. It would be a waste or resources and time to save all the settings for both groups of users if one group only needs Visio and another Office. Therefore, you could create two different configuration files and apply the appropriate one based on group membership. An example of such as script follows.

```
IfMemeber.exe "BWPTC\Citrix_Office"
if errorlevel 1 C:\ profkit\proflwiz.exe /S
F:\Settings\Office.ops /I C:\profkit\Office.INI /p
IfMemeber.exe "BWPTC\Citrix_Visio"
```

```
if errorlevel 1 C:\ profkit\proflwiz.exe /S
F:\Settings\Visio.ops /I C:\profkit\Visio.INI /p
IfMemeber.exe "BWPTC\Citrix_ALL"
if errorlevel 1 C:\ profkit\proflwiz.exe /S
F:\Settings\ALL.ops /I C:\profkit\ALL.INI /p
```

This single logon script controls the settings which users save based on group membership. Implementing a single script in this manner is often simpler than breaking the script into several individual scripts and applying them via GPOs.

Why should you care about user profile design?

The options you choose when designing the profiles for your Terminal Server environment will impact several areas, including:

- The administrative effort needed to add a server or a user.
- The amount of manual configuration a user must make to begin using Terminal Server applications.
- A user's ability to customize his environment.
- The overall continuity of the user's environment.
- The time it takes to launch an application or server session.

Let's take a look at each of these areas.

Adding Users or Servers

If user profiles are designed properly, adding a server or user will be as simple as adding it to the domain. You won't have to worry about custom configurations or settings. However, if user profiles are not designed properly, you will need to perform manual customization before bringing new servers or users into your environment.

Amount of User Configuration

The first time a user logs on to a 32-bit (NT/2000/XP/2003) Windows system, a profile must be created. If this profile is created from scratch, the user must manually configure everything himself. That could take a fair amount of time, and there's always the risk that the user won't configure things properly. On the other hand, if you pre-configure the user's profile then the user can begin working immediately. All of the options will be set up properly.

Users' Ability to Customize Their Environment

If you give users mandatory profiles without telling them, they may try to save their settings only to find that their settings were not retained the next time they log on. Mandatory profiles prevent users from saving any preferences or settings to their application environment. Roaming profiles allow them to save those settings at the cost of increased profile maintenance and logon/logoff times.

Continuity of the Users' Environment

If you use local profiles in an environment where users will try to save the settings from their Terminal Server sessions, the users may become confused because their environment could change from day to day as they connect to different servers. This would decrease productivity and increase users' frustration.

If your users use the same roaming profile on their local computer as they do when running sessions on Terminal servers, configuration settings or data could be lost from one of the sessions, since whichever session is logged off last will overwrite the master profile.

Application Launch and Session Start Time

When a user with a roaming profile logs onto a Terminal Server session, he must wait as his profile is copied from its network storage location to the local Terminal Server. If the profile is large or if the network connection is slow, the user will be forced to wait a long time.

Remember that roaming profiles are entirely copied down from the network when the user logs onto a Terminal Server. They're then copied back up to the network when the user logs off. Profiles can easily be several or even dozens of megabytes in size. If many users simultaneously log on and try to download their roaming profiles, it could negatively impact the network. You must consider the size of the profile, the speed of the network, and the number of users logging on or off together to determine if your network can support your users' profiles.

What are the User Profile Design Options?

When creating your strategy for managing the profiles of your Terminal Server users, there are many configuration options available. You'll need to provide answers to several design questions:

- Will you pre-configure any user profiles?
- What types of profiles will be used?
- Will you limit the size of roaming profiles?
- Where will roaming profile master copies be stored?
- How will you manage cached copies of roaming profiles?

- If you choose flex profiles, which registry settings will be retained from the session?

Will you pre-configure user profiles?

All settings and configuration information contained in a user profile must be configured at some point. You can either preconfigure it so that it's ready to go the first time the user logs on, or you can let users configure their settings after they log on.

When you're using local or roaming profiles, a copy is made of the local computer's "Default User" profile whenever a user who does not have a profile already created logs on. As an administrator, you can use this to your advantage. Any changes that you make to the "Default User" profile will be included in each new copy of it, thereby allowing you to modify it to "preconfigure" user profiles.

There are two ways to configure the "Default User" profile. The first is manually:

1. Open the registry editor using regedit.exe.
2. From the menu, choose Registry | Load Hive.
3. Browse to the local "Default User" profile folder.
4. Load "ntuser.dat" from the default user's profile.
5. When the dialog box appears asking for a name for the new hive, enter any name you want. This name is what the newly loaded hive will be called within the Registry Editor. This name is temporary.
6. Make any changes to the newly loaded registry hive.
7. When you have finished, choose Registry | Unload Hive.
8. From Windows Explorer, copy any files and folders that you want to be part of the profile into the "Default User" profile folder. (Be sure that the "Show hidden files and folders" option is checked.)

Rather than configuring the "Default User" profile manually, there is a shortcut that is much easier to use:

1. Create a dummy user on the Terminal Server called "Profile Template."
2. Configure that user with the same rights and options as your new users.
3. Log onto the server as that "Profile Template" user.

4. Configure each option as you'd like the default to be for all of your new users. This could include file "save as" locations, the Internet Explorer home page, or any other desktop or application settings.
5. Log out and log back on as the administrator.
6. Copy the entire contents of the "Profile Template" user profile folder into the default user profile, overwriting everything.

Either of these methods will update the "Default User" profile, causing new users to receive their profiles based on this modified default user profile. You can make additional changes to the default user profile at any time, but be aware that any changes you make will not affect the current profiles that have already been created.

The process above can also be used to create a mandatory profile. Instead of copying the "Profile Template" profile to the Default User, you would simply copy the contents of the profile to the location where you wish to store your mandatory profile.

If you have more than one Terminal Server, you should copy the "Default User" profile that you modified to all of your servers since new user profiles are always generated from the local "Default User" path. If you don't copy the profile, you might get users with profiles based on the wrong template depending on which server they logged on to.

Advantages of Pre-configuring User Profiles

- All users are ensured to receive the proper settings.
- The Terminal Server environment will be ready for users as soon as they log on.

Disadvantages of Pre-configuring User Profiles

- Pre-configuration is more work for you.
- All users are forced to get same the profile template.

Instead of pre-configuring user profiles, you can simply choose to have your user profiles generated from the generic "out of the box" profile. Or, if you have scripting skills, you can use a logon script to configure users' environments the first time they logon. (More information about scripting user environment changes is available later in this chapter)

Advantages of not Modifying the Default User Profile

- Allows users to configure things just as they like them.

- Good for environments in which nothing will be the same across users.
- Good for environments in which policies will be used to enforce settings. (See the next section for information about policies.)
- Less administrative work.

Disadvantages of not Modifying the Default User Profile

- Users must manually configure everything.
- Users might misconfigure a component.

What type of profile will be used?

At some point you must decide whether you will use local, roaming, mandatory, or flex profiles. As you're making this decision, keep in mind that you don't need to have an "all or nothing" solution. You may want to give some users flex profiles, while still restricting another group's ability to change any settings with mandatory profiles.

Local profiles can be used where the settings in the profile don't matter. This is usually the case when you're using policies to define desktop settings or when users are connecting to a single application that does not depend on the user profile at all.

Also, if you're just starting out and you only have one Terminal Server, you can begin with local profiles. As your environment grows, you can copy the existing local profiles to network share locations allowing them to be used as roaming profiles.

Advantages of Local Profiles

- Local profiles are the default option that works right out of the box.
- No administrative configuration is needed.
- Users can create a full, custom environment.
- Users can configure and change any settings.

Disadvantages of Local Profiles

- Only applied to local servers (meaning they don't transfer from server to server in multi-server environments).
- Users can configure and change (break) any settings.

The next option is roaming profiles. Roaming profiles are used most often in real world environments for the convenience they provide over local profiles.

Advantages of Roaming Profiles

- The same user profile can be applied across servers.
- Users can create a full, custom environment.
- Users can configure and change any settings.

Disadvantages of Roaming Profiles

- The network share location where the master profile is stored must be close to the Terminal Server where users log on.
- Left unchecked, their size can increase substantially, leading to slow logon and logoff times and increasing the risk of profile corruption.
- Users can configure and change (break) any settings.

Mandatory profiles are most often used in locked-down environments, although they're not necessary if policies are configured properly.

Advantages of Mandatory Profiles

- Good for locked-down environments.
- Generally faster than roaming profile since they don't typically contain customized configuration files.
- Users cannot configure or change any settings.

Disadvantages of Mandatory Profiles

- User cannot configure or change any settings.
- No user settings are saved between sessions.
- There is no way to disable a mandatory profile for users on specific machines

Finally, Flex profiles are most often used in environments where speed, security and user perception are all a concern. (Of course, these are a concern in all environments, which is why this solution is rapidly growing in popularity.)

Advantages of Flex Profiles

- Allows you to lock down certain configuration settings.
- Allows you to let the users configure certain settings.
- The same user profile can be applied across servers.
- Generally faster than roaming profiles
- Less chance of profile corruption

- Settings that can and cannot be changed can be "layered" onto users with group memberships, logon scripts, and GPOs.

Disadvantages of Flex Profiles

- Not "officially" supported by any vendor (yet).
- Some versions do not support files located within the profile. (They support registry entries only.)

Limiting the Size of Roaming Profiles

By default, user profiles contain many files and folders. Because every user's roaming profile is copied to the Terminal Server at logon and copied to the master network share location at logoff, it's important to keep the roaming profile as small as possible.

Left unchecked, a user's profile can easily grow to dozens or even hundreds of megabytes. When a user logs on, she must wait for the entire profile to be copied to the Terminal Server from the master network share. If the profile is large, the logon process will be slow. It will seem to "hang" while the profile is copied. This is easily the most frequent cause of slow logons in Terminal Server environments.

There are a few strategies that you can use to limit the size of roaming profiles:

- Redirect certain folders to network locations outside of the user's profile.
- Exclude certain default folders from the roaming profile.
- Apply an artificial size limit which will not allow the profile to exceed a certain size.

Let's now examine what each of these strategies entails.

Redirect Folders to Locations Outside of the User's Profile

By default, any folders that contain user-specific information are part of the user profile. As you saw back in Figure 6.1, this includes folders that contain configuration information, application settings, and user data. For example, the "My Documents" folder is part of a user profile.

In using your Terminal Server, most of your users will make extensive use of their "My Documents" folder. In roaming profile environments, this can cause the profile to increase in size as users store more and more documents. (Recall that when using roaming profiles, an increase in size is a bad thing.)

To mitigate this size issue, you have the option of redirecting certain profile folders to locations outside of the user's actual profile. (This is part of the Windows IntelliMirror technology.) For example, redirection could allow the "My Documents" folder to point to a static network location that never changes instead of a folder inside the user's roaming profile. Users with a redirected "My Documents" folder continue to open, save, and browse "My Documents" as usual. They would not be aware that any redirection was taking place.

The advantage to redirection is that the contents of the "My Documents" folder would be stored in one location (like the user's home folder). This content would not be copied to and from the Terminal Server with the rest of the roaming profile. Users would access a single "My Documents" network location no matter what Terminal Server they used.

As an administrator, you'll need to choose which folders to redirect from user profiles. Choosing these folders creates a balance between keeping the user profile as small as possible while allowing users to have fast, local access to their data.

You have a lot of flexibility in the implementation of folder redirection, allowing you to evaluate which folders to redirect on a folder-by-folder or user-by-user basis. If a folder contains configuration information that will be accessed in every session then you should probably not redirect it. However, folders containing user data files are good candidates for redirection since not all user files are used during every session. A user's "My Documents" folder might be 50MB containing 200 Word documents. However, throughout the course of a Terminal Server session, a user will only actually use a fraction of those documents. There's no reason that all 200 documents should be copied to the Terminal Server every time the user logs on.

In Terminal Server environments, the most common implementation of this strategy is to redirect the "My Documents" and "Application Data" folders, although experimentation in your environment will tell you which folders work best for you.

While it's technically possible to redirect the "Desktop" folder, you should really only redirect this across the network if it's actually necessary. Since the "Desktop" folder corresponds to the actual user's desktop, redirecting it means that the user's desktop is a view to a remote network drive. The problem with this is that as long as the desktop is visible in the session, Windows will continuously refresh the contents of the desktop across the network. This doesn't affect anything in single server environments, but it has the potential to add unneeded traffic to your network when a Terminal Server is full of users whose desktops are redirected.

Advantages of Redirecting Folders

- Redirected folders are not part of the roaming profile that is frequently copied across the network.
- Profiles can be smaller. This allows quicker logon and logoff times and reduces the chance of profile corruption.

Disadvantages of Redirecting Folders

- Redirected folders must be accessed across the network from within Terminal Server sessions.

Procedure for Redirecting Folders

Redirecting folders is a "user" registry setting (in the HKCU hive) of the Terminal Servers. Folder redirection can be set manually with the registry editor or applied via a policy. Windows 2003 lets you redirect any of the 18 default folders.

When specifying a target for the redirected folder, you may enter a UNC name instead of a hard-coded path. If you configure your target path so that it ends with the %username% variable (example: \\servername\sharename\%username%), then the path will automatically be created so long as the user has "modify" share and NTFS rights.

Registry Location for Redirecting Folders

A user's folders can be redirected in the registry by the following path:

```
HKCU\Software\Microsoft\Windows\Current Vesion\Explorer\User
Shell Folders\
```

This registry key contains a values entry for each profile folder. By default, each folder points to a location in the *%USERPROFILE%* location. You can change these to point to any path you want. You may use hard-coded paths, UNC paths, and system variables (such as *%HOMEDRIVE%*).

Group Policy Location for Redirecting Folders

Within the Windows Group Policy MMC snap-in, you can redirect the Application Data, Desktop, My Documents, and Start Menu folders. To do this, navigate to the following path: User Configuration | Windows Settings | Folder Redirection | Right-click on the folder | Properties.

Note that in order to access this option, you must connect to a live Active Directory environment. You can't simply run *gpedit.msc*.

When configuring your GPO, you can set folder redirection on a group-by-group or a computer-wide basis (all within the same GPO). You can also graphically configure options such as whether you want to redirect all users to a single folder or redirect each user to their own folder.

Exclude Certain Folders from Being Copied to the Roaming Profile

You may determine that some folders in a user's profile contain data not worth saving from session to session. In order to further decrease the size of roaming profiles, you can choose to exclude those folders from the roaming profiles altogether. Excluding folders causes them not to be copied up to the master profile network share after a user logs off.

When a user with a roaming profile logs onto a Terminal Server, the entire contents of the roaming profile are copied to the Terminal Server from the user's master profile network share, regardless of whether you have excluded certain directories.

Directory exclusion only affects roaming profiles as they are copied from the Terminal Server back to the master profile network share, after the user logs off. This only indirectly affects the size of the profile at the master location because if you implement directory exclusion after a user has established a roaming profile with a master copy stored on the network share, the directory exclusion will not make the profile any smaller.

The reason for this is that the excluded folders will already be part of the user's master roaming profile on the network share. They were put there when the user logged off with a roaming profile before you configured the directory exclusion. Even though the newly-excluded directories will never be copied from the Terminal Server up to the master profile location when the user logs off, they will already exist in the master copy, and so will be copied down every time a user logs on.

If you want to exclude directories from the roaming profiles of existing users with established roaming profiles, you need to manually delete the folders from their roaming profile master locations. You won't need to do this for new users that have never logged on since their master profile will be created on the network only after they log off of a Terminal Server that has the exclusion applied.

If you choose to exclude directories from roaming profiles, be sure to set the same exclusions on each of your Terminal Servers. Even one server without set exclusions would cause the unwanted folders to be copied to the master profile network share, becoming a permanent part of the user profile copied down every time a user logs on. You would then need to manually delete the folders from the master profile.

Advantages of Excluding Certain Folders

- Reduces the size of the roaming profile.

Disadvantages of Excluding Certain Folders

- Information in the excluded folders is not retained between sessions.

Procedure for Excluding Certain Folders

By default, Windows Server 2003 automatically excludes the History, Local Settings, Temp, and Temporary Internet Files folders from roaming profiles. You only need to configure folder exclusion if you identify additional folders that do not need to be part of your users' roaming profiles.

Folder exclusion is a registry setting that can be set manually in a default or mandatory profile or that can be set via a group policy. (Group policies are covered in detail in the next section.)

Registry Location

In the registry, folders can be excluded via the following path:

Key: HKCU\Software\Microsoft\Windows NT\Current Version\Winlogon

Value: ExcludeProfileDirs

Type: REG_SZ

Data: Directory names to be excluded, relative to the root path of the profile. Multiple directories can be separated by semicolons. The default setting is "Local Settings;Temporary Internet Files;History;Temp."

Group Policy Location

For Windows 2003 domains
User Configuration | Administrative Templates | System | User Profiles | Exclude Directories in Roaming Profiles

For Windows 2000 domains
User Configuration | Administrative Templates | System | Logon / Logoff | Exclude Directories in Roaming Profile.

Apply an Artificial Size Limit

In addition to the various methods by which roaming profile size is kept under control, there is another method that can be used as a last resort if other methods fail. As an administrator, you can specify the maximum size, in kilobytes, of roaming profiles on Terminal Servers. This size limit acts as a sort of "circuit breaker," kicking in when the profile gets too large.

In addition to the actual size limit specification, there are several other options that can be configured:

- Should the user's registry file be included in the calculation of the profile size?
- Should users be notified when their profile exceeds the maximum?
- Do you want them to be notified with a custom message?
- How often should that message be displayed?

Advantages of Setting a Profile Size Limit

- Guarantees that a profile won't get too big.
- Works in concert with other methods.

Disadvantages of Setting a Profile Size Limit

- Should not be used as a surrogate for other methods.
- Can cause user confusion when the limit is reached.

Procedure for Setting a Profile Size Limit

Limiting the size of a roaming profile can be accomplished by configuring a series of registry keys manually or through a policy. The artificial limit can be set up to 30MB. Even though 30MB is an extremely large profile, you can set it larger by modifying the ADM file (covered in the policies section of this chapter) as outlined in Microsoft Knowledge Base article 290324.

Group Policy Location

User Configuration | Administrative Templates | System | User Profiles | Limit Profile Size.

Choosing Not to Limit the Roaming Profile Size

Even after reviewing the options available for limiting the size of user profiles, you might make the decision not to limit the size. In small environments, it is often not worth the extra effort that goes into managing profiles.

Advantages of Doing Nothing

- Least amount of work.

Disadvantages of Doing Nothing

- Logons can be slow.
- Terminal Servers can run out of disk space.
- If the environment grows, you will need to address profile size at some point.

Where will roaming profile master copies be stored?

The convenience of using roaming profiles produces one side effect: the roaming profile must be copied over the network when the user logs on and logs off. In a perfect world, you would always be able to store the master copy of a user's roaming profile near the Terminal Servers that he will be using. In the real world this is not always possible, specifically with users that travel or connect to multiple Terminal Servers in multiple locations. Consider the environment illustrated in Figure 6.7.

Figure 6.7 Users often connect to multiple Terminal Servers

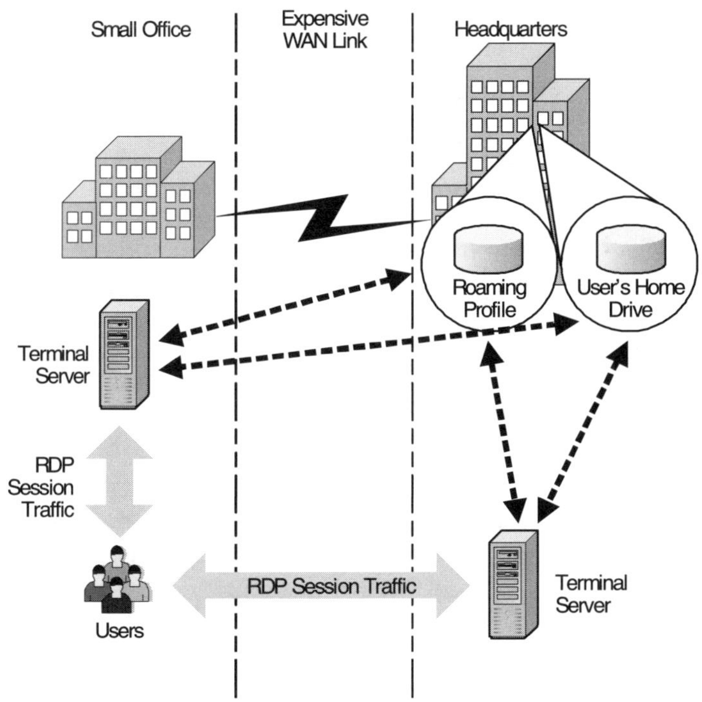

In environments such as this, where users logon to Terminal Servers in multiple locations, the decision as to where to store the master roaming profile becomes more difficult. You need to either: (1) choose a location from which the user can copy the profile no matter where they log on; or (2) move to the flex profile system to make the size of the data copied across the network much smaller.

Advanced Profile Customization Options

Now that you understand the basics of profile design, there are some advanced design options to consider for your environment. Think about how you're going to manage cached copies of roaming profiles, and how you can customize the default "all-or-nothing" usage of roaming profiles.

Managing Cached Copies of Local Profiles

When a user with a roaming profile logs on to a Terminal Server, the profile is copied from its network storage location to the local Terminal Server. After the user logs off, the profile is copied from the local Terminal Server back up to the network location. At this point, by default, the Terminal Server retains a local copy of the user's profile. This copy is saved locally so that if the user logs onto that server again before the roaming profile changes, the roaming profile does not need to be copied across the network, saving time and bandwidth.

However, in large environments, this profile "caching" could cause the Terminal Server to run out of disk space since there could potentially be hundreds of user profiles saved locally. After all, any user that logs on once will have a locally cached profile taking up space. Plus, the more servers you have, the less likely it is that a user will actually connect to the same physical server twice in a row.

To combat this, you can configure your Terminal Servers so that they do not retain the locally cached copy of roaming profiles. In doing so, whenever a user logs off of a Terminal Server, his profile is copied back up to its master network share location and the local copy is deleted.

Deleting locally cached profiles from Terminal Servers will allow you to save disk space. However, this free space could come at the price of logon speed. By configuring a Terminal Server to delete all locally cached copies of roaming profiles, users' profiles will be copied across the network when they log on without exception. If the Terminal Server had an up-to-date locally cached copy of a user profile, logon speed is faster because the profile wouldn't have to be copied across the network.

Some wonder if it is worth trading hard drive space for logon speed. Consider this situation:

If a user with a session on Server A logs off, her profile will be copied to her master network profile location. Her locally cached profile on Server A will have the same timestamp as the roaming master copy.

If the user then runs a session on Server B, her profile will be copied to her master profile location when she logs off. Her locally cached profile on Server B will now have the same timestamp as the roaming master copy. At the next logon, if she logs on to Server B, no network copy will be needed because the locally cached profile is the same as the network version.

However, if she logs back on to Server A, the network copy will take place because the master profile has been updated since she last logged onto Server A. Even though Server A originally copied the profile to the network share, Server B overwrote it later.

In this two server environment, the user has only a 50% chance that she will log on to the server that has the same profile as the network, thus saving the network transfer time. If there were ten servers, she would only have a one in ten chance. Twenty servers would be one in twenty.

Saving locally cached copies of roaming profiles was designed for traditional (non-Terminal Server) environments in which users were logging on to the same workstation every day.

Having the locally cached copy of the profile helps only if the local profile is as new as the remote roaming profile. In Terminal Server environments, the hard disk space is usually more important than the chance of good network speed, causing most administrators to configure their servers to delete locally cached roaming user profiles.

Advantages of Deleting Cached Copies of Roaming Profiles

- Saves drive space.

Disadvantages of Deleting Cached Copies of Roaming Profiles

- Could cause slower logons.

Procedure for Deleting Cached Copies of Roaming Profiles

This feature, like so many others, is simply a registry setting on your Terminal Servers. You can configure it manually with the registry editor or you can specify it in a policy.

Registry Location

Key: HKLM\Software\Microsoft\Windows\System\

Value: DeleteRoamingCache

Type: REG_DWORD

Data: 1 (enable)

Group Policy Location

Computer Configuration | Administrative Templates | System | User Profiles | Delete cached copies of roaming profiles.

Instead of deleting user profiles to save storage space, some people choose to store them in a location other than the default system drive. This allows the profiles to be stored on a large drive, since many of the Terminal Servers' system drives are extremely small.

There's no real disadvantage to moving cached profiles to another drive, so long as that drive is local. If you try to put cached profiles on a remote drive or network share, you will get extremely poor performance. All session interaction between the Terminal Server and the local profile assumes that the profile is local.

Advantages of Changing Cached Copy Location

- Often Terminal Servers have large drives other than the system drive.
- Get the performance of cached profiles without the risk of running out of disk space.

Disadvantages of Changing Cached Copy Location

- Cached drive must be local to each server.

Procedure for Changing Cache Copy Location

When you change the profile path, you can only change the root directory for all profiles. This means that the "Default User" and "All Users" profiles are also moved to the new location.

Registry Location

Key: HKLM\SOFTWARE\Microsoft\Windows NT\Current Vesion\ProfileList

Value: ProfilesDirectory

Type: REG_EXPAND_SZ

Data: The local folder where you want to store user profiles. By default, this is "%SystemDrive%\Documents and Settings."

Selectively Implementing Roaming Profiles

A great new feature of Windows Server 2003 (technically this feature was introduced in Windows XP) is the ability to selectively enable or disable certain roaming profile functionality on a server-by-server basis. You can configure roaming profiles for your environment while excluding their use on certain servers.

This functionality is implemented via policies (which are fully covered in the next section). As you'll learn, you can apply these options locally to individual servers or to entire groups of servers via Group Policy Objects.

Preventing Servers from Downloading Roaming Profiles

If you have certain servers in which you do not want a user's roaming profile to be used, enable the following policy:

Computer Configuration | Administrative Templates | System | User Profiles | Only allow local user profiles

In the real world, this policy is used only when you have multiple types of Terminal Servers hosting different applications. Often there will be some servers that host applications that do not require user profiles (large line-of-business or ERP applications, for example). Why waste network bandwidth and time downloading a remote roaming profile to a server if the application doesn't use it anyway?

Preventing Servers from Uploading Roaming Profiles

In Windows 2003 you can also configure a policy that prevents the changes made to a roaming profile from being uploaded back to the roaming profile's master storage location.

Computer Configuration | Administrative Templates | System | User Profiles | Prevent Roaming Profile changes from propagating to the server

In a way, implementing this option on a server causes that server to treat all roaming profiles as if they were mandatory profiles.

Giving One User Multiple Profiles

In some situations you might want to give a single user multiple roaming profiles. Imagine that users are connecting to two (or more) sets of Terminal Servers separated by a WAN. On each set of servers they need to use a roaming profile to enable their settings to follow them from server to server in the load-balanced cluster. The problem is that if you put the master profiles on a segment near one of the sets of Terminal Servers, the system will have to copy the profile across a WAN link every time the user logs on to the other set of Terminal Servers. It will also have to copy it back across that WAN link every time a user logs off of those servers.

In order to fully appreciate the complexity of this scenario, take a look at Figure 6.8.

Figure 6.8. A situation that might require multiple profiles for each user.

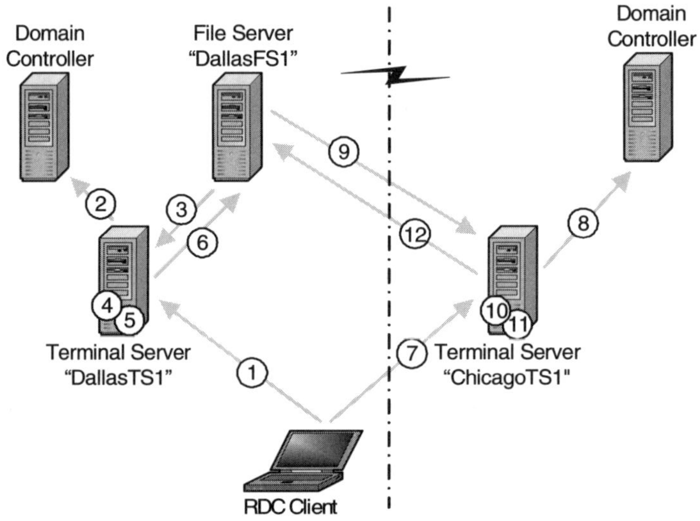

1. The user logs onto the server DallasTS1 in Dallas.
2. The user's Active Directory account is checked and a Terminal Server profile path is found that points to a share on DallasFS1.
3. The user's 1MB Terminal Server roaming profile is copied from DallasFS1 to DallasTS1 in a few seconds.
4. The user's session is loaded and ready to go
5. User logs off the DallasTS1 server.

6. The roaming profile is copied back to its storage location on DallasFS1 in a few seconds
7. The user now logs onto ChicagoTS1.
8. The user's account is checked and a Terminal Server profile path is found again.
9. The user's 1MB Terminal Server roaming profile is copied from DallasFS1 across the WAN link to ChicagoTS1. (The amount of time it takes for this depends on the size of the link and its current utilization.)
10. The user's session is loaded and ready to go.
11. User logs off the ChicagoTS1 server.
12. The roaming profile is then copied back from to its storage location on DallasFS1. (Again, the amount of time this takes depends on the size of the link and current utilization.)

In this scenario, the performance of the sessions on the Chicago severs may be just fine. Nevertheless, the users will complain about slow logon and logoff times due to their profiles being copied back and forth.

To combat this, you can configure some of your servers so that users that log on to them get their roaming profiles from alternate locations. This is commonly called a "user profile override" because the server will override the profile that's specified in the user's AD account object.

You can enable user profile overrides via a policy. (Policies are fully detailed in the next section of this chapter.) There is no real limit to the number of overrides you can implement. (If you have 55 servers, you could technically give a single user account 55 different user profiles—one for each server—if you really wanted to.)

The only downside to configuring multiple profiles per user is that you introduce a situation in which the user's environment changes depending on which Terminal Server he connects to. This is not usually a problem if one server runs a specific application like JDEdwards and the other set runs Microsoft Office, but you could wind up creating a new problem if both servers run Office and users want their settings to be maintained across both servers.

Group Policy Location

Computer Configuration | Administrative Templates | Windows Components | Terminal Services | Set Path for TS Roaming Profiles.

Advantages of Assigning Multiple Profiles to One User

- Eliminates the need to copy roaming profiles across WAN links.
- Speeds up user logons when done right.

Disadvantages of Assigning Multiple Profiles to One User

- Profiles will be out of sync between Terminal Server clusters.

Considerations when Designing User Profiles

Now that we've reviewed all of the options available when choosing how to apply user profiles, let's consider the questions that you need to answer. Answering these questions should make your design simple:

- Does each user need his own customized environment?
- How much network bandwidth is available?
- What are the locations of servers that users will log on to?

Custom User Environments

If all of your users will share the same environment then your profile design job is straightforward—you won't need to worry about custom profiles for each user. If users do need custom environments, then you will need to spend time thinking about how user profiles will be used.

Network Bandwidth Availability

If bandwidth is plentiful, you won't need to worry as much about the location of the master roaming profile network share or the size of roaming profiles. If bandwidth is scarce, you may spend significant time designing these components.

Server Location

If all of your Terminal Servers are in the same location then it's relatively simple to decide on the location of the server that will contain master roaming profiles. Of course in reality, it's usually not that easy. If you have users that log on to Terminal Servers in different physical locations or across WAN links, the decision of the master profile server location becomes difficult. You need to balance profile size and functionality with loading speed and network bandwidth availability.

User Policies / Group Policies

While user profiles allow users to customize the settings of their own environments, policies allow you (the administrator) to force settings in your users' environments. Policies (and their mandatory configuration settings) can be applied to servers globally, affecting all users that logon, or conditionally, affecting only specific users that logon. This conditional application can be based on user accounts, group memberships, or OU membership.

While most of the policy settings that are used to restrict or control a user's environment are available in policies from NT 4.0 through Windows 2003, some Group Policy settings discussed in this chapter are only available when to Windows Server 2003-based Terminal Servers that are members of a Windows 2003-based Active Directory domain.

Windows User Policies

Before we look at the details of how Microsoft Windows policies work, it's important to understand the differences between policies and user profiles.

Differences between Windows User Policies and Profiles

Both policies and user profiles affect registry settings. A user profile contains registry settings (in the *ntuser.dat* file) that are used to create the user's unique HKEY_CURRENT_USER registry hive when they log on. Policies also contain registry settings. They dictate which values are or are not allowed in the HKEY_CURRENT_USER registry hive as its being created from the user profile. Policies can also affect computer-wide HKEY_LOCAL_MACHINE settings, which are applied as the computer is booted before any users log on.

Application settings and configurations that are maintained in the registry can be set with either a user profile or a policy. If there is a conflict, the policy setting will take precedence over the user profile setting. (Registry settings for user can also be manipulated via logon scripts, which will be covered later in this chapter).

A user might configure his desktop background to be bright red, thus setting the bright red color value in a desktop settings registry key in the user's HKEY_CURRENT_USER registry hive. This updated value would become part of the user's profile, taking effect at every logon. At any time, the user could decide to change the desktop background color.

However, if you wanted to force the user's desktop to be a specific color, you would apply a policy. The policy would affect the exact same value in the same registry location as when the user set it (in their profile), except that the policy could not be changed by the user. That's in essence what a policy is—an administrator's way to force settings onto users.

Of course, you don't generally use policies to set the desktop color in Windows. You would use policies to set elements that affect how the users use the system such as Start menu items, file save locations, search options, and local drive access.

Figure 6.9 Differences between profiles and policies

User Profile	Policy
Applied to a user	Applied to a computer, group, or user
Only one per user	Many can be layered per user
Settings are the user's choice	Settings are the administrator's choice
Affects the user's registry hive	Affects the user's or server's registry hive
Registry settings, folders, files	Registry settings only

People often wonder whether they should use profiles or policies to manage the user environment. In the real world, the two are meant to complement each other and are used together. Situations are rare in which one is used to the exclusion of the other.

Creating and Editing Windows Policies

In Windows 2000/2003 environments, policies are created and managed via an MMC snap-in called *gpedit.msc*. Since policies are essentially no more than a collection of registry keys and values, policy editing snap-ins are merely graphical interfaces that allow you to set registry values. These registry values can then be directly applied to the local server or saved as policy files.

When editing and creating policies, you'll need at least one "ADM" policy template file. ADM files contain all of the policy settings and options, as well as the corresponding registry keys and values needed to create a policy. ADM template files are added as plug-ins to the policy editing utilities. Without any ADM template files plugged-in, the policy editing tools are useless, like the MMC without any snap-ins. Once the ADM files are plugged-in to the policy editing utility, you can point-and-click your way through the configuration of policies.

ADM policy templates are simply text files with the ".adm" extension, such as *winnt.adm* or *common.adm.* The MMC-based policy editors for Windows 2000 and 2003 come with several ADM files plugged-in out of the box. These default ADM files allow you to configure policies for several Windows options. However, if you have other applications installed, such as Microsoft Word, you'll probably want to extend your policy editor to include Microsoft Word options. Since the default ADM templates only cover Windows options, you can't use them to configure any Microsoft Word options.

In order to create policies that include Microsoft Word options, you must obtain a Microsoft Word ADM policy template file. There are hundreds of Microsoft Word templates available. You can download the "official" ones from Microsoft's web site. (They are included as part of the Office Resource Kit.) As soon as you add the Microsoft Word ADM template to your policy editing utility, you will instantly see options for configuring Microsoft Word settings. For example with Microsoft Word, these policy settings include paths to office assistants, the ability to disable certain features, and menu options.

You will need to find (or create) ADM policy templates for all the applications that you want to regulate with policies. Check out the THIN list at `http://thethin.net` for a great collection of ADM policy templates.

ADM policy template files essentially are nothing more than interfaces that provide you a graphical means of setting and forcing desktop and application settings onto users.

Why should you care about user policy design?

Now that you understand the basics of what policies are, you can appreciate the two reasons that you need to think about user policy design on your system:

- Policies affect users' ability to customize their own environments.
- Policies affect the security of your system.

Users' Ability to Customize Their Environment

If policies are too restrictive, users will not be able to do their jobs or fully use the system. Many over-zealous administrators go extremes when implementing policies, not realizing, for example, that users need the ability to access local drives, the control panel, or printer settings.

Security

User profiles and policies will directly affect the options and settings users see in their Terminal Server sessions. Properly designed policies will allow users to use the servers without risk of them changing inappropriate settings or accessing unwanted areas.

Shane Broomhall, a Citrix and Terminal Server instructor, says it best:

Most likely, you have a certain user in your environment with a copy of "MCSE for Complete Brain-Dead Idiots in 24 Hours" on his desk. This person is the really dangerous one. The one with a little knowledge and even less common sense. The one who, just by reading one thing, can completely break his desktop computer. From your perspective, if this person has broken his desktop by playing around with it (because it was not locked down) it's no big deal, because he has only really affected himself. However, now that you're using Terminal Servers, when this user does the same thing with a session desktop that has not been locked down properly, he's affecting potentially hundreds of other users. It is this user that forces us to spend time designing policies and profiles.

What are the user policy design options?

When it comes down to actually designing your policies, you have a few options. To decide on the type that best fits your environment, you first need to understand the options and how they are applied to users.

(*Note:* This book is not meant to be an exhaustive study of Windows 2003 policies. Rather, we review the basics and focus on the specifics and best practices that you should know in order to implement policies in a Terminal Server environment.)

What type of Windows 2003 Policies will you use?

There are two types of policies that you can apply in Windows 2000/2003 environments: local policies and group policies. Both affect the registry settings of your Terminal Servers. Let's highlight the differences between the two.

Windows 2003 Local Computer (System) Policies

Local computer policies are a fancy way of saying "the local registry settings" of a Windows 2003 computer. They are applied with the Group Policy MMC snap-in (gpedit.msc). By default, there is no shortcut for this snap-in. You have to launch it manually (Start | Run | gpedit.msc).

Changing settings of the local computer policy sets registry values on the local server. After you are done changing policy settings, you can simply close the Group Policy editor. Nothing needs to be saved since the Group Policy editor (in this case) is basically a direct connection with the local computer's registry.

The downside to editing the registry directly with Group Policy editor is that any policy settings you change will only apply to the local computer.

Advantages of Local Computer Policies

- Simple to apply.
- Easy to change.
- Work well for single-server environments.
- Allow each server to have unique policy settings.

Disadvantages of Local Computer Policies

- Must be manually configured at every server.
- Since these settings affect every user that logs on to the server, all users get the same settings.
- Do not scale very well.

Windows 2003 Group Policies

If your Terminal Servers are part of an Active Directory domain (whether Windows 2000 or Windows 2003-based), policy application becomes flexible. In Active Directory environments, policies can be stored in the directory as "Group Policy Objects." A Group Policy Object (GPO) is a single policy file containing policy settings for users and computers. GPOs are stored in the directory itself, and there is no limit to the number that can be stored. Once they are created and stored in the directory, GPOs are applied to Active Directory Sites, Domains, or Organizational Units. The policies defined within the GPO apply to those objects (such as users and computers) that are in the container where they are applied.

In small environments (1, 2 or even 3 servers), it might not be necessary to implement GPOs. As your environment grows, you'll find it is much easier to put your server into a specific OU and find it "auto-magically" configured like the other servers. This approach is the surest way to ensure that your server settings are identical between servers without having to manually configure or verify them all.

(Note: Terminal Servers running on Windows Server 2003 can receive policies from Domain Controllers and Active Directories running on Windows 2000, and vice-versa.)

Don't let the name fool you. Group Policy Objects have nothing to do with Windows user groups. The word "Group" in Group Policy Objects derives from the fact that a GPO is a policy applied to a "group" of objects.

Advantages of Group Policy

- Ensures uniform settings across Terminal Servers
- Changes to Server settings are done in one place instead of server-by-server
- Ensures that only administrators with rights to modify the GPO can modify the server settings
- Extremely flexible
- Granular application

Disadvantages of Group Policy

- Requires Active Directory.
- Requires the ability to edit a GPO (rights and skill)
- If different settings are required on different servers the GPOs will have to be filtered or multiple GPOs will be required

How will you apply policies?

Before applying any policies in your environment, you need to understand how they will affect servers and users. Since you can apply policies to servers, sites, domains or OUs, you must know the precedence that each takes when multiple policies are applied to the same server.

Policies are applied in the following order:

1. Local policies (stored in the local server's registry and configured via the gpedit.msc MMC snap-in).
2. Site (GPOs applied to the AD site to which the server belongs).
3. Domain (GPOs applied to the AD domain to which the server belongs).
4. Organizational Unit (GPOs applied to OUs that contain the server).

Such architecture allows you to create extremely flexible policies. For example, you can put all of your Terminal Servers into one OU. Then, you can create a locked-down Group Policy Object and apply it to the OU, effectively securing your Terminal Servers while not restricting user access to other systems not part of that OU.

Because policies can be applied at multiple levels, designs can become complex very quickly when you apply different policies at different levels to the same objects.

The details of Active Directory GPO design will not be covered in this book. If you plan to make heavy use of them, there are several excellent white papers on Microsoft's website that explain how they are applied and how settings are inherited between levels. GPOs are often used with great success in Terminal Server environments.

When applying policies to Terminal Servers, the biggest design decision that you will have to make is whether: (1) you will require different policy settings for different groups of users; or (2) whether all users using the server will receive the same policy.

Typically, you would only use a local policy if you do not have Active Directory or have a small single-server or (at most) a couple of servers in your environment. Once an environment begins to grow the granularity level of the policies generally does also.

Let's assume that you have a small two server environment that will host 50 users running a single application. In this environment, a local system policy may be adequate since few (if any) different policy settings will be required for different groups of users.

On the other hand, what if you have an environment with 50 servers spread across three clusters and numerous types of users using various applications and configurations? In this scenario it is more likely that you'll need the ability to filter policies based on group membership within the domain. Local policies cannot accommodate here since they affect every user that logs on and they can't differentiate between users or groups. You will have to use domain-based GPOs to achieve the results you are looking for.

Applying Policies to Users on a Terminal Server

Remember that each group policy object has two sections—a section that contains computer settings and a section that contains user settings.

What happens when a user from one OU (with a GPO applied) logs on to a Terminal Server that's in another OU (with another GPO applied)? Logically, you would think that the settings from the user section of the GPO applied to the user's OU would apply to the user, and the settings from the computer section of the GPO applied to the computer's OU would apply to the computer. Unfortunately, that's not how it works at all.

When a user logs on to a computer that's part of an Active Directory, the GPO that's applied is determined by the location of the *user's* account object in Active

Directory. If a user object is located in one OU and the Terminal Server (or any machine they log on to for that matter) is in another OU, the Group Policy applied to the user is applied as a result of the OU that the user object resides in and not the OU that the Terminal Server resides in.

This could be a problem for an administrator attempting to lock down a Terminal Server desktop without affecting users when they log on to their normal workstations.

To remedy this, you can configure a GPO to merge the settings from the Group Policy of the user's OU and the Group Policy of the computer's OU. Alternately, you can configure the GPO applied to the computer's OU so that it completely replaces the user's policy. You thus completely control users' Terminal Server policy without the interference of their original policies.

To do this, enable "loopback processing" in the GPO that's applied to the Terminal Server's OU. Loopback processing works in one of two modes:

- *Replace* (default) specifies that user settings normally applied from the user's GPO are ignored and replaced with the user settings as configured in this GPO instead.
- *Merge* specifies that user settings from the user's "normal" GPO will be applied along with the user settings from the GPO applied to the Terminal Server. If any two settings conflict with each other, the Terminal Server's GPO takes precedence.

Loopback processing is almost always a necessity in Terminal Server environments of any size. Without loopback settings enabled, you would have the same policy settings (and restrictions) applied to users at their workstations' desktops and on their Terminal Server sessions.

In most environments, you will need to implement much more restrictive settings on the Terminal Servers as compared to users' desktop workstations.

Loopback Processing Group Policy Location

GPO | Computer Configuration | Administrative Templates | System | Group Policy | User Group Policy Loopback Processing Mode

Advantages of Using the Loopback Processing Mode

- Allows you to specify GPO settings that are specific to the Terminal Server session.
- Allows for the merging or complete replacement of user GPO settings.

Disadvantages of Using the Loopback Processing Mode

- User environments will have different configurations between the Terminal Server sessions and the normal desktops.
- Additional complexity can be harder to administer.

What settings will you configure in the policy?

If your Windows 2003 Terminal Servers are members of a Windows 2003-based Active Directory, then you'll find that there are dozens of Terminal Server-specific policy settings available to you. These policies work just as any other policies in Windows. When enabled or disabled they basically edit the registry, which in turn changes the way the system works or is configured.

One interesting fact about these "Terminal Server" policy objects is that they're only meant to control Windows 2003 servers with Terminal Server installed. They're not meant to control the administrative Remote Desktop connection.

These settings can be found by using the group policy editor and navigating to the following location:

Computer Configuration | Administrative Templates | Windows Components | Terminal Services

In the root of this folder, you'll see a number of policy options and several sub-folders. Let's take a look at the various Terminal Server options that are available.

Keep Alive-Connections: These settings enable the server to determine the proper session state when the client disconnects its session. It is possible for a session that is disconnected to remain active and not go into a disconnected state, causing the client attempting to reconnect to wind up with a new session instead of reconnecting to the disconnected session.

By default, keep-alive connections are disabled and can only be enabled by editing the registry or enabling this policy.

Automatic Reconnection: When enabled, this policy configures RDC clients that get disconnected to automatically attempt to reconnect to the server, such as when there is a temporary loss of network connectivity. If a network disconnect occurs when this policy is enabled, the client will attempt to reconnect to the server 20 times at 5 second intervals.

Enabling this policy is basically equivalent to enabling the "Reconnect if connection is dropped" feature on the Experience tab in Remote Desktop Connection client.

If the policy is disabled, automatic reconnection of clients is not allowed, even if the client is configured for it.

This feature is especially useful to remote and Internet users that may experience frequent drops or short disconnects from the server.

Restrict Terminal Services users to a single remote session: As the name implies, this policy will limit each user account to a single session on your Terminal Server. When enabled, it will verify that a user does not have an existing session open *before* allowing him to load his session. If the user has an existing session, the new session connection is connected to the existing session and the first connection to that session is dropped.

This policy is ideal for environments in which users share passwords or are known to leave sessions open, only to open new ones from other workstations.

If you leave this policy set as "Not Configured," you can control this functionality with the Terminal Services Configuration MMC snap-in.

Enforce Removal of Remote Desktop Wallpaper: This option allows you disable all those pretty background pictures that users tend to put on their desktops. On a normal workstation wallpaper might not be a big deal, but in a Terminal Server environment these images eat up bandwidth and can degrade session performance. When enabled, a user does not have the ability to set or use wallpaper for their desktop session.

When disabled or not configured, the Wallpaper for the session will be displayed.

Deny log off of an Administrator logged on to the console session: One of the new features of Windows Server 2003 is the ability for administrators to connect to the server console (or *session 0*) via an RDP session. When this happens, the server's real console screen displays the "locked" message just like a normally locked computer. Enabling this policy prevents someone from being able to kick off the remote *session 0* session by unlocking the server console.

When not configured or disabled, the default action is to allow one administrator to unlock or logoff another administrator, potentially causing her to loose work since she might be logged in and active when she's kicked off.

Limit number of connections: This policy allows you to specify the maximum number of Terminal Server sessions that can run on a server. This is not a "per-user" setting, rather, it limits the total sessions on the server.

If you read the product documentation from Microsoft, they make a point to tell you that valid values for this policy range from 1 to 999,999 (just in case you have a really, really big server).

If this policy is left unconfigured or disabled, no limit is specified and users can keep connecting until the server runs out of system resources.

Limit maximum color depth: As its name implies, this policy allows you to place a server-wide limit on the maximum color depth for Terminal Server sessions. Enforcing this limit can save bandwidth and generally works well in low-bandwidth environments.

By default, Windows 2003 Terminal Servers will limit client connections to 16-bit color, although Terminal Server will support up to 24-bit color.

Keep in mind that this is a maximum setting. If you configure it for 24-bit color, clients that can't aren't configured for that much will still be able to connect at lower color depths.

Allow users to connect remotely using Terminal Services: Quite simply, disabling this policy lets you "turn off" access to a server via Terminal Services. If you set this policy to "disabled," existing sessions will continue to function on the Terminal Server even though it will deny new connection attempts.

This policy shouldn't be used to manage Terminal Server access. Most people use it when applying policies to non-Terminal Servers as a way to ensure that no users accidentally connect to them.

Do not allow local administrators to customize permissions: This policy is useful if you have people on your IT staff who like to play with permissions. It sets the security on individual connections (as configured via the Terminal Services Configuration tool) to "read only." When enabled, local administrators of a server will not be able to modify any of the security settings found in the tool.

The default action for Terminal Server is to allow local administrators to modify these settings as needed.

If you do choose to enable this policy, keep in mind that you'll have to wait for a Terminal Server to get the new policy update if you disable this policy in order to make "a quick change" to the security settings of a server.

Remove Windows security item from Start menu: This policy (one of the few that also works on Windows 2000 Terminal Servers), removes the Windows security shortcut from the Start menu. (Remember that in Terminal Server sessions the "Windows security" item is the equivalent of pressing *CTRL+ALT+DEL* on a regular computer.) Enabling this policy can help you prevent users from getting confused and accidentally logging off the server.

If you enable this policy, users will have to log off a computer by typing the Windows security hotkey sequence, which is usually *CTRL+ALT+END*. Alternately, you might decide to tell users to disconnect from their sessions and let the server automatically log off disconnected users after a few minutes.

Remove Disconnect option from Shut Down dialogue: Whenever a user selects "log off" from a Terminal Server session, he is presented with a log off dialogue that allows him to either log off or disconnect his session. If you want to force users to logoff (by not allowing them to leave a disconnected session), you can enable this policy.

This policy only removes the disconnect option from that one dialog box. It does prevent a user from disconnecting his session via other means (by simply closing the client window, for example). In practice, this policy is really only a good choice in thin client-type environments.

Set path for TS Roaming Profiles: This setting overrides the Profile Path or TS Profile Path that's set as part of a user attribute whenever a user logs onto this server via Terminal Services. It's a lifesaver in several different scenarios, including:

- Users who access two different versions of Terminal Severs and you don't want to mix the Profiles between the two systems.
- Users who access two different sets of Terminal Servers across WAN links and you want to use Roaming Profiles without having to copy the profile across the WAN link.
- You have two sets of servers that require different User Profile settings that conflict with each other. This is common when running multiple versions of the same application.

When enabled, you'll be asked to provide a UNC path to where you want to store the master copy of the roaming profile. This should be formatted as *\\ServerName\ShareName.* Do not append the *%username%* variable or anything else to the end. The Terminal Server will use this share location as the root directory then add the user profiles in directories matching their usernames under the root folder.

If this policy is set to Not Configured or Disabled, then the Terminal Server will store profiles as it normally would.

TS User Home Directory: Much like the previous policy, this policy overrides the home folder attribute normally associated with the user's domain or AD account object. This policy allows you to specify a "custom" home folder for users that log on to the specific Terminal Servers where this policy is applied.

Like the profile override policy, you'll need to specify a UNC path to the share that will hold users' home folders (such as *\\ServerName\ShareName*) and pick a drive letter that you want to use for the mapping. If you choose a local path, (such as *c:\homedirs*), the drive letter field is ignored and local path is used instead. This approach is basically the same as when you configure a home folder as part of a user's attribute in Active Directory, except that in this policy you don't specify any user-specific variables at the end of the path (such as *%USERNAME%*). Terminal Services automatically appends that at logon and connects the user to the proper folder within the share.

If this policy is Enabled, Terminal Services creates the home folder in the specified location as the user connects to the server. The home folder path for each user is the specified "Home Dir Root Path" field of this policy with the user's alias appended to the end.

Using this policy to override the default home folders is useful in several situations. We'll review those situations in the "Home Folders" section of this chapter.

Set rules for remote control of Terminal Server user sessions: This policy allows you to configure what type of access (if any) IT staff or users will have to a user's session when they remote control (or "shadow") it. It's important to note that this setting does not give you the ability to determine *who* can remote control which users' sessions. Instead, it sets the rules for the remote control session after the permissions for remote control have already been established in the Terminal Services Configuration tool.

Just like the normal configurations allowed with remote control settings, when this policy is enabled, you have five options to choose from:

- *No remote control allowed* disables remote control of sessions on the server.
- *Full Control with user's permission* causes a little box to pop up on the user's screen when a remote control attempt is made. If the user accepts the remote control, then the remote controller can view the user's session and control his mouse and keyboard remotely.
- *Full Control without user's permission* is identical to the previous option, except that the user is not given the option to accept or decline the remote control.
- *View Session with user's permission* is also similar to the previous options, although this policy setting prevents remote controllers from actually being able to take control of a remote user's keyboard and mouse. This is like a "remote viewing" option.
- *View Session without user's permission* is the same as the previous option, except that the user is not given the choice as to whether they want to be remotely viewed.

Remote control rules policy setting is also available in the "User Configuration" section of a group policy object (User Configuration | Administrative Templates | Windows Components | Terminal Services). If there is ever a situation in which this policy setting is configured differently in the Computer Configuration and User Configuration settings of the same policy, then the configuration in the Computer Configuration section will override the setting in the User Configuration. (This is one of the rare instances in which the "most restrictive" rule does *not* apply.)

Remote control rules can also be configured on a per-connection basis in the Terminal Services Configuration MMC snap-in (Start | All Programs | Administrative Tools | Terminal Services Configuration | Right-click on the connection | Properties | Remote Control tab) or via the user's AD account properties (Active Directory Users and Computers | Right-click on user object | Properties | Remote Control tab).

In cases where this policy setting conflicts with the remote control properties of the user object and/or the connection properties, the most restrictive settings are enforced. This allows you to apply the settings at the appropriate layer to fit your exact requirements.

Start Program on Connection: This policy setting allows you to specify the "initial program" (as discussed throughout this book) that's run when a user connects to a Terminal Server. Enabling this policy and specifying a program to run causes the server automatically to run the program and obscure the desktop and Start menu from the user. If the application is closed, then the whole session is ended.

If this policy is enabled and the program specified in the path and working directory is not valid, then the user will be presented with an error message and the session will abort.

If the policy object is set to Disabled or Not Configured, the Terminal Services sessions will start with an entire desktop or with a program specified by the end user in the RDC client.

As for the previous policy, this policy setting can also be specified in the "User Configuration" section of a policy (User Configuration | Administrative Templates | Windows Components | Terminal Services). In cases where an initial program is specified in both locations, the server will override the User Configuration setting and run the program that's specified in the Computer Configuration setting.

Client/Server Data Redirection Policy Subfolder

The policy objects contained in this subfolder all deal with the virtual channels of the RDP protocol. All of these policy settings can also be configured as a property of the RDP listener port in the Terminal Services Configuration MMC snap-in. In case of a conflict, the most restrictive setting will take precedence. (After all, if you configure a port so that audio is disabled, then all audio will be disabled through that port regardless of what the policy says.

Allow Time Zone Redirection: One of the most useful enhancements that Microsoft added to Terminal Server in Windows 2003 is the ability for the server session's time zone to be dynamically set based on the client device's time zone. The clocks in users' local and remote applications can be the same, and that one Terminal Server can host users from multiple time zones.

By default, this automatic session time zone adjustment is disabled, and the session time zone is the same as the server time zone. However, enabling this policy setting will cause the server to calculate the proper time zone from the RDC client.

It's important to realize that this functionality is "time zone offset synchronization," not "clock synchronization." The server will look at the time zone of the client, and adjust the time zone of the session to match. If the server's clock is set correctly *and* if the server is configured for the proper time zone then everything will work out.

server base time + client time zone offset = actual session time

Time zone redirection tends to cause problems for some users. Generally when it is enabled you will receive several calls from users in the same time zone as the server complaining that their clocks are *way* off. This discrepancy can usually be traced back to the client computer's time zone being set incorrectly, fouling up the server's calculation. Remember that RDC client does not send its clock time to the server. It only sends its time zone, causing the server to adjust the session time regardless of what the client clock says.

Since this time zone synchronizing functionality is rather new, you need to have client software that supports it. Microsoft introduces this support in the "5.1" versions of the RDC client software.

Do not allow clipboard redirection: As the name implies, this policy setting allows you to disable the RDP virtual channel that is used for sharing clipboard contents (cut & paste) between the server and a client computer using a Terminal Services session. This functionality is enabled by default.

Clipboard redirection can also be enabled or disabled as a property of an RDP connection port (Start | All Programs | Administrative Tools | Terminal Services Configuration | Connections | Right-click on the connection name | Properties | Client Settings tab | Clipboard mapping checkbox).

In the event of a policy setting conflicting with an RDP listener port setting, the most restrictive setting takes precedence.

Do Not Allow Smart Card Device Redirection: As discussed in Chapter 12, Windows 2000 and newer clients can use smart cards to authenticate to their Terminal Server sessions instead of standard (manual) credentials. Ordinarily, whether a user can use a smart card (or whether a user is forced to use a smart card) is configured as part of a user's Active Directory account object.

In some cases, you might want to prevent users from being able to use a smart card on some Terminal Servers, and enabling this policy setting allows you to do so.

Allow Audio Redirection: Audio redirection is a new feature of Windows Server 2003 that enables your users hear their session sounds on their local client devices (such as the Windows "ding!"). Enabling this policy setting turns on this functionality.

Audio redirection does consume bandwidth, so it should only be used when it's actually needed.

Enabling this policy does not automatically "force" users to hear audio. Instead, it gives them the option (via their client settings) of having audio redirected.

Similar to the other policy settings, you can also enable or disable audio redirection as part of the RDP listener port properties in the Terminal Services Configuration MMC snap-in. By default, audio redirection is enabled here. Conflicting settings revert to the most restrictive setting taking precedence.

Do Not Allow COM port, client printer, LPT port, or drive redirection: These four policy settings are grouped together here because they all are simple "on and off" switches for basic RDP functionality. As with the previous policy settings, if one of these settings is enabled then that particular virtual channel is disabled.

Also like the other settings, each of these four items can be configured as part of the RDP listener port's properties, and the most restrictive setting takes precedence when conflicts occur.

Do Not set Default Client Printer to be the Default in the session: By default, a Terminal Server will automatically set the client's default printer as their default printer within the Terminal Server session. This policy allows you to override that and not allow it to happen.

This setting is useful if the application you are running on the Terminal Server uses a local IP port or UNC on the server to send print jobs that you want to keep as the default.

Some people get confused by this setting since they enable it and the user's default printer still becomes the default in their session. This is often the case when the user has only one printer and no local printers are installed on the Terminal Server. The only printer available is the client's default printer and of course that has to become the default.

As with previous Policy settings, if this option is configured as "disabled" the exact opposite occurs and the user's client printer becomes their default. This setting can also be configured as part of the RDP listener port properties.

Encryption and Security Policy Subfolder

Based on the name, you would think that this section of the policy would involve some complexity, but it actually doesn't. It only has three available options, two of which have very little to do with server security and more to do with the traffic between the client and the server.

Always prompt client for password upon connection: If enabled, this policy setting tells the Terminal Server to ignore any credentials the client has passed to it, instead forcing them to log on to the Windows logon screen from the server when they make their connection. This option is generally used when you suspect that your users are using other peoples' machines with stored passwords on them.

If this setting is disabled, any credentials passed from the client will be used for authentication. Of course if there aren't any credentials passed to the server or the passed credentials are incorrect, the user will still be prompted for a username and password.

As with most of these policies this option can also be set in the Terminal Services Configuration tool.

Set client encryption level: This policy setting is very straightforward, allowing you to specify a minimum RDP protocol encryption level. The different levels (FIPS, Client, High, and Low) are detailed in Chapter 12.

If you enable this policy and the client device can't meet the minimum standard you've set, then the client connection will be refused. You can also enforce encryption levels on a per-connection basis as a property of the RDP listener port in the Terminal Services Configuration MMC snap-in. Conflicting settings between the two will cause whichever encryption scheme is more secure to be applied.

RPC Security Policy | Secure Server: This policy setting allows you to specify whether RPC calls to the Terminal Server must be secured. In Windows Server 2003 environments, this RPC interface is used for administration and configuration of Terminal Server settings and properties. While the details of a secure RPC environment are outside the scope of this book, enabling this setting will deny RPC requests unless they are secure. If this policy is set to "disabled" or not configured, the server will still request secure RPC connections at first, but will accept unsecured communications if secure ones are not available.

Licensing Policy Subfolder

The licensing subfolder of a Group Policy object contains two policy settings. (Unfortunately, the ability to specify a preferred licensing server is *not* one of them.)

License Server Security Group: As discussed in Chapter 4, one of the great new features of Terminal Server on Windows 2003 is your ability to control which servers are authorized to receive licenses from a TS License Server.

You can enable this functionality by enabling this policy setting on a TS Licensing Server. When you do this, a new local security group is created called "Terminal Services Computers." The license server will then only distribute licenses to Terminal Servers that are members of this local group. In order for your servers to be granted licenses, you'll have to add their domain computer accounts into this group. (Most people actually create a domain global group that contains Terminal Server computer accounts. They then place that global group into the Terminal Services Computers local group on each license server. That way, they can manage group memberships via the one global group instead manually at each license server.)

This license server security group feature is great for companies that buy licenses by department. Since it's possible for one department's Terminal Servers to discover another department's TS license servers, licenses could be accidentally transferred across departments. This policy setting prevents that from happening.

If this setting is disabled or not configured, the license server will default to issuing a license to any server that requests one.

Prevent License Upgrade: This policy setting lets you prevent your license servers from "wasting" a Windows 2003 license on a Windows 2000 Terminal Server. If this option is disabled or not configured, the TS License Server will first try to issue a Windows 2000 CAL to Windows 2000 Terminal Servers but will "upgrade" to a Windows 2003 CAL if no Windows 2000 TS CALs are available. Chapter 4 explains this functionality.

Temporary Folders Policy Subfolder

This subfolder of a policy object delineates how temporary folders are handled in Terminal Server sessions. You won't usually need to change these settings unless you're dealing with a particularly crabby application.

Do not use temp folders per session: By default, a Windows 2003 Terminal Server assigns the user's *TEMP* and *TMP* variables to a location in the user's profile *(%USERPROFILE%\Local Settings\Temp\<SessionID>)*. Enabling this policy setting lets you override the *SessionID* part of the TEMP path, turning it into *%USERPROFILE%\Local Settings\Temp*, causing every user on the server to share the same temp folder.

If this policy is disabled or not configured, specific per-session temp folders are created for the user at each login.

Do not delete temporary folder on exit: By default, a user's temporary files and folders are deleted from a Terminal Server when the user logs off (helping to reduce the profile size). When enabled, this setting allows you to override that default behavior and causes the server to retain those files. The setting only works if you do not enable the "Do not use temp folders per session" policy. If that policy is enabled, this policy will not function.

Session Directory Subfolder

These policy settings allow you to configure your servers to participate in a Session Directory. As discussed in Chapters 3 and 7, the Session Directory directs users to the server hosting their previously-disconnected sessions in clustered environments.

These Session Directory policies only apply to Terminal Servers running the Enterprise or Data Center editions of Windows 2003, since the Standard edition does not have the ability to participate in a Session Directory.

The easiest way to apply these Session Directory policy settings is to create an OU for your Terminal Server cluster. Then, you can configure the settings for the entire cluster simply by changing the settings of a GPO applied to the OU. This OU-based cluster method is much easier then trying to configure GPO security based on computer names.

Terminal Server IP address redirection: This policy option lets you configure how the routing works in a Session Directory environment—either based on an IP address or routing token. If you're not yet familiar with the details of Session

Directory, then this setting will be meaningless to you. Windows 2003's Session Directory is covered in Chapter 7.

If this is set to "Not Configured," the IP address redirection setting in the Terminal Services Configuration tool is used.

Join a Session Directory: As its name implies, enabling this policy setting will cause the target Terminal Server to participate in a Session Directory. This setting doesn't do any good on its own. You must configure the next two settings as well.

Session Directory Server: This setting is where you enter the name of the Windows 2003 server that's running the Session Directory service.

Session Directory Cluster Name: Since each Session Directory server can host multiple Session Directories, you also must specify the name of the specific cluster that you want the target Terminal Server to be part of.

Sessions Policy Subfolder

The final subfolder containing Terminal Services policy settings contains settings that apply to user sessions. There are five session settings available:

- Set a time limit for disconnect sessions.
- Set a time limit for active Terminal Services sessions.
- Set a time limit for active but idle Terminal Services sessions.
- Allow reconnection from the original client only.
- Terminate the session when time limits are reached.

Within a policy file, sessions settings can be configured as a property of both the Computer Configuration (Computer Configuration | Administrative Templates | Windows Components | Terminal Services | Sessions) and User Configuration (User Configuration | Administrative Templates | Windows Components | Terminal Services | Sessions). If there are ever conflicting values within the same policy file, the computer policy will take precedence over the user setting.

In addition to being configured as part of a policy, these settings can be configured as part of the RDP listener port properties (Start | All Programs | Administrative Tools | Terminal Services Configuration | Connections | Right-click on the connection name | Properties | Sessions tab). They can also be configured as part of a user's AD account object (Active Directory Users and Computers

MMC snap-in | Double-click on a user account | Sessions tab). In case of a conflict, the most-restrictive setting will take precedence.

Things to Consider when Designing User Policies

Now that you know what your user policy options are, you can begin the actual policy design process. As you design your policies, consider the following:

- Will users run full desktops or just an individual application?
- How important is security?

User Applications

If users are running full desktops on your Terminal Servers, it's important that you lock down those desktops with policies. On the other hand, if users only run an individual application then you don't need to worry as much about policies as you would with a full desktop.

Security

The tighter you lock down your policies, the more secure your environment will be. Of course this will also lead to a more restrictive, less flexible environment. See Chapter 12 for the full details about securing your Terminal Server environment.

Home Folders

As in any computing environment, home folders (previously known as "home drives" or "home directories") in Terminal Server environments provide a private location where users can store their personal files and data. In Terminal Server, home folders can also be used in addition to user profiles for storage of application configuration information.

The first rule for home folders in a Terminal Server environment is this: the more users store in their home folders, the less they are forced to store in their user profile. This is crucial, because a user's entire roaming profile must be copied on to the Terminal Server when they log on, and copied off of the server when they log off.

The second rule for home folders in a Terminal Server environment is that all users should have a home folder configured to allow not only for the first rule to be followed but also for ease of configuration. With a home folder, individuals have a location to store data, and administrators have a destination for redirected folders. The home folder is used in Terminal Server environments as a location to store windows and system information within the Windows subfolder of a user's home folder.

Traditionally, users' home folders are network shares mapped to drive letters when the users log on. In some Terminal Server environments, users won't need to save their own files, so you won't need to make use of explicit home folders for each user. However, users in these environments will still *technically* have a home folder location, even though they wouldn't have an explicit drive letter mapped to it. To understand this, let's take a look at how Windows 2003 home folders work.

How Windows Home Folders Work

Whenever a user logs on to a Terminal Server, the server designates a specific folder to be the user's "home folder." You can specify the exact location of the folder that becomes a user's home folder via the user account properties in the Users and Computers MMC snap-in (or in the Computer Management snap-in for single-server, non-AD environments).

Similar to a user's profile path, you can specify two home folder locations per user—one that is used when users log on to regular computers and one that is used when users log on to Terminal Servers. In either case, the home folder can be a local path on the computer where the user logs on or a drive letter that is mapped to a UNC share.

Configuring a user's home folder as a property of his user account is an easy way to give each user his own private storage space while ensuring that drive letters will be mapped properly and permissions will be set correctly. Other than that, there's really nothing special about home folders configured as part of the user's account—they simply provide a location for users to store personal files and data.

When a user logs on to a Terminal Server, the server contacts a domain controller to retrieve the user's home folder location. It first checks for a Terminal Services home folder (as configured in the "Terminal Services Profile" tab of a user's account properties). If no home folder is specified, the server will then check for a regular home folder location (as configured in the "Profile" tab of a user's account properties). If no home folder is specified in either place, the server will use the user's local profile as the home folder location. This process is outlined on the next page in Figure 6.10.

Figure 6.10 Home folder Mapping Process

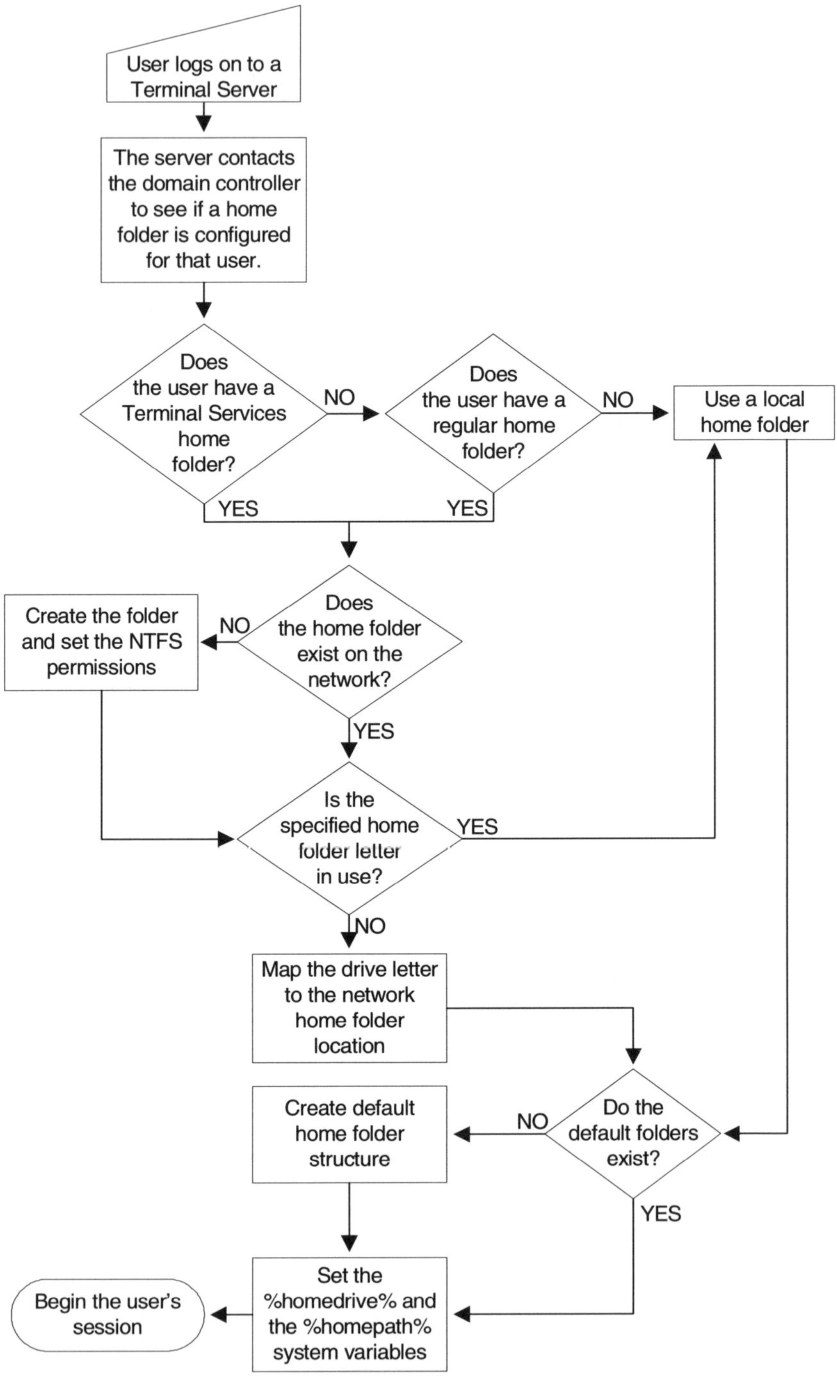

Whenever a user logs on, the server sets two system variables to indicate the path of the home folder: *%homedrive%* and *%homepath%*. These variables allow Windows applications to locate a user's home folder wherever it's located. For example, let's assume that a user's home folder can be found in the following location: *h:\home*. In Windows 2003 environments, the *%homedrive%* variable would be set to "*h:*" and the *%homepath%* variable would be set to "*\home*".

Breaking up the home folder into two variables allows you to map directly to a folder even if it's not the root of the share. If the home folder is the root of the share (such as "*h:*"), *%homedrive%* would be set to "*h:*" and *%homepath%* would be set to "\."

If you're not sure what the *%homedrive%* and *%homepath%* variables are in your environment, you can always check them from the command prompt by typing "*echo %homedrive%*" or "*echo %homepath%*." You can also view all of the environment variables that are set by typing "*set*."

How are Home Folders Used?

Most people think incorrectly that home folders are only used to store users' personal files. While this is a primary use for them in Terminal Server environments, home folders also serve a few other important purposes. In Terminal Server, home folders are used for:

- Windows system configuration information.
- Application data and configuration information.
- Personal files.

Windows and System Configuration Information

By default, the system creates two folders in each user's home folder: *windows* and *windows\system*. Any application looking for the server's *windows* or *system* directories to read or write .INI or configuration files is transparently routed to the appropriate directory in the user's home folder. That way, each user has his own configuration for applications.

These two folders are the only items automatically created in a user's home folder and should not be removed. Most users will create many more folders on their own.

Application Data and Configuration Information

Many applications require configuration folders to store user settings and data. Often these folders are created in addition to the *windows* and *system* folders. By putting this data in the user's home folder, an application can ensure that its settings will be unique for each user.

Personal Files

Perhaps the most important use for home folders is to store users' personal files. In addition to the data files that users store directly in their home folders, many administrators configure a policy that redirects users' "My Documents" and "Application Data" folders into their home folders (as described previously in this chapter).

By utilizing a user's home folder for personal data storage, you can leverage the advantages of roaming profiles without them growing too large since all personal files would be located in the home folder instead of the roaming profile.

Why should you care about Home folders?

There are several factors impacted by the way the home folder system is designed in Terminal Server. Because home folders are used throughout users' sessions, it's important that they're designed to support the needs of the users. Areas that are specifically impacted include:

- Logon speed
- File open/save speed
- User data integrity

Logon Speed

If the home folder is part of the user's profile that must be copied down to the Terminal Server every time the user logs on, logons will be slow. On the other hand, if the home folder is located on a separate network share, allowing the profile to be small, user logons will be fast.

File Access Speed

Many files will be read from and written to the user's home folder throughout the course of the user's session. If that home folder is located across a slow WAN link from the server running the user's Terminal Server session, opening and saving files will be slow.

User Data Integrity

A well-designed home folder environment will protect the data and the files that users store on their home folders. If the home folder design is sloppy, or worse yet, if home folders are kept on Terminal Servers, user data could be lost in the event of a problem.

What are the Home Folder Design Options?

There are a few options that you need to think about when deciding how home folders will be used in your Terminal Server environment. These options include:

- Home folder size
- Home folder location
- Number of home folders
- Methods of specifying home folders

Home folder Size

Remember the golden rule to roaming profiles? (Hint: Keep them as small as possible.) Home folders make this rule attainable. In order to shrink the size of a profile you need a place to store what you took out of the profiles.

While roaming profiles should always be kept as small as possible, there is nothing wrong with a home folder that is several gigabytes or more. They're only limited by the amount of hard drive space you have on the server that stores the home folders and how much data you can handle via your backup. From the network bandwidth standpoint, large home folders do not pose a problem since data is only copied across the network as it is needed (just like any network share).

So far, everything we've mentioned about home folders reduces to the idea that it's fine if they are large. However, there may be situations in which you actually need to limit the size of users' home folders. In Windows 2000/2003 environments, it's possible to limit the size of home folders using disk quotas.

Disk quotas allow you to specify the maximum drive space that a user can consume on an NTFS volume. Users are only "charged" for files and folders they own. You can set two limits per user per disk volume. A "soft" limit produces an event log and a warning for users that they are nearing their disk limit. A "hard" limit is the actual disk limit. When this limit is reached, users receive an "out of disk space" error if they try to copy anything else to their home folder.

In many environments, politics prevent disk quotas from "officially" being used. Even so, you might want to set quotas anyway. Set them high, just in case a slick user decides to store his entire MP3 collection in his Terminal Server home folder.

Advantages of Disk Quotas

- Helps prevent servers from running out of space.
- Different users can have different quota sizes.

Disadvantages of Disk Quotas

- Users are charged per volume, not per directory.
- Requires Windows 2000 or newer on the file server.
- Hastily-configured quotas could prevent users from doing their jobs.
- Disk space is cheap, and quotas might be more trouble then they're worth.

Procedure for Implementing Disk Quotas

Disk quotas only work on NTFS volumes on Windows 2000 and 2003. On both versions they're managed through the "Computer Management" MMC plug-in (Administrative Tools | Computer Management | Storage | Disk Management | Right-click on Disk Volume | Properties | Quota Tab).

Configuring disk quotas is fairly easy. You can set both the limit and warning levels for new users. You can also click the "Quota Entries" button to configure a custom list for existing users. Interestingly, the drop down box for the quota limit starts at "KB" and goes all the way up to "EB," which is one billion Gigabytes, in case you have users that you want to "limit" to a certain number of EB's.

You can also implement disk quotas on a file server via a GPO (Computer Configuration | Administrative Templates | System | Disk Quotas).

Location of Home Folders

In addition to home folder size, you also need to decide where your home folders will be located. Be careful when choosing the locations of home folders in relation to your network. While home folders must be located on a server that has the storage and processing capacity to support them, they should also be located in close proximity to the Terminal Servers so users have quick access to their data from their Terminal Servers sessions.

When you specify the location of your users' home folders, it's important that you *not* put them inside your users' profiles. This does not mean home folder can't be on the same server as the profiles, it just means that home folders should not be part of the directory structure that is copied to and from the Terminal Servers as part of a user's profile. If you put the home folders in the user profile, then all the work you do to minimize the size of the roaming profile is wasted.

When it comes down to the actual physical location of home folders, there are two choices:

- UNC share
- Local drive on the Terminal Server

Option 1. Home Folders Accessed via UNC Shares

In most environments, the appropriate home folder location will be on a server that is available to all Terminal Servers. The home folder is accessed through a UNC share name, and a drive letter is automatically mapped when the user begins his Terminal Server session.

Advantages of UNC Share-Based Home folders

- The home folder server can be built with redundancy, including Windows Clustering and RAID or SAN-based storage volumes.
- Individual Terminal Servers can be taken offline without affecting the availability of user data.

Disadvantages of UNC Share-Based Home folders

- A file server is required in addition to your Terminal Servers.

Procedure for Creating UNC Share-Based Home Folders

To create a home folder for a user, specify the home folder in the user's profile configuration (via the Users and Computers MMC snap-in). From the "Terminal Server Profile" tab, choose the "connect to" drive letter and type the full UNC path to the home folder location. You may use the %username% variable. If you specify the home folder as "*\\server\share\%username%*," then the system will automatically create the home folder and set the appropriate permissions. (Be sure to double-check that the selected drive letter is not in use for that user. If it is, you will not receive any error messages, but the home folder will map to a local drive (see below), not the UNC path.)

Option 2. Home Folders Stored on Terminal Servers

In some situations, you may choose to store users' home folders on the Terminal Server. This is usually done in small environments in which the Terminal Server is only one server.

Advantages of Storing Home folders on Terminal Servers

- Cheap and easy.

Disadvantages of Storing Home folders on Terminal Servers

- The contents of users' home folders are not available when they log on to another server.
- A new home folder will be created on each server where a user logs on.

Procedure for Creating Home Folders on Terminal Servers

A local home folder is also configured in the user account properties in the "Local Path" section. The entry takes the form of "*c:\path1\path2\ %username%.*" Again, using the *%username%* variable will cause the drive to be set up automatically the first time a user logs on.

Number of Home Folders

In most environments, each user will only have one home folder. However, there's no reason that each user needs to be restricted to only one home folder, or that multiple home folders for one user have to exist in the same physical location. Consider the following environment.

Figure 6.11 Some users need data in multiple locations

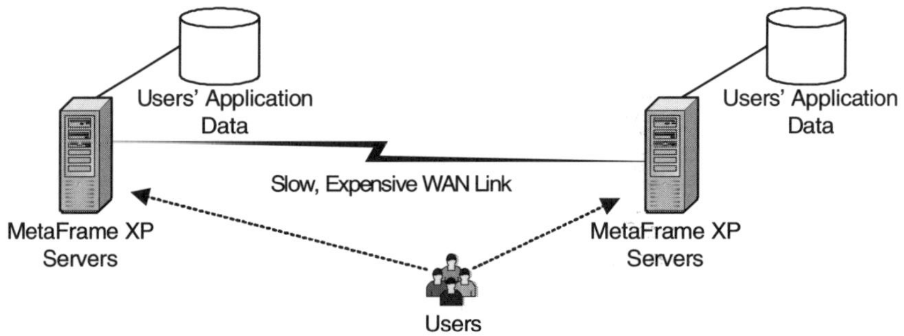

There are specific reasons that the user in Figure 6.11 must run his applications from Terminal Servers in two different locations. This company will never have both applications installed on the same Terminal Server because the databases are in two different locations. There is no reason that the user's personal data for the application should be in one single location. The user can have one home folder at each location—each containing files that are needed for that location.

Multiple home folders would make sense from a network standpoint, allowing the user to always have fast, local access to personal files from within sessions on both Terminal Servers. However, if you use multiple home folders, be careful. Don't try to make both home folders look the same to the user. You should probably not have both home folders mapped to the same drive letter (each in its own respective session). While there is nothing technically wrong with doing so, it is confusing for the user to have a *P:* drive in two different sessions that maps back to two different network locations. Users may switch back-and-forth between applications on different Terminal Servers. They won't understand, for example, drive *P:* from Microsoft Word has one set of files and drive *P:* from the data warehouse application has another. Using multiple drive letters gives the user an idea that there are multiple network locations.

Advantages of Multiple Home folders

- Local data access from sessions on remote Terminal Servers.

Disadvantages of Multiple Home folders

- Can be confusing if both drives have the same letter.

Procedure for Configuring Multiple Home Folders

In Windows 2003 environments, you can override a user's default home drive by applying a policy to a Terminal Server. (In case you skipped the policy section of this chapter, this override can be found in the following location within a policy object: User Configuration | Administrative Templates | Windows Components | Terminal Services | TS User Home Directory).

Home Folder Replication

Instead of having multiple local home folders for each user throughout your enterprise, it's possible to configure directory replication so that the contents of one home folder are replicated to multiple servers throughout the environment.

Home folder replication may sound good in theory, but it turns out to be a nightmare in real life. Data in home folders usually change frequently, making bad candidates for replication. Also, the replication process takes time, so a user simultaneously using sessions on two Terminal Servers that are far apart might have different versions of the same data if the replication process has not completed.

Home folder data replication is mentioned here for the sake of thoroughness and because it has been used with limited success in some cases. In general, it is more trouble than it's worth.

Advantages of Replicating Home folders

- The same user data is locally available to a user's session throughout the enterprise.

Disadvantages of Replication Home folders

- Data can get out of sync.
- Replication times can be long.
- Bandwidth is wasted during the replication process.
- Additional management is required.
- Replication software costs money.

Methods of Specifying Home Folders

So far, we've focused on how home folders are configured as part of a user's domain account properties. While this is the main method of specifying home folders, there are other methods that can be useful in certain situations. In this section, we'll take a look at all the methods you can use to specify a home folder for a user, including:

- User account properties configured in the domain or Active Directory.
- Home folder configuration via a GPO.
- Logon script.
- Folder redirection via a GPO.
- Do nothing (let the system create a home folder automatically).

Method 1. User Account Home Folder Configuration

Before we look at some of the "alternative" methods of configuring home folders, let's review the official way of doing it. In Active Directory or Windows NT 4.0 domains, domain users can be configured with a home folder that will be automatically mapped upon logon as part of their user account. Then, whenever that user logs on to a Terminal Server, his home folder is mapped and set to the specified location without any extra configuration or scripting.

Advantages of Specifying Home Folders via User Properties

- Easy to do.
- The "homedrive" and "homepath" variables are automatically set.
- This is the "official" method of creating home folders.
- The home folder is created and permissions are set automatically.

- Easy way to specify different home folders for Terminal Servers and non-Terminal Servers.

Disadvantages of Specifying Home Folders via User Properties

- No flexibility.
- The home folder settings apply to the user regardless of the computer that he logs onto.

Procedure for Specifying Home Folders via User Properties

In Active Directory environments, you configure home folders with the Users and Computers MMC (MMC | User Properties | Profile tab | Home Folder | Connect X: to UNC or local path).

You can use the following procedure to create home folders in Windows 2000 or 2003:

1. Create and share a root folder to use for your home folders in the location of your choice.
2. Give the "Everyone" group "Change" permissions on this folder.
3. For each user, specify the home folders as "\\your folder\%username%."

In this case, you should literally type "*%username%*" in the box (a percent sign, the word "username," and another percent sign). Do not substitute the user's real user name for the *%username%* variable.

When the user logs on for the first time, the system will automatically create the subdirectory for the username and give it the appropriate permissions. (Administrators get special access at the directory level only, the user maintains full control.) The *windows* and *windows\system* directories will also be automatically created, with administrators having full control.

Method 2. Group Policy Home Folder Configuration

As we discussed in the policies section of this chapter, you can use policy objects (either Group Policy or local policies) to specify home folders on a site, domain, OU, or local server basis. (Can't quite remember where that setting was? From within the policy editor MMC snap-in: User Configuration | Administrative Templates | Windows Components | Terminal Services | TS User Home Directory.)

The advantages and disadvantages of specifying home folders via a policy object are the same as specifying any setting via a policy object.

Method 3. Logon Script Home Folder Configuration

Another way to specify a home folder is to use a logon script to map a drive to a network share and then to execute a command that sets the home folder environment variable to point to that drive. (See the below for more information about logon scripts.)

Advantages of Specifying Home folders via Logon Scripts

- Extremely flexible implementation of home folders.

Disadvantages of Specifying Home folders via Logon Scripts

- Scripts must be manually configured.
- "*Homedrive*" and "*homepath*" variables must be manually set.
- Permissions must be manually configured.

Procedure for Configuring Home folders via Logon Scripts

Specifics of this method are addressed in the logon script portion of this chapter.

Method 4. Group Policy Folder Redirection

Active Directory group policies can be used to redirect local folders to network locations on computers running Windows 2000 and participating in Active Directory domains. For example, a user's "My Documents" folder can be redirected to a network share location that is centralized, so that no matter what computer the user logs on to, he would have access to the same data in his "My Documents" folder. Because this is a function of group policy, it can be applied only to the specific organizational units containing Terminal Servers.

While redirecting the "My Documents" folder to a static network point can eliminate the storage of too much data in a user's profile, this is not technically a "real" home folder. In addition to a location for storing personal files, a home folder also contains certain system information, and a home folder is the target of the *%homedrive%* and *%homepath%* variables. That being said, if your users will store all of their files in their "My Documents" folder, you can probably get away with redirecting that folder and not worrying about the "official" home folder location. (You could always manually reconfigure the *%homedrive%* and *%homepath%* variables to point to the *My Documents* folder.)

Advantages of Specifying Home folders via Folder Redirection

- Folder redirection can be used in addition to "official" home folders.
- Easy way to keep data out of profiles. (Isn't that the only reason we really care about home folders anyway?)

Disadvantages of Specifying Home folders via Folder Redirection

- Not a "real" home folder.
- "Homedrive" and "homepath" variables will point to other locations unless you manually set them.

Procedure for Specifying Home folders via Group Policy

Detailed information about folder redirection can be found in the User Profiles segment of this chapter.

Method 5. Do nothing. Let the system create a Home folder.

Finally, the "do nothing" approach is also a valid option with home folders. If no home folders are specified anywhere, the system will automatically create a user's home folder in their local user profile (by creating a *windows* directory and setting the *%homedrive%* and *%homepath%* variables).

This solution can work in small environments where users will not store their personal files in the home folder. However, there can also be several problems with this method. If a Terminal Server is configured to delete cached copies of roaming profiles at logoff, or if the local profile is overwritten by a roaming profile at logon, the data in the home folder will be lost.

Advantages of Doing Nothing.

- Least amount of work.
- Might be sufficient in small, single-server environments.

Disadvantages of Doing Nothing.

- If local profiles are not cached, home folder data will be lost.
- If local profiles are overwritten by roaming profiles at logon, home folder data will be lost.
- The "doing nothing" approach will not work in multi-server environments.

Things to Consider when Designing Home Folders

Now that you know all of the options, answering the following two questions should get your home folder design headed in the right direction:

- Does each user need to store personal files?
- Will users be logging on to multiple Terminal Servers at different physical locations?

User File Storage

If your Terminal Server environment is used for specific applications only, it's possible your users will never need home folders during their sessions. Of course, if your users are running applications that only open and save files, or applications that rely heavily on personalized configuration (such as email), then it will be important to ensure that users have fast, reliable access to their home folders.

Single Users with Multiple Server Locations

If users will be connecting to Terminal Servers in multiple physical locations requiring access to home folders, your design will need to reflect this. The result will be a much more complex design than if each of your users only connects to one Terminal Server.

When placing home folders, you also need to consider whether users will be using them just from Terminal Servers sessions or if users will need to access them from anywhere on the network.

Logon Scripts

Logon scripts in Terminal Server environments are no different from those in any other type of environment—they are simply batch files that run whenever a user logs on to the server. As with other components of Terminal Server environments, there are several different ways to use logon scripts and some are more effective than others. Before discussing how logon scripts are used, let's take a look at how they work.

How Logon and Logoff Scripts Work

Both logon and logoff scripts are batch files that execute when a user logs on or logs off of a Terminal Server. These scripts can use system environment variables and can call other scripts and executables.

Logon Scripts

With logon scripts, you can assign a batch file to run when certain users log on or when a certain Terminal Server computer is used. They allow you to influence certain aspects of a user's environment without taking full control of it (as when policies or profiles are used). Terminal Server logon scripts can be used to:

- Define and map a user's home folder (if this is not done automatically).

- Set up an application's environment in the user's home folder, by creating subdirectories and copying the necessary configuration files from a template directory.
- Modify the user's profile/registry.
- Verify or set permissions in a home folder.
- Start background processes.
- Configure and prepare any Windows components for use.
- Map network drives.
- Create icons and shortcuts for the user.
- Map printers.

Logoff Scripts

In addition to logon scripts, you can configure logoff scripts that run whenever a user logs off of the Terminal Server. These scripts serve several purposes, including:

- Deletion of unwanted temporary folders.
- Backup of important files.
- Copying of files to network locations.

Why should you care about logon script design?

In most Terminal Server environments, logon scripts are used in addition to profiles and policies to create the user environment. If your system requires logon scripts, then you will need to use them. When designing logon scripts, the decisions you must make relate more to *how* the logon scripts are implemented than to *what* they do when they run.

If you don't carefully consider all logon script options available, you could limit the flexibility within your environment. For example, some logon script languages are more flexible than others, allowing more powerful scripts to be created.

What are the logon script options?

When designing logon scripts, you'll most likely spend most of your time writing the script itself, but there are a few decisions that you can make to help implement your scripts. Make these decisions by answering the following questions:

- What script language will be used?
- How will the scripts be launched?
- Will you use the same script on all of your servers?

Script Language

There are hundreds of languages available for creating logon scripts with few differences between them. In this section, we'll focus on two of the most popular scripting languages. If you have another preferred language, use it with Terminal Server.

The two scripting languages that we will mention here are Windows batch scripts and Kixtart scripts.

Windows Batch Scripts

Windows batch scripts are regular BAT or CMD files. Batch scripts are the most popular and easiest to use of all the available scripting languages, mainly because this is the script language that most of us have been using for fifteen years.

With Windows batch scripts, you can use system environment variables and create conditional logic. There are several advanced features built into this powerful scripting language. In many environments, you'll be able to do everything that you need to with Windows batch scripts. If there is anything that you can't do with the native scripting language, you can always call another command-line utility from your script.

Advantages of Windows Batch Scripts

- No third-party interpreter is needed.
- Scripts run in their own native language without needing to be compiled.
- Everyone knows how to write batch files.

Disadvantages of Windows Batch Scripts

- Limited native advanced features.

Kixtart scripts

The Kixtart scripting language and interpreter is a free script environment originally included in Windows NT Resource Kits. (You can download the Kixtart utilities for free from `www.kixtart.org`.) Kixtart scripts are more powerful and flexible than batch scripts but are written in their own proprietary scripting language. Many administrators use Kixtart scripts for advanced features, such as the ability to conditionally branch based on a logged-on user's group membership.

Advantages of Kixtart Scripts

- More advanced than batch scripts.

Disadvantages of Kixtart Scripts

- Written in a proprietary language.
- Requires the kix.exe script player.

Launching Scripts

After you write your logon scripts, you'll need to decide how the scripts will be launched. In the past this was easy (there was only one option). Today, there are five different methods that can be used to launch a logon script for a given user. Some of these methods apply to all users that log on to a particular computer. Other methods apply to a particular user and follow that user to all computers. The five methods are:

- User's Domain or Active Directory account object properties.
- Group policy.
- Startup folder.
- Launch scripts via the registry.

Method 1. User's Domain / AD Account Properties

Most people configure logon scripts on a "per user" basis as part of the user's domain or Active Directory account configuration. This is the standard way of configuring logon scripts, and scripts configured in this manner will run whenever the user logs on to any computer in the domain. It's easy to apply different scripts to different users using this method.

On the other hand, a disadvantage of applying scripts this way is that they run no matter where the user logs in—whether or not the system is a Terminal Server. This is not usually considered a show-stopper, as it's relatively straightforward to build intelligence into a script to detect whether or not it's running on a Terminal Server.

Advantages of Scripts via Users' Domain Account Properties

- Easy to set up.
- Scripts are automatically replicated between domain controllers (via the *Netlogon$* shares).
- "Standard" way of configuring scripts.

- Different scripts can be applied to different users.

Disadvantages of Scripts via Users' Domain Account Properties

- No way to prevent a script from running when a user logs on.

Procedure for Scripts via Users' Domain Account Properties

In Windows Active Directory environments, logon scripts are configured through the MMC (User properties | Profile Tab | Logon Script).

Method 2. Group Policy

Group policy objects can contain logon and logoff scripts (in addition to computer startup / shutdown scripts) that are executed wherever the policy is applied. By using group policy, it is possible for you to "layer" scripts on the user, with different scripts applying at the site, domain, and OU levels. If a user is part of an OU structure several containers deep, it's possible to apply different logon and logoff scripts to each OU in the layer. All of the scripts will run for each user.

This method, when used in conjunction with the Group Policy Loopback processing mode is a great way to ensure that the script only runs when the user logs on to a Terminal Server.

Advantages of Launching Scripts via Group Policy

- Each group policy can have its own script, allowing for layering of scripts.
- Scripts (via policies) can be applied to specific OUs.

Disadvantages of Launching Scripts via Group Policy

- Requires Active Directory.

Procedure for Launching Scripts via Group Policy

Add the script names to the appropriate group policy via the group policy MMC snap-in (User Configuration | Windows Settings | Scripts).

Method 3. Startup Folder

The "Startup" folder in a server's Start Menu contains programs that are run automatically when a user logs on. There are two startup folders that can be used. The first is in the "all users" profile. Logon scripts or application shortcuts placed in this folder are executed by every user when she logs on. The second startup folder location is unique for each user. Any scripts stored in the "Startup" folder in the user's profile will execute every time the user logs on. If the user has a roaming profile and the scripts are stored in the "Startup" folder of that profile, the scripts will execute on any server where her profile is applied.

Of course these scripts only run once the user's environment is completely loaded. This sometimes leads to problems when scripts are modifying applications and users are trying to launch those same applications.

Advantages of Launching Scripts via the Startup Folder

- Different scripts can be configured for different users.
- If Terminal Server roaming profiles are used, you can easily create a logon script that only runs in Terminal Server environments.
- Each user can have multiple logon scripts.
- User-specific and server-specific logon scripts can be easily combined.

Disadvantages of Launching Scripts via the Startup Folder

- If the profile doesn't load, the script won't run.
- Script sometimes runs after the user is already opening applications.

Procedure for Launching Scripts via the Startup Folder

To launch logon scripts via a startup folder, all you need to do is copy the script into the appropriate startup folder. For "all users," the folder is unique on each server (*Local Profile Root*\All Users\Start Menu\Programs\Startup). For specific users, the logon script must be copied to their master profile locations (*User Profile Root*\Start Menu\Programs\Startup).

When you put a logon script in the startup folder, you might wonder whether you should copy in the actual script or shortcuts to the script. Even though "best practices" dictate that you should only place shortcuts in the Start Menu, in this case you should put the entire script in the startup folder. Even the longest logon scripts are relatively small in size, and it's much easier to manage if the actual scripts are in the startup folder.

Method 4. Launch Scripts via the Registry

Another method by which to launch logon and logoff scripts is to add entries to your Terminal Server's registry. Every server has a registry key that specifies programs that are executed when the server is booted or when users log on. Adding your logon scripts to the list of programs executed when a user logs on is an easy and effective way to establish a logon script for all users on a particular server.

Advantages of Launching Scripts via the Registry

- Script always runs, without exception.
- No dependency on profiles or network drives.

Disadvantages of Launching Scripts via the Registry

- Must be configured manually on every server.

Procedure for Launching Scripts via the Registry

The logon and logoff programs that are run when users log on or off are specified in the following locations:

Logon Script

Key: HKLM\Software\Microsoft\Windows\Current Version\Run

Value: Free-form name of your script.

Type: REG_SZ

Data: Full path and executable of script. Each script requires its own "value" entry.

Logoff Script

Key: HKLM\Software\Microsoft\WindowsNT\CurrentVersion\Winlogon

Value: LogoffApp

Type: REG_SZ

Data: List of applications that are to be run, separated by commas.

Launching Different Scripts on Different Servers

Each of the four methods of launching logon scripts has its own advantages and disadvantages. In large environments, you'll probably need to be able to launch different scripts for different groups of servers. If you're using Active Directory, you can simply apply scripts via GPOs. However, if you're not using AD, there's a simple solution that still allows you to launch different scripts on different servers.

Add a line to your logon script that checks to see if a certain condition is true. If it is, the script will run. If not, part of the script can be skipped. This allows you to conveniently configure a logon script to run on all servers that is smart enough to know where it's running and which parts should run.

An easy way to accomplish this is to create a logon script that checks for the presence of a flag file on the server. If the flag file is present, the script is executed. If not, the script is aborted. Simply copy the empty flag file to the servers where you want your script to run. For example, you might add the following line of code to your logon script:

```
if exist %systemroot%\yourflagfile.txt goto exit
```

This would cause the script to exit if *yourflagfile.txt* was found on the server.

Real-World Logon Script Usage

Most new Terminal Server administrators don't focus on logon scripts for user customization. Instead, they often focus on the default profile that users will use and the policies in place to secure the desktop. Unfortunately, one problem that's often overlooked when using a preconfigured default profile for configuring the environment is that new changes will have to be added to that profile and existing user profiles will have to be deleted to allow the change to take effect.

Most experienced Terminal Server administrators use logon script to customize their user environment. These scripts (in any language) often accomplish some common tasks, most frequently:

- E-mail or E-mail profile configuration.
- Modification of per-user registry entries for specific applications.
- Creation of network printers.
- Copying of application files to the user's home folder.
- Configuration of Windows desktop settings.

Let's assume that you already have a 10-server load-balanced cluster deployed. The cluster hosts Office XP (including Outlook) and a document management software package. Now, imagine that a new update has been tested for the document management package, but it will require that several registry entries be changed for each user. What's the best way to go about this?

Of course if you're using roaming profiles, you could make the change to the default user profile and then delete all of your users' current profiles, but this would cause the loss of all your users' personalized settings in Microsoft Office.

A better option in this case would be to write a script that modifies the required registry keys at logon, leaving the rest of each user's profile intact while still satisfying the requirements for the software upgrade.

Considerations when Designing Logon Scripts

When you begin to design your logon scripts and decide how they will be invoked, there are two questions to consider:

- Do you need scripts to run on a "per-user," "per-server," or "per-application" basis?
- Do you need different scripts to run on different servers, depending on which the script is running on?

The answer to the first question will help you determine how to launch the logon scripts. Figure 6.12 provides a snapshot of which script launching methods can be used in which situations.

The answer to the second question will help you determine what type of logic you will need to include in your logon scripts. With that, you should have all the information you need to design effective and efficient logon scripts, in turn making your Terminal Server environment easy to manage.

Figure 6.12 The various methods that can be used to launch scripts

Method	Per-User	Per-Server
Domain Account	•	
GPO	•	•
Startup Folder	•	•
Registry		•

Real World Case Study

Parker HealthNet, A Regional Healthcare Network

Parker HealthNet has decided to use Windows 2003 Terminal Services to provide applications for 5000 users at nine hospitals and thirty remote healthcare facilities. Many of their users will need to access applications from multiple client devices. For example, doctors often travel between hospitals and remote medical offices, and nurses will use terminals spread throughout many locations in hospital complexes.

A project team was assembled to create a design for the Terminal Server environment. Their design was based on the current environment as outlined in Figure 6.13.

Figure 6.13 Parker HealthNet's WAN Architecture

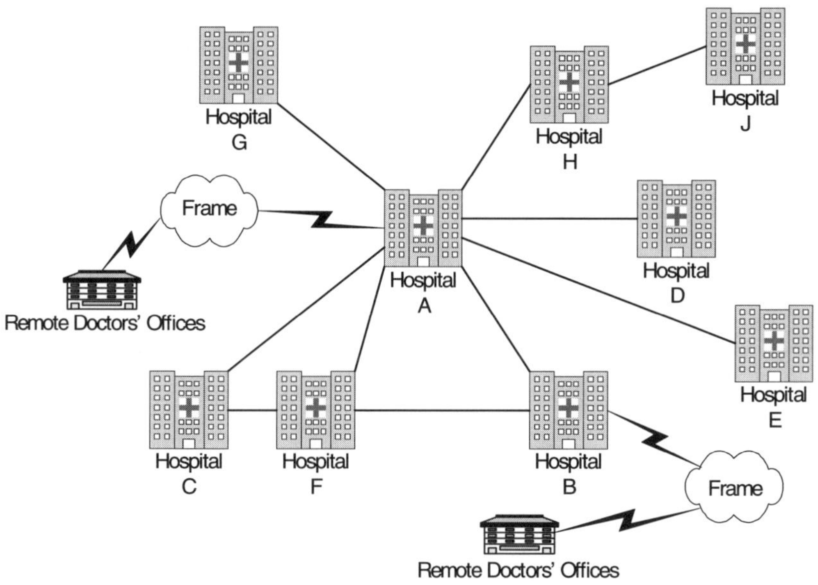

The project team first outlined their objectives. For the Parker HealthNet environment, several objectives were identified, including:

- *Security.* A secure environment was needed, since most of their applications are integral to patient care and must be HIPAA compliant.
- *Availability.* If applications were not available, patient care would suffer.
- *Mobility.* Many users would need to simultaneously access applications running on multiple Terminal Servers in multiple locations.

Based on their current environment and future needs, the project team was able to make several design decisions. First, they decided to place Terminal Servers locally at each of the nine hospitals. Each hospital would be configured with its own Terminal Server cluster. They decided that users would primarily access applications running on Terminal Servers installed locally in each of their own hospitals, but that there would also be some central medical applications for all users running on a Terminal Server cluster in the central datacenter. Figure 6.14 shows a typical hospital and how its users would access applications.

Figure 6.14 Typical Hospital with Terminal Server application access

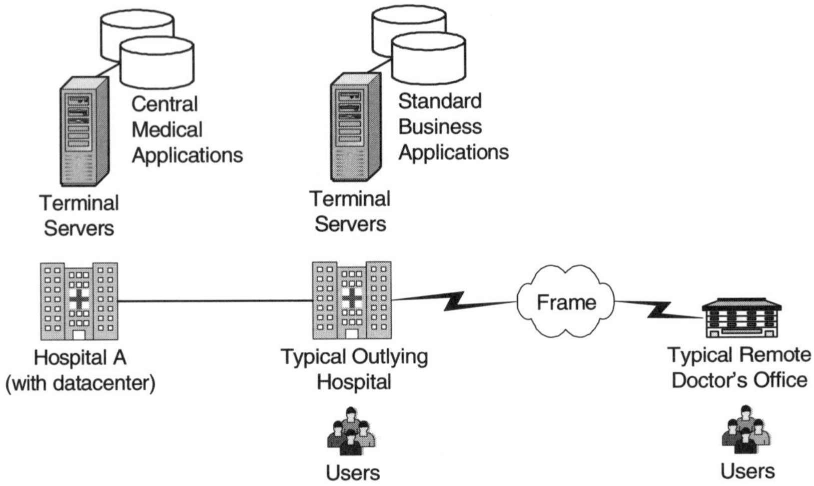

Parker HealthNet migrated to Windows 2000 Active Directory two years ago, and they'll be running a Windows 2003-based Active Directory by the time the Terminal Servers are deployed. They have one Active Directory domain with separate Active Directory Sites configured for each hospital.

Once these basic design decisions were made, the project team deliberated at length on more complex questions. They were able to consolidate all of their questions into two core issues:

- Should they use mandatory profiles, flex profiles, or group policies to lock down the desktops?
- Considering that many users travel between locations, where should the master roaming profiles be located? What about the home folders?

Let's take a look at how the Parker HealthNet project team dealt with these design issues.

Issue 1. Desktop Lockdown

The major discussion around desktop lockdown was not "if" they should lock them down, but "how." Should they use mandatory profiles, flex profiles, or group policies? Initially the project team thought that they had to use group policies, but some members pointed out that mandatory and flex profiles contain the same registry data as policies. By using mandatory roaming or flex profiles, they could create locked-down template users and use those to manually create the mandatory roaming profiles.

After reviewing the options, the project team quickly threw out the pure mandatory profile option. They figured that since the flex profile was basically built on top of a mandatory profile, they could implement it across the board with very little risk. For users who don't need to customize their own environments, the flex profile works just like a mandatory profile. However, for the users who would need to customize any parts of their environments, the flex profile would allow them to do that without the "bloat" associated with standard roaming profiles.

To bolster the security offered by the mandatory components of the flex profiles, Parker HealthNet also chose to create policies and apply them to the OUs containing the Terminal Servers to further limit the capabilities of their users.

Issue 2. User Profile and Home Folder Locations

After determining which types of profiles and policies would be used, the project team needed to decide where on the network to store users' roaming profiles and home folders. The easiest way to determine this was to look at how users would access the Terminal Servers. From there, it would be easy to determine where to store user data.

The project team planned for all users across the health system to run the "standard" applications from Terminal Servers at their respective local hospitals. Additionally, many users would need to access medical records applications that would reside on Terminal Servers in the central datacenter in Hospital A. Those users would therefore need access to two Terminal Servers—one at their local site and one in the central datacenter. Generally, users would not need access to multiple Terminal Servers at different local sites.

Now that the project team knew where the Terminal Servers would be located and how they would be accessed, they needed to decide where on the network to store roaming profiles and user data. They knew that they should try to keep the data as close as possible to the Terminal Servers. They decided to create several storage locations throughout the health system, with one storage location at each of the nine hospitals. The exact data location for a specific user would depend on where that user was based. The project team appreciated the fact that just having data stored in multiple locations on the network does not mean each that user's data would be located in multiple locations. It just means users' home folders and roaming profiles would be sprinkled throughout the WAN.

For users in the remote medical offices, roaming profiles and home folders would be stored at the nearest hospital. (See Figure 6.15.) This arrangement is due to the fact that there would not be any Terminal Servers at the remote office facilities, and remote office users would access Terminal Servers located at the nearest hospital.

Figure 6.15 Roaming profile and home folder Locations

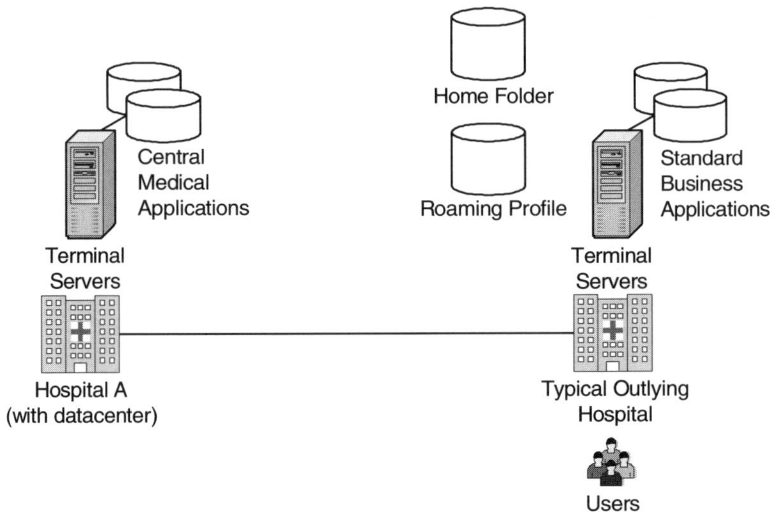

Because some users need simultaneously to access applications from Terminal Servers in the central hospital and their local hospitals, the project team needed to decide where those roaming profiles and home folders would be located. Right away they discarded any notions of using data replication to copy user profiles or home folders to multiple locations throughout the WAN. They knew that by introducing data replication, they would needlessly complicate their environment and waste money on additional storage devices and replication software.

Ultimately, the project team decided to keep the user data at the local hospital site since the medical applications that ran on the central Terminal Servers didn't require access to the users' home folders. They could enable home folder overrides for those servers. As for the profiles, it wasn't a major issue for users with sessions on those servers to load their profiles from their local hospital servers since using the flex profiles allowed the project team to limit the size of the profiles.

Once that was settled, all the project team had left to do was to decide how to deal with users that travel between hospitals. Should those users access applications from local Terminal Servers in the hospital they are visiting, or should they access Terminal Servers from their home sites?

After a brief discussion, the project team decided that traveling users would run applications off of Terminal Servers at their home sites, not the sites to which they traveled. This decision was made for several reasons:

- Easier to manage, as there would be no need for any script logic to determine from where the user was connecting.
- Easier to size the servers, as the user base for each site would be constant.
- Master copies of profiles and home folders would be stored at the same local site as the Terminal Server.
- Users could easily reconnect to disconnected sessions from any location, as the sessions would always be running in the "proper" location.
- The RDP protocol is efficient and is the preferred protocol for WAN communication. (If local Terminal Servers were used, then the RDP protocol would only be used on the local LAN, and inefficient file transfer traffic would traverse the WAN. See Chapter 3 for details.)

Parker HealthNet Implementation Summary

Ultimately, Parker HealthNet was able to successfully implement the Terminal Server environment as outlined. Though it has been only six months since they completed the implementation, patient care has been positively affected. In fact, Parker HealthNet is planning on acquiring two or three hospitals in the next 12 to 18 months, and view their Terminal Server environment as one of the key components that will allow them to quickly integrate the new hospitals into their existing business environment.

CHAPTER 7

Designing High Availability Solutions

This chapter describes the options you have, the steps you must take, and the money you must spend to ensure that your Terminal Servers are highly available for your end users.

In most environments, the use of Terminal Services starts out small. A single server usually provides a few applications to a few users. Over time, those environments reach the point of users depending on the applications hosted on Terminal Server. Then it becomes necessary to administrators to think about building multiple servers and systems that can automatically carry users through a failure of one system.

By thinking about how Terminal Server and its supporting systems work and how your users will use them, you can create a strategy to guarantee that the system has the redundancy needed to absorb small "hiccups" and is properly backed up to survive major disasters.

The redundancy of many Terminal Services components is discussed throughout this book. This chapter pulls those components together creating a holistic strategy that you can apply to your entire Terminal Server environment.

Terminal Server Availability in Today's World

In environments where availability is of utmost importance, administrators usually implement clustering technologies. Clustering technologies are usually applied to database, email, or web servers. If a server fails, another "node" is able to pick up where the first left off, and in many cases users are completely unaware that a failure occurred.

Unfortunately, seamless clustering failover technology is not available with Terminal Server, and is unlikely to be for some time. In fact, no Terminal Server-based technology can do this—not Microsoft, not Citrix, and not Linux. Now, before you slam this book down and tell everyone that this technology is completely bunk, think about what this means.

If a user is using a remote application on a Terminal Server and that server fails, the user's application will not magically appear on another Terminal Server right where she left off. That would require mirrored disks, shared memory stacks, dynamic program executables, and all sorts of other tools that haven't been invented yet.

What *is* possible with today's technology is load-balanced redundant environments. You can build your Terminal Server environment so that if a server fails (obviously ending the sessions of any users connected to it), the user can *imme-*

diately reconnect to a new server and launch her application again. (This is much better than in traditional environments where applications run on users' desktops.)

It is also possible to configure redundant hardware on your servers and manage them in a way to minimize the chance that they'll go down.

Microsoft Terminal Server "Clustering"

Now that we just made such a big deal about how you can't create "real" clustering with Terminal Servers, we should point out that Microsoft has started using the terms "load-balancing" and "clustering" interchangeably when discussing multi-server Terminal Server environments. This duplicity tends to cause confusion, so keep in mind that for the next few years, when you hear the word "cluster" in the context of Terminal Services, it really means "a load-balanced group of Terminal Servers." It has nothing to do with Windows 2003's Cluster Service.

What affects Terminal Server availability?

In order to determine what is required for your environment, let's look at the various components of a Terminal Server system from the perspective of redundancy. Figure 7.1 (next page) shows a generic view of the technical components required for a user to access an application hosted on Terminal Server.

The majority of this chapter will focus on how to configure your Terminal Servers in a load-balanced group. However, as Figure 7.1 illustrates, when creating a highly available environment, you can't just focus on the Terminal Servers. It does no good to build a fantastic load-balanced Terminal Server environment only to have your web server go down. Therefore, we'll first discuss high-availability strategies for several components of a Terminal Server environment, including:

- Client devices.
- Network connections.
- Web interface servers.
- Terminal Servers.
- User and application data.

Throughout the remainder of this section, we'll analyze how each component in Figure 7.1 affects overall redundancy and what can be done to that component to strengthen the redundancy of the overall system. All of these components work together as a system. Refrain from thinking about the redundancy of one component without considering the redundancy of others. Your Terminal Server environment is only as strong as its weakest link.

Figure 7.1 The Terminal Server components that must be functional

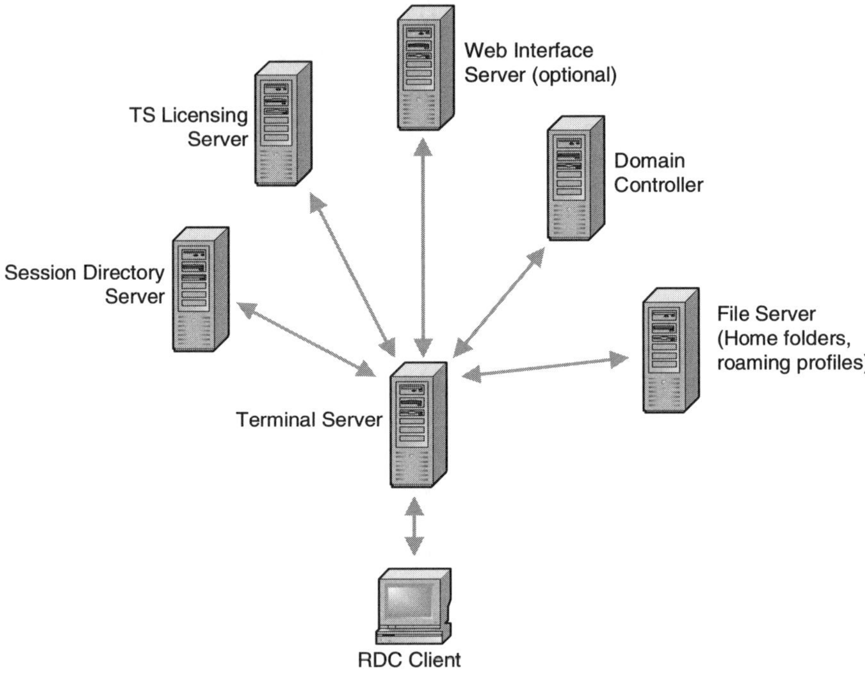

Client Device Redundancy

By this point you are well aware that a major architectural advantage to thin client environments is that any user can connect from any client device. If a client device ever fails, a user can begin using a different device and pick up right where he left off.

Chapter 9 will present the issues to consider when designing your client device strategy. These issues can be summarized as follows: With RDP clients, apply "high availability" not by changing anything on the client itself, but rather by having a spare client device available to quickly replace a failed unit. Many companies that employ true thin clients at business locations will keep one or two spares at each site as quick replacements in the event of device failures.

Network Connection Redundancy

In a Terminal Services environment (or any thin client environment), users instantly become unproductive if their network connection is lost. Short of running dual network cables to every user's client device, you can configure clients to point to multiple Terminal Servers on multiple network segments (as covered in Chapter xx).

If your users connect to Terminal Servers over a WAN link, it's a good idea to provide some type of failover should that line go down. Generally the decision to do this will be dependent on the cost of the failover connection.

The costs associated with network bandwidth in a large Terminal Server environment can be complex. Terminal Server users require approximately 15 to 30 Kbps per concurrent user of bandwidth between their client and the Terminal Server. While fairly efficient on its own, the amount of bandwidth required to provision hundreds or thousands of end users can be considerable.

Think about a single remote site environment. Assume you have a remote site connected to your LAN via a T1. There are 30 users at that remote site using Terminal Server to access one of their primary applications. If that link is down due to either a router failure or line failure, how much down time would be acceptable for those users?

If only a few users required immediate access to the application and the rest could be down for several hours then a backup ISDN dialup line might be acceptable. However, if all 35 users required immediate access to the application, you may have to configure a full T1 as a backup line.

This example is very simplistic. To make any network system fully redundant you must ensure that all of the components in the chain are redundant, including the WAN lines, the routers the lines are connected to, and the switches that the routers are connected to. If any of the components between the client and the server were to fail, connectivity would still be available.

On Terminal Servers you should also ensure that the network components are redundant all the way to the server. This process would include putting dual network cards in your Terminal Servers and configuring them for failover in case one stopped working. Best practices suggest that each network card be connected to a different switch so that the servers can still function if a switch is lost.

Web Interface Server Redundancy

If the TS advanced client or a custom portal is used to provide access to applications (as covered in Chapter 11), you must take the necessary steps to make certain that a working web page appears whenever users enter the URL into their browsers. Let's examine the steps that can be taken to ensure that the web server does not become the Achilles' heel of your Terminal Server environment.

Ensuring Users can find a Web Server

How will you guarantee that your users will always be able to connect to a functioning web server, even if your primary server is down? Luckily, people have been focusing on creating redundant websites for years, and there's nothing proprietary about Terminal Server environments that would prevent your web site from working like any other. Four common ways of ensuring website availability are:

- Connection to the server via a DNS name.
- Use of smart DNS or load balancing for server connections.
- Clustering the web servers.
- Creation of a manual backup address.

Option 1. Use a DNS Name to Connect to the Web Server

By connecting to an RDP website via a DNS name rather than an IP address, the DNS name can be configured to point to any IP address. If something happens to the main server, the DNS table can be modified to point to a backup server. The disadvantage here is that the failover must be done manually.

Advantages of Using a DNS Name for Redundancy

- Quick to implement
- Transparent to end users
- Inexpensive

Disadvantages of Using a DNS Name for Redundancy

- Manual failover

Option 2. Use Load Balancing or Third-Party Smart DNS to Connect to the Web Server

Windows web servers can be configured in a load balanced cluster just like Terminal Servers, allowing multiple servers to respond to web page requests. In the event that one server goes down, the other will accept all the requests. (Load balancing is covered later in this chapter.)

Some third-party load balancers allow for "health checks" to be performed constantly on the servers they are load balancing. These products can generally be configured to poll the service you are attempting to load balance (such as IIS) to ensure that the server is alive and responding to the proper requests.

In addition, some third-party products offer what they call "Smart DNS." These packages are a step up from normal load balancing that usually will only work when the servers are on the same subnet. These types of products (such as an F5 Big IP DNS controller) tie in at the DNS level where the URL is resolved and provide the ultimate availability since they can load balance across IP subnets. In addition to being able to lose a web server, an entire site or connection to a site can be lost and your users will still be able to connect to another server.

The disadvantages to using this type of product are that it must tie into your DNS and is generally very expensive if you are only going to use it for a set of web servers.

Advantages of Using Third Party load balancing or Smart DNS

- Provides health checks that native load balancing does not.
- Transparent to end users.
- The ultimate in cross-site redundancy

Disadvantages of Using Third Party load balancing or Smart DNS

- Extremely expensive for a simple solution.
- Must tie into your DNS solution.
- Can be complicated to configure.

Option 3. Create a Web Server Cluster

Many web servers can be configured in a cluster, allowing one web server to take over if the other fails. Cluster failover is automatic, although the hardware and software needed to run them can be expensive. (Web server clustering with Internet Information Services requires the Enterprise edition of Windows 2003 which is much more expensive than the standard edition.)

Advantages of Building a Web Cluster for Redundancy

- Fast, automatic failover.

Disadvantages of Building a Web Cluster for Redundancy

- Specialized cluster hardware and software can be pricey.

Option 4. Manual Backup Address

Some people decide to configure two identical web servers and instruct their users to try the alternate address if the first is not available. This option is cheap and easy to implement, although it requires that your users remember a second address.

Advantages of Using a Manual Address for Redundancy

- Inexpensive.

Disadvantages of Using a Manual Address for Redundancy

- Requires user competence.

Terminal Server Redundancy

Two different strategies can be used to increase the redundancy and availability of your actual Terminal Servers:

- Try to make each individual server's hardware as redundant as possible.
- View each Terminal Server as "expendable." Build redundancy with extra servers.

Chapter 5 outlined strategies for the "cluster / silo" model of deploying Terminal Servers and detailed the advantages and disadvantages of building large or small servers. This section builds upon those two chapters by addressing the design option of whether you should approach server redundancy with "quality" or "quantity."

The exact approach that you take will depend on your environment. How would you define "high availability" as it relates to your environment? Does it mean that users' sessions can never go down, or does it mean that they can go down as long as they are restored quickly?

Option 1. Build Redundancy with High Quality Servers

One approach to making Terminal Servers highly available is to increase the redundancy of the systems themselves. This option usually involves servers with redundant hardware including disks, power supplies, network cards, fans, and memory. (Today's newest servers have RAID-like configurations for redundant memory banks.)

Advantages of Building Servers with Redundant Hardware

- By using redundant server hardware, you're assured that a simple hardware failure will not kick users off the system.

Disadvantages of Building Servers with Redundant Hardware

- No economies of scale. Every server must contain its own redundant equipment.
- Employing this strategy still doesn't mean that your servers are bullet-proof.
- What happens if you lose a server even after all of your planning? Will you have the capacity to handle the load?

Option 2. Build Redundancy with a High Quantity of Servers

As outlined in Chapters xx and xx, you'll most likely need to build multiple identical servers to support all of your users and their applications regardless of your availability strategy. In most cases it's more efficient to purchase an extra server (for N+1 redundancy) than it is to worry about many different redundant components on each individual server.

Advantages of Building Extra Servers

- Better economies of scale.
- You'll have the capacity to handle user load shifts after a server failure.

Disadvantages of Building Extra Servers

- If a simple failure takes down a server, all users on that server will need to reconnect to establish their RDP sessions on another server.
- An extra server might cost more than simply adding a few redundant components as needed.

If you have applications that cannot go down (because users would lose work), you'll have to spend money buying redundant components for individual servers. However, if it's okay to lose a server as long as the user can instantly connect back to another server, you can use the "high quantity" approach. Even without redundant components, losing a server is a rare event. Users are always safer on a server than on their workstations since the configuration and security rights are configured properly on the server. Traditional environments don't have redundant components on every single desktop and are still widely accepted. It should be acceptable not to have redundant components on servers as long as users can connect back in as soon as a server fails.

User and Application Data

To correctly determine which actions you should take to ensure that your data is highly available, you must first classify your data. All data can be divided into two categories:

- *Unique data* is crucial to your business and unique to your environment. This category includes user profiles, home drives, databases, and application data.
- *Non-unique data* is anything that you can load off of a CD from a vendor, such as Windows Server 2003, SQL Server, and your applications.

As outlined in previous chapters, you must ensure that your Terminal Servers only contain non-unique data. Unique data should be stored elsewhere, such as on a SAN or NAS device, as shown in Figure 7.2.

Figure 7.2 Redundant servers with data on a SAN

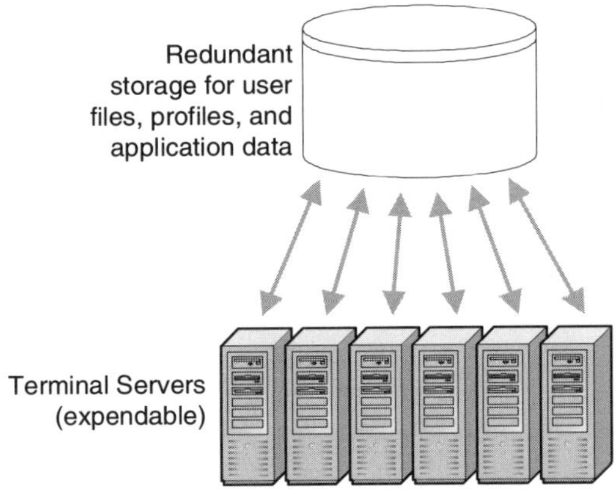

In this environment, your data is protected if you lose one or more Terminal Servers. Your SAN should have the necessary redundancy built into it, such as RAID, multiple power supplies, multiple controller cards, and multiple interfaces to the servers. Instead of using a SAN, you can use a standard Windows 2000 Server file share driven by a Microsoft Cluster.

Advantages of using a SAN or RAIS for Data Redundancy

- Quick recovery in the event of a failure.

Disadvantages of using a SAN or RAIS for Data Redundancy

- Doesn't work in smaller environments.
- Requires an "extra" server (for N+1 redundancy).
- Since all your non-unique data is on a SAN or NAS, you'd better make sure that's backed up.

Terminal Services License Service

As you know from Chapter 4, after your Terminal Server has been active for 120 days it must be able to contact a license server. If it can't, users' connections are refused. Make sure that you have redundant license servers since a failure there could render all of your Terminal Servers useless.

Configure two license servers, one as a "primary" and one as a backup. The Primary server will contain all TS CALs for the site, and the secondary or backup server will contain no licenses.

The primary server services all license requests since it has licenses that are installed and ready to hand out to the servers. The backup will be there as a "just in case" and acts as a place to which you can restore the license server database if required.

If the primary license server fails, the secondary license server will provide temporary services until the primary is available again. There are three possible outcomes in this situation:

- Clients that already have licenses will continue to connect since Terminal Server does not look to the licensing server unless it requires a license.
- Clients with temporary licenses that are expiring are giving a seven day grace period to contact a licensing server with active licenses. You have a full week to get your primary license server running again.
- Clients without any type of license will be issued a temporary license by the secondary licensing server. These licenses (as stated in Chapter 4) allow for full use for the system for 90 days.

In the event of a failure of your primary license server, you have a minimum of seven days to restore your primary license server and its license database or to restore your license database to the secondary server.

When designing your redundant license server solution, resist the urge to install licenses on multiple license servers (unless you have business reasons for doing so as outlined in Chapter 4). The scenario laid out in the pervious paragraphs represents a tried and true method.

Using the Session Directory when Load Balancing

We touched briefly on the Session Directory service back in Chapter 3 when we discussed the design of your Terminal Server network environment. Since the Session Directory is only used in multi-server load balanced environments, we'll explore it fully here.

The Session Directory is a database that keeps track of which users are running which sessions on which servers. This information is used when a user wants to disconnect from a session and then reconnect back to it in multi-server environments. Without the Session Directory, the system would not know that the user had a disconnected session on a server and might route her to a different server where she would start a new session. In addition to being annoying for the user, this is a waste of resources. A single user could leave many orphan sessions throughout the environment.

Not every multi-server load-balanced environment needs a Session Directory. For example, if your environment is configured so that users are not allowed to leave disconnected sessions on a server, then you won't need a Session Directory.

By itself, a Session Directory does not enable load balancing. It's merely one of the components that make up a load-balanced cluster of Terminal Servers. Figure 7.3 (facing page) outlines these components.

- *Terminal Servers* host users' sessions.
- *A Session Directory* is the optional component that allows users to reconnect to previously disconnected sessions.
- *A load-balancing mechanism* routes users' inbound connections. (Load balancing is discussed in the next section.)

Prior to implementing the cluster, determine if a Session Directory Database will be required. In addition to allowing users to reconnect to disconnected sessions, a Session Directory can restrict users to a single Terminal Server session in the cluster. If you wish to use this feature or have the ability to reconnect users to disconnected sessions, you will have to implement a Session Directory.

Figure 7.3 The elements of a Terminal Server cluster

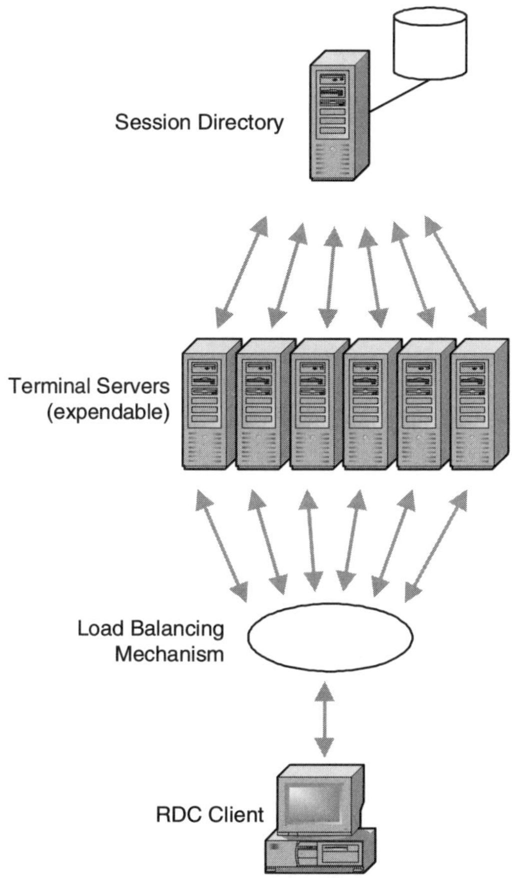

The downside to using a Session Directory is that the Terminal Servers that participate in it must run at least Windows Server 2003 Enterprise edition, costing about $3000 more than the standard edition of Windows 2003.

Advantages of using Session Directory

- Allows users to reconnect to disconnected sessions.
- Allows you to enforce single-session only user policies.

Disadvantages of using Session Directory

- Requires at least the Enterprise edition of Windows 2003.
- Requires an external load-balancer.

How the Session Directory Works

The Session Directory is a simple Windows service and a small database that run on a Terminal Server in your environment.

When a Terminal Server is configured to participate in a Session Directory, a record is created in this central database each time a session is started. These records are queried or updated by the Terminal Servers in the cluster whenever users log on, log off, or disconnect his session. Users can quickly reconnect to their existing disconnected sessions even though the client has no idea to which server they were attached. The Session Directory service (the database itself) is light on required resources and one Session Directory server can handle multiple Terminal Server clusters.

To use the Session Directory in your environment, two configurations are needed:

1. Install the Session Directory database on the server that will host it.
2. Configure each of your Terminal Server member servers to participate in that Session Directory.

Configuring the Session Directory Database

You can make any Windows 2003 server into a Session Directory server. It need not be running Terminal Services. Furthermore, the Session Directory service is "preinstalled" on every Windows 2003 server. To use it, simply enable the service (Start | Administrative Tools | Services | Double-click "Terminal Services Session Directory" | Change Startup type to "Automatic" | Apply | Click "Start" button).

Several things happen as soon as you start the Session Directory service. First, a folder called "*tssesdir*" is added to the system32 folder. This folder contains the database and some supporting transaction log and check files.

Also, a local group is created on the server called "Session Directory Computers." At first this group is empty, but each Terminal Server's computer account must be added to this group to use the Session Directory on that server. It should be noted that if the Session Directory is started on a domain controller, the "Session Directory Computers" group will be created as a Local Domain group.

As this service is fairly light, it can easily be run on a file server for smaller implementations. With thousands of users, however, you might consider a dedicated server (or redundant servers).

That's all there is to it. No GUI configuration tool in needed for the Session Directory service. The task of defining Session Directory clusters falls to the individual Terminal Servers themselves.

Creating High Availability Session Directory Service

The Session Directory can be used to ensure that Terminal Servers are highly-available. However, what happens if the Session Directory itself fails? In addition to losing the ability to make use of the Session Directory features, your users' logon times will dramatically increase as each Terminal Server tries to connect to the Session Directory server. Therefore, in larger environments, it's worth spending the money to cluster your Session Directory server. (In this case the term "cluster" is used in its proper sense.)

Since Session Directory is nothing more than a simple database, the only way to make it fault-tolerant is to cluster it. Fortunately, Microsoft wholly supports Session Directory clustering on a Windows Server 2003 Microsoft cluster. (Of course clustering requires at least the Enterprise edition of Windows 2003.) While some might feel that clustering such a small service is overkill, losing a Session Directory in a production environment can cause major problems.

Clustering is a complex technology. Entire books have been written about Windows clustering, so we won't address it here. However, we will discuss the Session Directory-specific cluster components.

At this point, we'll assume that a two-server Windows 2003 cluster has been created and you're getting ready to create a new resource. In order to cluster the Session Directory Service, follow these steps:

1. Set the Terminal Server Session Directory service to "Automatic" on any Windows Server 2003 (Enterprise or Datacenter edition) servers that will host the service.
2. Verify that the cluster group already exits with the IP address, network name and disk resources to be used for the Terminal Services Session Directory server.
3. Create a Generic Service resource (MMC Cluster Administrator Snap-in | File | New | Resource).
4. The New resource wizard is launched. Enter the following information on the first screen:

- Name (This doesn't really matter. Most people use something like "TS Session Dir.").
- Description (not required for functionality).
- Configure the Resource type as a Generic Service.
- Configure the group as the cluster group name already configured for the cluster.

5. On the next screen, select the nodes in the cluster on which you wish to host the Session Directory Service.
6. On the Dependencies screen, specify that two resources need to be online before bringing the Session Directory service resource online. These two resources are:
   - The "Physical Disk" resource.
   - The "Network Name" resource.
7. On, the Generic Service Parameters screen, configure the Service name as "TSSDIS," and check the box next to "Use Network Name for computer name." TSSDIS.EXE is the EXE that loads the service. Using the network name for the computer name allows computers to connect to this service despite which physical server they actually get connected to.
8. On the Registry Replication screen, the Terminal Services Session Directory Service requires the following: *System\CurrentControlSet \Services\Tssdis\Parameters*. Notice that this entry does not contain "*HKEY_Local_Machine*." Type the entry just as it is listed above to configure the nodes in the cluster to replicate these registry entries between them and allow service settings between servers to be identical.
9. Once you're finished with the wizard, verify that the resource appears in the Cluster Administrator and bring the service online (Right-click on the service name | Bring On-line).
10. Finally, since your Session Directory service is running on multiple servers, create a domain group for use in the Terminal Servers Session Directory local groups on your clustered servers. This domain group should contain all of the computer accounts of the Terminal Servers that will act as clients to the Session Directory Cluster. Once the group is created, add it to the local group on each Session Directory server.

Configuring Servers to Use the Session Directory

Each Terminal Server in your environment must be configured to participate in a Session Directory. At the most basic level, you need to tell each Terminal Server which server it should contact to find the Session Directory and what cluster name it should use. Think of this as a restaurant reservation. In order to meet your friends, you need to know both the name of the restaurant (the Session Directory server) and the name on the reservation (the cluster name).

We've mentioned previously that a single Session Directory server can support multiple clusters (just as a single restaurant can support multiple parties). What's interesting about this is that you don't configure these cluster names on the Session Directory server itself. Instead, you configure each Terminal Server so that it looks for a specific cluster name on a specific Session Directory server.

In order host multiple clusters on the single Session Directory server, simply specify the same server for multiple Terminal Servers and give each group of Terminal Servers a unique cluster name in its Session Directory settings. The Session Directory server will manage each cluster separately without any other configuration.

Keep in mind that all Terminal Servers that use a particular Session Directory server—regardless of cluster name—must have their computer account in the "Session Directory Computer" group on the server hosting the directory.

Use the following procedure to configure a Terminal Server to use a Session Directory:

1. Open the Terminal Services Configuration MMC snap-in and select the "Server Settings" item in the left pane.
2. Open the Properties page of the "Session Directory" item in the right pane.
3. On the Properties page, check the box labeled "Join Session Directory."
4. Add the cluster domain name to the "Cluster name" field. The actual name you choose is inconsequential and never revealed to clients. Just make sure the name is identical on each server that you want in that cluster.
5. Enter the Session Directory server name or IP address to the "Session Directory server name" field. (If you're using a clustered Session Directory, this will be the Network Name of the cluster.)

6. Ensure that the "IP Address Redirection (uncheck for token redirection)" box is checked. Token redirection is used with some hardware load balancers and is covered later in this chapter.
7. The final setting on the server is the "Network adapter and IP address Session Directory should redirect users to." This setting tells the session directory which IP address to send to client computers for redirection, allowing you to control to which network card the client will connect. It also allows you to isolate RDP traffic to a single network card and use a second network card for backend traffic (more on this later).

Configuring Session Directory Options Using a GPO

Since Active Directory will be used in almost every environment where a Terminal Server 2003 Session Directory is used, it's easiest to configure each server's Session Directory settings via a GPO (Computer Configuration | Administrative Templates | Terminal Services | Session Directory).

The only setting that you can't configure via a GPO is the server's IP address used for IP Address Redirection. This setting doesn't matter if you are using Routing tokens, but since it's unique for each server it can't be set within the GPO. It will have to be set in the Terminal Services Configuration for each server.

Load Balancing Options

Let's look now at the actual mechanisms that can be used to load balance your Servers. There are three different ways this can be achieved:

- Windows Network Load Balancing.
- Third-party hardware load balancing routers.
- Third-party software load balancing products.

Windows Network Load Balancing

Microsoft Windows Network Load Balancing ("NLB") is the "free" out-of-the-box software load balancing solution available for Windows 2003-based Terminal Servers. NLB is available with all editions of Windows Server 2003, although your Terminal Servers must be running at least the Enterprise edition of Windows to use the Session Directory.

Network Load Balancing works by assigning a single virtual IP address to those multiple servers that can respond. You then assign a DNS name to the virtual

IP address. RDP clients connect to this DNS name, and the system responds by automatically connecting the user to the least-busy server.

Under the hood, Network Load Balancing enables all of the configured nodes on a single subnet to detect incoming network traffic for the cluster's virtual IP address. (When using Windows NLB, all servers must be on the same subnet.) On each Terminal Server in the cluster, the Network Load Balancing driver acts as a layer residing between the cluster driver and the TCP/IP stack. A portion of the incoming network traffic can be received by the host.

Windows Network Load Balancing works at the network level by distributing the network client request between hosts. Windows NLB is limited to a maximum number of 32 possible hosts in any one cluster.

Also, as its name implies, Windows Network Load Balancing is only able to determine which server is the least-busy based on *network* load. If one server has failed but is still responding to the network, the NLB system will continue to send users to it.

Advantage of Load Balancing with Windows NLB

- It's the "free" solution that's built-in to Windows.

Disadvantages of Load Balancing with Windows NLB

- Load calculations are only based on network load.
- You can't natively load-balance more than 32 servers.
- All servers must be located on the same subnet.
- What if you need to load balance more than 32 Terminal Servers?

One major limitation of Windows Network Load Balancing is that you can only use it to load balance 32 servers. If you need more than 32 servers in your cluster, you must implement one of the following options:

- Move to a third-party hardware or software load balancing solution as described later in this chapter.
- Combine multiple groups of NLB clusters with round robin DNS servers.

Let's take a closer look at this second option. In this case, your DNS servers should be configured with entries for both of the clusters' virtual IP addresses in a round robin entry so that clients connect to either one in a one to one ratio.

Make sure that each cluster has the same number of servers, or adjust your round robin ratio accordingly.

At this point you may be thinking that a DNS round robin solution could suffice for simple load balancing. Before you go down that path, remember that there are reasons why it's called DNS round robin and not DNS load balancing.

If a server failure in an NLB cluster will be detected by the other servers (through the cluster's heartbeat packets), new RDP connections will be distributed only among the remaining Terminal Servers. However, a DNS round robin scheme will continue to send connections to the server that has failed until a change is manually made to the DNS entry.

Configuring Windows Network Load Balancing

This book is not meant to an exhaustive study of Windows Network Load Balancing. However, we'll cover some of the Terminal-Server specific items that you probably won't find in other papers covering NLB.

There are only a few requirements that all servers must meet to use Windows NLB:

- Have at least one network interface configured for Load Balancing.
- Use TCP/IP.
- Be on the same subnet.
- Share a common (virtual) IP address.

In an ideal world, each of your Terminal Servers within in the cluster would have two network cards. The first would be used for the "front-end" RDP traffic between clients and server. The second would be used for "back-end" services and data access.

All versions of Windows Server 2003 come with Network Load Balancing installed. To use it, all you have to do is enable it on the network card that you intend to use for RDP connections (Control Panel | Network Connections | Right-click on your network card | Properties | Check the box next to the "Network Load Balancing" option).

Once you enable NLB, you must configure it (Network adapter properties | Highlight "Network Load Balancing" | Click the "Properties" button). There are several configuration options to understand when using NLB in a Terminal Server environment.

The Properties button leads you to a window with three tabs—Cluster Parameters, Host Parameters, and Port Rules.

Cluster Parameters

On the Cluster Parameters tab, you'll first enter the virtual IP address, subnet mask, and DNS name that your cluster will use. These should be the same on all Terminal Servers in the cluster.

Then you'll select a cluster operation mode. Windows NLB has the ability to work in two different modes: "unicast" and "multicast."

Regardless of the mode you choose, NLB creates a new virtual MAC address assigned to the network card that has NLB enabled, and all hosts in the cluster share this virtual MAC. Then, all incoming packets are received by all servers in the cluster, and each server's NLB drivers are responsible for filtering which packets are for that server and which are not.

When in unicast mode, NLB *replaces* the network card's original MAC address. When in multicast mode, NLB *adds* the new virtual MAC to the network card, but also keeps the card's original MAC address.

Both unicast and multicast modes have benefits and drawbacks. One benefit of unicast mode is that it works out of the box with all routers and switches (since each network card only has one MAC address). The disadvantage is that since all hosts in the cluster all have the same MAC and IP address, they do not have the ability to communicate with each other via their NLB network card. A second network card is required for communication between the servers.

Multicast mode does not have the problem that unicast operation does since the servers can communicate with each other via the original addresses of their NLB network cards. However, the fact that each server's NLB network card operating in multicast mode has two MAC addresses (the original one and the virtual one for the cluster) causes some problems on its own. Most routers reject the ARP replies sent by hosts in the cluster, since the router sees the response to the ARP request that contains a unicast IP address with a multicast MAC address. The router considers this to be invalid and rejects the update to the ARP table. In this case you'll need to manually configure the ARP entries on the router. (Don't worry if you're lost at this point. Just be aware that if you're using multicast mode, you'll need to get one of your network infrastructure people involved.)

The bottom line is that you don't want to use unicast in a Terminal Server environment unless you have two network cards. (That way, you can still connect to a specific Terminal Server if you need to via another adapter and another IP address.) If your servers have only a single network card, then you'll want to use the multicast mode.

Host Parameters

The "Host Priority" is a unique number assigned to each server in the cluster. This number (an integer) identifies the node in the cluster and determines the order in which traffic is delivered to the servers by default. The priority is organized by lowest to highest with the lowest number handling all traffic not otherwise handled by the set of load balancing rules.

Port Rules

The Port Rules tab allows you to configure how load-balancing works within the cluster. By default, a rule is created that equally balances all TCP/IP traffic across all servers. To use NLB for a Terminal Server cluster, you'll need to change some settings.

First add a new rule (Port Rules tab | Add button) that will specify how RDP traffic is to be load-balanced. Configure the port range for 3389 to 3389 to ensure that this new rule only applies to RDP traffic. Select the "TCP" option in the protocols area and the "Multiple Host" as your filtering mode.

The "Affinity" determines if a specific client's requests will continue to be routed to a specific server (such as the first server they were connected to) based on the client's IP address. If you're using the Session Directory then a specification here is not required or can be set to "none." If you are not using the Session Directory, set this rule to "single affinity" so that a client will always be serviced by the same server and users can reconnect to their disconnected sessions.

Finally, the "Load weight" setting determines the amount of users/load this server should handle. The cluster algorithm will divide the server's load weight setting by the total of all the servers' settings to calculate a load index value for each server, allowing you to route more connections to larger servers.

A simple example is a two-server cluster, the first server having a quad processor configuration and the second having a dual processor configuration. Through load testing, you have determined that the quad can handle exactly twice the number of users as the dual. One server (the dual) can be configured with a load weight of 50 while the other server (the quad) can be configured with a load weight of 100. In this configuration, the second server would receive twice as much traffic as the first. The default load weight setting is "Equal" and assumes all servers in the cluster can handle an equal amount of load.

Baseline NLB Configuration

As we discussed earlier, NLB clustering is extremely complex. Nevertheless, you should be able to create a basic configuration for lab testing fairly simply. The following settings will work for almost every environment and allow you to easily configure RDP load balancing:

Cluster Parameters Tab	
Cluster IP Address	Common IP shared between all servers
Subnet Mask	Common Subnet
DNS name of cluster	Shared DNS name (should refer to the Common cluster IP)
Operation mode	Unicast
Host Parameters Tab	
Priority/Host ID	Start at 1 and work up as you add servers. Each must be unique
Dedicated IP	IP Address of NIC that will accept load balanced requests
Subnet Mask	Subnet mask of NIC configured for Load Balancing.
Default State	Started
Port Rules	
Cluster IP Address	If only using one, leave the default at "All"
Port Range	3389 to 3389
Protocols:	Default of "Both" will work so will "TCP"
Filtering	Multiple Hosts, Affinity set to None. (If you're not using Session Directory you can set this to "single.")

Leave the remaining settings at their default values. (You can also use these settings for load balancing your web servers. Just change the port rule from 3389 to 80.)

Once your cluster is up and running:

- Check that each server's dedicated IP address must be unique, and the cluster IP address must be identical for each server in the cluster.
- Verify that any load-balanced applications are installed and configured on all cluster servers. Remember that Windows NLB is not aware higher level applications and does not start or stop applications or services on each server.
- Ensure that the dedicated IP address is always listed first (before the cluster IP address) in the Internet Protocol (TCP/IP) Properties dialog

box to ensure that responses to connections originating from a host will return to the same host.

- Make sure that both the dedicated IP address and the cluster IP address are static IP addresses. They cannot be DHCP addresses.
- Do not enable Network Load Balancing on a computer that is part of a "real" Microsoft cluster services cluster. Microsoft does not support this configuration.

Limitations of Windows Network Load Balancing

Even though it's "free," Network Load Balancing has some weaknesses. In addition to the disadvantages listed previously, some people want load-balancing tools to check the health of individual servers or create load indexes based on CPU utilization or the number of active sessions.

For this functionality, you'll need to turn to third-party tools. There are hardware- and software-based solutions for load balancing Windows 2003 Terminal Servers.

Configuring Servers for Hardware Load Balancers

One alternative to Windows Network Load Balancing is to use a hardware load balancing device. This is a piece of hardware that sits between your Terminal Servers and your users and is able to intelligently route users to the least-busy Terminal Server.

Often referred to as "layer 7 switches" or "layer 7 load balancers" (due to the layer of the OSI model they in which they operate), examples include Cisco's LocalDirector, F5 Networks' BIG-IP, Nortel's Alteon, and Foundry's ServerIron.

How Hardware Load Balancers Work

RDP traffic is sent to the switch using a single IP address (a virtual IP for the cluster). The switch then load balances the traffic between the Terminal Servers based on the algorithms programmed into the device. Additionally, the manufacturers will often use a heartbeat ping against the servers in the cluster to make sure they're still available.

Some of the more advanced hardware load balancers come with software agents that can be installed on the Terminal Servers. These agents can return even more information about the server's current load to the load Balancer. F5 has an agent that is installed on your servers that performs health monitoring of the devices in the cluster, including CPU, memory, and disk utilization, helping to ensure the most efficient load balancing of RDP traffic. NLB doesn't look at any of these components.

Using a hardware load balancer is ultimately more stable and scalable than using NLB or Round Robin DNS. They are expensive, however (some are in the $30,000 to $35,000 range), and you'll need multiple switches to avoid making the switch a single point of failure for your Terminal Server cluster.

Advantages of Hardware Load Balancers

- Load balancing calculations are based on several server metrics, including CPU usage and the number of current user sessions.
- As "closed" systems they are extremely reliable.

Disadvantages of Hardware Load Balancers

- They are expensive.
- You'll need more than one to achieve true redundancy.

When dealing with a load balancing device, it's important to understand how that device works on the network since it affects how your users connect to the Terminal Server and how session reconnection with the Session Directory service works.

Figure 7.4 (next page) outlines the process that takes place when a user connects to a Terminal Server through a hardware load balancer.

1. A client connects to a cluster via the cluster's DNS name, in this case "clus01."
2. The load balancer routes the client to the least busy Terminal Server within the cluster—TS01.
3. The client logs onto the server.
4. TS01 authenticates the user and then queries the Session Directory to see if that user has a disconnected session on any other server in the cluster.
5. In this case, the Session Directory indicates that the user has a disconnected session on TS05.
6. TS01 sends its authentication information back to the client in an encrypted format. It also sends back a load balance packet containing the IP address of TS05.
7. The client uses this information to seamlessly connect to TS05.

8. TS05 then reconnects the user to their disconnected session.

Figure 7.4 The user connection process through a hardware load balancer

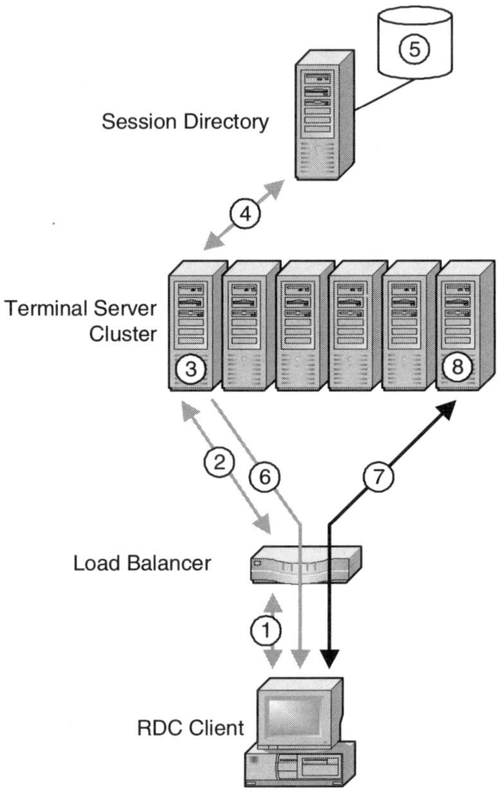

As you'll learn in Chapter 12, sometimes Terminal Servers are on a private network behind a firewall. (A firewall might use NAT with your Terminal Servers all on the private 10.x subnet.) In these cases, you'll need to make special provisions to use the Session Directory.

The IP address of the Terminal Server that's recorded in the Session Directory is not valid to the RDP client device. To address this issue, configure your Terminal Servers so that they pass a routing token back to the client device instead of the actual server's IP address. In turn, the RDP client presents this token to the load balancer, and the load balancer deciphers it and routes the user to the proper server. This process is outlined in Figure 7.5 (facing page).

Figure 7.5. Load balancing in NAT environments

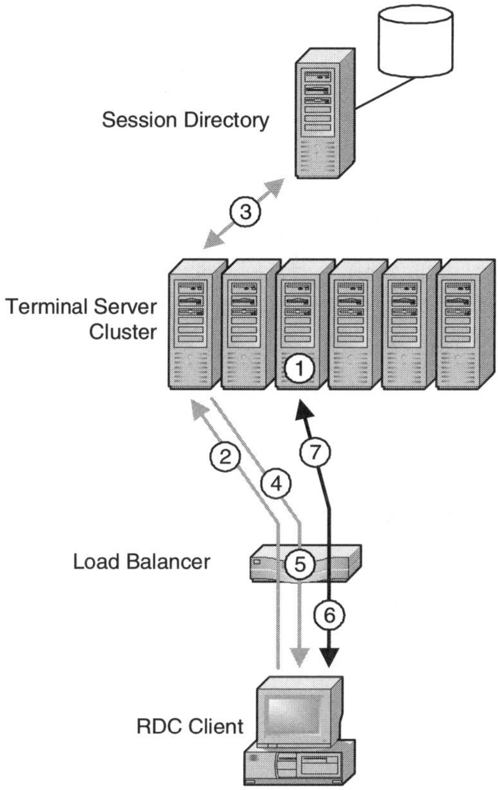

1. The user has an existing disconnected session on TS03.
2. When the user reconnects, the load balancer decides that TS01 has the least load, and the user is routed to it.
3. Since TS01 is configured to use a Session Directory, it queries the Session Directory once the user authenticates and discovers that the user has a disconnected session on TS03.
4. TS01 passes the new server information to the client. The IP address is the same (the IP address of the load balancer), but it also embeds a routing token into the package for the client.
5. Internally, the load balancer associates this routing token with TS03.
6. The client reconnects to the cluster's virtual IP address, but this time it also provides the routing token.
7. The load balancer notices that the client has presented a routing token. Therefore, instead of sending the user to the least-busy server, it routes

the user to the server it has associated with that particular routing token—TS03 in this case.

To configure your Terminal Servers to use a routing token with a hardware load balancing, uncheck the "IP Address Redirection (uncheck for token redirection" box in the properties of a server's Session Directory configuration (Terminal Services Configuration MMC snap-in | Server Settings | Session Directory).

Third Party Software Load Balancing

Hardware load balancing, while a huge improvement over Windows NLB, has some significant drawbacks. Primarily, the hardware load balancers are very expensive. If your company is lucky enough to have existing hardware load balancers then you can simply "add" your Terminal Servers to them (if you have enough spare ports, that is).

Alternately, many people choose to use third-party software products to add sophisticated load balancing capabilities to Terminal Server. Among these products are:

- Citrix MetaFrame Presentation Server
- DAT Panther Server
- Jetro CockpIT
- Tarantella New Moon Canaveral iQ
- Terminal-Services.NET WTSportal Pro

All of these software products improve upon Terminal Server's "out of the box" functionality. The prices vary drastically. Some of these products cost almost $400 *per user*, but they add functionality across the board. Other products only add load-balancing features to Terminal Server for only $100 *per server* (with unlimited users).

Since many of these products are useful in many different ways (in addition to load balancing), they are covered fully (and are compared to each other) in the Appendix.

CHAPTER 8

Printing

At some point during your Terminal Server system design you'll remember that your users will probably want to print something sooner or later. Printing is an important function to users within their Terminal Server sessions, yet it has traditionally been the biggest nightmare for administrators of server-based computing systems. Ideally, printing from applications via RDP sessions should be no different than printing from any other application. It should be relatively seamless to the users, allowing them to click the print button within their application, easily select a printer, and quickly receive their printouts.

All server-based computing environments pose unique challenges to printing. This is not due to any Microsoft design flaw, but rather with the way processing occurs in server-based architectures. Because all application processing occurs on the server, users' print jobs are also created on the server. However, users' printers are usually located near and configured at their client devices. The process of getting server-generated print jobs to a client-specified printer can be complicated.

On top of that, Windows Server 2003 uses the same printing subsystem that was designed way back in the Windows NT days. The original architects of NT built the Windows printing engine as a single process meant to run on a single device. This is fine for desktop printing but can lead to problems in server-based computing environments.

In this chapter, we'll look at how Windows printing works and the printing options that are available when using Terminal Server. We'll also look at what it takes to assign printers to users when you have dozens or even hundreds of users connecting to the same server. We'll close this chapter with an in-depth case study that examines the challenges faced by one company's multifaceted printing environment.

How Windows Printing Works

Before we explore the challenges of Terminal Server printing and the many solutions, you need to understand how Windows printing works. After all, the actual process by which a Terminal Server prints is no different than any other Windows computer.

When you look under the hood, there are a surprising number of steps that take place whenever a document is printed. We could write an entire book detailing the exact printing process that takes place, but to be able to successfully design Terminal Server environments, you just need to know the basics.

The printing process varies slightly depending on whether you're printing to a local printer or a network printer, but the same basic steps take place in each case. Behind the scenes, there are three phases that take place from the moment you hit the "print" button in your application to the moment the finished print job appears on the printer:

- Phase 1. Windows Application.
- Phase 2. Print Spooler.
- Phase 3. Printer (or "Print Device" as Microsoft calls it).

Figure 8.1 The Windows printing process

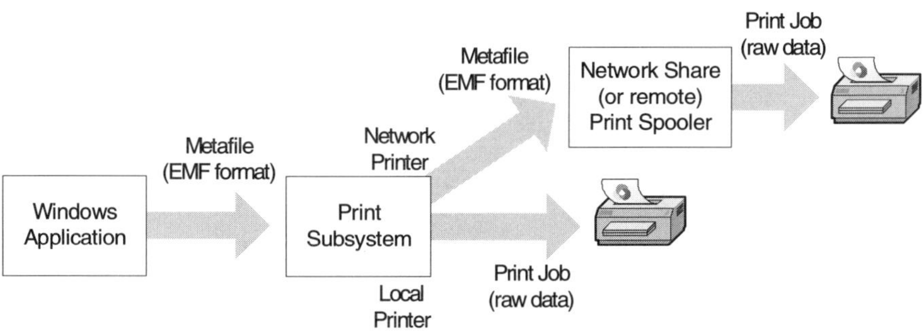

Phase 1. Windows Application

When a user requests a printout from a Windows application, the application is responsible for generating its own output in preparation for printing. This output includes items such as formatting the pages properly and adding page numbers. The application processes its printer output via a Windows subsystem called the Graphics Device Interface (GDI). The GDI generates the application's output in the form of a metafile that contains data and instructions for the printer. (This metafile is usually referred to as "print data.")

The preferred format of this print data is Microsoft's own enhanced metafile (EMF format). EMF print data is preferred over RAW format because EMF processing is less processor-intensive and it allows for background printing.

EMF files are not printer-specific. An application would generate the same EMF file for a printout no matter what kind of printer it was printing to. The file is the common middleman between the application and the printer driver. In order to understand this, let's consider how the following line of text would be printed:

All people seem to need data processing.

The EMF file for this line of text would contain instructions for the printout, including things like the color, font, characters, and the spacing. The EMF file is a vector-based document that is very small in size.

Once the GDI has written the EMF file to disk, the print data is passed into the Windows print subsystem.

Phase 2. Print Subsystem

The Windows print subsystem performs many printing-related functions. The easiest way to understand what it does is to break it up into logical steps. This subsystem is responsible for several tasks:

- Receiving the EMF file from the GDI.
- Determining whether the target printer is a local printer or a network printer.
- Using the print driver to translate the EMF file into the printer's raw format. (At this point the "print data" becomes a "print job.")
- Temporarily holding the print job if the printer is offline or otherwise unavailable.
- Ensuring that the print job is successfully transferred to the printer.

The exact process that takes place depends upon the type of printer that the print job is being sent to. A printing component called the "print router" sends print data down separate paths depending on whether the printer is a network or local printer.

For remote printing, the unprocessed EMF file that was received from the GDI is sent to the print server to be rendered with the proper print driver.

On the other hand, if the print job is destined for a local printer, the local print spooler uses the print drivers to translate the EMF file into the printer's raw data format. This time-consuming and processor-intensive process is called "rendering." The rendered print job contains the raw data (print job) that is specific to the printer. Take another look at our example:

All people seem to need data processing.

In this case, the rendered print job would contain the printer-specific detailed instructions and formatting needed for printing in the printer's native language.

This would include resolution, paper tray information, form feed data, and the rasterized image of the page. Rendered print jobs vary in size depending on the type of printer and how well the drivers are written. In most cases, however, the rendered print job files are much larger than the EMF print data files.

Once the print job is created, the print spooler ensures that the file is transferred to the printer.

Phase 3. Printer

In the final printing phase, the printer receives the rendered print job from the print spooler. The printer prints this file regardless of its format. This is why printers will print garbage if the wrong drivers are used. Using the wrong drivers creates print jobs that are not compatible with the printer. However, the printer doesn't know this and it tries to print whatever it receives.

How Terminal Server Printing Works

Now that you understand how printing works in standard Windows environments, let's see how printing can be configured in Terminal Server environments. Before we get too far into the details of Terminal Server printing, we need to "redefine" some standard printing terms for the Terminal Server environment.

Even with the infinite number of printing scenarios available in the real world, there are only two major types of printing scenarios available with Terminal Server. All Terminal Server printing is a variation on one of the following two themes:

- *Server Printers*. Server printers in Terminal Server environments are printers in which the Terminal Server has direct access to the print queue. This can include standard network printers that are accessible via a \\servername\printername share. It can also include printers where the print queue is located locally on a Terminal Server itself, even including printers that are directly connected to the Terminal Server. Think of server printers as printers that are "installed" on the server.
- *Client Printers*. These are printers that are available to a user's client device before an RDP session is launched. This can include printers that are physically attached to a client device or printers that are logically mapped through the network. Think of these as printers that are "installed" on the RDP client.

Figure 8.2 The various types of Terminal Server printers

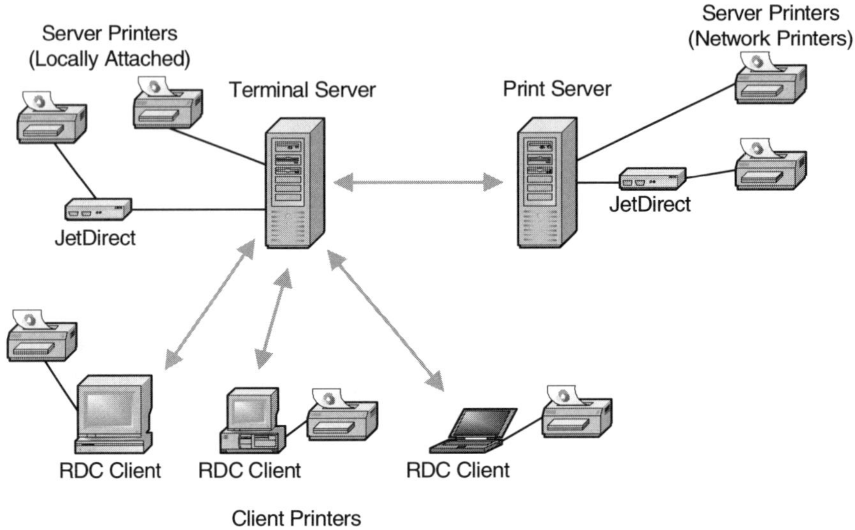

It's important that you understand the differences between server and client printers in Terminal Server environments. Each type has advantages and disadvantages and is used or configured differently. For these reasons, we'll look at server printers and client printers separately in this chapter, beginning now with server printers.

Server Printers

A "server printer" is any printer that is installed on a Terminal Server. In technical terms, this means that the server has direct access to the print queue. This print queue can be Windows or NetWare, client or server based. Basically, any printer that can be accessed via a *\\computername\printername* share is a server printer.

A server printer can also be a printer that has a print queue directly on a Terminal Server. This could be a printer that is physically connected to a local LPT or USB port of a server or an IP printer that has a print queue locally on a Terminal Server.

In Terminal Server environments, server printers work just like "regular" printers in traditional environments. Figure 8.3 outlines this process.

Figure 8.3 Server Printers in a Terminal Server environment

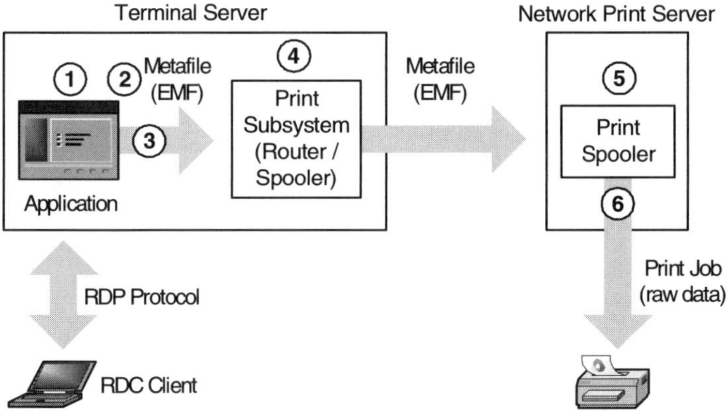

1. The user prints from his application running on the Terminal Server.
2. The GDI creates the EMF file on the Terminal Server.
3. The GDI sends the EMF file to the printer subsystem.
4. The print router on the Terminal Server sends the EMF file to the network print server.
5. The network print server receives the EMF file and transfers it to its print spooler. The spooler renders the print job in preparation for printing.
6. The print job is transferred to a printer port where a print monitor service transfers it to the physical printer.

In most environments, users' network printers are already being mapped via logon scripts or they're configured as part of a user's roaming profile. In these cases, you don't really have to do anything special to make them available via Terminal Server sessions. Users can even set up their own network printers if they have the permissions to connect to them.

In general, you'll notice that if the print servers are on the same network as the Terminal Servers, then printing performance is excellent. In fact, printing in this type of environment is no different than printing in any network environment. This is most often seen when the users, Terminal Servers, and printers are all located in the same building.

Unfortunately, this server printer performance is not as good in remote environments where the users and printer are located on one side of a WAN and the

Terminal Server is located in another. In such cases, (as shown in Figure 8.4) the voluminous print jobs have to reach the print server over the WAN link which is also shared with all the RDP session traffic.

Figure 8.4 Server printers are not efficient when the Terminal Servers are remote

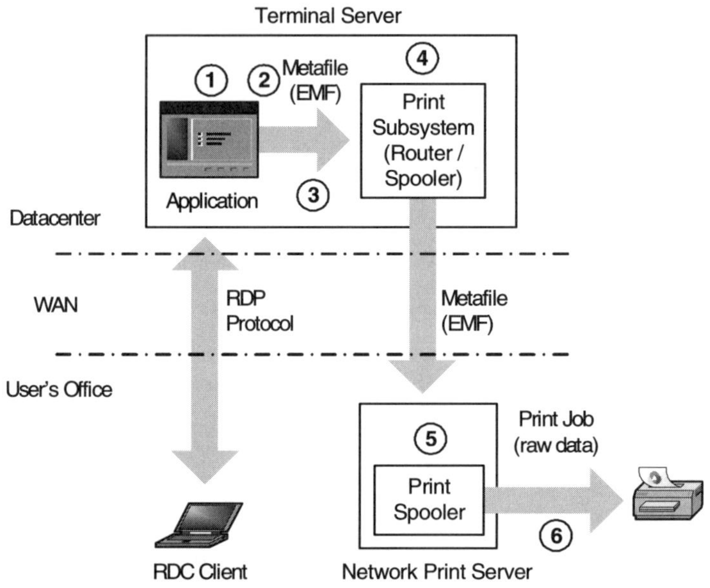

Advantages of Using Server Printers

- Decent performance when the Terminal Server and print server are on the same LAN.
- Reliable.
- Users receive the same printers no matter where they log in.

Disadvantages of Using Server Printers

- If "fat" clients are used, you'll need to set up the printer for the user on the client and the Terminal Server.
- Users must browse the network for printers that are not preconfigured.
- Printers must be manually configured by user or group.
- To get good performance, the print server and the printer must be located on the same LAN as the Terminal Server.
- Users receive the same printers no matter where they log in.

Client Printers

In Terminal Server environments, any printer that's available on a user's client device is known as a "client printer." Client printers can be printers that are physically attached to the client device (perhaps via a USB or LPT port) or they can be network printers that were mapped before the user's RDP session started. Either way, Terminal Server 2003 can automatically make client printers available on the server via a user's RDP session. This lets users print to printers that they are familiar with.

Both the RDP ActiveX control (web client) and the full RDC client support printing to client printers. Some third party RDP client software is available for other operating systems, but their printing capabilities are pretty varied. (These clients are discussed in full in Chapter 10.) For the sake of this chapter we will focus only on the RDP clients from Microsoft.

How Client Printers Work

Before we can look at how client printers are configured, it's important to understand how client printers are used by Terminal Server.

When a user connects to a Terminal Server, his local RDP client software automatically makes the printers he has installed locally available to him from within his server session. It does this by dynamically creating printers that print to special printer ports (also dynamically created) that point back to the client device. These printers will have a name like "*Printer name (from Client name)in Session #*." (For example, "Lexmark Optra E312 (from LAPTOP42) in session 14.") Furthermore, these printers are configured on special ports with names like "TS001" and "TS002" (as seen from the "Ports" tab of the printer's property page. Each printer is created with permissions that allow only that user to print to it.

Technically, power users and administrators can print to any printer, so they'll see all the printers from all users on the server. Regular users, however, will only see their own printers. When a user needs to print a document from within a Terminal Server application, he invokes the print job as usual. From within his session, he'll see his client device's printers listed within the application's printing interface. To the user, these printers look like regular printers. The user has no idea that these printers are actually mapped back to his local printers through the RDP protocol.

When the user prints to one of his client printers, the process outlined in Figure 8.5 (next page) takes place.

Figure 8.5 Printing to a client printer attached locally to a client device

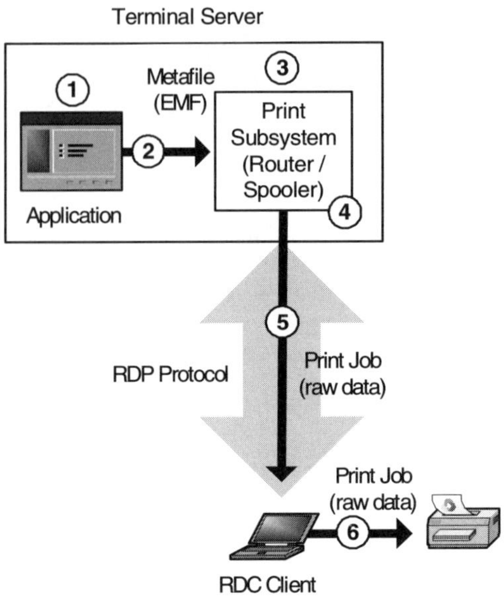

1. The user prints from his application running on the Terminal Server.
2. The GDI creates the EMF file on the Terminal Server.
3. The EMF file is sent to the print spooler (via the print router) on the Terminal Server.
4. If the print drivers for the client printer are load on the Terminal Server, the Terminal Server's print spooler renders the print job. If the proper drivers are not loaded on the Terminal Server, the user's print job cannot be completed.
5. The print job is sent from the Terminal Server to the client device via a printing virtual channel as part of the RDP protocol.
6. The client device receives the print job. Because the server had the print drivers loaded for the client's printer, the print job is rendered specifically for the client's printer, and the client device's local printer subsystem can immediately process the job and send it to the printer.

Upon looking at the client printing process in Figure 8.5, you can probably see that there is the potential for a severe performance problem. The raw print job is usually quite large, and it can take a long time to transmit to the client's printer, especially if the user is connected via a dial-up line. Additionally, the performance of the RDP session can be degraded because bandwidth is being consumed by the print job that is being sent to the client.

Now consider what happens when printing to a client network printer. (Remember that a client network printer is a network printer that was mapped from the user's client workstation before their session with the Terminal Server was started.)

Conceptually, this process is similar to printing to a locally-attached client printer. However, since this is a network printer, the client must take the additional step of sending the print job to the network print server once it's received from the Terminal Server. Figure 8.6 outlines this process.

Figure 8.6 Terminal Server printing to a client network printer

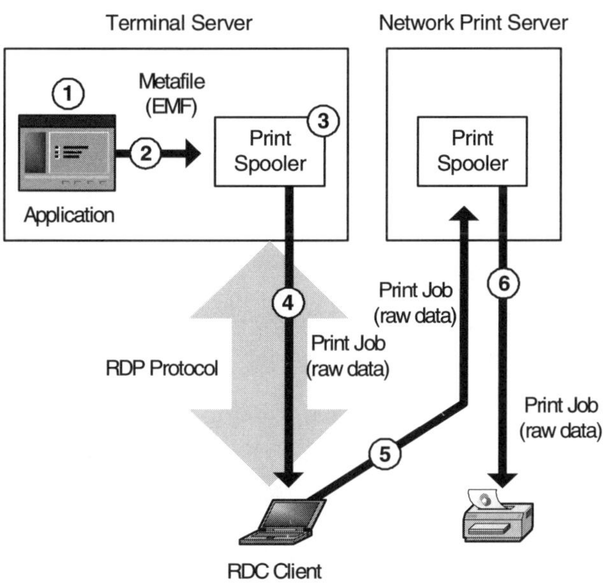

1. The user prints from his application running on the Terminal Server.
2. The GDI creates the EMF file on the Terminal Server.
3. Since the printer is a client-mapped printer, the print job is rendered on the Terminal Server.
4. The Terminal Server sends the print job to the mapped port through the printing virtual channel of the RDP protocol.

5. The client device receives the print job and forwards it to the network print server.
6. The print server receives the print job and sends it to the printer.

At first glance you might wonder why Terminal Server is not smart enough to print directly to the network print server. It would seem that doing so would alleviate the need for the EMF file to travel down from the server to the client and back. Unfortunately, in reality, this is not feasible. For example, there can be situations where the print server from Figure 8.6 is only available to the client device and not to the Terminal Server., or maybe there's a firewall on the network that only allows RDP traffic on port 3389 through.

Regardless of the specifics of a situation, the folks at Microsoft who designed Windows knew that they couldn't guarantee that Terminal Server had access to the print server. Therefore, they had to take the lowest common denominator and send the print jobs down to the client, even if that meant that in some cases the client turned around and sent the print jobs right back up to the server.

Of course an easy way to combat this potential inefficiency would be to simply map the network printer from within the user's Terminal Server session, thereby allowing the server to send the print job directly to the network print server. Sound familiar? It should, because this would be the exact description of a server printer as outlined back in Figure 8.3.

Another way to combat this inefficiency would be to use a third-party printing product, as discussed later in this chapter.

In addition to the performance issues, there's one more potential downside to using client printers. As you saw in Figures 8.5 and 8.6, a user's print job is initiated on the Terminal Server when client printer mappings are used. Because of this, the *server* needs to have the necessary drivers installed for the client's printer so that it can create the print job. After all, it's the server that will be creating print jobs from user sessions, not the client device.

If you're lucking enough to have an environment in which your users have only a few different types of printers, then this might not be a problem. However, if you have hundreds of users with hundreds of different printers, installing and configuring printer drivers on your Terminal Servers can be a nightmare. We'll study the use and management of printer drivers on Terminal Servers a bit later in this chapter.

Another downside to using client printers in Terminal Server environments is that in order for a user to be able to use a printer, it must (by definition) be installed and configured locally on their client device. If your users have a lot of printers already configured on their workstations, then this might be okay. However, this could also be the exact opposite of what you're trying to do by using Terminal Server. Most likely, you want to move away from having to configure things on individual users' workstations. If a user installs, deletes, or otherwise modifies their local workstation printers (not your problem), it will affect how they print from their Terminal Server session (definitely your problem).

Advantages of Printing with Mapped Client Printers

- Seamless connection of printers.
- Users see printers that they are familiar with.
- All supported local printers are available.
- Quick setup for existing client printers.

Disadvantages of Printing with Mapped Client Printers

- Poor print performance.
- Bandwidth intensive.
- Print jobs must be rendered on the server, which is processor-intensive.
- Printer drivers must be installed on the Terminal Server.
- Printers must be installed and configured on local clients.
- Users can update, modify, or delete their local printers, directly impacting the client printer mappings.

Enabling Client Printer Support

By definition, client printers are already set up and configured on the client devices, so there is nothing else that you need to do there. All client printer mapping configuration is done on your Terminal Servers. From a high level, allowing users to print to their client printers involves two steps:

1. Install the printer drivers on your Terminal Servers.
2. Configure your servers to use client printers.

Step 1. Install Printer Drivers

Since client printers will only work when the printer drivers are installed on the Terminal Server, the first thing you need to do when using client printers is make sure that the proper drivers are installed on your server. In the real world, there are many issues associated with the installation and management of printer drivers on Terminal Servers. We'll look at the specific details in the "Managing Printer Drivers" section of this chapter.

Step 2. Configure the Terminal Server to Connect Client Printers

After the printer drivers are installed, you need to configure your Terminal Server to connect clients' printers when their RDP sessions are started. To do this, you'll have to configure Terminal Server permissions, the RDP connection listener, and the user's domain account properties.

Step 2A: Verify Terminal Server Permissions for Printing

In order for users to be able to print on a Terminal Server, users will need Read, Write, Execute, and List Folder Contents access to the print spooler's directory, *%SystemRoot%\System32\Spool.* Even though these are not the default settings for Windows Server 2003 "out of the box," these settings have been a Terminal Services best practice since the beginning of Terminal Services.

Step 2B: Verify RDP Listener Configuration for Client Printer Use

With the Terminal Services Configuration tool, you can configure the client printer options for all users that use a particular connection. In the "client settings" tab section of the connection properties, make sure that the "Windows printer mapping" and "LPT port mapping" boxes are *not* checked in the "Disable the following" section. Obviously, checking either one of these boxes will prevent client printers from being mapped.

Also, if the "Use connection settings from user settings" option is checked, then you will need to verify that the user's account is properly configured for client printer mapping.

Instead of configuring these options as an RDP connection property on each server, you can apply them via a GPO. (See Chapter 6 for more information about GPOs.) These client printer mapping properties can be found within a GPO via the following path:

Computer Configuration\Administrative Templates\Windows Components\
Terminal Services\Client Server Data Redirection

The settings configured here will then apply to any Windows 2003 Terminal Server that is in an OU where this GPO has been applied.

Step 2C: Configure User Account Settings

You can also configure client printer connection settings on a user-by-user basis. In Active Directory environments, the client printer mapping properties are part of the user's AD object (Active Directory Users and Computers | User Object | Environment Tab).

Selecting "Connect Client Printers at Logon" will cause the user's client printer to automatically be created when they log onto a Terminal Server. When the user logs off and all his print jobs have printed, the printer is automatically deleted. If you do not set the "Connect Client Printers at Logon" option, a user will still be able to manually map to his client printer, it just will not be created for him automatically.

Printer Driver Problems when Using Client Printer Mapping

Remember that your Terminal Server must have the proper printer drivers installed for users to be able to print to their client printers since the print jobs are rendered and spooled on the server.

At first glance, this doesn't seem like it would be too much of a problem. However, there can be complications. For example, how does a Terminal Server know if it has the proper driver installed for a user's client printers?

When a user with client printer mapping enabled starts a Terminal Server session, the server checks the driver names of the printers install on the user's client device. It then looks at all the names of the drivers that are installed on the server. If the two names are the same, the server knows that it has the appropriate drivers installed to support that printer and the printer is automatically mapped for that user's session. However, if there's not an exact match, then that printer is skipped and the Terminal Server moves on to the next client printer.

For example, if the Terminal server has a driver installed called "HP OfficeJet 40xi" and the RDP client has a printer installed that uses a driver called "HP OfficeJet 40xi," the server will know that there's a match. However, if the client has a printer that uses a driver called "HP DeskJet 500," then obviously the server knows that there is not a match.

This works fine in when Windows 2000 and Windows XP clients connect to Windows 2000/2003 Terminal Servers. Since all these platforms use the same printer drivers, the names of the drivers are guaranteed to match. However, this leads to an interesting situation if your client devices are running anything prior to Windows 2000, including ME, 98, 95, or NT. The problem arises from the fact that the same printer driver written for two different versions of Windows doesn't necessarily use the exact same printer driver names. For example, the Windows 95/98 version of the driver for a LaserJet 5P printer is named "Hewlett Packard LaserJet 5P," while that printer's Windows 2000/XP/2003 driver is named "HP LaserJet 5P." To humans, these two names are the same, but to Terminal Server, the fact that the client's printer uses a driver that starts with "Hewlett Packard" and the server's driver starts with "HP" means that the server thinks these two names are different. To a Terminal Server, these two names are no more similar than the names "HP LaserJet 5P" and "Tandy LP-1000."

In the situation of a client connecting from Windows 98 with an HP LaserJet 5P printer attached, the server would not map that printer—even if it had the proper drivers installed—since the print drivers' names didn't match.

Workaround Solution: Client to Server Print Driver Mapping

To address this, it's possible for you to correlate the names of printer drivers on your server with the names of printer drivers on your users' clients. For example, you can tell the server that the client print driver "Hewlett Packard LaserJet 5P" is the same as the server print driver "HP LaserJet 5P." Keep in mind that you only need to do this if (1) you are using client printer mappings and (2) your clients are not running Windows 2000 or Windows XP.

In order to enable printer driver mapping, you need to place a file on your Terminal Server that contains the pairs of client and server driver names. In previous versions of Terminal Server, this was done via a mapping file called "*wtsuprn.inf*" located in the *%systemroot%\system32* folder. However, this file does not exist by default in Windows Server 2003, and Windows does not look for it.

To create a mapping file in Windows 2003, you must add two registry values:

> *Key:* HKLM\SYSTEM\CurrentControlSet\
> Control\Terminal Server\Wds\rdpwd
> *Type:* REG_SZ
> *Value:* PrinterMappingINFName
> *Data:* Name of the .INF file that contains printer driver name mappings. (For example, c:\winnt\inf\printsubs.inf)

> *Key:* HKLM\SYSTEM\CurrentControlSet\
> Control\Terminal Server\Wds\rdpwd
> *Type:* REG_SZ
> *Value:* PrinterMappingINFSection
> *Data:* Name of the section in the .INF file that contains the actual mappings. (For example: Printers)

Once you've finished adding your registry entries you should restart the spooler service or reboot the Terminal Server to allow these changes to take effect. After you add the new registry values, you'll need to create an .INF file that includes the driver names you want to use for client-side to server-side mappings. You file will look something like this:

```
;PRINTSUBS.INF
;This file contains Mappings for Client driver to
Server driver printer connections

[Printers]
;"Client Printer Driver Name" = "Server Printer Drive
Name"

"Hewlett Packard LaserJet 5P" = "HP LaserJet 5P"
```

You can create this file with Notepad and save it within an .INF filename extension in the *%SystemRoot%\System32* directory. Using this example, you would specify the *printsubs.inf* file name that you just created in the *PrinterMappingINFName* registry value and "Printers" in the *PrinterMappingINFSection registry value*.

The printer driver names you place in this file are case sensitive and space sensitive. Basically, everything between the quotation marks must match the printer name *exactly*. As with many .INF files, the leading semicolon (;) indicates that the line is a comment and should be ignored. When you use this file, be aware that you can have more than one client printer mapped to a single server print driver.

Creating a printer driver mapping file is more of an art than a science. Fortunately, the some very kind people run a website called `www.printingsupport.com`. This site has downloadable printer mapping files that you can use in your environment.

Once you get your mapping file created, you'll need to make sure that it exists on every Terminal Server where you want these printer driver mappings to be applied. Keep in mind that this mapping file merely tells the server which of its already installed drivers correlate to client printer drivers. You'll also need to install the actual printer drivers on your Terminal Server when you use this file.

If your .INF mapping file contains any syntax errors (other than a misspelled driver name inside the quotes), you may receive the following messages in the event log:

Event 1110: "Error processing ntprint.inf. If the file on the system is corrupt, you can restore it from the installation media.

This message is misleading since it refers to "ntprint.inf" and not your custom filename. This error usually means that the custom .INF file that the system is processing has errors in it. The most common error is that you will create a custom mapping file with no entries in it. You new .INF file must have at least one mapping in its printer name mapping section and the lines containing your mappings must not start with a semicolon. If the custom .INF file has a blank name-mapping section, you'll receive the Event 1110 errors in the event log.

Finding the Exact Printer Driver Names

In order to be able to map printer drivers between your Terminal Server and clients, you need to know the exact printer driver name for both the server and the client. You can get this information from the printer properties dialog box (Right-click Printer | Properties). On Windows 9x computers, the driver is listed in the "Print using the following driver" box. On Windows 2003 servers the driver box is on the "Advanced" tab. Because the name of the printer driver can vary on the workstation depending on the platform, make sure you have the right driver name for the each client platform that is being used. For example, if you see "HP LaserJet 4000 Series PCL 5/5e," be sure to note all the punctuation, spaces, and case sensitivity.

If you already have the driver installed on your Terminal Server, but you do not have a printer installed where you can check the properties, you can always view the driver name from the list of drivers installed on the server. Just open the Printers applet in control panel and use the "Drivers" tab from the File | Server Proprieties applet. This will show you a complete list of drivers installed on your Terminal Server.

Once the driver names have been added to your mapping file, your users will be able to print to their client printers from Terminal Server sessions. You do not have to reboot your server after you change the mapping file. Simply log the user off and then back on.

Sequencing of Client Printer Driver Mapping

When a user with client printers logs on to a Terminal Server, the server goes through several steps to try to find an appropriate printer driver to use:

1. The list of the client's local printers is enumerated from the registry.
2. The server queries the printer driver string names on the client.

3. The server looks for the client printer driver name in the printer driver mapping .INF file.
4. If no match is found, the server looks for a driver name match in the [Previous Names] section of built-in "*ntprint.inf*" file.
5. If the server still cannot find any mapping information, it checks to see if the driver is already installed. To do this, it looks at *HKLM\System\CurrentControSet\Control\Print\Environments\Windows NT x86\Drivers* in the registry.
6. If it can't find the printer driver information in the registry, that means that the printer driver is not installed. As a last resort, the server will check to see if the client's printer is one of the hundreds of standard printers that are available with Windows. To do this, it goes back to the built-in *ntprint.inf* file and looks in the *[Manufacturer]* section. If a match is found, the server automatically installs the driver by extracting in from the built-in *Driver.cab* file located in the *%systemroot%\Driver Cache\i386* folder on the server.
7. Once any of these steps is successful, the server creates a dynamic printer port that maps back to the real printer on the user's client device. This port is mapped through an RDP virtual channel. Then, the server creates a printer object with the appropriate permissions (and using the appropriate drivers) for the user.
8. If the server is not able to find an appropriate driver using any of the previous methods, then the client's printer is not mapped for the session and an event that states that the printer could not be redirected is written to the event log.
9. The server starts this entire process over again for the next printer on the client's list.

In general, Terminal Server 2003's printer driver installation process works fairly well. There used to be problems with incompatible drivers getting installed and crashing the server, but that hasn't really been a problem since the NT 4 days. (Back then, a lot of regular drivers would blue screen the server if multiple users tried to print at the same time. Ouch!)

Limiting the Number of Drivers Installed

One of the big concerns that many administrators have is the number of printer drivers that are installed on their servers. Since users with all types of printers cause drivers to be installed on the Terminal Server, the server will need to manage a lot of drivers. This can be a problem whenever client printers are used, regardless of the client operating system. (Remember that the mapping file is helpful when using older clients, but even new Windows XP clients still cause printer drivers to get installed on your Terminal Servers.)

In order to prevent too many drivers from getting installed on your server, there are two options that you can implement:

- Map multiple client printer drivers to a single server driver.
- Use a third-party "driverless" printing solution (discussed later).

Let's look at how we can use the printer driver mapping .INF file to control the number of drivers that are installed on a Terminal Server. Thinking back to the previous description of this file, you'll remember that it can contain multiple client driver entries for a single server driver. This means that you can use a single printer driver on your server to support dozens (or even hundreds) of different client printer models. For example, it's widely known that many LaserJet drivers will work with other LaserJet printers. You might decide that you want all client printers called HP LaserJet 4, HP LaserJet 4M, HP LaserJet 4 Plus, HP LaserJet 4M Plus, HP LaserJet 4L, and HP LaserJet 4ML to use the same "HP LaserJet 4" driver. This will let you provide a single server driver for six different printer models. To do this, you could configure your .INF mapping file to look like this:

```
[Printers]
;"Client Printer Driver Name"  =  "Server Printer
Drive Name"

"HP LaserJet 4M" = "HP LaserJet 4"
"HP LaserJet 4 Plus" = "HP LaserJet 4"
"HP LaserJet 4M Plus" = "HP LaserJet 4"
"HP LaserJet 4L" = "HP LaserJet 4"
"HP LaserJet 4ML" = "HP LaserJet 4"
```

In fact, HP has a completely "generic" LaserJet driver (called "HP LaserJet") that you could use for every single LaserJet printer, and a generic DeskJet driver (called "HP DeskJet") that you could use for every single DeskJet printer. Adding all these entries to your .INF file would allow you to support hundreds of different types of printers with only two different drivers.

You can also use these "alternate printer mappings" to map a driver from one vendor to support a printer from another vendor. In addition to having fewer drivers to support on your servers, this can also lead to a potential performance gain. This can happen because the spooled print file, which is transmitted down the RDP stream to the RDP client, is created with the printer driver. All printer drivers are not created equal. Some printer drivers are very efficient and create very efficient spool files. This is usually the case with name-brand printers. However, the whole reason that we need to use client printer mapping in the first place is because we, as administrators, do not have control over the printers that our users have connected locally to their clients. They probably didn't buy the name brand printer that we recommended. Instead, they bought the cheapest $25 printer that they could find at Walmart. These printers tend to have very inefficient drivers, which means that they can easily create spooled print files that are several megabytes per page. (To be fair, the people who created these drivers probably never imagined that anyone would actually want to transmit the spooled print files across a slow network.)

To combat this, you can usually find alternate drivers that work for some printers that are much more efficient than the printer's native drivers. You can also use alternate black-and-white drivers for color printers. By definition, black-and-white drivers will produce smaller spool files since they're monochrome instead of full color. Of course, your users will not be able to print in color, but monochrome printing is better than nothing.

All this alternate printer driver mapping leads to one question: Which drivers can successfully be substituted for which printers?

Of course you can find out by trial and error on your own, but most likely you have better ways to spend your time. Fortunately, the Internet is full of free resources like www.printingsupport.com whose sole purpose is to provide printer driver mapping information for Terminal Server administrators.

The only real drawback to using alternate printer driver mapping is that some of the functionality of the original printer driver on the Terminal Server may not work on the printer. These functions are usually minor, like multiple paper tray settings, stapling, or duplexing options.

Advantages of Alternate Printer Driver Mapping

- Allows users to print to printers whose native drivers are not supported.
- Controls the total number of printer drivers in your server farm.
- Allows you to substitute efficient printer drivers for inefficient ones.

Disadvantages of Alternate Printer Driver Mapping

- Some printer functionality could be lost by using alternate drivers.
- You need to figure out which alternate drivers work for each printer.

- You must manually map the generic driver to the exact name of every driver it is to replace.
- If you make this change on one server, it needs to propagate to the other servers.

Improving the Performance of Client Printing

As discussed previously, the architecture behind the use of client printers is fundamentally inefficient since large spooled print jobs must be sent via the RDP stream to the client to be printed. Even though some of the other printing methods (such as server printers) are much more efficient than using client printers, the convenience of client printers is a compelling reason to use them. Because of this, there are some aspects of their performance that can be addressed, including:

- Reducing the DPI of the printers.
- Implementing a third party printing solution.

Reducing the Printer DPI Settings

Because the entire spooled print job must be sent to the client when client printer mapping is enabled, users with slow connections may see degraded session performance. This amount of degradation is generally proportional to the size of the print job being sent. Therefore, reducing the size of the print job reduces the impact printing has on the client session. By reducing the DPI of the printer from 600 DPI to 300 DPI, you essentially reduce the print job size by 75%.

Of course an additional benefit of this is that print jobs finish faster since the amount of data being transmitted is smaller. The drawback to this is that jobs that require a high resolution will look "grainy" and this will not be acceptable to some users. For normal text, however, 300 DPI is just fine.

Advantages of changing Printer DPI settings

- Increases overall RDP session performance while printing, especially over slow connections.
- Can possibly speed up printing.

Disadvantages of changing Printer DPI settings

- Documents requiring a high-resolution may look grainy.

Managing Printer Drivers

Whether you use client-mapped printers or server printers, you'll need to have printer drivers installed on each of your Terminal Servers. Consequently, you will need to spend some time thinking about how to manage those printer drivers. Before we address this issue, however, let's look at what printer drivers really are, how they work, and how they're stored on Windows servers.

How Windows Printer Drivers Work

Fundamentally, Windows printer drivers translate print jobs from an enhanced metafile format, which is printer-independent, into the native language that can be understood by a printer. This is why a printer prints garbage when you use the wrong driver. Printer drivers need to be installed and registered on a computer before they can be used.

Two things happen when you install a printer driver onto a Terminal Server or Windows 2000 server. First, the necessary printer driver files are copied from the source location to the server. The server stores printer driver files in the *%systemroot%\system32\spool\drivers\w32x86\3* folder. In this path, the "*w32x86*" signifies an Intel Windows 32-bit platform, and the "*3*" signifies the version of the printer driver (3 = Windows 2000/XP/2003).

Second, the driver's details are written to the registry in this path: *HKLM\System\CurrentControlSet\Control\Print\Environments\ Windows NT x8 6\Drivers\Version-3\<printerdrivername>*. Similar to the file path, a Version-3 key means that the driver is a Windows 2000/XP/2003 driver.

User's individual printer settings, such as print, duplexing, and paper tray options, are stored in the *HKCU\Printers* registry key. These settings are user-specific and stored in their profile, just like any other customized Windows settings.

Installing Printer Drivers

Installing print drivers onto a Terminal Server is no different than installing printer drivers onto any Windows computer.

The easiest way to install a driver without actually installing a printer is via the "Printers and Faxes" applet. (Start | Printers and Faxes | File Menu | Server Properties | "Drivers" tab | "Add" button) On a Terminal Server, it's only necessary to add the Windows 2000/XP/2003 version of the driver, since you're only installing the driver so you can print from server sessions.

If you have a lot of drivers to install, you can script the process using *rundll32.exe* to call the printui.dll (the Printer Properties User Interface).

If you're only using printers whose drivers are built-in to Windows 2003 (via the "*driver.cab*" file discussed previously) then you don't really have to worry about driver installation since the process is automatic when the printer is installed. However, if you have a number of drivers that are not part of the Windows 2003 install, you can script the following command to install a large number of printer drivers at once:

rundll32 printui.dll,PrintUIEntry /ia /m "*Driver Name*" /h "Intel" /v "*Version of driver*" /f *Source\print.inf*

To use this command, replace *Driver Name* with the driver's name as it appears in the .INF file, replace *Version of Driver* with the platform for which it was written, (generally Windows 2000 or XP) and replace the *Source\print.inf* with the path and .INF filename for the printer driver. For more information on using rundll32.exe for installing and removing printers and drivers, run "*rundll32 prinui.dll,PrintUIEntry /?*" from a command prompt. When using this command, note that there is a comma with is no space between the word *prinui.dll* and *PrintUIEntry*.

Removing Printer Drivers

When you delete a printer from the "Printers" folder on one of your Terminal Servers, the drivers are not uninstalled from the server. This can be a problem if you've identified that a certain printer driver causes problems, since you need to be able to remove that driver from the server to prevent clients from using it.

Fortunately, the Printers and Faxes applet in Windows 2003 (and 2000) can also be used to remove drivers from your Terminal Server. (Start | Printers and Faxes | File Menu | Server Properties | "Drivers" tab | "Remove" button) Of course this will only remove the driver if no printers are currently using it.

Alternately, you can also use the "rundll32" command we used previously to remove the print driver. All that is required is the modification of a couple of switches. The cool thing about using the rundll32 method is that it can even be done from remote machines. Here are some examples of how to use the command line to remove a local driver and a driver from a remote server.

To remove a driver from a machine you are logged into:

```
rundll32 printui.dll,PrintUIEntry /dd /m "HP DeskJet 500" /h
"Intel" /v "Windows 2000"
```

To remove a driver from a remote machine:

```
rundll32 printui.dll,PrintUIEntry /dd /c\\Computername /m
"HP DeskJet 500" /h "Intel" /v "Windows 2000"
```

Make sure to replace *Computername* with the name of the server you are removing the driver from.

If all else fails (which unfortunately still happens, even with Windows 2003), you can manually remove a printer driver and all traces of its existence by following this procedure:

1. If you haven't done so already, remove the printer by deleting it form the "Printers" folder.
2. Stop the spooler service.
3. Browse to the following registry location: *HKLM\System\ Current-ControlSet\Control\Print\Environments\Windows NT x86\Drivers\Version-x\<printerdrivername>*, where x is the version of the driver (2 = NT 4.0, 3 = Windows 2000/2003).
4. Note the names of the files listed.
5. Remove the registry key *yourprinterdriver*.
6. Delete the referenced driver files from the *%systemroot%\ system32\ spool\drivers\w32x86\x* folder. If you have multiple printers installed, you may want to copy the driver files to a temporary location before you delete them outright, because many similar types of printers use the same driver files.
7. If you're not able to delete the files, you will need to disable the spooler, reboot, and delete the files again. After you do this, reset the spooler to "automatic" startup.
8. After the print drivers have been removed, you should reboot the server.

What driver does a Printer Use?

Occasionally you will need to figure out which drivers a printer uses that you haven't installed yet. This is especially handy if you allow your Terminal Server to automatically install any needed printer drivers.

Every Windows 2000 and Windows 2003 server has a "master list" of default printers that it supports and the drivers that each printer needs. That master list is stored in the *%systemroot%\inf\ntprint.inf* file. You can open this file in a text editor to see which drivers each printer will request. *Ntprint.inf* is organized by manufacturer, with individual printers and their drivers listed under the manufacturer's section, as shown below.

```
[HP]
"HP 2000C" = HPV2000C.GPD.ICM
```

Printer and Driver Replication

One of the printing-related challenges that you'll face as an administrator of a multiple server environment is that each Terminal Server maintains its own list of configured printers and locally installed print drivers. Each Terminal Server is completely unaware of the printer configuration and installed drivers of the other Terminal Servers.

Further complicating this is that as an administrator, you'll have no idea whether a printer driver has been updated or installed unless you view each server and driver individually.

In addition to this, server printers and their configurations are stored locally on each server and must be added, removed, or modified on every server to maintain a consistent environment. This leads to a management nightmare in environments with hundreds different client printers.

In a load-balanced or clustered server environment, each server must be configured identically. This means that drivers, printers, and printer configurations should match on all servers in the cluster. Doing this manually in a server cluster of 5 servers with 100 printers would be extremely time consuming. Now imagine those same printers in a 20- or 30-server cluster, and you'll quickly realize that you need a better way to manage drivers.

There are really only a couple of ways to get both the Windows print drivers and the server printers you have created on a Terminal Server to other servers:

- Replication using Print Migrator.
- Manual replication.
- Use a third-party printer management tool (discussed later in this chapter).

Method 1. *Using* Print Migrator to Replicate Drivers

Print Migrator is a tool from Microsoft that can be used to replicate printer drivers between servers. (Since Microsoft is always changing things on their website, the easiest way to find this tool is to do a search on Microsoft.com for "Print Migrator." The version discussed here is 3.1.)

Printer Migrator allows you to back up printers, print queues, ports, printer drivers, and printer shares to a .cab file. You can then restore the settings of that .cab file to another server. You can even use this tool to migrate printers between different versions of Terminal Server.

Advantages of Print Migrator Replication

- Drivers and settings can be replicated to remote servers.
- Drivers can be replicated from network print servers to Terminal servers.
- Print Migrator can be command-line driven, allowing you to script and schedule it with the command scheduler. (Run printmig /? for a list of command-line options.)
- This too is really easy to use.

Disadvantages of Print Migrator Replication

- Migration must be manually invoked.
- The spooler service is stopped while this tool is used.
- Since this tool packages drivers into the CAB file, the CAB file can become quite large.
- Target Terminal Servers must be placed into "install" mode.

Method 2. Manual Print Driver Replication

The other option for replicating printer drivers is to do it manually. You must manually install or copy all of the needed printer drivers onto each of your Terminal servers.

Advantages of Manual Print Driver Replication

- No learning curve.
- Allows you to install different printer drivers to different servers.
- Works well in small environments with only a few drivers.

Disadvantages of Manual Print Driver Replication

- Drivers must be manually installed onto each Terminal server.

Configuring Printers for Users

Now that you've completed the work needed to ensure that various printers will be available to the users on your Terminal Servers, you need to provide a method for users to access their printers. This is easy if you're using client mapped printers because the printers are automatically created for the users.

However, client printers aren't always an option in the real world, so server printers must be used. When using server printers, you need to think about how your users will access these printers. Will you assign certain printers to certain users? If so, how will you do this? Maybe you want to allow all users to be able to use all printers? If this is the case, how will users know which printers they should use? We'll look at two strategies to answer these questions:

- Assigning printers to users.
- Methods of letting users choose their own printers.

Assigning Printers to Users

Once you decide that you would like to control which printers your users are able to print to, you need to determine how to provide that access. Setting permissions on printers is important, but permissions alone won't configure a printer for a user. For example, if you want the user "brian" to print to the *\\printerserver\fastlaser* printer, you can edit the properties of that print queue and grant "brian" print permissions. However, how will Brian know how to access that printer? Is he smart enough to be able to browse the network to the *\\printserver* computer, and then select the *fastlaser* printer? Most likely, if you decide that Brian should use the *\\printserver\fastlaser* printer, you need a way to assign that printer to him so that when he selects "print" from a Terminal Server application, the *\\printserver\fastlaser* printer shows up in his printer list.

There are three methods that you can use to assign server-based printers to users:

- Map printers in users' logon scripts.
- Map printers as part of a user's profile and policy settings.
- Install the printer locally on the server and configure its permissions.

Method 1. Configuring Printers via Logon Scripts

One of the most tried-and-true methods of making printers available to users is to map them via a logon script. (Logon scripts were covered in detail back in Chapter 6.) When it comes to printing, there are a few different ways that you can use logon scripts to map users' printers.

One of the cool things about using logon scripts to map printers is that you can incorporate conditional branching into the scripts based on a user's group membership. That way, you can give a user access to a printer simply by adding them to the appropriate Windows group. You can even set the permissions of a printer based on the same user group.

Command-Line Printer Mapping

You can use the same "rundll32" from the printer drivers section of this chapter to map user connections to network printers. (This method replaces the older, less-flexible "*con2prt.exe*" utility.) To do this, add the following line to a logon script:

```
rundll32 printui.dll,PrintUIEntry /in \\printserver\printer
```

Again, make sure that you have a comma with no space between the words "*printui.dll*" and "*PrintUIEntry*." You can add this command multiple times in a script if you need to map multiple printers.

Mapping Printers with Kixtart

If you've chosen to use Kixtart as the language for your logon scripts, you can use its own native capabilities to connect to network printers. For example, the following Kixtart code checks to see whether the user is in the "*PrinterGroupName*" Windows group. If he is, it adds the *\\printserver\fastlaser* printer connection and sets it to be the default printer for the user.

```
if ingroup("PrinterGroupName")
  addprinterconnection ("\\printserver\fastlaser")
  setdefaultprinter ("\\printserver\fastlaser")
endif
```

Many Terminal Server administrators use code like this, adding this code segment for each printer in the environment. This can allow them to create an all-encompassing logon script that maps the proper printers based on users' group memberships.

Advantages of Assigning Printers with Logon Scripts

- You can assign printers on a per-user or per-group basis.
- You can assign different printers for different servers.
- Logon scripts can be used in many different ways.

Disadvantages of Assigning Printers with Logon Scripts

- Requires knowledge of the logon script language.

Method 2. Configuring Printers via User Profiles

Another option for ensuring that users can easily access their printers is to use roaming profiles. By doing so, your users will only have to connect to a printer once. After that, the printer connection will become part of their profile and will automatically be restored whenever they logon. See Chapter 6 for full information about using roaming profiles.

Advantages of Assigning Printers via Roaming Profiles

- This method works without using logon scripts.
- The same printers will be available to the user no matter where they log on.

Disadvantages of Assigning Printers via Roaming Profiles

- Roaming profiles must be configured for your environment.
- The user (or you) will have to manually configure the printer the first time for the user.
- The same printers will be available to the user no matter where they log on.

Method 3. Installing Printers onto the Terminal Server

The last method of assigning printers is not exactly a "best practice," but it can work well in smaller LAN environments that don't have too many printers. To use this method, you install the printer "locally" onto a Terminal Server. This does not mean that the printer must be physically attached to the Terminal Server. It just means that you add the printer to the Terminal Server as a local printer instead of a network printer. To do this:

1. Logon to the Terminal Server as an administrator.
2. Start the "Add Printer" wizard.
3. Select "Local printer attached to this computer."
4. Make sure that the "Automatically detect and install my Plug and Play printer" box is unchecked.
5. When asked, create a new port instead of using an existing port.
6. Select Standard TCP/IP port.
7. Type in the IP address of the printer or print server.
8. Configure the options for type of port detected on the IP address you specified.

Following this procedure creates a shared print queue on the Terminal Server. Even though this queue is for a remote printer, the server treats it as a locally installed printer. By default, all users that run sessions on a Terminal Server are able to print to local printers on a server, meaning that all users will "automatically" have access to this printer.

You can modify the permissions of one of these newly-installed local printers so that only certain users or groups can print to it. What's cool about this is that users won't see a printer that they don't have rights to print to, so you don't have to worry about any additional configuration.

The major downside to this method is that since the print queue is local to the Terminal Server, the server's printing subsystem will spool the file locally and send it across the network in its raw data format instead of as an EMF file. (In some cases, such as when some types of JetDirect cards are used, this is always the case anyway.)

Advantages of Installing Printers on Each Server

- You can assign printers to users simply by editing the permissions of the printer.
- All users that use the Terminal Server will automatically see the printer.

Disadvantages of Installing Printers on Each Server

- Each printer must be configured on each server. (Although printers can be replicated with tools such as Microsoft's free Print Migrator.)
- This method bypasses the "real" print servers in your environment.
- Print jobs are spooled on the Terminal Server instead of on the print server.
- All users share the same print queue.

Letting Users Choose Their Own Printers

Instead of assigning printers to your users, you may have an environment in which users need to be able to choose their own printers. This makes your job much easier. If security is important, you can still set the printing permissions on the printers that you don't want everyone to be able to print to.

If you simply give a user permissions to print to a network printer, that printer will not be automatically set up for the user. However, the user will be able to browse the network and connect to the printer if he needs to print to it.

Advantages of Letting Users Choose Their Own Printers

- You can still set security for printers that need limited access.
- There is less for you to configure.

Disadvantages of Letting Users Choose Their Own Printers

- Users need to know how to connect to printers.
- Users need to know which printer they are looking for.

If your users are able to configure their own printers via Windows Explorer or the "Printers" folder in the Start Menu when using a desktop session this may be fine. However, in the real world, many people choose not to allow users to connect to the Windows desktop or Windows Explorer and instead only use single application connections, and thus users are not able connect to network printers since they have no interface to do so.

With that problem in mind, many administrators will give the users a connection to the server that launches the Printers folder. Of course this is an extra step for the end user but it allows them access to a resource without giving them a full server desktop.

Configuring Printers Folder as an Initial Application

Connecting to the Printers folder is very easy to do. The Printers folder does not have its own executable; it's actually built into the Windows shell (explorer.exe). These types of Explorer shell components are called "shell extensions." Each shell extension has its own GUID, which is like a serial number that differentiates it from all other shell extensions. Information about different shell extensions are contained in the following registry location: *HKEY_CLASSES_ROOT\CLSID\<unique guid>*.

In this case, the Printer folder's unique GUID is *{2227A280-3AEA-1069-A2DE-08002B30309D}*.

Any Windows program can access a shell extension by calling *explorer.exe* and requesting the GUID of the extension it wants. You can even create an initial application that points to the Printers shell extension. Here's a neat trick to show how that shell extension will work:

1. Create a new folder on your Windows desktop.
2. Name the folder "Printers.{2227A280-3AEA-1069-A2DE-08002B3030 9D}" with no spaces anywhere in the name.

As soon as you press Enter, the icon for the folder will change into the Printers folder icon. When you open that folder it will look just like the Printers folder from the start menu. To make the Printers folder available as a stand-alone application, you need to create a command line that launches a folder like this. Here are the steps to take:

1. Create a folder called "Printers.{2227A280-3AEA-1069-A2DE-08002B30309D}." Make sure that there are no spaces anywhere in the name.
2. Put that folder somewhere it can be launched. For example, use the *c:\print* directory, so that the full path of your folder is *c:\print\Printers.{2227A280-3AEA-1069-A2DE-08002B30309D}*.
3. Now, all you need to do is launch that folder with certain command-line switches. However, you need to first make a copy of explorer.exe. Your copy can be called anything except explorer.exe. This will force your command to open a new instance of explorer.exe, since yours will have a different name than the background copy that is already running.
4. Put the new copy of explorer.exe (Let's call it printexplorer.exe) into the *m:\print* folder.
5. Access your new folder via the following command: C:\print\printexplorer.exe /n,/root, C:\print\Printers.{2227A280-3AEA-1069-A2DE-08002B30309D}.

That command line begins by launching *printexplorer.exe* with several command-line options. The */n* option tells explorer to open a single-paned window. The */root* option tells explorer to open this window as the root, preventing users from being able to click the "Up" folder to browse back up through the directory structure. The command ends with the full path to your custom folder, telling explorer which folder should be used as the root.

Simplifying with Third-Party Printing Solutions

By this point we've examined all aspects of printing in Terminal Server environments related to out-of-the-box tools and techniques. However, even considering everything we've seen so far, troubling issues can still arise, including:

- Printer drivers must be installed and managed on every Terminal Server for each client printer in use in your environment.

- Client printing performance is poor, both in terms of the amount of data that must be sent across the network and the server resources required to render the print jobs.
- There are no good out-of-the-box solutions for situations in which RDP clients and print servers are on one side of the WAN while the Terminal Servers are on the other (as outlined back in Figure 8.4).

Fortunately, several third-party software printing solutions are available to address these issues. The four most popular vendors now, in alphabetical order are:

- *Emergent Online (EOL)*: a fairly large consulting and training company that also creates various software packages to help administrators with many thin-client situations. They offer several printing products that can help with many different aspects of printing. Their website is `www.go-eol.com`.
- *ThinPrint*: a German company with a large US presence. As their name implies, they focus entirely on printing in mobile and low bandwidth environments. You can find them at `www.thinprint.com`.
- *triCerat Software:* offers several products that can help you simplify the management of server-based computing environments, including several printing products. More information is available at `www.tricerat.com`.
- *Qnetix*: a company whose Uniprint product family provides printing solutions for server-based computing environments. Visit `www.uniprint.net`.

Because there are drawbacks to Terminal Server's out-of-the-box printing solutions, and because third-party tools are so popular, it's worth considering them. As for recommendations, we'll study the printing challenges and how third-party tools are used to address them from a technical standpoint. We will *not* analyze each vendors' products and provide reviews. (Product review information is available online at `www.brianmadden.com`.)

After reading this section, you'll have a true understanding of why these products are needed and how they can help, enabling you to explore the different printing vendors and accurately assess their offerings. All four vendors named here offer 30-day trial versions of their products. You can find a complete list of links with more information in the Appendix.

The technical design information provided here together with the online information about these four vendors should provide you with enough information to decide how to support the printing challenges that arise in your environment.

Understanding the Third-Party Tools

The printing software tools of the above-named vendors can be divided into two groups:

- Products that install a "universal" driver on the Terminal Server that works with any printer. EOL, Qnetix, and (for those interested) Citrix's universal print driver fall into this group.
- Products that enable EMF-based printing, including those from ThinPrint and triCerat.

At first glance, it may seem that the two descriptions are the same. Products from each group differ in how they solve printing challenges.

Universal Print Driver (UDP) Products

The universal print driver products from EOL, Qnetix, and Citrix allow you to install a single "universal" print driver on your Terminal Server that is then used for every printer. (This driver does not, however, work with specialty printers such as vector plotters, label printers, and barcode printers.)

When a user prints, the Terminal Server's print subsystem uses the universal driver to render the print job into either a PDF file or PCL file (depending on the product). Then, the print job is transmitted to the client device where the local printing subsystem forwards it to the appropriate print queue. This entire process is laid out in Figure 8.7.

Figure 8.7 The Third-Party Universal Print Driver Process

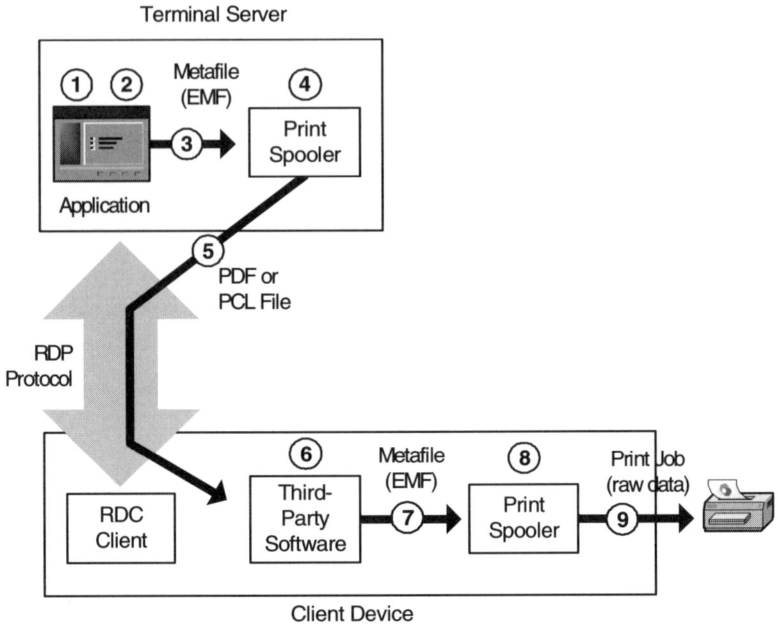

1. The user prints from an application on the Terminal Server.
2. The GDI generates an EMF file.
3. The Terminal Server's printer subsystem sends the EMF file to the local print spooler.
4. The print spooler uses the "universal" driver to render the print job into a universal format. (PDF or PCL, depending on the product.)
5. The PDF/PCL file is transmitted to the RDP client. Some products send the file through a virtual channel in the RDP protocol, and some send it via TCP/IP.
6. A third-party software component on the client receives the PDF/PCL file.
7. The third-party software on the client invokes the local print process. The client device's local GDI generates an EMF file on the client device.
8. The client device's local printer spooler renders the print job with a locally installed printer driver.
9. The print job is transmitted to the client's printer, just like any print job in a non-Terminal Server environment.

Advantages of Universal Print Driver Products

- Universal print driver products allow printing to any printer without having to install different drivers on your Terminal Servers.
- You don't have to worry about what kind of client printer is used. It can be replaced without having to notify the server administrator.
- PDF / PCL files are smaller than raw print jobs, thereby increasing the speed of the printout and lowering the impact on the network. (Furthermore, some of the products compress the PDF/PCL print data.)

Disadvantages of Universal Print Driver Products

- Print jobs are rendered on the server, which means that the server must spend resources generating the printout.
- Since the PDF / PCL documents are fully rendered, any compression that is used affects the quality of the printout.
- Printer features are limited to the "lowest common denominator" capabilities of the universal driver.
- These products do not work with all printers.

Metafile-Based (EMF-Based) Printing Products

ThinPrint and triCerat's products fall into the second group of third-party printing products known as "EMF-based" printing products. TriCerat has a product called "ScrewDrivers," and ThinPrint's product is called "ThinPrint."

EMF-based printing products are technically superior to UPD-based printing products, but they are also more expensive.

Both triCerat ScrewDrivers and ThinPrint install a simulated print driver on the server that receives print data from the GDI. This approach is similar to that of UPD-based products. However, unlike those products, these EMF-based products do *not* render the print job on the server. Instead, they send the device-independent EMF file to the client device. From there, triCerat or ThinPrint client software forwards the EMF print data to the client's print subsystem. The client device renders the print job and sends it to the appropriate printer. Figure 8.8 illustrates this process.

Figure 8.8 The third-party EMF-based printing software process

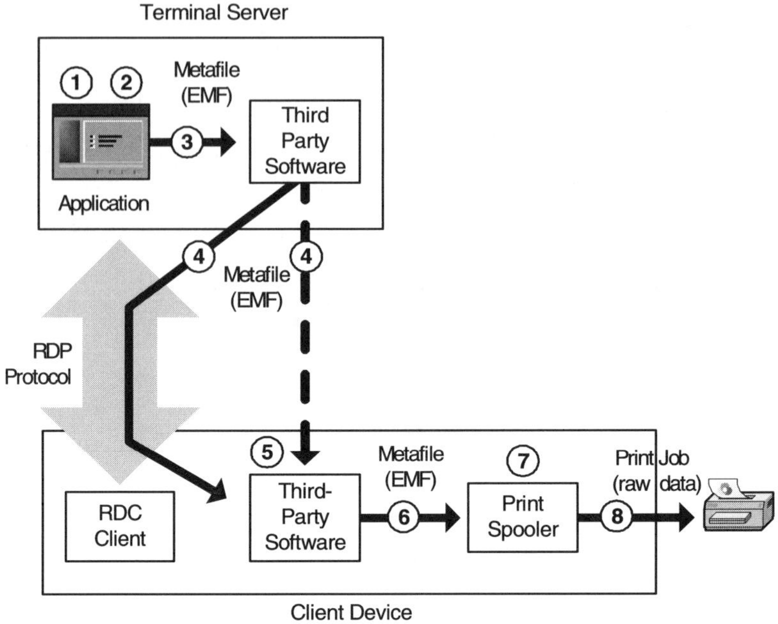

1. The user prints from an application on the Terminal Server.
2. The GDI generates an EMF file.
3. The third-party software component running on the Terminal Server receives that EMF file.
4. The third-party software compresses and transmits the EMF file to the RDP client. It is usually transmitted through a virtual channel of the RDP protocol, although ThinPrint has the additional option to transmit it directly to the client via TCP/IP outside of the RDP protocol.
5. A third-party software component on the client receives the EMF file.
6. The third party software transfers the EMF file to the local print spooler on the client device.
7. The client device's local print spooler spools and renders the print job.
8. The print job is transmitted to the client's printer, just like any print job in a non-Terminal Server environment.

Advantages of EMF-Based Printing Software

- EMF-based printing software allows printing to any printer without having to install different drivers on your Terminal Servers.
- EMF print data is smaller than raw print jobs, thereby increasing the speed of the printout and lowering the impact on the network.
- EMF print data is also smaller than PDF / PCL files (used by the UPD-based products). Also, the compression ratio of EMF files is higher than PDF / PCL files.
- You don't have to worry about what kind of client printer is used. It can be replaced without having to notify the server administrator.
- Since the print job isn't rendered until it hits the client, you can automatically use the full capabilities of your printer.
- Since the print jobs are not rendered on the server, you will not experience as large a performance hit in heavy printing environments as compared to UPD-based products.
- Documents are printed with 100% of the original quality, since lossless compression is used.

Disadvantages of EMF-Based Printing Software

- More expensive than universal print driver software.
- More complicated than universal driver solutions.

Third-Party Solutions for Low Bandwidth Clients

Often, Terminal Server environments are designed so that the users are at one location and the Terminal Servers are at another location. This design is preferred in many cases because it's desirable to place the Terminal Servers close to the data sources, usually located at corporate offices. One problem with this architecture is printing. Typically, the location that houses the users has its own print server, as is often the case with remote offices or factory floors, shown in Figure 8.9.

Figure 8.9 Terminal Server in a WAN environment

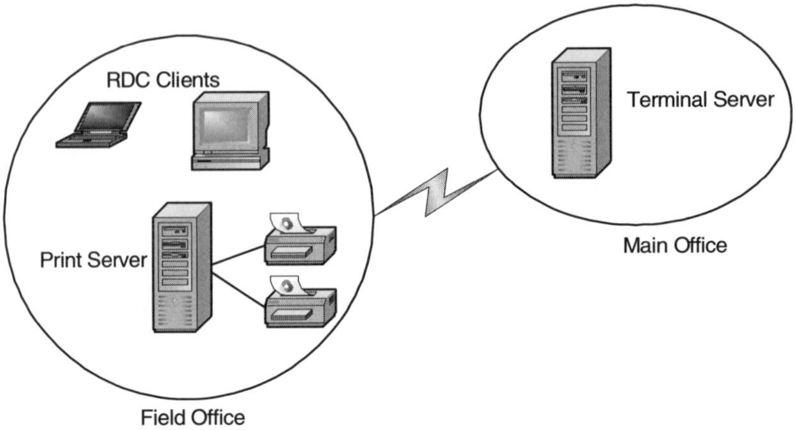

The problem with this design is that the WAN is not used efficiently. If client printers are used (see again Figure 8.5), the Terminal Server will spool the entire print job before it's sent across the WAN. Alternately, the printer could be configured as a server printer (see again Figure 8.3). However, with this configuration, the print job would still be spooled on the Terminal Server. Either way, inefficient print traffic is sent across the WAN.

The third-party tools outlined previously offer some relief in this scenario as well. The UPD-based tools send the PDF or PCL data to the client, and the client then invokes its local print subsystem and prints the document as normal.

The EMF-based solutions send the compressed EMF data to the client, where (again) the client invokes its local print subsystem and prints the document as normal.

On the surface, it doesn't appear that there are any problems with the third-party tools as outlined. But what happens if your client device is connected via a low-bandwidth connection? Or if your client device is running on a platform not supported by the products listed previously?

Fortunately, there is a solution here as well. Some third-party vendors offer products by which the print information is sent directly to the print server, completely bypassing the client device. (In effect, the print server becomes the third-party software client.)

The exact implementation of this process depends on the vendor. UPD-based vendors such as EOL and Qnetix have solutions by which they can send PDF files directly to print servers, and ThinPrint can send EMF print data directly to the print server.

The "standard" advantages and disadvantages of UPD-based and EMF-based solutions apply in this scenario also. The EMF-based solution offers better performance and quality at a higher price than the UPD-based solutions.

Real World Case Study

Dina's Gourmet Food Service

Dina's Gourmet has decided to implement Windows 2003 Terminal Servers to provide several core applications for their users. They have 13 office locations and about 950 users. At this point, the project team has taken an inventory of their locations and users. Based on inventory findings, they were able to put together the basic design of their Terminal Server environment. Now all they need to do is figure out how to print. The project team decided that it would be easiest to create a solution based on the type of printing scenario. In looking at their Terminal Server system design, they realized that there were basically four different printing scenarios:

- *Main Office.* There is 1 main office with 550 users and 14 Terminal Servers. All printing is handled by local print servers.
- *Regional Offices.* There are 2 regional offices, each with 150 users and 5 Terminal Servers. All printing is handled by local print servers. However, these users will also need to print from sessions running on Terminal Servers at the main office.
- *Small Offices.* There are 10 small offices, each with 5 to 15 users. These offices do not have local Terminal Servers—all their users run applications off of Terminal Servers at the main office. Each of these small offices has a local file server that doubles as a print server, with a laser printer and a color ink jet printer.
- *Home Users.* There are fifty users that work from their homes. Each has a local printer connected to his laptop computer. The IT department had issued a "Home Office Supported Equipment" list to the departments that listed four different printer models that would be supported.

In addition to identifying the different printing scenarios, the project team also created a list of business goals for their Terminal Server printing environment. These goals included the following:

- Users should be able to log in anywhere and be able to print.
- The printing process cannot be too confusing for the users.
- The printing process must work at a reasonable speed.

Keeping these three printing goals in mind, the project team decided to address each printing scenario separately, beginning with the main office.

The Main Office

All of the printers at the main office are standard network printers. Most of the print servers are running Windows 2000. The network printers are fairly standard and all have JetDirect cards.

Figure 8.10 Network printers at the Terminal Server location

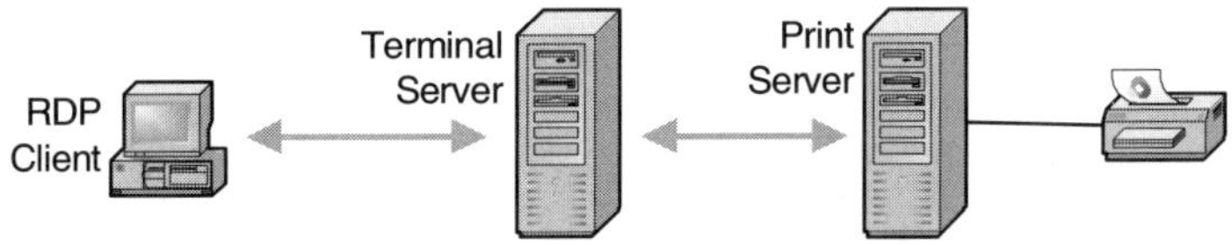

At the main office, users' printers are automatically mapped via their logon scripts. Because the project team wanted the users to have the same environment when they logged onto a Terminal Server as when they logged onto their local workstation, the users will run their standard logon scripts (except for the virus update section which does not run if it detects that the user is logging on from a Terminal Server). Because the printers are configured via logon scripts, there will be no issues configuring printers for different users.

Some project team members commented that printing performance would actually be faster when printing from Terminal Server than when printing from workstations since the Terminal Servers are in the data center two racks down from the print servers. Print jobs generated by users on Terminal Servers don't even have to leave the data center.

There was only one issue with the network printers at the main office that the project team had to address. That issue dealt with printer drivers and the drivers that need to be installed onto the Terminal Servers. Some project team members wanted to install all of the drivers for all of the printers; other team members thought that only basic, generic drivers should be installed. To fully understand the difference of opinion, let's probe deeper into this issue.

Dina Gourmet has eight different types of network printers in their main office. Three-quarters of these are HP LaserJets. The rest are more specialized, such as color printers and dot-matrix printers for multipart forms. Some project team members felt that all of the LaserJet printers should use the same driver, most likely a LaserJet 4 driver. While they might lose some functionality of the more advanced printers, they would not have to support very many drivers.

Other team members felt that they could easily support eight different printer drivers. They pointed out that because these were all network printers, there was no chance that non-supported printers would ever be used. There was no risk that they would ultimately have to support hundreds of printer drivers.

In the end, this driver issue was escalated all the way up to the CTO. His vision was pretty compelling. He said, "We have already spent a lot of money on fancy printers that can duplex, collate, staple and bind. With our vision of moving everything to a server-based computing model, it seems that Terminal Server will be a key part of our infrastructure for the next few years. For that reason, we should do everything we can to ensure that we are able to realize the full benefits of our printers in the Terminal Server environment."

With that, the project team decided to install all of the native printer drivers on their Windows 2003 Terminal Servers.

The Regional Offices

Dina Gourmet has two regional offices, each with about 150 users. Most applications that users need to access will be served from local Terminal Servers. However, a few users will need to access some database applications from Terminal Servers located at the main office. In either case, all printers at these regional offices are network printers. The print servers, which are all Windows 2000, are located locally at the regional offices.

Figure 8.11 Network printers at the regional offices

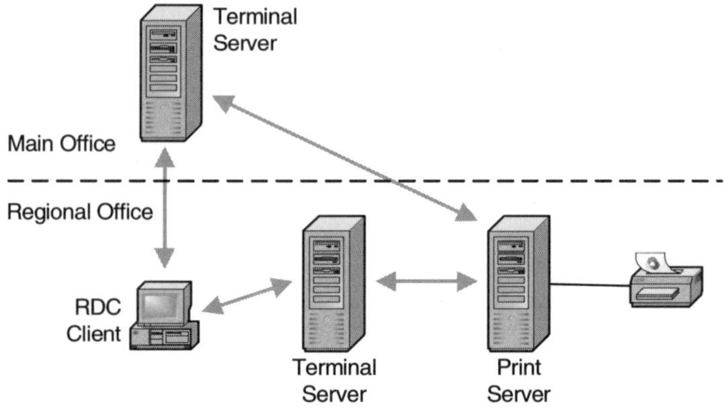

For the most part, printing in the regional offices mirror the main office, with users receiving their printer mappings via logon scripts. The users running RDP sessions on local Terminal Servers will have extremely fast and reliable access to the printers.

The only issue here relates to those users who need to print from applications running on the Terminal Servers located back in the main office. In order to figure out how printing should be configured for them, the project team conducted an interview in order to create a "printer user's profile." Their questionnaire addressed all printing information that the project team would require to determine the type of printer support needed.

The following questions were asked of users to create the printer user's profile:

- How many different printers do you use? Why?
- Do you use any advanced printer features, such as duplexing, collating, copying, or hole-punching?
- Do you print in color? How often?
- Do you ever use different paper types or sizes?
- Do you have any other special printing needs?
- Do you print forms, Word documents, images, or presentations?
- Who views your printouts?
- How many times per day do you print?
- What type of client device do you have? What operating system does it run?

- How many pages are usually printed at once?

In addition to surveying individual users, the project team also chose to look at the printers that they used and to collect the following information about them:

- What is the printer's rated speed, in pages per minute?
- How often is the printer used throughout the day?
- How is the printer connected to the network? Can it be accessed via an IP address, or must it be accessed via a print server?
- What special features does the printer support that might be lost by using alternate generic drivers? How many people use these special features?

Remember, as far as the project team was concerned, they were only collecting printer information to evaluate printing options for users at the two regional offices (with local print servers) that had to print from applications running on Terminal Servers located at the main office.

The evaluations revealed that only about twenty people from each regional office needed to print from Terminal Servers at the main office. Most of these were using Windows XP workstations, although a few in the Customer Service Department were using HP Evo thin client terminals. Some users needed to print in color, and they did print quite often from their central applications. The printers they used were HP LaserJet 8000N's, and they often printed on both sides of the page.

Based on this analysis, and the information that the project team received from their interviews, they built this list of requirements:

- Client platforms of Windows XP and Windows CE.
- Monochrome and color printing.
- High speed.
- The printer must support duplexing.

The project team determined that a third-party printing software solution was their best choice to meet these requirements. As outlined in Figure xxx, their users would be able to print to any printer without administrator intervention.

A third party utility would provide the best overall solution for the regional office users that needed to print from applications running on the main office Terminal Servers. The only real disadvantage to that approach was the fact that the third party tool had to be purchased in addition to their Microsoft software. However, the team figured that increased performance and decreased configuration effort would allow the new software to pay for itself very quickly.

The Small Offices

All of Dina's ten small offices have local print servers, but all Terminal Server application execution takes place at the main office. Again, because the print server is not located near the Terminal Server, the spooled printer files must be sent from the Terminal Server across the WAN to the print server, which can be time consuming.

Figure 8.12 Network printers at remote office locations

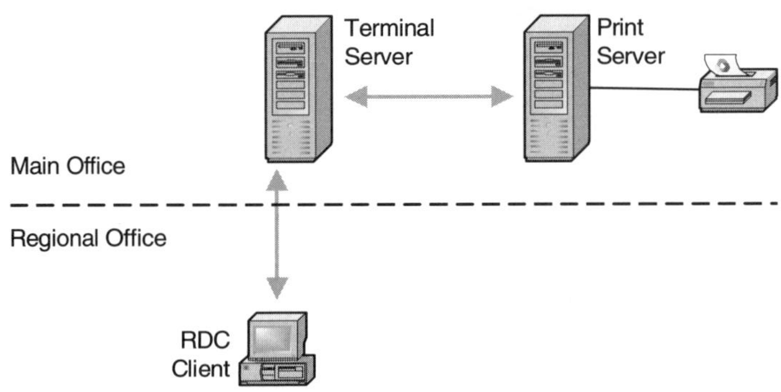

In this case, the project team was able to quickly make a decision without any disagreement. They decided to use the same third-party printing utility that they will use for the regional offices, allowing the users at those facilities to make full use of their color and laser printers without the need to install any client software on users' workstations.

Home Users

Finally the project team addressed the printing needs of the home users. The home users all run Terminal Server sessions off the servers at the main office. Almost all of the fifty home users have local printers installed. The printers are connected to their laptop computers via USB or the parallel port. As the project team discussed earlier, the big challenge concerning these users was that no one can be sure of what kind of printers they have. Some team members estimated that there may be as many as thirty different types of printers out there.

Figure 8.13 Local printers attached to client devices

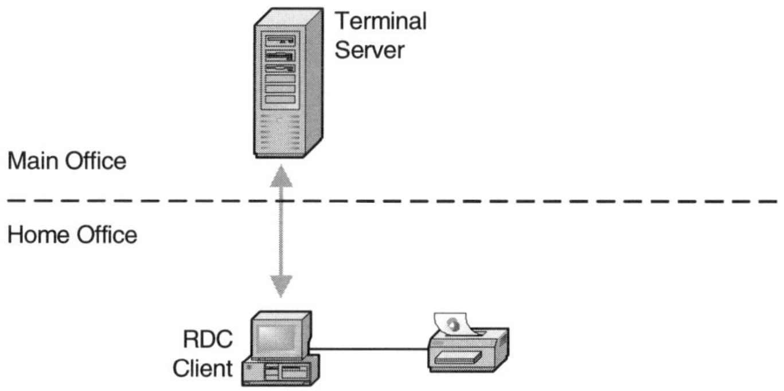

Fortunately, the printing technology decision for the home users was also easy to make. The project team knew that they were working with these requirements:

- Any client computer make and model.
- Any operating system.
- Any printer make and model.
- Extremely slow network connections (dial-up).
- No user intervention.

All of these requirements naturally lead the team to one solution: third party printer management software. The server component of this software would be installed on each of the Terminal Servers. A client component would be installed on every RDC client device. Once this client software is installed, the Terminal Servers send small, unrendered metafile print jobs to the client. The third party software installed on the client computer renders the print jobs locally, allowing any printer to be used, as shown back in Figure 7.8.

Summary

By carefully analyzing all of the unique requirements of each printing scenario, the Dina Gourmet Food Service project team was able to successfully design a Windows 2003 Terminal Server printing solution that allows users to print documents with the speed and flexibility they need.

CHAPTER 9

User Access Methods and Client Devices

This chapter guides you in connecting your users to their applications running on your Terminal Servers. Clearly, you've already made the decision to use Terminal Server to make this access easy. Now you just have to work out the details. There are two basic questions you'll need to answer:

- What process and methods will your users use to access their applications?
- What types of hardware devices will be used to access the applications?

To answer these two questions, we'll present the myriad of available options and the advantages and disadvantages of each. Additionally, we'll outline the issues you should think about when planning your own environment. As far as client device options, we'll explore everything from full-blown Windows PCs to Linux workstations to Windows-based thin client devices. We'll also consider the time and effort it takes to configure, manage, and troubleshoot these devices, as well as the situations in which different types of devices are appropriate.

Let's begin with the methods by which users can access Terminal Server applications.

Methods of End User Access

The primary reason that anyone uses Terminal Server is to provide simple end-user access to Windows applications. By "methods of end user access," we're talking about how your users actually launch their applications on your Terminal Servers. Do they have icons for Terminal Server applications in their Windows Start Menu or on their Windows desktop? Do they launch applications through the web? Are they running complete remote desktops or only specific applications?

Why is the method of access important?

By spending some time up front to consider how your users will access their applications, you can build an environment for them that's easy to use. This will make your life easier as a Terminal Server administrator.

How you configure user access will directly affect several aspects of your users' experience, including:

- What users can do with their applications
- How easily users can get access to and use their applications

- How easy the system is to administer
- How quickly the users can access the system and switch between applications
- How secure the system is
- Total cost of ownership

What are the user access method options?

Ultimately, all users will access your Terminal Servers via some form of RDP client software from a hardware device that supports that software. Once a user is connected, his experience is controlled by the server—it doesn't really matter how he connected or what kind of client device he has. All of the user access method options really what steps the users must take to establish their connections.

From the management standpoint, the various user connection options fall into two general categories:

1. Options that require configuration on client devices, such as the traditional Remote Desktop Connection client.
2. Options that do not require configuration on client devices, such as deploying applications via RDP files and web portals.

Regardless of the access methods you choose, your users will need some form of client software loaded onto their client device. Some access methods require that you manually configure or update the client configuration on every single client while others allow you to make configuration changes one time at the server, with clients receiving the new settings automatically.

Let's look closer at each of the following methods of end user access:

- Placing icons on your users' desktops and in their Start Menus.
- Creating websites or web portals with links that launch applications.
- Installing and configuring the full Remote Desktop Connection client software on each client workstation.

Option 1. Standard Remote Desktop Connection Client

Using the standard Remote Desktop Connection (RDC) client, users can choose the servers they wish to connect to and even configure peripheral device mappings. These connections can be saved to the clients' local machine so they can be reused. The RDC client comes installed on every Windows XP workstation, meaning you have very little to install on the client side.

To your users, though, this would be like accessing an application to launch another application, and could be very confusing. In addition, few users are savvy enough to use the client properly. This method of connection will most likely prompt calls to the helpdesk for assistance with configuring or reconfiguring the client.

Advantages of Remote Desktop Client

- Users have more control over the client.
- Connection settings can be saved by the user for later use.
- Client software already is installed on Windows XP clients.

Disadvantages of Remote Desktop Client

- Users have more control over the client.
- Any application configuration changes must be done manually.
- Shortcuts to remote RDC connection application might have icons that look different from "normal" icons

Option 2. Web Page / Web Portal

Another option is to provide users with web access to applications using the Terminal Services Advanced Client (TSAC). These web pages can be configured to automatically install the RDP client software onto the user's client device if it's not installed when users visit the site.

Several third-party products such as Citrix MetaFrame, Tarantella Canaveral iQ, and Jetro CockpIT offer advanced Terminal Server application web portals that can be configured to provide the user with a login screen when he first accesses the site. After successful authentication, the list of applications is custom-built for the user based on his credentials. This application list consists of hyperlinks and icons for each application. Clicking one of these application hyperlinks launches a session fully integrated into the user's desktop experience.

See Chapter 10 for details on creating web application portals for your Terminal Server environments, and refer to the appendix for a complete list of third-party products and their features.

Advantages of Connecting via a Web Page

- Access to applications can be from any machine, without preconfiguring client software.

- Since many organizations already use web pages and intranets for important information and announcements, Terminal Server applications can be configured as part of a user's home page or corporate portal.
- Because application configuration is done at the web server, you can easily change parameters or options. The client device would use the changes the next time it accesses the web site. There is no need to manually configure every client.
- One web page can contain links to applications from multiple servers or server clusters.

Disadvantages of Connecting via a Web Page

- Visiting a web page for applications may be an added step for your users.
- This introduces a single point of failure. If the web server goes down, users lose access to their applications.
- You'll have to maintain the web server in addition to all of your Terminal Servers.

The advanced web portal technology requires the use of third-party products.

Option 3. Centrally-stored Links to RDP files

You can also choose to install the Remote Desktop Client on all desktops and then store RDP connection files in a central location. Shortcuts to these RDP connection files can then be placed in the users' Start menu (either manually or using an Active directory GPO). This method allows you to centrally manage users' connections with very little desktop configuration. More information on the Remote Desktop Connection client and RDP files is available in Chapter 10.

Advantages of Storing Central RDP Files

- Connections can be configured and managed centrally.

Disadvantages of Storing Central RDP Files

- Client upgrades will have to be done manually at the client or via a software distribution package.
- Users will have to enter their credentials each time they launch an application, since the Central RPD files cannot maintain user information

Remember to Focus on Applications

When determining how your users will launch their Terminal Server applications, it's important to remember that your users only care about their applications. The ideal environment will allow them to access their applications in an easy and intuitive manner, and to remain productive.

Client Device Planning Considerations

A major advantage of server-based computing technology is that the type of client platform and device that determines which applications you can use is removed from the equation. While good from a business perspective, it can have the negative effect of making your technology decisions difficult. It was easy when applications only worked in Windows environments. If a user needed to use the application, they needed a computer running Windows—period.

Now that Terminal Server has come along, users can access Windows applications from virtually any platform and device. Each platform and device combination offers slightly different options for you (the administrator) and your users.

In order to evaluate which types of client devices are best suited to your environment, you must answer a series of questions. These questions can be grouped within five categories:

- Technology management issues.
- Political issues.
- Cost.
- Environment and facilities aspects.
- Applications.

Technology Management Issues

How will the client devices be configured?

Do you need client devices that pull all configuration parameters from a central area and thus do not require local configuration? If you have devices that require local configuration, do you have the skill, software, and ability to automatically script and push out this configuration, or will you need to visit each client device manually?

How much time should be spent troubleshooting the clients?

If each client device contains custom data and configuration information for its user, then IT support personnel could potentially spend significant amounts of time troubleshooting and hunting down problems within each client device. Traditionally this has been the case with Windows-based PC workstations.

In the thin-client world, troubleshooting doesn't require that kind of time. Many companies deploy generic client devices to end users with all users' applications executing on Terminal Servers and their data stored on network drives. If a client device were to stop working properly, the IT staff doesn't have to waste valuable time troubleshooting it. They can pull it out and replace it with a new device.

What kind of local IT support is available?

If your user environment is located at a main corporate campus or if you have local IT department staff, it's possible to use client devices that require some manual configuration or expertise to install. However, lacking an IT staff at the users' site, you must use client devices that a non-technical person can troubleshoot; usually, thin client devices. If one stops working, a non-technical person can go to the closet, get a new one, and plug it in in place of the broken one. The cables are color-coded, and all configuration information and application information is either preset or downloaded from a server.

Political Issues

What is the quality of the relationship between the IT department and the users?

Do your users respect the IT department or are they hostile? (Believe it or not, there are some environments in which the users actually respect IT.) In the presence of mutual respect, it will be easier to introduce new technologies and devices to the end users. If the relationship is strained, every detail of the IT department's technology decisions will be scrutinized. Any aspect of the new technology that the users feel is lacking could cause a user revolt.

Have users become attached to their ability to "personalize" their computers?

In traditional environments where full PC workstations reside on each user's desk, many users have become accustomed to "personalizing" their computers, as seen in custom desktop themes, screen savers, wallpapers with pictures of users' kids, and animated dinosaur mouse pointers.

You might choose to replace your users' customizable PCs with thin client devices that are managed as generic company assets and can be replaced if broken, much like the telephone.

Though these thin client devices provide a 100% identical look and feel of business applications, users can be put off if they were to lose some "freedoms," such as the ability to customize settings and use floppy disks.

How adept are your users?

Will your users be able to adapt to new solutions or technologies, or will they call the helpdesk every day for a month? Even worse, are they too smart (or crafty)? Will they try to break or get around whatever procedures are put in place? You should spend time trying to understand what your users' true needs are. Keep in mind that some users are never happy. No matter what you do, they will always want more.

How easy is it for users to break the client devices?

Most users tend to meddle with whatever configuration settings and options they can find on their client computers. When considering client devices, it's important to assess how easily they can be "locked-down," preventing users from breaking them.

What is the security level needed in the user environment?

Will end users need secure access over the network, or will they need secure authentication, such as smart cards or biometric authentication? How about the client devices themselves? If they are located somewhere in which theft is a problem, thin client devices are preferable to PC workstations since they are worthless outside of an office environment (unless the thieves set up a Terminal Server in their hideout). If they are stolen, thin client devices are cheaper to replace.

Cost

Is there a significant investment in the current client devices or licenses?

Sometimes Terminal Server is deployed in environments that haven't updated desktop technology for many years, so it's easy to justify the cost of new client devices that are purchased as the Terminal Server applications are rolled out.

More common, though, are the environments that lease or refresh their desktop technology every few years. Even if the IT department decides that thin client devices are the cheapest, easiest, and coolest client devices they could use, they may not be a possibility if the end user departments "just got new PCs last year, we're not pulling them out now."

If politics force you to use existing client devices, then your client device selection process shouldn't take long.

Who pays for new end user hardware?

Often end user departments pay for their own client devices. In these cases, you need to know whether they typically purchase what the IT department recommends or if they purchase whatever they want (usually based on cheapest price). If they go by IT recommendations, are there particular vendors that must be used or price caps that must be observed?

Of course, even if the IT department pays for the end user devices, these same political and pricing issues may still apply.

Environmental / Facilities

Are there any special environment site needs?

If the end user environment is harsh or dirty, client machines may break more often, requiring ones that are inexpensive and easy to replace. If the client environment has sanitary requirements, as in hospitals, the client devices might need to be hermetically sealed or have the ability to be easily disinfected.

What are the power consumption requirements?

Many traditional computers require 200 to 300 watts to operate, while many thin client devices operate on 25 watts or less. When you consider that these devices are used for at least 2000 hours per year, and with energy prices always increasing, the power cost savings can be tremendous, even with a few hundred users.

Applications

What types of applications will be used?

If only Terminal Server applications will be used, then any client devices will work (thin client, Windows CE, full PC, etc.). But, if users will ever need to access an application that is not delivered via the Terminal Server, they will need client devices that support other applications. Interestingly, this issue drives the balance between the number of applications in the Terminal Services environment and the complexities and expenses associated with different client devices.

How many different applications will be used?

In addition to the types of applications that are used, you must evaluate how many applications a user will need.

If the user is using less than five applications every day (word processor, email, web, and a line of business application), then it makes it easy for you to recommend thin client devices. However, the more applications a user requires, the tougher it becomes to use thin client devices. You might also need to consider other factors, such as the length of application usage. How many times is the user switching between applications per day?

What kinds of graphics and sound support will clients need?

Do the users have applications with high graphics requirements? Some thin client devices have better graphics performance than others, evident in high resolutions and color depth.

Do the users need audio support on their client devices? Remember that although audio support might not be perceived as necessary by the IT department, the users may be very upset if they "lose" sound when moving to a Terminal Server-based solution.

Do the end users require wireless mobile access?

If users need to be able to move around while using their Terminal Server applications, is this movement confined to one area or one building, or will they need to access their applications from anywhere in the country?

How will mobile devices be used? The requirements of users that need access primarily from one location with the ability to roam are different from those of users that primarily need to roam. Battery life is also a factor.

What types of peripherals are used?

Some environments may require specific peripherals, such as bar code readers or scanners. If this is the case in your environment then you will need to evaluate whether applications will support the barcode readers through thin client devices and Terminal Server sessions or if the applications will need to be installed locally on traditional PCs.

Will the users travel with their client devices?

If users will be traveling with their client devices, such as laptops, then you must make provisions for them to have access to applications when they are offline. You won't be able to use Terminal Server, at least while the laptop users are not connected.

Types of Client Devices

There are literally hundreds of different types of client devices that can be used to access Terminal Server environments. While that list is always changing and it's not practical to discuss all of them here, these client devices can be broadly broken down into four groups:

- Traditional computer workstations, including standard Windows PCs and Macintosh computers.
- Thin client devices, including devices that are based on Windows CE, Windows XP Embedded, or Linux on-a-chip. These devices have no local hard drives and typically boot off of servers or have embedded operating systems. While some of these devices may have local web browsers or terminal emulators, they usually run most applications from backend servers.
- Traditional computers, managed as thin client devices. These devices are usually standard computers, complete with local operating systems and hard drives that are created with disk "images." If one stops working properly, it's replaced with a new computer or it's "re-imaged." Significant troubleshooting time is not wasted.
- Mobile wireless devices, including dedicated wireless devices and palm-sized computers.

Option 1. Traditional Computer Workstations

Traditional computer workstations are currently deployed in almost every organization throughout the world. From a Terminal Server standpoint, if traditional computers are out there and paid for, then why not use them? Terminal Server works well when accessed from standard computers, whether users access their hosted applications through the locally installed RCD client or through a web portal.

Additionally, because traditional computers have local processors and hard drives, the RDC client can cache certain information and graphics locally. This increases performance, especially over high-latency/low-speed connections.

However, as more applications become server-based and as more companies use Terminal Server, traditional computers quickly become overkill for many users. They are expensive to maintain and users often break them through "trial and error" misconfiguration.

Advantages of Traditional Computer Workstations

- Already deployed in most locations.
- Users are comfortable with them.
- Local processor and storage allows for better session performance.
- No perception of "IT is taking this away from us."
- Local, non-Terminal Server applications can also be used.
- Many peripherals are available and compatible.

Disadvantages of Traditional Computer Workstations

- Expensive to purchase and maintain.
- Proprietary for each user.
- Difficult to troubleshoot.
- Must be manually configured or complex scripts and policies must be created.
- Require local IT staff for support.
- Prone to being broken by "curious" users.
- Increased risk of "accidental" local data storage, which is not secure and not backed up.
- Target for thieves in unsecured environment.
- Many more options and models make it harder to enforce standards.
- High power consumption.
- Many moving parts that can break or get dirty.

Option 2. Thin Client Devices and Appliances

Thin client devices and appliances are purpose-built machines used primarily for accessing server-based computing environments, including web browsing, terminal emulation, and Terminal Server sessions. These devices usually have no local hard drives or moving parts.

There are several flavors of thin client devices, most easily categorized by their local operating system. Most of these devices run some form of chip-based Windows (Windows CE.NET or XP embedded), Linux, or Java. In order to connect into the Terminal Server environment, they need to have the appropriate local RDP client software installed.

There are several advantages to using thin client devices. Because they don't have any in-depth local configuration, users are not able to break them as easily as a standard PC. They have few (if any) moving parts, so there is less to break. If something does break, it's usually cheaper and easier to replace the entire terminal.

For example, one company headquartered in Euclid, Ohio has manufacturing facilities in Ontario, Canada. Their entire manufacturing shop floor is run off of applications on Terminal Servers located in Euclid. All application access in Canada is done via thin client devices. Due to the harshness of the manufacturing environment, traditional PCs were always breaking. The thin client devices they chose had no moving parts—not even cooling fans—so they don't break nearly as often. When a thin client device does break, the shop foreman goes to the closet and grabs a replacement terminal. The user connects back into his session right where he left off with only a few minutes of total downtime.

However, be careful that you're not fooled by the seemingly endless advantages of thin client devices, because several major drawbacks exist.

First and foremost is the fact that with thin client devices, all major processing must be done somewhere else. With full-blown PCs, you have the *option* of running applications centrally. With thin clients, all applications *must* be run centrally. Do you, as an administrator, really want your clients surfing the web or writing email to their kids with valuable server processing time? Of course, many thin clients now have local browsers and local email programs, but you get the idea.

Advantages of Thin Client Devices

- Low maintenance costs. If one breaks, throw it away, plug in a replacement, connect back into the session, done.
- No local user troubleshooting.
- No local IT staff is needed.
- Little-to-no local user configuration, so users can't break them (as easily).
- Low power consumption.
- No black market value, so they're less likely to be stolen.

Disadvantages of Thin Client Devices

- Less flexibility than PCs.
- Essentially, all applications must run through host server.
- If they are purchased to replace PCs, people will be upset. ("We just spent $2500 on new PCs, and now they're replacing them?")

- In politically charged environments, users perceive that their full PC's are being "taken" from them.

Thin client devices are a great option, but unless you have a compelling reason *not* to use PCs, be careful of the "nothing" approach (as in "all or nothing") that you get with thin clients.

Option 3. Traditional Workstations, Managed as Thin Devices

It is possible to combine the traditional computer workstation hardware with the management style of thin client devices to create a solution that has some of the advantages of each.

This option entails keeping full computer workstations for every user, but building a standard workstation image that is deployed to all users. All applications (except maybe a web browser) are server-based. The idea is that if a computer workstation breaks, a new hard drive or new workstation can be brought in to replace it.

One company that did this created a "five minute rule." Basically, the desktop computer technicians would visit an end user whenever they had a problem and called the helpdesk. If it was something simple, they fixed it. However, if the desktop technician could not fix the problem within five minutes, the user's computer was wiped clean and a new image was put on.

This worked well because all of their applications were delivered via Terminal Server and all of the users' data was stored on the network. All of the users' computers in the entire company had the same image, which was just a base operating system, a web browser, and the RDP client software.

Advantages of Traditional Workstations Managed Like Thin Clients

- Current hardware can be utilized.
- Efficient use of time for IT staff.

Disadvantages of Traditional Workstations Managed Like Thin Clients

- The hardware still breaks.

Option 4. Mobile Wireless Devices

"Mobile wireless devices" are a legitimate option when deciding how your users will access their applications. As with all mobile wireless devices, the primary drawback is still battery life. There are two classes of wireless devices, LAN devices and public WAN devices.

LAN devices are usually laptop computers or Windows CE / Pocket PC devices with 802.11 wireless network cards. Most people just buy full-blown laptops with wireless LAN cards.

The wireless public WAN is the system that for which you pay a monthly access fee. There are many networks throughout the world, and most are based on CDPD, CDMA, PCS, GPRS, GSM, or similar networks. Of the millions of palm-sized computers out there today, many of them run the Microsoft RDP client. They can be used for wireless, go-anywhere access to business applications.

Advantages of Mobile Wireless Devices

- Access to critical applications from anywhere.

Disadvantages of Mobile Wireless Devices

- Expensive service (US $30-$100 per user per month).
- Tiny screens on devices.
- Not practical for everyday use.
- Battery life.

CHAPTER 10

Deploying and Configuring Remote Desktop Clients

Throughout this book, we've discussed as one of the great advantages of using Terminal Server that users can access any application from any client device. We've even looked at the different types of client devices and where they work best.

To this point, however, we have not yet looked at the actual Terminal Server client software that must be installed on the client devices so that they can run remote sessions on Terminal Servers via the RDP protocol.

In this chapter, we'll review the available Terminal Server client software options and take a look at the client configuration process. We'll also examine how the different configuration options can impact client use. We will not discuss how these clients integrate with websites. That topic deserves its own discussion, and is covered in Chapter 11.

RDP Client Functional Overview

The RDP client software is the fundamental element that allows a computing device to attach to and run sessions off of a Terminal Server. Without the client software installed, a device cannot run RDP sessions. From the Terminal Server's perspective, it doesn't matter which client is used or how a client connects to the server. This is the true beauty of Terminal Server. All users get the same application experience—regardless of their client platforms.

RDP Client to Terminal Server Communication

Fundamentally, the RDP client software does three things:

- It allows you to find a Terminal Server to connect to.
- It establishes the remote sessions via the RDP protocol with that Terminal Server.
- It connects and manages client peripherals.

In order for the RDP client software to connect to a Terminal Server, the client software must be able to find the Terminal Server. Generally this is done through a DNS name, but it can also be accomplished by IP address, by enumerating the domain, or by clicking a link in a web page.

Once the user selects which server they want to connect to, an RDP session is established. As that session is being established, the RDP client software works with the Terminal Server to map various client components (drives, ports, printers, the clipboard, etc.) to the server for use in the user's session.

Some versions of the RDP client software allow users (or administrators) save their settings into configuration files. Then, for future sessions, a user can simply double-click the configuration file to launch the RDP client software with the saved configuration.

Types of RDP Client Software

All RDP client software falls into two basic categories:

- RDP clients available from Microsoft.
- RDP clients available from everyone else, including licensed, unlicensed, open source, hobbyist, and experimental clients.

RDP Clients Available from Microsoft

In 1998, Microsoft licensed the core Terminal Services technology (called "MultiWin") from Citrix Systems. Part of the licensing agreement specified that Microsoft would only provide RDP clients for select platforms. To that end, Microsoft has written and provides full official support for RDP clients on the following three platforms:

- 32-bit Windows platforms
- Windows CE / Pocket PC
- Mac OS X 10.1

Today's version of the RDP client from Microsoft is called the Remote Desktop Connection Client, or simply, the "RDC client" (not to be confused with the "RDP" protocol).

Although your choice of platforms is limited, the individual clients themselves have quite a bit of functionality. The latest RDC client (version 5.2 ships with Windows 2003) for 32-bit Windows computers lets you to manipulate the entire session configuration from the client. This is the primary client that Microsoft supports and recommends.

An extension of this client is "RDC for the Web" (or what was formally known as the Terminal Server Advanced Client). This client is in the form of an ActiveX control, and allows users to connect to Terminal Server applications via web portals. (This client is fully covered in the Chapter 11.)

The Windows CE / Pocket PC RDP client is often preinstalled on thin client devices, although you can download it from Microsoft for use on PDAs. The

Windows CE client supports most of the RDP 5.2 functionality, though its interface is not as advanced as the full RDC client.

A more recent addition to the official Microsoft client roundup is the RDC client for Mac. While only Mac OS X 10.1 and newer are supported, this client allows you to connect to a Terminal Server just as you would a normal Windows-based RDC client.

RDP Clients for Other Platforms

A few years ago, you had to use third-party server software (such as Citrix MetaFrame) if you wanted to connect to a Terminal Server from a client platform that wasn't supported by Microsoft. However, times have changed and you can now get third-party RDP client software for any platform which allows you to connect to a native Terminal Server without any third-party server software.

For Linux, UNIX, and any other environment you want to compile it for, an open source RDP client is available from `www.rdesktop.org`. Like most Linux software, this client is freely available under the GNU public license (GPL). This client is popular for use with old desktops. You could potentially take a large number of older PCs, reconfigure them using Linux as a base OS, and use the client to connect to the Terminal Servers. This approach falls along the lines of the "traditional desktop managed as a thin client" outlined back in Chapter 9. The rdesktop.org client is also very popular in Macintosh environments since the official Microsoft version requires Mac OS X 10.1.

If Linux is not really your bag, you can do the same thing using DOS. Cláudio Rodrigues has developed a DOS version of the RDP client available for purchase from his website, `www.terminal-services.net`. Although the Linux client from rdesktop.org is free, the DOS client could be an alternative if you don't have time to learn Linux.

HOB sells a Java version of the RDP client at `www.hobsoft.com`. Their Java client works on just about every Java platform.

Finally, a company called DDH Software has even developed RDP client software for Palm OS. You can purchase that from `www.ddhsoftware.com`.

Between the Windows and Macintosh versions from Microsoft and the third-party open source, Java, DOS, and Palm clients, you should be able to provide your Terminal Server applications to users regardless of their client platforms.

RDP Client Features

Today's RDP clients (both official and non-official) offer many capabilities. We'll take a look at the various features, although keep in mind that not all of these features are supported on every platform. (We'll talk about the specifics of each platform later in this chapter.)

Also, as you're reading, remember that most of these features can be configured in multiple locations. For example, audio mapping can be enabled or disabled as a property of the Terminal Server's listener port and as a property of the RDP client software. In order to use audio, it must be enabled in both locations. The Appendix of this book has a feature chart that lists every single Terminal Server feature and all the locations at which it can be configured.

Now, let's look at the myriad of features available from RDP client devices.

Local Resource Capabilities

Certain hardware elements of RDP client devices can be configured so that they may be accessed through RDP sessions running on remote Terminal Servers. This process is called "mapping" because it is similar to mapping a network drive or printer port on a server, except that RDP client device mapping occurs in the opposite direction. Mapping local resources involves several steps:

1. When the RDP session is established with the Terminal Server, the client software on the client device sends the server a list of local components that are available to be mapped.
2. If the appropriate mappings have been enabled on the server, the mapping process continues and a dynamic mapping is made to the client device.
3. Part of the RDP protocol, called a "virtual channel" is used for the mapping. One channel is used for each of the different types of device mapping. This channel allows the mapping data to flow back and forth between the RDP client and the Terminal Server.

These mappings are dynamic. They only exist for the current user and the current session. As soon as the user logs off, the mappings are deleted.

There are several types of devices that can be mapped to client devices in RDP sessions.

Client Disk Drives

Terminal Servers have the ability to connect to and map client drives from the local client device to the sessions running on the Terminal Server. When this is done, users have the ability to access data stored on their local hard drives or floppy drives from within their Terminal Server sessions. By default, client drives are connected as network resources. They show up in the user's explorer session as "*C on Clientname*." If you look at the open network connections in the session, you'll see a connection to *\\TSClient\C*. This connection allows users to access their local drives via a name they'll recognize.

In some situations, you may want to configure your Terminal Server so that it does not automatically connect to the client drives. If you do this, you can still configure it so that users can browse to their client drives through network neighborhood. To do this, make a change to the properties of the connection, which means that you must use the Terminal Server Configuration utility to configure it. Use this utility to edit the properties of the connection, and ensure that the "Connect client drives at logon" box is not checked (Terminal Services Configuration | Edit Connection | Client Settings). In order for this to work, the RDP client device must also be configured to allow client drive mapping.

Whenever any client devices are mapped from within RDP sessions, your users will see a "Microsoft Terminal Services" item in their Network Neighborhood (Network Neighborhood | Entire Network | Microsoft Terminal Services). Underneath the Microsoft Terminal Services item will be a computer called "*TSclient*." Browsing this computer will reveal the local drives shown as *\\TSClient\C*. These drive share names are made up of the drive letter as seen on the local client device, so they will see the shares as *\\TSClient\C* or *\\TSClient\D*.

If you would like to disable all access to RDP client devices' local drives, check the "Disable Client Drive Mapping" box in the connection's properties (Terminal Services Configuration | Edit Connection | Client Settings) or configure this setting via a GPO (as described in Chapter 6).

By default, most RDC clients do not auto-connect client drives for security purposes. It must be enabled on the client device.

Printer Mapping

Similar to the drive mappings, printers can be mapped with the RDP client software. Many different parameters will affect your printing solution in your Terminal Server environment. For that reason, you can find everything that you need to know about printing in Chapter 8.

Port Mapping

You can map LPT and COM ports from the local RDP client devices so that they are available to users via their server sessions. This is also configured as a property of the connection (Terminal Services Configuration | Edit Connection | Client Settings | Ensure that "Disable Client LPT Port Mapping" or "Disable Client COM Port Mapping" is not checked) or as part of a user profile. When you enable port mapping, the ports are not mapped in Terminal Server sessions automatically. Instead you can manually map them with the "*net use*" command much like a drive is mapped. (`net use LPT1: \\TSclient\LPT1`). The name of the client does not need to be known since the client device is always known within its own session as "*TSCLIENT*."

Audio Mapping

If your users' client devices have speakers, they can hear audio from their sessions on the Terminal Server. This arrangement is known as "client audio redirection" and works in a way similar to the other client mapping features.

If you decide to enable client audio mapping, you should know that only certain kinds of sounds are redirected to the RDP client devices. Only audio from applications in which the programmers "properly" used the Microsoft sound APIs fall into this category. Certain types of sounds that are played from server sessions do not make it to the client.

You'll need to test any applications that require sound. Microsoft designed the audio mapping capabilities of the RDP client so that the general "beeps" and "bings" that users receive throughout the day can be sent to the client. It's not meant to enable users to watch multimedia presentations from the server (although that can be done in many of cases).

On your Terminal Servers, enable client audio mapping as a property of a connection (Terminal Services Configuration | Edit Connection | Client Settings | Disable Client Audio Mapping box unchecked) or as part of a GPO (see chapter 6).

Clipboard Integration

When users run a combination of local and remote applications, they'll often need to cut and paste data from their local applications to their remote applications. Since both sets of applications are running on two different computers, this clipboard integration is not inherently possible. Fortunately, the RDP client software allows local and remote applications to share clipboard data.

When this feature is enabled, any data that is written to the clipboard of either the client or the server is instantly replicated to the clipboard of the other.

As with other configurations, clipboard integration is enabled or disabled as a property of a connection (Terminal Server Configuration | Edit Connection | Client Settings | Disable Client Clipboard Mapping check box) or via a GPO.

Window's Key Combinations

Within Windows environments there are several key combinations used to focus Windows or bring up the security menu. An example of these is ALT+TAB, or CTRL+ALT+DEL.

By default, these key strokes are captured locally on the client device and are not sent to the Terminal Server session. In some environments, users might need these keystroke combinations within their RDP sessions. Imagine that an application running on a Terminal Server requires the user to press CTRL+ALT+DEL. How would the user do that from her Terminal Server session? If she presses CTRL+ALT+DEL on her local client device, the local CTRL+ALT+DEL screen will pop up, not the one on the server.

In order to send CTRL+ALT+DEL to the server, the user must configure her RDP client to send these combinations to the server for execution. This is truly a client side setting that cannot be configured on the server. The only place to configure this is on the "Local Resources" tab of the RDC client. You can configure it to use the key combinations on the local client only (default), the remote server only, or send to the remote server while you are connected to it in a full screen mode.

Color Depth

One advancement of Windows Server 2003 is the introduction of support for up to 24-bit color in RDP sessions. The new client supports 8-, 16-, and 24-bit color. In general, the higher color depths add overhead to the bandwidth used by the client. The amount of overhead varies greatly depending on the types of applications being run, but testing shows it's about a 2-3kbps increase each time you increase color depth.

Client Performance Enhancing Options

In addition to the various features they support, several of the RDP clients also have capabilities to increase the performance of the RDP session. This is done in several ways. (Full performance tuning details are discussed in Chapter 13.)

Bitmap Caching

Some RDC clients have the ability to cache bitmap images from the Terminal Servers increasing the performance of a session since popular screen objects can be retrieved from the local cache instead of from the Terminal Server. Bitmap caching is generally beneficial, especially with applications that have a few main screens that most users flip through. It also works well in WAN environments.

In Windows 32-bit RDC client, bitmap caching is enabled via the "Experience" tab. Once enabled, the client begins to cache bitmaps into a BMC file located on the client device in the *c:\Documents and Settings\<username>\Local Settings\Application Data\Microsoft\Terminal Server Client\Cache* folder.

As you can see by this path, the bitmap cache is stored under the "local Settings" folder, meaning that it's not replicated as part of a roaming profile. Writing this chapter via a Terminal Server session with Microsoft Word 2003 created two cache files that were 8 and 19MB in size.

Themes

You can use the RDP client to disable Windows Server 2003 "Themes." Disabling themes simplifies the graphic layout of the Terminal Server session, thereby decreasing the amount of graphic data that must be sent to the client.

Menu and Window animation

You can also adjust how the Terminal Server shell draws its menus and windows. By default, Windows 2003 "rolls" the menus down. While pretty to look at, it also means that more graphic data would be sent to the client device in Terminal Server environments. Most RDP clients allow you to disable menu and window animations for their sessions, potentially saving bandwidth.

Show Contents of Windows while Dragging

As the name implies, you can choose to not show window contents while dragging (causing window dragging to look as it did in the old days—a simple wireframe outline is drawn instead). Just like the other animation-related client performance options, disabling this option can increase performance since less graphic data is sent to the client.

Desktop Background

The final option that you can disable to increase performance is the Windows desktop background image. Again, this option can be disabled on a client-by-client basis. When disabled, a blank Windows desktop background is displayed instead of any images or active desktop content that users have stored in their profiles.

Which features are supported on which platforms?

The previous section outlined the generic options available with RDP clients. It's important to note that not all of these options are available on all client platforms. The chart in Figure 10.1 shows several popular RDP client platforms and the specific options supported on them. (An up-to-date version of this table is always available at `www.brianmadden.com`.)

As you examine this chart, keep in mind that it only shows the options that could be used on different client platforms. As an administrator, you have the ability to restrict certain options from users, and many of these restrictions can be configured in several places. The Appendix of this book contains a chart detailing every configuration option (those shown below and then some), and the location at which each option can be configured.

Figure 10.1 RDP clients and the features they support.

	Win32	WinCE	Mac OS X	RDesktop	HOB Java	TS DOS	Palm OS
Drive mapping	•	•	•		•		
Printer mapping	•	•	•	•	•		
Port mapping	•	•		•			
Audio	•	•	•	•	•		
Clipboard Integration	•	•	•	•	•		
Windows Key Combinations	•	•	•	•	•	•	•
Bitmap Caching	•	•	•	•			
Compression	•	•	•				
Encryption	•	•	•	•	•		
Smart card redirection	•	•					

Now that you've seen the options available to various client platforms, let's take a detailed look at the most popular client for the most popular platform.

32-bit Windows Remote Desktop Connection Client

Since most users who access Terminal Server environments do so from 32-bit Windows client devices, this is the client platform that Microsoft has spent the most effort on. In order to study the 32-bit Windows RDP clients, we'll look at the following areas:

- Technical overview of the 32-bit remote desktop connection client.
- Client configuration.

RDC Client Technical Overview

The 32-bit Windows Remote Desktop Connection client is very sophisticated. This is the new name of what formerly was known as the "Terminal Server Client." As we mentioned earlier, though, most administrators still call this (and will probably forever call this) simply, the "RDP client."

Out of the box, Windows Server 2003 comes with version 5.2 of the Remote Desktop Connection client. This version is newer than the one that comes standard with Windows XP and newer than the one included in Service Pack 1 for Windows XP. However, there's no significant difference between the versions.

When you install Windows Server 2003, the installation files for the RDC client (version 5.2 of course) are automatically copied to the *\Windows\System32\clients\tsclient\win32* folder. You can use the *msrdpcli.msi* install package to load the RDC client onto any Microsoft 32-bit operating system dating back to Windows 95.

RDC Client Installation

The installation of the RDC client is fairly straightforward. RDC client version 5.2's installation program automatically installs it to the *\Program Files* folder, and it only asks users for their names and for them to accept the license agreement. Otherwise the installation is almost silent.

Since it's a standard MSI package, you can easily change the default options you want or configure it for a silent install to be used with SMS or a logon script. (As you probably know, the "/q" switch will perform a silent installation of an MSI package.) The details of configuring MSIs for installation are outside the scope of this book; however, you can find good information by going to `www.microsoft.com` and doing a search for "Windows Installer."

In the real world, most people are content with the version 5.1 RDC clients that are built in to Windows XP. For new installations, however, you're always better off going with the newest version. Like all new software, there are two installation methods:

- *Electronic software distribution.* Fortunately, the RDC client is a very simple MSI. You can actually generate a software distribution package directly from the command line. This package can easily be deployed with Microsoft Systems Management Server, Wise, or Altiris products. The only drawback to this method is that you need to have some form of software distribution product in place, although it's rare that environments of significant size don't have this already. Worst case, you can simply script a silent install and run it as a part of users' login scripts.
- *Manual installation.* If you can't deploy the RDC client via with a software distribution product, you could always put it on a network share and have users manually install it. Alternately, since it's so small (less than 1MB), you could even email it to your users.

Configuring the Remote Desktop Connection Client with RDP Files

When a user fires up the actual Remote Desktop Connection client, the interface configures itself with several defaults. The only option you *need* to configure is the name of the server you want to connect to. The RDC client uses the default configuration information to set up the session and the virtual channels as soon as you hit the connect button.

If you want to change any of the session settings, disconnect from the session, make the changes to the client, and then reconnect with the new settings. There is no interface (as with previous Terminal Server clients) that allows you to save multiple configurations right in the application. Instead, the Remote Desktop Connection client allows you to save its current configuration as an RDP file. (Even the "default" client settings are saved in a hidden file called "*default.rdp*" in the root of each user's "*My Documents*" folder.)

As mentioned previously, an RDP file is simply a text file containing the information needed to make a connection based on settings you've specified in the GUI. This idea is based on the huge success of Citrix ICA file type which has been the cornerstone of their application launching mechanisms for the web for the last few years. Figure 10.2 shows the contents of a basic RDP file.

Figure 10.2 An RDP file that launches Microsoft Word 2000 on tsserver01

```
screen mode id:i:1
desktopwidth:i:800
desktopheight:i:600
session bpp:i:16
winposstr:s:2,3,0,0,648,507
full address:s:tsserver01
compression:i:1
keyboardhook:i:2
audiomode:i:0
redirectdrives:i:0
redirectprinters:i:1
redirectcomports:i:0
redirectsmartcards:i:1
displayconnectionbar:i:1
autoreconnection enabled:i:1
username:s:
domain:s:
alternate shell:s:C:\Program Files\Microsoft Of-
fice\Office\winword.exe
shell working directory:s:C:\Program Files\Microsoft
Office\Office
disable wallpaper:i:1
disable full window drag:i:1
disable menu anims:i:1
disable themes:i:0
disable cursor setting:i:0
bitmapcachepersistenable:i:1
```

As you can see, this file consists of a set of RDP options that are enabled (1) or disabled (0), along with the name of the server to which it's connecting (tsserver01) and the path for the executable (winword.exe).

The biggest limitation of the RDC client (and therefore also to using centrally-stored RDP files) is a security "feature." The RDC client does not have the ability to pass the credentials of the locally logged on user into the Terminal Server session. In addition, the RDP file stores any saved credentials in an encrypted format, meaning that they'll only work from the workstation on which they were created and log in as the user by which they were saved.

When using centrally-stored RDP files, your users will need to manually log on to the remote Windows session. When compared to the alternative (users manually configuring their own clients), RDP files don't seem that bad.

Creating RDP Files

Creating RDP files for central deployment is easy.

1. To begin, launch the Remote Desktop Connection client (mstsc.exe).
2. Click the "Options" button to expand the client.
3. Configure the General tab with your required options. The computer can be the Terminal Server name or a DNS name if you're using load balancing.
4. Remove any user name or password entry fields and ensure that the "Save my password" option is *not* checked. Saved cached passwords will only work for the user that saved it on the machine where it was created, so there's no use for it when creating RDP files that will be shared among users.
5. Configure the Display Tab with your required options.
6. Configure the Local Resources Tab with your required options
7. Configure the Programs tab with your program path. Check the box that says "Start the following program on connection." The executable and working directory are the paths on the server, not the workstation. Place the path to the executable and its name in the appropriate fields.
8. Configure the Experience tab. For users connecting via the Internet, you shouldn't set the speed any higher than 56k, giving the user a good experience while still reducing the bandwidth required by the session.
9. Check the box "Reconnect if connection is dropped," allowing the Terminal Server client to automatically reconnect to the server if the network connection is dropped and the stream lost.
10. Return to the General Tab and save the connection with a recognizable name to create an RDP file with all of your connection information for that application.

Repeat this process as many times as necessary for each of your applications.

Launching the RDC Client from RDP Files

Chapters 5 and 9 focused on how your users could connect to your Terminal Servers. If you chose to have users connect to initial applications, then they'll need to launch their RDC client software with an RDP file. There are two ways to do this.

The first involves placing your customized RDP file on a network share. Then, add shortcuts to this centralized RDP file on your users' Start menus. This allows your users to launch the Terminal Server applications just as they would any other application since the RDP file type is associated with the locally installed RDC client. At the same time, since the RDP file is centralized, you can maintain control and easily update it.

Alternately, use command line options of the RDC client executable (*mstsc.exe*) to launch a connection based on information contained in an RDP file, such as:

```
mstsc.exe application1.rdp
```

There are several command line options for the RDC client. You can specify your screen size with "/w" and "/h" switches, or full screen with the "/f" switch. Administrators can also use the "/console" switch to connect directly to the server's console via RDP instead of connecting to a Terminal Server session.

CHAPTER 11

Accessing Terminal Servers via Web Portals

One of the greatest aspects of Terminal Server is that because your applications are centralized, your users can access them from any location or any device. Throughout this book, we've focused on how to design your server environment and how to get the RDP client software installed on your users' client devices. But what happens if you have a mobile workforce that needs to access applications from multiple locations and clients?

One solution that's gaining in popularity is to deploy applications via websites or web portals. In this scenario, users simply connect to a web page to access their Terminal Server applications. In some cases, the RDP client software can be in the form of an ActiveX control, so the remote application is actually embedded directly into the web page.

Advantages of Using Web Connections

- All users can access their Terminal Server applications via one URL.
- You do not need to visit users to make configuration changes since application and server connections can be stored on the web server and re-configured there.
- Users can have access to applications from anywhere in the organization.

Disadvantages of Using Web Connections

- Some thin client devices do not support these types of connections.
- You need a web server.

Web Connectivity Options

The first decision to make once you decide to deploy Terminal Server applications via a website is how you want your users to experience the applications. You have two choices:

- The applications can be embedded into the web page itself. Closing the web browser disconnects the server session. In this case, the RDP client software is an ActiveX control that's downloaded from the web server.
- The user can click a link on a web page that launches the "standard" RDP client software (as discussed in Chapter 10).

Embedding Applications into Web Pages with the ActiveX Control

In order to illustrate how the system works when you embed applications into a web page, we first need to review the components that make up this system. Then, we can look at how they work together to deliver applications to your users.

Web Embedded Application Components

Three primary components are used when embedding remote Terminal Server applications into a web page.

- Web server hosting the RDW.
- Terminal Servers to host the applications.
- Active X Client.

Component 1. Web Server

You web server is obviously the primary interface for users in this environment. After all, the whole purpose is to allow users to access their server desktops through the web, and this is done with the web server. The ActiveX control we're discussing here works with IIS servers version 4.0 and later, (although if you're looking to use another web server you can use custom pages and the client described later in this chapter).

Component 2. Terminal Servers

A Terminal Server or a cluster of Terminal Servers must be available to accept the inbound connections and host the applications. The Terminal Servers host the users' RDP sessions after the user launches a connection. When a user clicks a link to launch a session, the user's session starts on Terminal Server just like any other session. In fact, there is no difference in a user's session whether he launches it from Web page or from a regular client.

Component 3. ActiveX Control

When embedding Terminal Server applications directly into web pages, a Microsoft ActiveX control replaces the full desktop RDC client. This ActiveX control is called the "Remote Desktop Connection Web Connection," or simply "RDW." (The RDW client replaces the "Terminal Server Advanced Client" that you may remember from a few years ago.)

The RDW ActiveX control provides virtually the same functionality as the full Remote Desktop Connection client, but is obviously designed to be used in a web browser for connections over the Web. When embedded in a Web page, the client connects to a Terminal Server session, even if the full Remote Desktop Connection client is not installed on the user's computer.

You can install this client on any Windows 2003 IIS Server. (Add/Remote Programs | Add/Remote Windows Components | Application Server | Internet Information Services | World Wide Web Service | Remote Desktop Web Connection) You can also download it for free from Microsoft.com.

When you install the RDW ActiveX control on an IIS server, a minimal set of sample web pages are also installed. These pages include default and connection pages that work together to create a terminal server web connection.

How the Remote Desktop Web Connection Client Works

Now that you understand the components that make up an RDW environment, let's look at how they all work together to deliver embedded applications to your end users.

Figure 11.1 shows the various RDW components and the processes that take place in the environment. Read through the steps while referring to the diagram.

Figure 11.1 How the remote desktop web connection client works

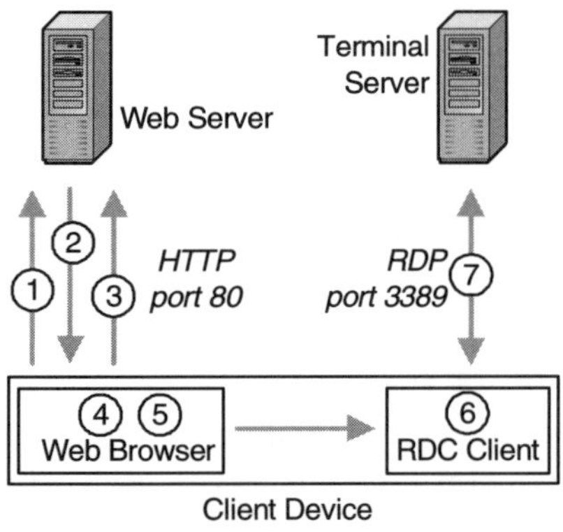

1. A user with a web browser requests the web page by typing in a URL.

2. The web server sends down the HTML login page via the HTTP protocol.
3. The web server checks to see if the user has the full RDC or the ActiveX control RDW client installed.
4. If not, or if the version installed is older than the version in the CAB file, the ActiveX control is downloaded, decompressed, and installed.
5. The web page is displayed in the client's browser.
6. The user enters a server or connection name and screen resolution and clicks "connect."
7. The ActiveX control running on the client workstation passes the startup parameters to the Terminal Server, and a session is launched.

In this case, the RDP session is running on the client device via the ActiveX control (which is also running on the client device). Once the session is running, the web server is no longer required. Even though it's in a browser, the RDW client is connected directly to the Terminal Server.

The RDW Installation Process

Installing the RDW is easy. Run the tswebsetup.exe package that you downloaded. This "installation" process is nothing more than an "unzipping" process that unzips some files into a folder of your choosing. Most people choose to unzip these files into a folder called "*TSWEB*" underneath their "*wwwroot*" folder.

There are only a few files contained in the zip. The main one is *msrdp.cab*. This cabinet file is only 304kb in size. It contains the actual ActiveX control (*msrdp.ocx*) and an INF file (*msrdp.inf*) that helps get the ActiveX control installed on client workstations. In addition to the CAB file, the main zip file also contains a sample web page (default.htm) and some supporting graphics. (To see what it looks like, just browse over to `www.brianmadden.com/tsweb`.)

Customizing the Default RDW Web Page

This default page leaves something to be desired. It's not at all configured for your Terminal Servers. At this point a user could technically use the web client, but he would be required to type in the name of the server or cluster he wishes to connect to.

When using the embedded RDW client, most people choose to customize the web page to make it simpler for the end user. Let's look at some different ways to customize the ActiveX client pages:

- Preconfiguring a server name.
- Selecting client features to be used.
- Embedding the RDW client into your own web pages.

Preconfiguring the Server Name and Resolution

Instead of keeping the default page and training users to type in a server name, you can preconfigure the web page so that the connection name (or names) are already in the HTML. This alleviates helpdesk calls when users can't remember the name of their connection. You can also change the list of available screen resolutions or even force all users to use a single resolution (useful if you want to force all users to connect in full screen mode).

To do this, edit the default.htm page with any HTML editor, although notepad is adequate for the simple edits you'll be doing here. When you open *default.htm* in your editor, search for the following section:

```
<!-- Column 3 -->
    <td id="ServerNameKeyWidth" style="width:10%;"
valign="middle">
        <label id=ServerNameKey accessKey="S"
for="editServer">
        <br><p align="right"> <ID
id=ServerName><u>S</u>erver:</ID></label></p>
        </td>

<!-- Column 4 -->
      <td id="ServerKeyWidth" width="40%"
valign="bottom">
      <br>  <input type="text" name="Server"
size="41" id="editServer">
      </td>
      </tr>

<!-- Row 2 -->
<tr>

<!-- Column 3 -->
<td valign="middle">
<p align="right"><label id=sizeKey accessKey="Z"
for="comboRes" class="sizespace"><ID
id=size>Si<u>z</u>e:</ID></p></td>
```

```
<!-- Column 4 -->
<td valign="bottom">  <select size="1"
name="comboResolution" id=comboRes class="topspace">
<option selected value="1"><ID id=option1>Full-
screen</ID></option>
<option value="2"><ID id=option2>640 by
480</ID></option>
<option value="3"><ID id=option3>800 by
600</ID></option>
<option value="4"><ID id=option4>1024 by
768</ID></option>
<option value="5"><ID id=option5>1280 by
1024</ID></option>
<option value="6"><ID id=option6>1600 by
1200</ID></option>
            </select> </label>
```

The code in the first section labeled "Column 3" creates the text field where users enter their server names. This field can easily be changed into a dropdown list with multiple entries for various servers, much like the resolution selection in the section labeled Row 2 Column 4. (A sample of a server dropdown list is available at `www.brianmadden.com/tsweb/serverlist`. Feel free to visit that page and "view source" to steal the code and do it yourself.)

Notice all the "option value" entries towards the end of this section of HTML code. These entries represent the options that the user may select which choosing the resolution. If you don't want any of the resolutions, then simply delete the option. Or, if you want to force all users to use the same resolution (by removing the resolution dropdown box altogether), visit `www.brianmadden.com/tsweb/resolution` and steal the code yourself.

Selecting Client Features to be Used

In addition to customizing the options that are visible to users via the web page, you can also edit the default.htm file to specify which advanced client functions are used. You can enable or disable client drive mapping, printer mapping, port redirection, and smart card redirection all by editing some simple HTML.

Simply open default.htm in your text editor and search for the following lines of code. Then, adjust the TRUE or FALSE settings accordingly, and you're all set.

```
MsRdpClient.AdvancedSettings2.RedirectDrives      =
FALSE
MsRdpClient.AdvancedSettings2.RedirectPrinters    =
TRUE
```

```
MsRdpClient.AdvancedSettings2.RedirectPorts       =
FALSE
MsRdpClient.AdvancedSettings2.RedirectSmartCards =
FALSE
```

Embedding the RDW Client into any Web Page

Rather than using the sample default.htm web page, you can instead embed the RDW ActiveX control in any page you want. This is no different from embedding an ActiveX control in any web page (which is easy for developers).

Just insert the following *<OBJECT>* into the *<HTML>* section of your web page.

```
<OBJECT ID="MsRdpClient"
    CLASSID="CLSID:9059f30f-4eb1-4bd2-9fdc-
36f43a218f4a"
    CODEBASE="msrdp.cab#version=5,1,2524,0"
    WIDTH=800
    HEIGHT=600
</OBJECT>
```

This sample code sets the embedded session to run at 800x600 resolution. There are additional parameters that you can pass to the *msrdp.ocx* ActiveX control. The easiest way to get a full list is to open the OCX with a utility from Visual Studio such as OLEview.

Launching Applications from Web Pages

Even though launching Terminal Server connections that are embedded into a web page is easy to do, there are some technical limitations. The default web page is limited to desktop connections, and this can be a problem if you've decided to have users launch individual applications instead of full desktops.

Instead of using the embedded ActiveX control, you can build custom web pages that have links to individual applications. You'll remember from Chapters 5 and 10 that it's possible to create an "RDP" file containing Terminal Server application connection settings. You can then deploy this RDP file to your users.

Take this process one step further in order to launch an application from a web page by placing links to RDP files within your web pages. By combining a little bit of HTML, an RDC client, and some preconfigured RDP files, you can create a portal-friendly HTML list of Terminal Server applications for a centralized location from which users can access Terminal Server applications. One URL can host links to applications for the entire environment, regardless of where your Terminal Servers are located.

Application Page Web Components

Similar to using embedded ActiveX RDW client, there are three key components to consider when designing web pages that launch RDP applications:

- Web Server.
- Client Device.
- RDP Files.
- Terminal Servers.

Web server

The web server serves the HTML pages to the end user. In this case, the web server can be just about any platform.

Client Device

To be able to launch RDP Terminal Server sessions this way, the client device must have the full RDC client installed locally. In theory, any platform can be used, so long as the client's operating system is capable of receiving RDP files and automatically passing them on to the RDC client software.

RDP Files

RDP files stored on the web server contain all the connection information for a particular application. They're passed down to the client device when requested. From there, the client's browser passes them on to the locally installed RDC software to launch the RDP session.

Terminal Server

As in all web-based scenarios, the Terminal Server in this case is essentially a bystander. It's not involved in the web server or application launch process, rather, it only receives the users' RDP sessions once they receive the RDP files from the web server.

How it Works

Getting this all to work is more complicated than when working with the embedded ActiveX RDW client. However, the extra configuration time on the front end makes the whole experience easier for your users.

Figure 11.2 The process of launching RDP applications from a web page

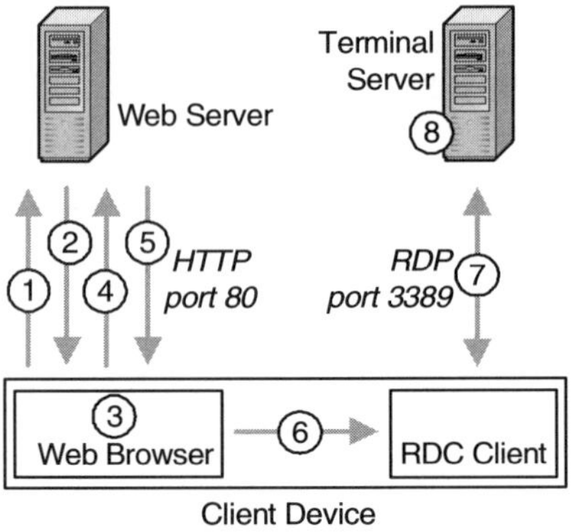

1. The user enters a URL into their browser
2. The web server sends down an HTML with a list of applications available in the Terminal Server farm. Each application is linked to an RDP file.
3. The user clicks an application icon or link.
4. The web browser requests the file from the web server.
5. The RDP file that is stored on the web server is downloaded to the user's client device.
6. The user's client device has a file association for the RDP file type that launches the RDC client and receives the RDP file.
7. The RDC client establishes a session to the application or server based on the preconfigured settings in the RDP file.
8. The user authenticates to the server and the application or desktop session is launched.

At first glance, this process may seem complicated. However, if you take a logical look at it, you'll see that it is probably something you do every day by clicking on web links to PDF files. If you click a link within a web page to open a PDF file, the PDF is sent to your machine and opened using your Adobe Acrobat reader. The same happens here, except instead of a PDF and Adobe Acrobat, you have an RDP file and the RDC client.

Configuring the Web Server

The only configuration change that you'll need to make to your web server will be to register RDP as a MIME type. We'll review this process for IIS, but it will need to be done to your web server regardless of its type.

By default, IIS servers only host and serve files to users that are of a registered MIME type on the server. Since an RDP file is unknown to the IIS server, it must be registered or it won't be served to clients. In IIS 6.0 running on a Windows 2003 server, do this by the following procedure:

Using Internet Service Manager on the web server, locate the website you wish to configure for use with the RDP client. (This may be the default website if you're using a test server.)

1. Right-click on the web site and select properties.
2. Select the "HTTP Headers" tab.
3. Click the "MIME Types" button at the bottom of the page.
4. Click the "New" button on the right.
5. In the new MIME type window, enter ".RDP" as the Extension (without quotes) and "`application/x-rdp`" as the MIME type (without quotes).
6. Click "OK" on each of the three open windows until you are returned to the main Internet Services Manager window.

If you're using another type of web server, the main difference is that ".RDP" is the file extension and "application/x-rdp" is the MIME type.

Configuring the Web Page

The basic web page you need to make consists of a few hyperlinks to RDP files. This page is so simple that it can be made in FrontPage or notepad in a just a few minutes. "Jazzing up" the web page should not be a problem for even a novice with no web programming skills.

The webpage is generally made after the RDP files are created, but for the purposes of continuity we'll step though this first assuming that you learned something about RDP files in the client chapters of this book.

The sample code below was created in Microsoft FrontPage and is a functional RDP Application list:

```
<html>

<head>
<meta name="GENERATOR" content="Microsoft FrontPage
5.0">
<meta name="ProgId" con-
tent="FrontPage.Editor.Document">
<meta http-equiv="Content-Type" content="text/html;
charset=windows-1252">
<title>New Page 1</title>
</head>

<body>

<p>This is a sample RDP app portal….</p>
<p><a href="excel.rdp">MS Excel 2000</a></p>
<p><a href="winword.rdp">MS Word 2000</a></p>
<p><a href="outlook.rdp">MS Outlook 2000</a></p>

</body>
</html>
```

As you can see, the HTML links to three RDP files. Since the web server is now configured to host RDP files, all that's required to "deploy" this solution is to copy the RDP files and this HTML file to the web server. A screenshot of the web page this code produces is on the next page.

If you're the creative type, the web pages can be reconfigured into any format with any look and feel (also shown on the next page).

Figure 11.3 A quick application launching webpage made with FrontPage

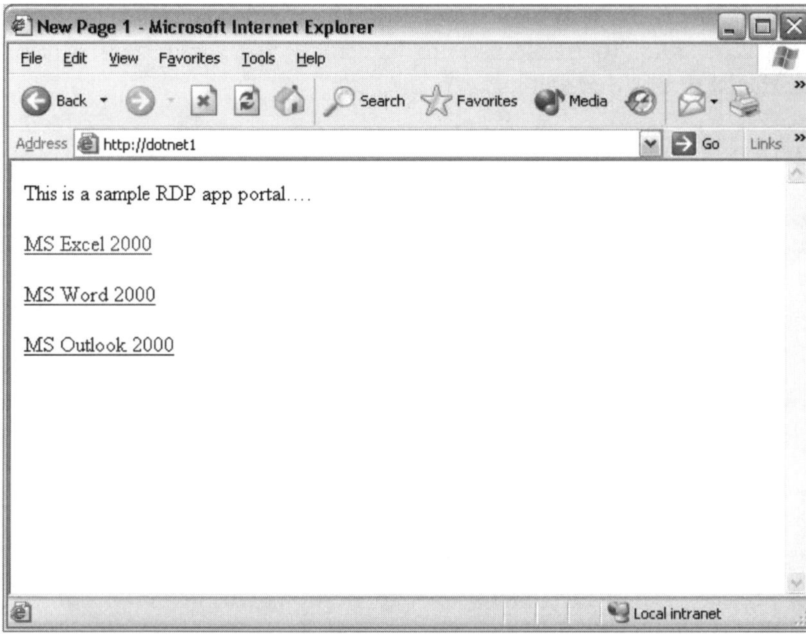

Figure 11.4 A more sophisticated looking webpage based on the same basic code

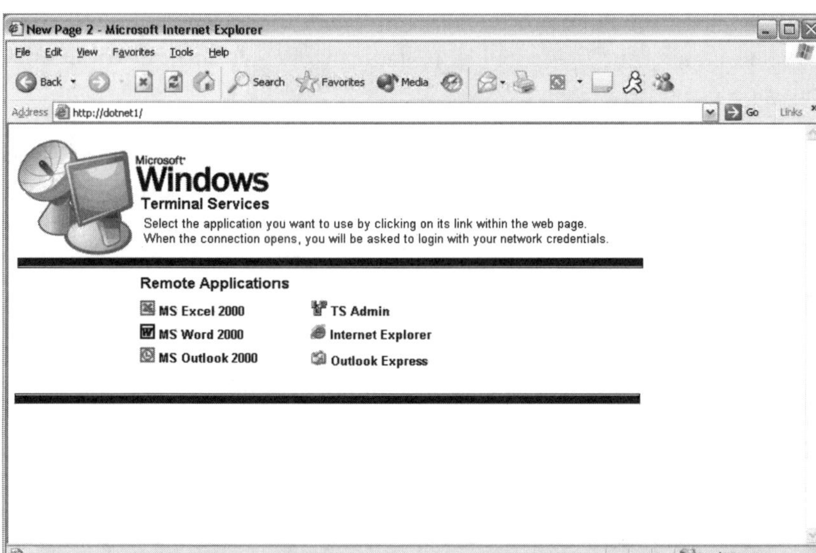

Configuring the RDP Files

At its basic level, the web page is nothing more than a mechanism providing links to RDP files. To enable users to launch specific applications, you must create the RDP files that will make up the list.

As you'll recall from Chapter 10, an RDP file is essentially a text file that's created when you save a connection configuration within the RDC client. All of the configuration settings within the client are stored within the RDP for use at a later time. Options stored in an RDP file include:

- Address to connect to (IP address, cluster name, or server name).
- Video resolution.
- Color depth.
- Client device configuration.
- Application to execute in the session.
- Experience settings.

You'll need to create RDP files for each application. This process is outlined at the end of Chapter 10.

Configuring the Client

The RDP client on the user's workstation shouldn't require any configuration other than making sure it's installed. (Chapter 10 details client distribution and installation options.)

In order for users to launch applications from web pages, they'll need to have the full client installed. The RDW ActiveX control will not suffice because the ActiveX control does not have the file type association support that the full RDC client does and cannot run outside of a browser window as can the full RDC client.

Most people add an "Install Client Now" link to their web pages that leads to an MSI package to install the client on the user's workstation.

All that's left to address on the client device is that the first time the user clicks an RDP web link, a "Save or Open" dialog box will appear asking the user what he wants to do. The user can click "Open" and "Do not prompt again for this file type," but that might be confusing for them.

Get around this by editing the registry of the client device. Most people make the registry modification at the same time that they install the RDC client. (For Windows XP workstations that have the RDC client preinstalled, you'll need to modify the registry via a logon script or SMS package.)

Can create a .REG registry merge file from the following text (or visit `www.brianmadden.com` to download this file):

```
REGEDIT4
; removes the prompt to download the RDP file.


[HKEY_LOCAL_MACHINE\SOFTWARE\Classes\Applications\msts
c.exe\shell\Connect\command]
@="mstsc.exe \"%1\""

[HKEY_LOCAL_MACHINE\SOFTWARE\Classes\Applications\msts
c.exe\shell\Connect]
"MUIVerb"="@C:\\WINDOWS\\system32\\mstsc.exe,-4002"

[HKEY_LOCAL_MACHINE\SOFTWARE\Classes\Applications\msts
c.exe\shell\Connect]
@="Connect"

[HKEY_LOCAL_MACHINE\SOFTWARE\Classes\Applications\msts
c.exe\shell\Edit\command]
@="mstsc.exe -edit \"%1\""

[HKEY_LOCAL_MACHINE\SOFTWARE\Classes\Applications\msts
c.exe\shell\Edit]
"MUIVerb"="@C:\\WINDOWS\\system32\\mstsc.exe,-4003"

[HKEY_LOCAL_MACHINE\SOFTWARE\Classes\Applications\msts
c.exe\shell\Edit]
@="Edit"

[HKEY_LOCAL_MACHINE\SOFTWARE\Classes\Applications\msts
c.exe\shell]
@="Connect"
  [HKEY_LOCAL_MACHINE\SOFTWARE\Classes\RDP.File]
"EditFlags"=hex:00,00,01,00

[HKEY_CURRENT_USER\Software\Microsoft\Windows\CurrentV
ersion\Explorer\FileExts\.rdp\OpenWithList]
"a"="mstsc.exe"

[HKEY_CURRENT_USER\Software\Microsoft\Windows\CurrentV
ersion\Explorer\FileExts\.rdp\OpenWithList]
"b"="IEXPLORE.EXE"
```

```
[HKEY_CURRENT_USER\Software\Microsoft\Windows\CurrentV
ersion\Explorer\FileExts\.rdp\OpenWithList]
"MRUList"="ab"

[HKEY_CURRENT_USER\Software\Microsoft\Windows\CurrentV
ersion\Explorer\FileExts\.rdp\OpenWithProgids]
"RDP.File"=hex:

[HKEY_CURRENT_USER\Software\Microsoft\Windows\ShellNoR
oam\MUICache]
"C:\\WINDOWS\\system32\\mstsc.exe"="Remote Desktop
Connection"
```

Once you complete all these steps, you'll have a custom application list that you can plug into any portal or simply use on its own for deploying Terminal Server applications to your end users.

Building Dynamic Application Lists

People who are familiar with third-party Terminal Server products point out a major drawback to the web techniques outlined in this chapter. Specifically, both of these techniques lack the ability to automatically create custom application lists for each user.

For example, wouldn't it be great if your users could log in to a website and then get a custom list of applications that was created just for them based on their group memberships? Actually, there are three ways to achieve that:

- Use a third-party product.
- Write a custom ASP page.
- Use Windows SharePoint Services.

The first involves the use of third-party products. These products are fully discussed and reviewed in the Appendix of this book, but Citrix MetaFrame, Tarantella New Moon Canaveral iQ, and Jetro CockpIT all have web portal capabilities that can do just this.

Second, some developers have taken the time to build ASP pages that automatically show or hide links to RDP files based on a user's group membership. Such an ASP page is simple to program for even a beginning ASP programmer.

The final method, and by far the most popular for pure Terminal Server environments, is to use Windows SharePoint Services, or "WSS." WSS is available for free with Windows Server 2003, and is the newest version of Microsoft's

SharePoint technologies that were first available with SharePoint Team Services and SharePoint Portal Server 2001.

WSS is a content and document management system allowing administrators to "publish" content for various audiences based on various group memberships. Using WSS, you can publish RDP files as content, and target them for specific groups. For example, you can create a domain group called "Word Users" and then publish an RDP file that launches MS Word to that domain group. Upon logging in to the portal web page, users in the Word Users group would see the RDP file, and users who weren't in the group wouldn't.

More information about using Windows SharePoint Services to create dynamic web application portals for Terminal Server environments is available at `www.brianmadden.com`.

CHAPTER 12

Security

A major part of any computing environment is security. We've not dwelled much on security in the preceding chapters due to the fact that when you focus on the security of your Terminal Server environment, you must do it from end-to-end. You can't just "do a little security here, and a little there." There would be no benefit to talking about security of profiles in the user profile chapter because even if you did everything profile–related to tighten security you might have overlooked a major security hole somewhere else.

To prevent this, we'll analyze the security elements of a complete Terminal Server system in this chapter. We will systematically analyze every Terminal Server component, taking note of what the potential security risks are and what to do to minimize each of them.

Let's begin by reviewing the components that make up a Terminal Server system. We can represent the individual components as layers in the complete Terminal Server system, as shown in Figure 12.1. (These layers like the OSI model applied to a Terminal Server.)

Figure 12.1 Terminal Server layers

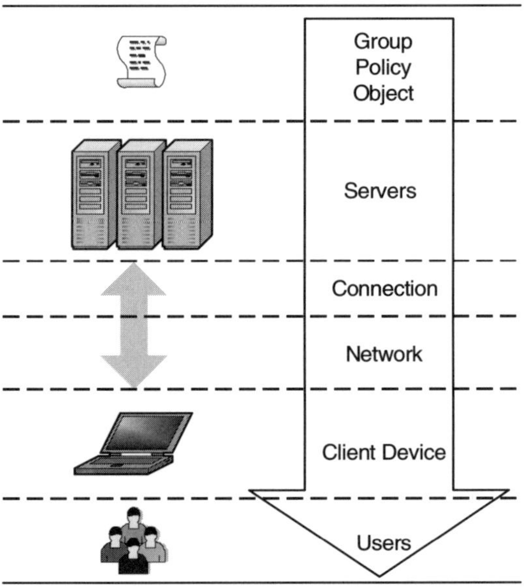

This chapter focuses primarily on the security of the Terminal Server components. It is not meant to be an end-to-end security manual. Your Terminal Server environment is only as secure as its weakest component, and often human elements are involved for which no technical manual can prepare you.

Security Configuration Layers

Let's take another look at the different layers in which many of the security-related settings can be made. For example, client drive remapping can be enabled or disabled as part of a user's AD account properties, via a GPO, as a setting on the RDP client, or as a property of a server's connection listener port. Beyond that, applications launched via an RDP file can also have the printer mappings configured within the RDP file itself.

Figure 12.2 The drive mapping security parameter configured at multiple layers

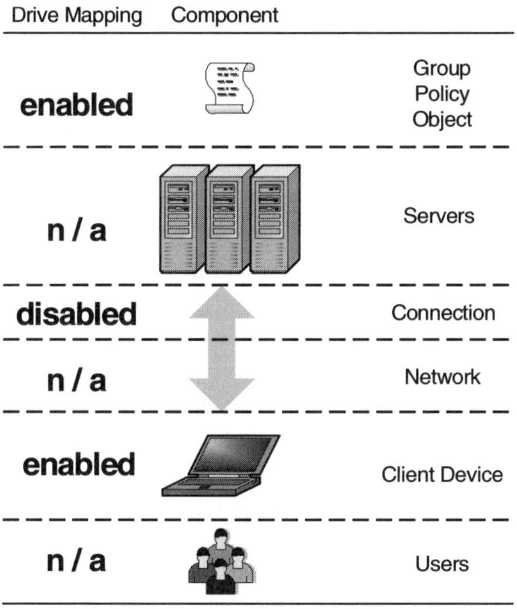

When a single parameter is configured in multiple locations with conflicting settings, the most restrictive configuration will always take precedence (unless a GPO is involved, in which case the rules change. See Chapter 6.) Referring to Figure 12.2, if the client device and the GPO were configured to allow drive mapping, but the server connection was set to prohibit it, no session connecting via that connection would be able to access client drives. Although the client is configured differently, users must still traverse the connection configured for the absence of drive mapping. In this example, we can say that the "client layer" was set to allow drive mapping, and the "connection layer" was configured to deny it.

Figure 12.3 shows all of the possible layers where a security parameter can be configured. Not every security parameter can be configured at every layer. It's important to look at the Terminal Server settings and determine the proper layer at which the security parameter should be applied. Do all users require drive mapping or only users connecting to certain servers? Might users only connecting to a server via a specific IP addresses need drive mapping?

Figure 12.3 Various configuration scope layers

Level	Scope.
GPO	All users logging into servers where the policy is applied.
Server	All users connecting to one server.
Connection	All users attaching via one defined server connection. Multiple connections can exist on one server.
Client	All users connecting from one RDP client device, regardless of the user rights or the server or farm hosting the RDP session.
User Account	User profile settings. These settings follow the user, regardless of the server or connection used.
RDP File	Settings affect anyone using the RDP file, regardless of settings in other locations.

Throughout this chapter we'll look at dozens more security settings configurable at all layers. Beyond that, the appendix of this book contains a "Terminal Server 2003 Component Configuration" chart detailing every setting within the Terminal Server environment and listing the layer at which it can be configured.

The rest of this chapter is divided into sections that each focus on a different security configuration layer, including:

- Server security
- Application security
- Connection security
- Network security
- User Account Security

Server Security

To adequately analyze server security in Terminal Server environments we must divide the servers into their multiple roles and look at the security of each role separately. We'll examine each of the following Terminal Service environmental roles:

- Terminal Server application hosts.
- Terminal Service licensing servers

Terminal Server Application Server Security

Since the actual user sessions are executed on the Terminal Servers, they figure greater into a discussion of security. The basic actions to consider when securing your Terminal Servers are:

- Using the NTFS file system.
- Configuring NTFS file permissions.
- Using GPOs to secure the user environment.
- Installing Terminal Services on a domain controller.
- Disabling the "Secondary Logon" Service.
- Remove unnecessary software
- Applying hotfixes and service packs.

Use the NTFS File System

Each user that runs a session on a Terminal Server is essentially running a remote control console session. Without an NTFS file system, you won't be able to set any file–level security permissions. Any user that is logged would be able to access files in use by other users. No mechanism would prevent users from deleting key system files, potentially crashing the server!

There is no reason not to use NTFS on your servers. Every user will be able to access NTFS files via an RDP session, even if his client is running on an operating system that cannot support NTFS, such as Windows 95.

Configure NTFS File Permissions

Using just the NTFS file system might not provide enough security with its default permissions in your environment. Even if you do not intend to fully lock-down your Terminal Servers or plan to run only initial applications, you should secure the basic file system.

When you install Terminal Services on a Windows 2003 server, you're asked whether you want to use "Full Security" or "Relaxed Security." (These options were known as "Windows 2000 Security" or "Permissions Compatible with NT 4.0" on Windows 2000 Terminal Servers.) This security setting has nothing to do with your domain configuration or your Active Directory environment. It affects only the level of security that users are given when they access your server via a Terminal Services session. To compare the two settings:

- *Full Security*. This setting results in Terminal Services users having the same permissions as regular members of the local users group. Regular users are not able to write to inappropriate registry keys or tamper with sensitive system files. Of course, with this level of security comes additional risk. In this case, users will sometimes not be able to run legacy applications. If you choose Full Security, you should thoroughly test your applications before enabling them for any users.
- *Relaxed Security*. This setting results in Terminal Services users having full access to many parts of the registry and many of the system files. This alternate level of security was developed to allow older applications to execute properly.

After selecting the "permissions compatibility" mode during the installation of Terminal Services you can change it at any time via the Terminal Services Configuration MMC snap-in (Administrative Tools | Terminal Services Configuration | Server Settings | Permissions Compatibility). Setting this compatibility affects the following registry key:

Key: HKLM\System\CurrentControlSet\Control\Terminal Server\

Value: TSUserEnabled

Type: REG_DWORD

Data: 1 = Relaxed permissions. 0 = Full Security mode.

Do Not Install Terminal Services on a Domain Controller

Individual domain controllers cannot be managed separately from each other. In order for a user to be able to log on to Terminal Server sessions she must have "log on locally" (called "log on interactively" in Windows 2000) rights. If the Terminal Server is a domain controller, granting the user "log on locally" rights on the server will allow her to log on to any domain controller, even ones that are not Terminal Servers.

Also, domain controllers in Active Directory environments must be located in the "Domain Controllers" OU. You can't use OU-based Group Policy Objects if your Terminal Servers are installed on domain controllers.

Lastly, several security holes are associated with the operation of the Local System Account on domain controllers. In order to have a secure environment, never let log on to a domain controller. Installing Terminal Services on a domain controller makes it difficult to follow this recommendation.

Disable the "Secondary Logon" Service

Windows 2000 introduced a secondary logon ability (then called the "Run As" service) which allows users to run programs with different user rights. Within Windows Explorer, a user can shift-right-click on a file and select "Run as..." from the context menu. Alternately, a user can enter the "runas" command into the command line.

Administrators often lock down Terminal Servers for those groups of users that should be using them. The secondary logon ability allows a user who's already connected to a Terminal Server to change his credentials, potentially bypassing any security measures the administrator has configured. (If you read the rest of this chapter, you'll know better than to build servers that exhibit this weakness.)

The secondary logon ability can be disabled at the server by stopping and disabling the "Secondary Logon" service. Disable the service after you stop it, or the system will start it again when it is needed.

Remove all Non-Essential Software

Any extra applications installed on your Terminal Servers represent an increased security risk. Each installed application brings introduces more vulnerabilities. Access to extra tools, (such as those included in the resource kits) makes compromising or abusing the server easier. You shouldn't give your users more than they need to do their job.

Apply Service Packs and Hotfixes

As in any computer environment, maintaining security requires that you frequently check for new hotfixes that address security issues, even if you already keep your servers up to date with the latest service packs.

Check for new hotfixes from Microsoft and from any other third party vendor (like Citrix or New Moon) at least once a week. Because history has shown that neither Microsoft nor these other vendors have a perfect track record for creating bug-free hotfixes, you should also check with an online discussion group (see www.brianmadden.com for details) to see if there are any issues surrounding newly released hotfixes.

To help maintain your hotfix environment, Microsoft has released at security hotfix checker utility (detailed in Microsoft Knowledge Base article 303215). This utility allows you to quickly and easily check the status of hotfixes on multiple servers.

Application Security

Next consider the applications that users run, how they access them, and what they can do with them. To begin, let's review how applications are launched by users. There are two ways that users can launch applications on a Terminal Server:

- By connecting to an "Initial Program" (or "Initial Application").
- By running the Windows desktop and launching applications from within established sessions.

When looking at application security, we must first examine the security of launching applications. Complete details of the ways by which users launch applications were covered in Chapter 9.

Securing your Servers when only "Initial Programs" are Used

Many people choose to use Terminal Servers for specific applications. They specify an "initial application" to be launched when the user connects. A quick check of the big feature chart in the appendix shows that you can actually configure an initial application as a property of a user account, GPO, connection listener, client device, or via an RDP file.

If you have a Terminal Server that hosts only a single application, then it's easy to configure the "initial application" as part of a GPO and apply permissions so that users logging in to that server always get that initial application. If you want to host multiple applications on a single server, but also want to use the "initial application" functionality (since it hides the remote task bar, etc), then you either have to use third party server-based computing software (as detailed in the Appendix) or have your users connect via RDP files.

Security Aspects of Launching Programs with RDP Files

In previous chapters we discussed connecting users to applications using RDP files. These files are preconfigured and usually stored centrally on a web server or network share point for users to launch applications. What we did not discuss was the security of these files.

These files contain the connection information for the RDP client to connect to a server or server cluster and launch an application. Beyond securing the server, the files should be secured so that users who have no need of these applications can not access the RDP file in the first place.

If the files are stored on a network share point they can be secured using normal NTFS and share permissions. Maintain them on a central share and only distribute shortcuts (.lnk files) to the users.

Security on these files should be configured in such a way that users needing access to the application have read and execute permissions and users who do not require these applications have no security configured on the files. Configuring security this way provides two benefits:

1. Users that require access can launch and use the files but will not be able to modify them.
2. Users that do not need access will not have the ability to launch the RDP file or open it up to look at its configuration.

In a web server scenario, these files can be secured much the same way. When placed in a public directory on an IIS web server, they are open to the world via the *IUSR_%computername%* account. Secure either the entire directory using NTFS permissions and domain groups (if the web server is in the domain) or create a login page with a web login (non-domain) that will not let the user access the icons without authenticating. (See Chapter 11 for more information about using web servers to access Terminal Server applications.)

Securing the Server when "Initial Programs" are Used

Many administrators make the mistake of assuming that once the RDP files are configured and security on them is set properly, there is nothing more to worry about. They forget that although only RDP files are available, any user can create a new Remote Desktop connection within his RDP client software. Using this new connection, he would be able to log on to a full Windows desktop. Even if you use web server to host your RDP files, anyone can download and install the full RDP client from the Internet and create a connection to one of your Terminal Servers.

If this happens, it usually results from the administrator not anticipating that the users would ever connect to the desktop. The administrator probably did not make any effort to lock down or secure the desktop and the user would have free access to inappropriate applications, data, or configuration settings.

While it is hard to prevent situation without some third party software (like Citrix or New Moon), you can secure your Terminal Server desktop in such a way that connecting to it would be useless. When using RDP files for your connections, you may want to create a GPO that completely removes every application and link from your Terminal Server's desktop. That way, if an adventurous user does get a connection he will only see an empty screen with a logoff button. (See Chapter 6 for details on configuring User GPOs).

Windows Desktop Application Security

Instead of worrying that users might "accidentally" find their way to the Windows desktop, you might instead decide to let users connect to the remote desktop and run several applications. If this is your plan, you'll need to ensure that the user environment is protected and secured so users can't do things they're not supposed to do. There are three strategies by which to secure your Windows desktops:

- Apply appropriate policies or profiles.
- Configure NTFS security.
- Prevent users from installing applications.

Applying Policies and Profiles

The Windows desktop shell can be "locked down" so that users are limited by their rights and the actions that they are able to perform. In the last section, we talked about desktop so totally locked down as would be completely useless to a user. However, you can also lock down a desktop so that it looks and feels like a standard desktop but has some of the more "dangerous" capabilities removed. For example, you might choose to remove the "Shutdown" or "Run" commands from the Start menu. The easiest way to do this is with policies as described in Chapter 6.

Advantages of Enforcing Application Security with System Policies

- Can be easily applied across multiple servers.

Disadvantages of Enforcing Application Security with System Policies

- Policies only watch over the Windows shell. If you restrict certain areas or applications, users can get around that restriction by launching applications via the command prompt.

Setting NTFS Security

Another way to restrict the applications that a user can access is to configure the NTFS security on the application executables themselves. The nice thing about setting NTFS-level security is that once set, there is no way around it. No matter how the user accesses the server, the application won't run if the user doesn't have NTFS rights to the application.

Additionally, in Windows Server 2003 environments you can manage NTFS file permissions with a GPO, just as if you were right clicking on the directory and setting the permissions manually. To do this, browse to the following location in a GPO: Computer Configuration | Windows Settings | Security Settings | File System (You'll must be in a real GPO to see this option, you can't just manually fire up *gpedit.msc* by itself.).

When you get to this section of the GPO, right-click on the File System object, then on "New File." Browse to the folder or file or create a new one. Once the folder has been selected, set the proper NTFS permissions on it, configure it to replace the existing permissions and propagate the permissions to the subfolders and files.

This feature makes life extremely easy when it comes to NTFS permissions since you can configure security across your entire Terminal Server environment without logging in to each server or changing the permissions via script.

Advantages of Limiting Application Execution with NTFS Security

- NTFS permissions that prevent users from accessing certain files or applications are absolute—there is no way for a user to get around them.
- Very granular control of who can and cannot access applications.

Disadvantages of Limiting Application Execution with NTFS Security

- NTFS permissions do not prevent users from running applications from other, non-local locations. Even if you restrict access to a local copy of Word, a user might find *winword.exe* on a network share and be able to execute it from there.

Preventing Users from Installing Applications

If users run remote Windows desktops on your Terminal Servers, you don't want them to be able to install any software applications. Remove the users' "write" permissions from the software installation registry key. Use *regedt32.exe* to browse to the following registry location:

```
HKLM\Software\Microsoft\WindowsNT\CurrentVersion\Terminal
Server\Install\Software
```

From the Security menu, choose "Permissions." From there you can configure your users with read-only permissions. Be sure that you propagate these permissions to the subkeys below the key where they are applied.

Applying a Software Restriction Policy

A new feature of Windows 2003 (well, technically it was introduced in Windows XP) is software restriction policies. While we previously discussed how to use GPOs to restrict which users can run which executables, you can apply software restriction policies to your Terminal Servers to enforce a broad, rule-based control of the types of applications that users can run.

For example, you can use software restriction policies to specify what types of executables can run, or to only allow signed executables to be launched. Software restriction policies are applied to servers as part of a GPO (Computer Configuration | Windows Settings | Security Settings | Software Restriction Policies).

Creating a Security Template for your Servers

One useful security tool that is often overlooked is the native ability of secedit.exe to create a security template for use on other servers. This tool (which is included by default on Windows 2003 servers) gives you the ability to create a "perfect server" and then copy its security settings to other servers. These security settings encompass several areas, including:

- Registry Permissions
- File System permissions
- Account policies
- Audit Policies
- Restricted group settings
- User Rights Assignments
- Service Settings

To use this tool, create a perfect server, configure its local policies and permissions exactly the way you want them, and then run secedit with a command line switch to export the settings. Here is an example of this command:

```
SECEDIT /EXPORT /cfg lockdown.inf
```

Secedit has many options. By default, *secedit* will read the security info from the local system security database. If you wish to export security settings from another database you can specify the */db* switch and the location of the database. Or, if you only wish to export the registry permissions and not the NTFS permissions, *Secedit* allows you to use the */AREAS* switch and specify the security from specific areas of the system. The areas you can specify are listed in the table below:

Figure 12.4 Secedit configuration options

Area	Description
SecurityPolicy	Copies account policies, security policies, and event log settings
Group_Mgmt	Copies the restricted group settings
User_Rights	Copies the local User rights assignments
Regkeys	Copies local registry permissions
Filestore	Copies File System permissions
Services	Copies System service settings

These settings can then be imported to another server using the /import switch and specifying which database to import to and which CFG file to import from. Unlike the */export* switch, the */import* does not assume the local security database. You must specify it. To import to the local security database, you would specify *%Systemroot%\Security\Database\secedit.sdb.*

Connection Security

Remember from Chapter 2 that "connections" in the Terminal Server environment refer to the groups of settings that apply to a specific Session Protocol / Network Protocol / Network Interface combination in the form of a connection listener port. There are multiple options configured at this "connection layer." Many of them directly impact the overall security of the system. Additionally, there are many neat tricks you can do to provide different levels of security to different interfaces.

Connection Properties

When configuring the properties of a connection listener port (Terminal Server Configuration Utility | Right-click on connection | Edit | Advanced Button), it's important to remember that those properties will affect all users that connect to the Terminal server via that connection unless you check the box for each item that allows the server to use the settings in each user's profile.

Let's examine each of the following connection layer security settings:

- Session timeouts
- Working with broken connections
- Client reconnection options
- Auto session logon
- Limiting the number of sessions per connection
- Disabling logons
- Encryption
- Using default Windows authentication
- Initial programs to be executed
- Remote Control
- The RDP TCP port

Session Timeouts

You can configure three different timeout periods for each connection: connection timeout, disconnection timeout, and idle timeout. Each of these choices allows you to specify the timeout in minutes. A checkbox allows the timeout settings of the connection to default to those specified in the user's account settings as opposed to by the connection itself. This allows for different settings on a user-by-user basis. Selecting "no timeout" disables that specific session timer for that connection.

The "End a disconnected session" limit causes the server to reset a disconnected session after the specified time has passed. The current user will lose any work that was in progress. The disconnection timer is a good way clean up any disconnected sessions that users have forgotten about. Many companies set this to approximately 2880 minutes (48 hours). If they have some situations requiring less time, they configure those in the user profile.

The "Active session limit" lets you specify the maximum time that an RDP session can stay connected. After this time passes, the server either disconnects or terminates the session. (The decision to terminate or disconnect the session is determined by "when session limit is reached" option further down on the screen.)

The "Idle session limit" specifies the amount of time that a live connection can stay in an idle state (no activity) before the server automatically disconnects or ends the session. From a security standpoint, the idle timeout works well as an "automatic lock-down." Many companies set their idle timeouts relatively low so that if a user leaves his desk with an active RDP session open, the server will disconnect the session after a few minutes. Then, when the user returns to his desk, he can conveniently reconnect to his disconnected session without losing any work. Like the active session limit, you can specify the action taken when the idle session limit is reached—the session is either ended or disconnected.

Extreme care must be taken when working with connection timeouts. Almost all environments that utilize connection timeouts configure them as a property of the user account (at the "user layer"), instead of configuring them here as a property of a connection. The one exception is the disconnection timeout, which is used to clean up any old sessions.

Working with Broken Connections

The term "Broken Connection" specifies what happens when an RDP client stops responding to the Terminal Server during an RDP session. Broken sessions can result from network failures, power failures, and crashed client devices.

At the connection layer, specify what action the server should take when a connection is broken (Terminal Services Configuration MMC snap-in | Connections | Double-click the connection | Sessions tab | "When session limit is reached or connection is broken" option). You have two options. The server can end the session or it can simply disconnect it. The choice you make here also affects the actions that take place when a session reaches its active or idle limits. From a security standpoint, the broken connection action does not pose much of a security risk because even if you allow disconnected sessions, users must successfully authenticate before they can reconnect to a broken session.

You might be wondering about the "Auto Client Reconnection" that is available with the latest Microsoft client and how it relates to the broken connection detection of a Terminal Server. On newer versions of the RDC client (at least version 5.2, which is newer than the one that ships with Windows XP), auto client reconnect allows RDP clients to automatically reconnect to a Terminal Server if their RDP sessions are interrupted. If you want users to be able to automatically reconnect to broken sessions, ensure that this option is set to "Disconnect from session" (which is the default).

Reconnecting From Any Client

You can also use the "Sessions" tab of the connection properties sheet to specify how users can reconnect to disconnected sessions (if disconnected sessions are permitted in your environment).

Some people view the ability to reconnect from any client as a security problem. In actuality, the security risk is not great since the user must authenticate on the new client before being able to reconnect to a session. Also, the user can only reconnect if the disconnected session was started with the same credentials as the new user. One user cannot reconnect to another user's disconnected session.

Potential security problems can arise, however, when multiple users log on with the same user account to access Terminal Servers. This is common in many environments for kiosks, common applications, or task-based workers. If a user authenticates with credentials that were used to start multiple sessions (which have since been disconnected) on one server, the user will be presented with an option to choose the disconnected session to connect to. It's possible that the user might pick a session that does not belong to him and be able to view privileged information or data. (Of course, one could argue that if there's any chance that a session could contain sensitive information, users shouldn't be logging on with shared credentials anyway.)

Auto Session Logon

The Logon Setting section of a connection's properties let you use one set of credentials to automatically log on any user that attempts to start an RDP session via that connection. Using this setting can pose a tremendous security risk, as any person could access to the system without being officially set up or authorized. It is relatively simple for a user or attacker to download and install the RDC client software and then to "discover" the Terminal Server, connect to it, and be automatically logged on.

Limiting the Number of Sessions per Connection

The maximum number of concurrent sessions can be limited per connection on the connection's main property page. In general, this setting is not used since this limit applies to all users—including administrators.

Disabling Logons

Disabling logons is useful if a custom connection is needed from time to time, but you do not want to have the connection open all the time or have to recreate the connection each time it is needed. Disabling the logons of a connection does not cause existing sessions to be broken—it merely prevents additional users from being able to log on.

Encryption

The required level of encryption can be set at the connection level, affecting all sessions on the connection. The details of the various levels of encryption will be discussed in the network security portion of this chapter.

Use Standard Windows Authentication

On the bottom of the main property page of the connection's properties is a fairly benign checkbox labeled "Use standard Windows authentication." Checking this box forces user authentication (over that connection) to occur through the standard Windows authentication DLL, *msgina.dll.*

If you install the Novell NDS Client on your Terminal Server, the Novell client authentication and logon DLL (*nwgina.dll*) will replace the Microsoft DLL. The "Press CTRL+ALT+DEL" logon screen is a Novell screen instead of the standard Microsoft screen after you install Novell's NDS Client. Checking the "Use standard Windows Authentication" checkbox will force RDP sessions to be logged on via the Microsoft client when that connection is used.

This is useful if you have two groups of users that connect to the same Terminal Server. You can create two separate connections—one for each group of users. Use one connection (call it "RDP1-TCP") for users that use the Netware Client can have the "Use standard Windows Authentication" box unchecked, allowing them to log on with the Novell authentication. Use the other connection ("RDP2-TCP") for users connecting to authenticate via the Microsoft logon DLL.

The end user experience is the same, regardless of whether the "Use standard Windows Authentication" box is checked or unchecked. The RDP client only passes the basic authentication parameters to the Terminal Server, and the checkbox merely specifies which DLL handles those parameters after they are received by the server.

Specifying an Initial Program to be Executed

A Terminal Server connection can be configured to set the initial program for every user that connects via the connection. This topic was fully covered back in Chapter 5, and the security aspects of configuring initial applications were covered previously in this chapter.

Setting the initial program at the connection layer functions in the exact same way as setting it for one specific user, except that the connection layer setting applies to all users on that connection without exception. As soon as the user logs on, the specified program is run. As soon as the user closes that program, he is automatically logged off. At no time will the user ever see a desktop unless the desktop is specified as the initial program to run.

Specifying an initial program to be executed is a good way to lock down your server if all users will need to use only one program. Users still need to authenticate before the program is run (unless the AutoLogon is configured). When the user closes that initial program, the connection is terminated.

Since this option is set at the connection layer, the initial program will affect everyone who connects, including administrators. (Administrators would be able to still remotely connect to the console session.) Setting the initial program at the connection level is most useful for Terminal Servers that serve as public terminals or kiosk devices.

As an interesting side note, even if a user connects to an initial application configured via his client or an RDP file, via a connection listener port that has the initial program specified, the initial program specified at the listener will run, not the one specified in the RDP file or at the client.

Remote Control

Basic remote control parameters can be set at the connection layer, such as whether remote controlling or view of another session is enabled and what type of notification or input the target sessions have. Many organizations choose to set different remote control parameters for different connections. Refer to the "Administrative Environment" segment of this chapter for more information on remote control.

TCP Port Used for RDP Sessions

By default, Terminal Servers accept inbound RDP sessions via TCP port 3389. For added security, some administrators like to change this port number. This port can be changed in the registry at the following path:

Key: HKLM\System\CurrentControlSet\Control\Terminal Server\WinStations\RDPConnectionName\

Value: PortNumber

Type: REG_DWORD

Data: Port number in hex (default 3389 = `d3d Hex`)

The "*RDPConnectionName*" in the above registry path is the name of the ICA connection you would like to change, for example "RDP-TCP." Because the RDP port configuration is a connection layer setting, you can configure different ports for different connections. After changing this port number, restart the server.

Remember that if you change the RDP port on the server, you must also change the port that the RDP client looks for.

In the real world, very few people choose to change the RDP port, mainly because there are plenty of other security measures that can provide excellent security and they don't want to deal with configuring all of their clients to use a nonstandard port. "Security through obscurity" is not generally viewed as a strong security measure.

Connection Permissions

You can specify which users and groups are able to connect over a particular connection listener port. However, you can also specify (from a permissions standpoint) just exactly what you want them to be able to do.

Like all security in Windows 2003, you can build extremely advanced custom sets of permissions, giving each user or group exactly the options they need. User and group permissions can be specified at the connection layer, with the permissions affecting the configured users for each connection.

Figure 12.5 Advanced connection permission properties

Advanced Permission	Allows the User or Group to...
Query Information	Obtain information about the current session
Set Information	Configure connection parameters
Remote Control	Remote Control other user's sessions
Logon	Connect via selected connection
Logoff	Log off other users
Message	Send popup messages to other sessions
Connect	Reconnect to disconnected sessions
Disconnect	Disconnect other peoples' sessions
Virtual Channels	Use virtual channel in a session

To make your life easier, Microsoft has "preconfigured" three different security levels: Guest, User, or Full Control. The permissions granted for each level are shown below.

Figure 12.6 Preconfigured connection permission levels

	Guest	User	Full Control
Query Information		•	•
Set Information			•
Remote Control			•
Logon	•	•	•
Logoff			•
Message			•
Connect		•	•
Disconnect			•
Virtual Channels			•

You can customize any of these levels or create your own by highlighting the user account or group and then clicking the "Advanced" button. For example, you might give one group "shadowing" permissions without having to give them full access rights. This setting would be accomplished by clicking the "advanced" button, selecting the group, clicking the "view/edit" button, and selecting the rights needed for that group. However, the preconfigured levels work well for most situations and save you from having to manually select each option.

It's important to understand that these permissions only affect the one connection at which they are applied. It is possible for one user to have "Full Control" rights on one connection and "No access" rights to another.

For each line-item property, there are two boxes: allow and deny. If you select the deny box, the option is explicitly denied for that user or group, and this "deny" takes precedence over any other allow permissions configured in any other group, similar to "no access" NTFS permission.

If you're using a third party software such as Citrix MetaFrame that uses its own connection listener port, some people recommended that you disable the RDP connection listener port. While doing this would minimize your security risk, it actually increases your overall risk. If there's a problem with your MetaFrame connection that prevents a session from connecting, you would have no recourse unless you are located physically near the server. In the real world, most people choose to leave the default RDP connection listener port active when using MetaFrame, but configure the permissions so that only administrators are able to connect. That way you protect the connection while giving your own group a backdoor connection in case of trouble. (Although if your administrator account is called "administrator" and its password is "password," keeping RDP active is a valid risk. If such is the case in your environment, put this book down and pick up a copy of *Security for Dummies*.)

Strategies for Using Multiple Server Connections

Terminal Server connection listener ports can be used in creative ways to provide different types of security. All security configuration settings that are applied at the connection layer apply to all users that connect via that port. However, there is nothing to say that you can't have more than one connection listener port for each protocol.

If you put multiple network cards in a Terminal Server, you can create multiple RDP-TCP connections, one for each card. To do this, change the LAN adapter for the connection's properties (Terminal Services Configuration MMC| Connections | Double-click the connection | Network Adapter). Change the network adapter from "All network adapters configured with this protocol" to just the network adapter that you want to use. Then create a new connection for the other network adapter (Terminal Services Configuration MMC | Right-click on "Connections" folder | Create New Connection). Because each network card would have a different IP address, each connection will be accessible via a unique IP address and therefore a unique DNS name.

This allows you to have a completely different set of properties for the same server, each accessible via its own unique address. This arrangement is useful if you want to provide different groups of users access to the same server, but want different connection–layer settings to apply to each group. One group could access `server1.yourcompany.com` and the other group could access `server2.yourcompany.com`. In reality, each would be using a different connection of the same server.

Advantages of Configuring Multiple Connections

- If you need different connection layer settings on one server, this is the only way to do it.

Disadvantages of Configuring Multiple Connections

- You need one physical network card for each unique connection.
- All users connecting to the server via its NetBIOS name will connect via the same network adapter.

Connection Configuration in the Registry

All connection listener port configuration information is stored in the registry of each Terminal Server in the following location:

HKLM\System\CurrentControlSet\Control\TerminalServer \WinStations\<*RDPConnectionName*>

Because this configuration information is stored in the registry, you can allow or deny specific users access to the appropriate registry keys. If a user has the ability to write to this registry key, then he will have the ability to change the parameters of Terminal Servers connections, regardless of the permissions that are configured elsewhere.

Network Security

Any traffic that crosses a computer network is susceptible to being captured and viewed by unauthorized individuals. Because of this danger, the networks must be secured in one of two ways:

- Protect the physical network connections so that no one can access the network to compromise the data.
- Protect the logical data on the network so that if the data is compromised it is meaningless to the person who found it.

Protecting physical connections is not practical in today's world, especially over the Internet. When addressing network security, most people focus on protecting the data that crosses the network. The common approach is "I don't care if you actually capture my data, because if you do, it will be totally meaningless to you." The networks over which Terminal Server traffic flows are no different from other computer networks. To secure your Terminal Server network, you need to look at two components:

- Network data security (Encryption).
- Network perimeter security (Firewalls).

Let's begin by examining your Terminal Server network's data security.

Terminal Server Network Data Security / Encryption

In Terminal Server environments, there are multiple types of network communications that need to be secured. Figure 12.7 shows all of the various network communications that take place in a standard Terminal Server environment. As you can see when using Terminal Server, users are not just accessing resources on that server. Users will have to authenticate, access file and print resources and any other backend servers (such as Exchange, SQL, Oracle, etc) for application data. As we analyze the security of a Terminal Server network environment, keep in mind that more is involved than securing data between the client and the server.

Figure 12.7 Terminal Server network segments

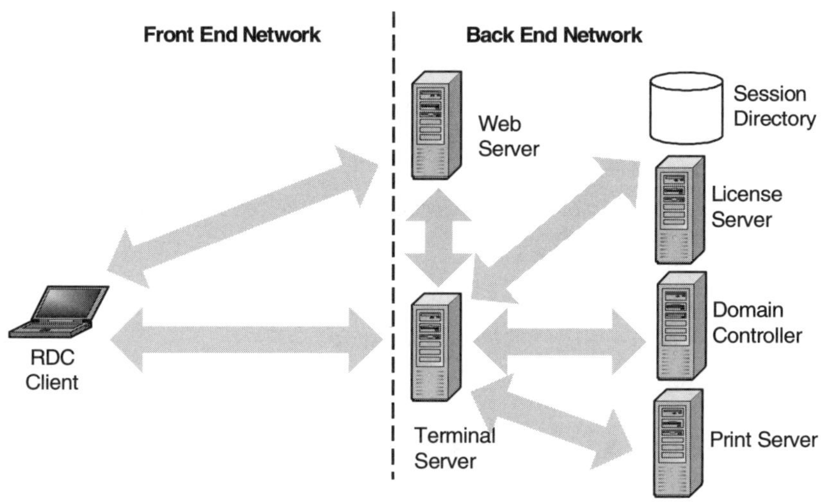

As you can see in Figure 12.7, the front-end communication includes all of the traffic that travels between client devices and the Terminal server, and the back-end communication includes all of the network traffic that travels between the various server components. Let's analyze the security needs of each of these network communication links, starting with the front-end.

Segment 1. Client Device to Terminal Server

In many scenarios, RDP session communication will travel across both trusted (or internal) networks and untrusted (public) networks. When addressing the security of this RDP communication, you must look at two components: session creation and session use.

- *Session creation.* When an RDP session is created, the user credentials are passed from the client device to the Terminal Server. This action poses a security risk because stolen user credentials could be used to invoke pirated sessions. Even worse, because many companies are consolidating their user directories, stolen user credentials from a session could most likely be used to access email or other network resources.
- *Session use.* While an RDP session is in use, a packet sniffer could be used to capture the RDP session packets. Because these packets contain all the keystrokes that a user types, anything that the user types could be compromised, including passwords.

Incidentally, you'll notice that during an RDP session, we're only really worried about the keystrokes, not the screen display data. It is highly unlikely that an attacker could capture the screen shot information from RDP session packets. Screen shot captures would require that the attacker crack the binary RDP protocol. Of course, there are many hacker websites with dedicated sections for Terminal Server, so this risk could change in future.

Either way, RDP session traffic must be protected. As with any other type of traffic, the most effective way to accomplish this is with encryption. Encrypting RDP traffic does not make it any harder for an attacker to obtain, but it does render the data unreadable to an attacker. There are two methods by which to encrypt RDP session traffic:

- Create an encrypted tunnel (VPN) between the end user and the server, through which RDP session data flows.
- Encrypt only the RDP traffic with the standard Microsoft encryption.

Segment 1 Method 1. Encrypt RDP Traffic with a VPN Tunnel

Virtual Private Networking (VPN) software can be used to create a secure, encrypted "tunnel" from the client device to the Terminal Servers. In these scenarios, each user has VPN client software installed locally on his client machine. This software utilizes the user's local ISP and the Internet to connect to the corporate office. Once this secure connection is established, a private tunnel is created connecting the local user to the corporate network. The local user can access the corporate network as if he were attached to the network locally. In actuality, the VPN software on the user's client device connects to the VPN software at the corporate office via the Internet. All traffic that flows back and forth is encrypted by the VPN software. Through this VPN tunnel, the user can launch Terminal Server sessions. The RDP protocol itself is not encrypted directly; rather, it is encrypted by the VPN software automatically.

Figure 12.8 An RDP session encrypted via a VPN tunnel

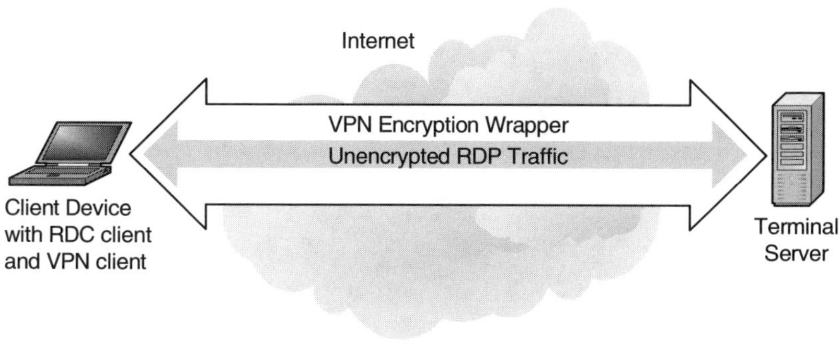

Many companies choose to use VPNs for their users to access Terminal Server applications from remote locations. In most instances, VPN access to Terminal Server applications is chosen because the company already has an existing VPN solution in place for remote access to other applications. They can easily extend their existing VPN environment to support RDP session traffic from remote users.

The major downfall to using these types of VPNs is that the VPN client software must be installed on every single client device. The degree to which this affects a user depends on the VPN software being used. For example, Microsoft's Internet Security & Acceleration Server product offers VPN capabilities, and the client software for it is built in to every version of Windows since Windows 2000. However, other vendors' VPN client software may have to be downloaded to each client device before it can be used, and this can pose a problem on a guest computer.

Imagine you were at a friend's house when your pager went off, notifying you that there was an urgent work–related matter that needed to be addressed immediately. Fortunately for you, your company built Terminal Servers that will allow you to connect from home. You can go to your friend's PC, log on to the Internet, and begin accessing your Terminal Server hosted applications. But, because your company chose to secure their servers with a VPN, before you can connect you must first go to your company's intranet site to download and install the VPN software. Only after this is configured are you able to access your applications. When you are done, you uninstall the VPN software from your friend's computer.

Advantages of Using VPN Tunnels

- All traffic is encrypted.

- Users are not limited to accessing only Terminal Server applications.
- If the VPN is already in place, it can be easily extended to support Terminal Server.

Disadvantages of Using VPN Tunnels

- VPN software must be installed on every client device.
- VPN software must be configured before it can be used.
- Some clients are not compatible with VPN software.
- Many corporate firewalls block VPN traffic.
- The VPN software costs money, and may be very expensive.
- Some bandwidth is wasted by the VPN tunnel overhead.

Ultimately, VPNs are a good solution if you have users that will use the same computer over and over to remotely connect to your Terminal Servers. VPNs are a not good solution if remote users will need to connect from many different random computers.

Segment 1 Method 2. Encrypt RDP Traffic with Microsoft Encryption

Instead of encrypting the entire network stream between the client and server with a VPN solution, it's possible to encrypt just the RDP session traffic itself, as shown in Figure 12.9.

Figure 12.9 Encrypting the RDP session

One method that can be used to encrypt RDP traffic is Microsoft's native RDP encryption. Unlike other products, Microsoft's RDP session encryption is driven by the server's connection settings and not by the client. Microsoft currently has four different configurations available for the connection level. The four options listed below are found on the general tab of the RDP connection properties pages:

- *Low*: This setting encrypts data using 56-bit encryption. It secures data sent from the client to the servers (the keystrokes) but does not encrypt data that is sent from the server to the client. This option would only be used to secure credentials and other keystroke-type information on an intranet environment.
- *Client Compatible*: This setting configures the client-to-server communication at the maximum key strength that the client supports. The latest RDP clients support 128-bit encryption. This option is useful if you want to use strong encryption without locking out users connecting with earlier versions of the RDP client.
- *FIPS Compliant*: This setting encrypts data traveling from client to server *and* from server to client with the Federal Information Processing Standard (FIPS) encryption algorithms by using the Microsoft cryptographic modules. Only RDC clients version 5.2 and higher can use this encryption setting. If configured at the minimum encryption level for a connection, older client connections will be denied.
- *High*: This level is the default used by Windows Server 2003 server. It encrypts the data in both directions (like FIPS) using a 128-bit key. It should only be used when the environment contains 128-bit clients only, since it will also deny connections to clients that don't meet the standard.

Since session encryption is configured at the connection level, people often wonder how the client knows which encryption type is being used.

The encryption level of the RDP session is negotiated when a connection is established. When the server is configured for a certain encryption level, it first determines if the connecting client supports this level. If so, a simple key negotiation takes place and the session is established via an encrypted pipe. If a user attempts to connect to a server with a level of encryption not supported by the client, the client connection is refused (Service Pack 1 for Windows 2003 changes this encrypted session negotiation. See `www.brianmadden.com` for details.).

The entire encryption process is transparent to the user. It does not add any overhead to the RDP network traffic, although it does add a touch of overhead to the server and client processor utilization as they encrypt and decrypt all RDP session data.

Advantages of Native RDP Session Encryption

- Works on any almost any client platform.

- Transparent to the user.
- Easy to configure.
- Can be configured at the server.
- Does not require an X.509 certificate.

The only real disadvantage to using native encryption is that you need to open a nonstandard port (TCP port 3389, for the RDP session) on your firewall to receive the RDP traffic from outside clients. This topic will be covered in greater detail in the "Perimeter Security" section of this chapter.

Disadvantages of Native RDP Session Encryption

- Requires nonstandard ports to be opened on the firewall when RDP clients connect across the Internet.
- Does not verify the identity of the Terminal Server like SSL does.
- The initial "handshake" is unencrypted.

Securing Back-End Network Communications

Thinking back to Figure 12.7, you can see that there are several backend servers that your Terminal Servers need to communicate with. Since this book is not about securing server-to-server communication but instead about Terminal Server, we're going to continue focusing on securing that environment. The purpose of Figure 12.7 is to point out that a Terminal Servers is not a stand-alone machine, and requires access to many resources.

Communication between the Terminal Servers and the backend servers can be secured in a number of ways. Database access connection between client and server can be secured easily. SQL connections can be encrypted with the native ODBC database tools and software. Connections to file and print servers can be secured with IPSec. All of your security options should be explored, but be aware of the servers with which your Terminal Servers need to communicate.

Fortunately, since back-end servers are usually all located on an internal network, encryption of that network is generally not as critical as encryption of the front-end network.

Network Perimeter Security / Firewall Configuration for Access from the Internet

In this section, we won't spend time talking about the importance of firewalls and why you need them. The truth is that most environments have them. Instead, we're going to focus on how firewalls relate to Terminal Servers. This leads to three questions:

- Where should I place my Terminal Servers in relation to the firewall?
- What ports do I need to open on the firewall?
- How do I make the Terminal Servers work if the firewall is using Network Address Translation (NAT)?

Terminal Server Placement in Relation to the Firewall

When deciding where to put the Terminal Servers that will provide RDP access to applications across the Internet, there are three basic options:

- Terminal Servers outside the firewall.
- Terminal Servers inside the firewall.
- Terminal Servers in a DMZ.

Option 1. Terminal Servers outside the Firewall

Figure 12.10 A Terminal Server outside the firewall

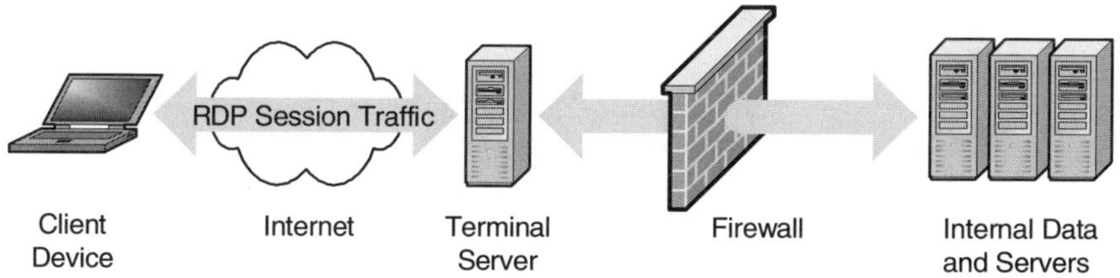

This configuration is primarily used when Terminal Server applications are standalone (they do not need to access any data from the inside of the firewall).

By putting Terminal Servers outside of the firewall, any Terminal Server application that accesses resources from servers on the inside of the firewall will need to have a port opened on the firewall. The more ports that are opened increase the likelihood that a breach of the firewall could occur.

Another point of worry is that Microsoft software is not known for being bulletproof. Very few organizations feel comfortable having unprotected Windows servers sitting on the Internet.

Putting Terminal Servers on the outside of the firewall raises complexities if you have users on the inside that need to access the Terminal Servers. Should they go through the firewall in the opposite direction? Should you have a Terminal Server environment with some servers on the inside and others on the outside? When users from both inside and outside need to access Terminal Server application hosts, the servers are usually not put on the outside of the firewall.

Advantages of Placing Terminal Servers Outside the Firewall

- Works well if no internal users will need to access the servers.
- If the Terminal Server is compromised, it *may* limit damage to the internal network.

Disadvantages of Placing Terminal Servers Outside the Firewall

- Application holes need to be opened in the firewall for access to internal applications.
- It can be difficult for some applications on the Terminal Server to get through the firewall to the resources they need on the inside.
- If the server is compromised, something like a keystroke logger could be installed to record passwords.
- Greater risk from automated scripts and Internet-based attacks.
- If users connect to the Terminal Servers with the same user accounts that they use on the inside, they must authenticate to the Terminal Server through the firewall.

Option 2. Terminal Servers inside the Firewall

Most companies choose to place their Terminal Servers inside the firewall. By doing this, they are leveraging the true definition of the "firewall," as it will take the brunt of all Internet traffic and attacks.

Figure 12.11 A Terminal Server behind the firewall

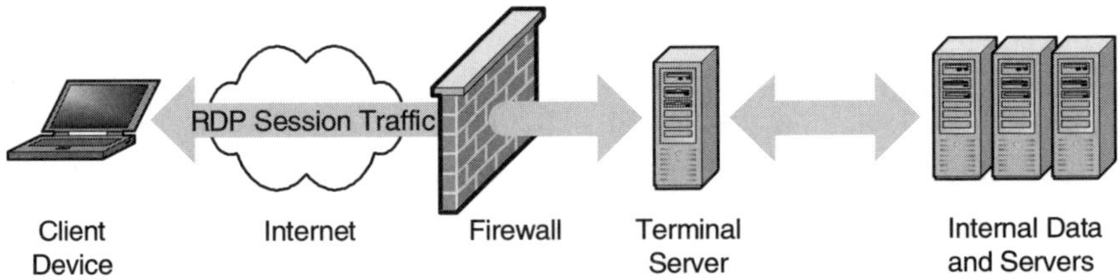

This tends to be the most secure of all possible configurations because the only holes that need to be opened on the firewall are for RDP traffic to the Terminal Servers. Most of today's firewalls also offer stateful packet inspection capabilities, meaning that they can validate certain types of traffic going to the internal servers.

Advantages of Placing Terminal Servers Inside the Firewall

- Only the Terminal Server addresses and ports need to be opened on the firewall.
- Reduces the complexity of the firewall configuration.
- Very Secure.

Disadvantages of Placing Terminal Servers Inside the Firewall

- If the Terminal Server is compromised, other servers behind the firewall could be compromised.
- The firewall must be configured to allow RDP traffic to flow to the Terminal Servers.

Option 3. Terminal Server in a DMZ

Some firewalls allow for the configuration of a DMZ (Demilitarized Zone). A DMZ can also be created with a pair of firewalls. This DMZ combines the above two methods. The Terminal Servers aren't totally exposed on the outside of the firewall, but they also do not have free access to devices on the inside of the firewall. In this configuration, no outside traffic has direct access to devices on the inside of the firewall. Instead, the firewall is configured so that outside clients can access only the Terminal Servers in the DMZ. Those Terminal Servers, in turn, can access (through the firewall) network resources on the inside.

Figure 12.12 A Terminal Server in the DMZ

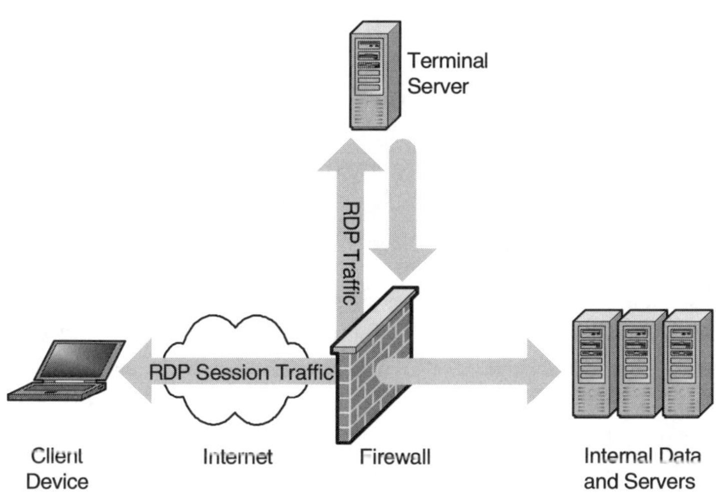

Advantages of Placing Terminal Servers in the DMZ

- Most secure solution.

Disadvantages of Placing Terminal Servers in the DMZ

- Most complex firewall configuration.

Firewall Port Configuration for Terminal Server Environments

If you decide to put your MetaFrame XP server behind a firewall or in a DMZ, there are several TCP ports that must be configured on the firewall.

Figure 12.13 Firewall port usage

Port	Direction	Destination	Description
3389	Inbound	All Terminal Server	RDP port needed for Server-client communication
1024-65535	Outbound	RDP Client	Terminal Server will dynamically select a unique port for each RDP session in this port range. This configuration is standard practice on firewalls.
80	Inbound	Web Server	If you are using web launched RDP files, and your Web server is behind a firewall
443	Inbound	Web Server	If you are using web launched RDP files and you require authentication to the pages, it is best to secure this traffic with SSL to protect the user credentials and the RDP files

This list allows for basic communication between the end user and the Terminal Server through the firewall. If your Terminal Server is in a DMZ, the exact ports that need to be opened from the DMZ to the internal network can become a little more complicated. If your Terminal Server is a member of a domain, users will be required to authenticate. If the application being run on the server uses an SQL database on the internal network, port 1433 needs to be opened between this server and the SQL server. You'll also need to open ports for access to SMB shares, printers, and other network services and applications.

Network Address Translation at the Firewall

Most companies that use firewalls configure them for Network Address Translation (NAT). Internal servers can then be configured with private IP addresses that are not valid to the outside world. Because all network traffic between the inside servers and the outside world is channeled through the firewall, the firewall maintains two addresses for each server. One address is valid to the outside world; the other address is valid to the inside network. When a request for the server hits the firewall from the outside, the firewall translates the address to the internal address of the server before passing it on to that server. Just the same, when the internal server sends network data to an external address, the firewall changes the existing sender's address (the server's internal address) to the server's valid external address. The server has no idea that its address is not valid to the outside world. Using NAT allows servers on the inside to be protected from the outside world by forcing all communication to travel through the firewall.

Figure 12.14 Network address translation at the firewall

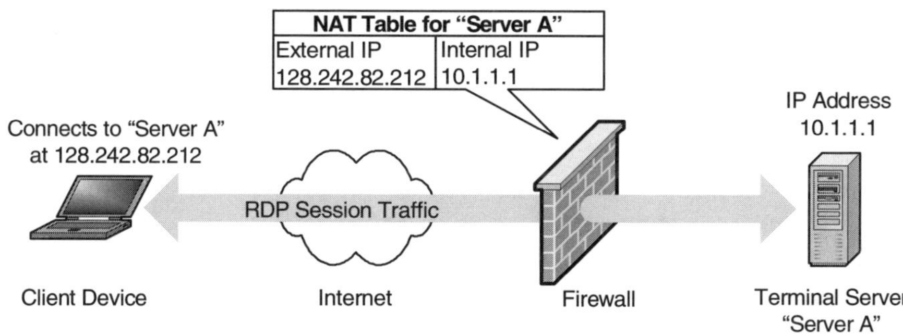

The advantage to using NAT is that because the internal IP addresses of the servers are not valid on the outside, it is technically impossible for an attacker to find a "back door" into the network. All traffic must flow through the firewall because the internal addresses are not valid to the rest of the world. Also, by using NAT, companies do not have to register the IP addresses for their internal devices.

In non-Terminal Server environments there are usually no issues with NAT because the internal server has no need of knowing that its IP address is being changed by the firewall. This is not the always the case in Terminal Server environments. To understand why, let's consider the following scenario.

An RDC client device connects to a Terminal Server via the Internet. The Terminal Server is accessible to the Internet via the IP address 128.242.82.212. A firewall running NAT sits between the Internet and the Terminal Server. The Terminal Server's IP address is configured to be 10.1.1.1. The firewall automatically translates between the two IP addresses for traffic going between the Internet and the MetaFrame XP server. This scenario is depicted in Figure 12.15.

Figure 12.15 The firewall translates the RDP client's request

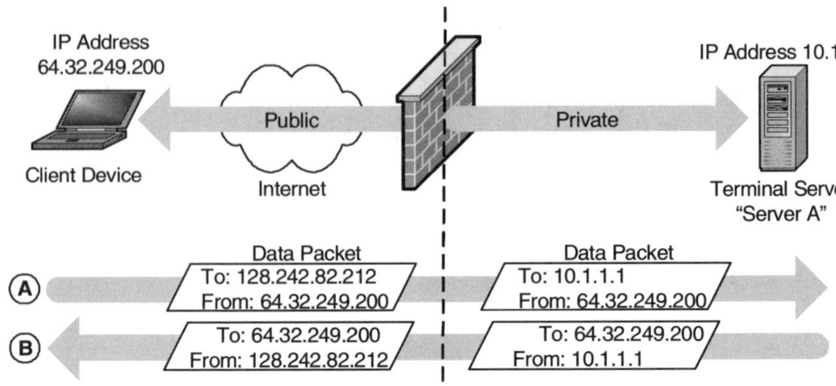

NAT Table for "Server A"	
External IP	Internal IP
128.242.82.212	10.1.1.1

If an RDP client on the outside of the firewall connects directly to the Terminal Server, there will be no issues. The firewall will use NAT to translate between the internal and external addresses of the Terminal Server. In this case, the RDP client and the Terminal Server do not know that the address is being translated. All translation occurs transparently at the firewall, and all is well.

However, if the Terminal Server is part of a cluster that's using Microsoft's Session Directory to reconnect users to disconnected sessions, the IP address returned to the client when they reconnect (after the Session Directory finds their existing session on another server) will be the server's internal address, not the NAT'd external address. The client would need to connect to the load-balanced external IP address, but the session that was found would be based on internal address. In this case, the client's traffic won't go anywhere since the 10.1.1.1 address is not valid from the outside. (Chapter 7 focused on clusters and load-balancing in-depth.)

In order for the RDP client to connect and be successfully reconnected to a session on a Terminal Server behind a firewall using NAT, one of two statements must be true:

- The terminal server MUST have a public IP address. The server is generally sitting in the DMZ or outside the firewall.

OR

- A third party load balancing solution that has the ability to accept Session Directory tokens and acts as a router or gateway for the load balanced devices must be used.

The first solution would require that at least one network card on the server has a valid, routable, external Internet IP address. This address would be used as the Session Directory adapter for reconnecting disconnected sessions. The caveat here is that you have to make this server publicly available with a port 3389 open which is less secure than being behind the NAT firewall.

In the second scenario, the hardware load balancer also acts as a pseudo-router. All load balanced traffic is routed through it. When a user disconnects from a Terminal Server using this configuration, a Session Directory token is returned to the client instead of the server's IP address. This token contains the IP address and credentials and is handed off to the load balancer at connection for routing. In this case, the server would not need a routable internet IP that could be accessed from the Internet, but instead would only require that the load balancer be able to connect to them.

User Account Security

Addressing security from a user perspective focuses on:

- The user account configuration.
- Secure user authentication
- The domain configuration and trust relationships.

User Account Configuration

You can configure several security options at the user layer. The advantage to configuring security at this layer is that the settings follow the user no matter where he logs on. In both Windows NT 4.0 and Active Directory environments, there are several user properties that affect the security of your Terminal Server environment. These user account configuration options can be broken down into three broad categories:

- Options that are configured as part of the user's domain account.
- Options that are configured per user or group as part of a server's local security rights.
- Options that are configured as part of a policy.

User Domain Account Configuration

The security options that are configured as part of a user's account properties are literally properties of the user account itself. In Windows NT 4.0, these properties are configured via user manager for domains and the configured options become part of a user's account in the SAM. In Active Directory, they are configured as part of a user's Active Directory account properties and the options become part of that user's Active Directory user object.

There are only a few user account properties specific to Terminal Services environments. (See the feature chart in the Appendix for a full list of settings that can be configured here.) First, each domain user that will use any Terminal Server must have the "Allow logon to Terminal Services" box checked in her account properties. If you have particular users that you do not want to use any Terminal Servers, uncheck this box. Unchecking this box results in the error "Your interactive logon privilege has been disabled" whenever the user attempts to log on to a Terminal Server.

In addition to this user right, the user must be a member of the Remote Desktop User's group on the Terminal Server itself or be a member of a domain group that is nested into this local group.

Each user's account also has properties similar to those that you can configure at the connection layer. These properties include timeouts for ending disconnected sessions, active and idle session limits, and whether the user can reconnect to disconnected sessions from any client or only from the original client. The settings apply to the user whether they connect to a Terminal Session via RDP or any other third-party protocol.

Not immediately obvious is how the "run program on startup" options work within a user's account properties. This option is similar to the initial program option that you can specify at the connection layer because when the user exits from the program, his Terminal Services session is ended. However, be aware that any initial program that you specify in a user's domain account property only affects him when he logs on to Terminal Services with the RDP protocol.

Server Local Security Rights

Each server can have a local policy in place that affects users' local security rights. These rights are configured via the local security policy of the server (Start | Administrative Tools | Local Security Settings | Security Settings | User Rights Assignments). You can configure local or domain users or groups with various user rights. While many user rights are not relevant to the security of Terminal Server environments, there are several that are. Some of the security-related rights include a user's ability to shut down the computer, change the system time, manage the auditing and security log, and take ownership of files. Again, the feature chart in the Appendix of this book shows which options can be configured here.

One of the security rights particularly useful in Terminal Server environments is the "log on locally" right. In order for a user to be able to use a Terminal Server, he must have the rights to log on locally to the server. In the real world, you might have 10 or 12 servers for 2 or 3 different departments. You can create a global group for each department, called "*Dept A TS Users.*" Then, on the Terminal Servers that serve applications for Department A, you can remove the "log on locally" right from "Domain Users" and grant it to "*Dept A TS Users.*"

Alternately, you can use the local group "Remote Desktop Users" and place your departmental users into this group since it is already assigned the "log on locally" right. Configuring the local security rights of the server gives you an extra level of protection beyond your NTFS security and Application Restriction policies.

In addition to the "log on locally" security right, you'll notice there is a "deny log on locally" security right. You might be confused as to why there are two of these and how each should be used. Normally, if you have users that you do not want to use Terminal Services, you can just choose not to give them the "log on locally" security right. That way, if the user is a member of multiple groups, they can get the "log on locally" security rights from any one of their group memberships. However, if you have specific users or groups that you definitely do not want to use the Terminal Server no matter what, then you can add them to the "deny log on locally" list. This security right will always take precedence if a user is on the list for both "log on locally" and "deny log on locally." Use the "deny log on locally" carefully because it is possible that one user might be a member of multiple groups with conflicting rights.

User Policies

All of the local security rights from the previous section can be deployed across multiple servers as part of a group policy. They are tied to specific user accounts only when those user accounts are added to the system policy or to an organizational unit where the group policy is applied. For detailed information regarding the use of policies in a Terminal Server environment, refer to Chapter 6. In all cases, domain policy or group policy settings will take precedence over the configured local security rights.

Secure User Authentication

One way that many organizations are securing their user environments is by implementing secure user authentication mechanisms. The three most popular methods are smart cards, two-factor authentication, and biometric authentication.

Smart Cards

In environments in which positive user identification is important, smart card technology if often used to authenticate users. Windows Server 2003 allows you to log on to a Terminal Server session in an Active Directory domain using a smart card. Smart cards allow you to require strong credentials from users, thus providing a more secure environment.

Smart cards offer several benefits:

- *Secure credentials*: Smart cards maintain credentials and private keys stored locally on the card. Furthermore, they provide tamper-resistant storage for that data. If a smart card is lost or stolen, it is almost impossible for anyone except the intended user to use the credentials that it stores. (Most smart cards have a “self destruct” feature that disables the card if the wrong PIN is entered a number of times in a row.)
- *Isolation of sensitive data*: Cryptographic operations are performed on the smart card itself rather instead of on the client or server. This feature isolates security-sensitive data and processes from other parts of the system.
- *Portable security*. Credentials and other private information stored on smart cards can easily be transported between computers at work, home, or other remote locations.

While smart card authentication is more secure than standard Windows authentication, you'll need to implement several things to use them in a Terminal Services environment. First, you'll need a public key infrastructure (PKI) before you can deploy smart cards in your organization. This can be a project in itself and can be expensive depending on the solution used. Next, you must have Active Directory deployed in your organization and your client computers must be running a client operating system with built-in smart card support, such as Windows XP or Windows 2000, and some versions of Windows CE .NET. Finally, you'll need to install smart card readers on the client computers.

In order for a user to log on to a Terminal Server, she inserts her smart card into the card reader. Her smart card contains a digital certificate which is transmitted to the Terminal Server. The server (which has its own X.509 digital certificate) checks the user's certificate from the smart card to verify that it matches the certificate on file. If so, the user is authenticated and her RDP session is launched.

For added security, policy options are usually configured on the Terminal Servers that dictate the action taken when the smart card is removed from the reader. Many companies configure their environments so that a user's session is immediately disconnected if her smart card is removed from the card reader attached to the client device.

Advantages of using Smart Cards

- Excellent two-factor security.
- Easy for users to use and understand.

Disadvantages of using Smart Cards

- Requires Windows 2000 or XP clients.
- Requires substantial smart card infrastructure (cards, readers, certificates, etc.).
- Users must remember to bring their smart cards with them.
- Users can lose their smart cards.

Before you begin using smartcards in your Terminal Server environment, you should have them working in your existing environment. You should have individual cards with users' certificates and PINs on them. Your backend directory (such as AD) should be ready to go. Your certificate authorities and digital certificates should be all set up. Once all this is in place, smart card usage with Terminal Server is easy to implement.

Token-Based Two-Factor Authentication Mechanisms

Since Terminal Server is based on standard Windows and Active Directory components, you can easily integrate third-party two-factor authentication. The most popular two-factor authentication products are Secure Computing's SafeWord PremierAccess (`www.securecomputing.com`) and RSA's SecurID (`www.rsa.com`).

Both of these companies offer keychain-sized electronic tokens that you distribute to your users. When a user attempts to log on to a Terminal Server, he needs his username, password, and the constantly-changing code from his token.

Two-factor authentication lowers the risk that stolen user credentials will lead to a breach of your system.

Advantages of using Token Authentication

- Excellent two-factor security.
- Easy for users to use and understand.
- You don't have to install any kind of hardware on the client devices.
- All types of platforms of client devices are supported.
- Tokens are cheap.

Disadvantages of using Token Authentication

- Users must remember to bring their tokens with them.
- Users can lose their tokens.
- Tokens take batteries.

Biometric Authentication

If two-factor authentication does not provide enough security for you, you can also use biometric authentication for your Terminal Servers. The term "biometric authentication" conjures up all sorts of mental pictures, but in today's world it usually means fingerprint scanners. There are dozens of companies that make these scanners, and you can now get them at any electronics store for under $100.

The problem with most fingerprint scanners is that they come with software that installs on a local workstation and memorizes your fingerprint and your passwords. It then "stuffs" your passwords into login boxes that appear on your workstation. While this is a great solution for individual users, it doesn't do much good in enterprise Terminal Server environments.

Fortunately, you can buy enterprise software that can pull together these random fingerprint scanners. One of the most popular is SAFsolution from SAFlink (`www.saflink.com`). This software incorporates biometric authentication into your Active Directory while letting your users choose any standards-compliant biometric device that they want. For example, if you use Terminal Server to provide applications to remote customers, you can tell them that they need a fingerprint scanner but that they can buy whichever one you want. You can then use the SAFlink software to ensure that they cannot authenticate to your Active Directory unless they have a fingerprint scanner installed.

Advantages of using Biometric Authentication

- Attackers cannot impersonate users' accounts.
- User does not have to remember to bring his smart card or token with him.
- There's nothing for the user to lose.

Disadvantages of using Biometric Authentication

- You must purchase biometric devices for each client.
- You must purchase enterprise biometric software to run everything.
- Some cheap fingerprint scanners can be fooled by photocopies and gelatin molds.

Secure System Administration Environments

The last thing that we need to look at when considering Terminal Server security is how your servers will be administered. This is often overlooked, but very important. Even the world's most technically secure environments won't actually be secure if too many people have administrative rights.

Another important part of the administration of your Terminal Servers relates to how the servers are actually used, including how administrators or help desk personnel shadow end users and how everyone's actions are logged, recorded, and audited.

As we look at the security of the Terminal Server administrative environment, we'll focus on two areas:

- Remote controlling users.
- Auditing and usage logs.

Session Remote Control

Terminal Server session Remote Control allows administrators to remotely view a selected end user's RDP session. There are several security and privacy concerns raised when deciding how to use shadowing stemming from the fact that a malicious user could shadow another user's session without him knowing it. He would potentially be able to view sensitive or personal information.

To mitigate this security risk, you have the option of choosing not to enable any of the remote control features or choosing to manage the remote control environment so that only authorized users are able to remote control other users. Let's look at how this can be applied in the real world.

Choosing not to Enable Remote Control

If remote control poses a great security risk in your environment, you can disable it at the connection listener port. This is the easiest way to prohibit remote control on a single server. If you have multiple servers, you can also disable remote control via a Group Policy.

Remote Control Rights

You also have the ability to configure which users are able to remote control other users.

You can give a user the ability to remotely control another user as part of his user account properties (AD Users and Computers | Double-click user account | Remote Control tab | Enable Remote Control).

Furthermore, you can configure granular remote control permissions at the connection level (Terminal Services Configuration | Connections | Double-click connection | Permissions tab). Anyone with "Full Control" permissions on that connection listener will be able to remote control other users. If you want users to be able to remote control other users without giving them full control of the connection (helpdesk users, for example), then add their group and click the "Advanced" button to give them the remote control right without giving them other rights.

Remote Controller / Controllee Interaction

Even with permissions to remote control users, there are two additional parameters that can be configured, "Require User's Permission" and "Level of Control."

Checking the "Require User's Permission" box will cause a message box to be displayed in a user's session before the remote control session starts. The user has to grant permission to the remote controller.

The "Level of Control" option lets you configure whether the person doing the remote controlling has the ability to interact with the remote session by using the keyboard and mouse, or whether they are just able to observe the remote session.

You can configure these remote control settings as part as a user account, GPO, or a connection listener property. You'll remember from Chapter 6 that GPOs always take precedence over user account settings. Beyond that, the most restrictive setting will apply if there is a conflict between the user account/GPO setting and the connection listener port setting.

User Auditing

Often Terminal Server administrators want to be able to create log files that they can use to audit specific Terminal Server user events, such as user session logons and logoffs. There are two ways that audit logs can be created:

- Windows user account auditing.
- Third party auditing and logging tools.

Logging Users with Windows Auditing

For simple user logging, it's best to think back to your Windows Administration 101 class.

In Windows 2000/2003 environments, auditing can be configured via a group policy in Active Directory environments (Group Policy Object | Computer Configuration | Windows Settings | Security Settings | Local Policies | Audit Policy), or via the local computer policy when group policies are not used (Administrative Tools | Local Security Settings | Local Policies | Audit Policy). When Active Directory is used, most people configure the audit policies for the Group Policy Object that has the OU that contains their MetaFrame XP servers.

You can configure auditing for any item (file, directory, etc.) via the audit dialog box (Item Properties | Security Tab | Advanced Button | Audit Tab).

You can also enable auditing of Terminal Server-specific activities at the connection level (Terminal Services Configuration | Connections | Double-click connection | Permissions tab | Advanced button | Auditing tab). Just add your user or group there, and configure whether you want to audit the success or failure of any Terminal Server activity on that connection.

All of the Windows audit events will appear in the security event log.

Logging Users with Third Party Tools

If you need heavy duty security auditing and logging in your Terminal Server environment, you'll probably be disappointed with the native components that are available from Microsoft. Fortunately, there are several third-party auditing tools available. Some of the most popular include Techtonik ONEapp (`www.oneapp.co.uk`) and Lakeside Software's Systrack (`www.lakeside`

software.com). New information about these and other third party tools is constantly available at www.brianmadden.com.

CHAPTER 13

Performance Tuning and Optimization

We initially discussed server sizing back in Chapter 5. Server sizing and performance tuning are closely related. The main difference between them is that server sizing is about choosing the proper hardware, and performance tuning is about making configuration changes that affect how efficiently the hardware is used. In this chapter, we'll look at several techniques and resources that you can use to tune your servers, their applications, and the network.

What is performance?

Although an odd question to ask right off the bat, this is an important one to help frame the context of what you can reasonably expect to achieve. Simply stated, performance (in this case) is getting expected results based on a fixed set of inputs. Terminal Servers perform well when they meet your expectations. Whether you have 10, 100, or 1,000 users per server is not as important as *knowing* that you'll reliably have 10, 100, or 1,000 users per server.

All Terminal Server performance problems really fall within one of two categories:

- You want something to happen faster.
- You want more of something.

There are an infinite amount of things that people want to happen faster in Terminal Server environments. They want faster logons, faster application response times, and faster screen updates.

Think about the speed of different activities on your Terminal Servers. Do you have dialog boxes that you want to pop up in one-tenth of a second instead of one-half of a second? Do you want to cut the logon time from thirty seconds down to ten seconds?

Instead of wanting things to happen faster, perhaps you want more of something. In most cases, people want to accommodate more users per server.

Approaching your Performance Problem

Before you even begin to assess the performance of a Terminal Server, it's important to understand that every Terminal Server has a limit. This limit varies from company to company, but is based on applications, user profiles, hardware, the network, and countless other factors. There are plenty of "finely tuned" environments in which only 25 users can be accommodated on a server. Then again, there are plenty of environments with 350 users per server.

Once you accept the fact that you'll never fit 750 users on a dual-processor server, the next step is to define your problem. What's the *real* performance problem in your environment? If you have a server that is slow with 100 users, does that mean that your server is not tuned properly, or does it mean that you have too many users on it? From a performance standpoint, those are just two different ways to look at the same problem.

Given that all Terminal Server performance issues can be reduced to the desire for "more" or "faster," your particular performance issue is likely to be one of the following:

- Logons are too slow
- The overall environment is too slow
- You want to get more users on your server
- The server erratically hangs, spikes, pauses, freezes, and/or slows

You might experience multiple (or all) of these problems in your environment, and quite often they are related. For this reason, it's recommended that you read through this entire chapter before customizing your strategy for addressing specific performance issues. Let's begin by troubleshooting slow logons.

Troubleshooting Slow Logons

All of the problems mentioned previously can be annoying, but slow logons seem to be the curse of so many Terminal Server environments. There are plenty of real-world situations in which people are completely happy with their servers except for the fact that logons are too slow.

What exactly is a "slow logon?" It depends on your environment. Logging on to a Terminal Server and establishing a new session will never be as fast as connecting to a previously disconnected session. Some companies have logon processes that complete in a few seconds, while others take a few minutes. Unfortunately, there are some environments in which the logon process takes several minutes, and even 20-30 minutes is not unheard of. This is the situation that we will troubleshoot here.

Understanding the Terminal Server Logon Process

The logon process in Terminal Server environments is interesting, especially since it doesn't necessarily relate to the usability and overall feel of the server in general. As you've learned thus far, a series of events happen on a Terminal

Server from the time a user clicks the "connect" button until the time his application or desktop is presented to him. In order to successfully troubleshoot slow logons, you need to fully understand what happens during the logon process. Only then can you begin to investigate which aspect of the logon process is holding things up.

Building on what was covered in earlier chapters, the following sequence of events occurs when a user logs on to a Terminal Server:

1. The user clicks the connect button.
2. In session directory-enabled Terminal Server 2003 environments, the server routes the user to the server that is hosting the user's disconnected session. (See Chapter 7 for details.)
3. The server negotiates with the requesting client for its encryption level and virtual channel capabilities.
4. The user is authenticated to the domain and his rights are checked for access to the connection.
5. The licenses are verified. The server client access license is verified first, and then the Terminal Server client access license is verified. (See Chapter 4 for details.)
6. The Terminal Server determines the user profile type and loads one if necessary. (See Chapter 6 for details.)
7. The Terminal Server applies any GPOs that have been configured. (See Chapter 6 for details.)
8. The Terminal Server launches any applications as specified in the policies. (See Chapter 6 for details.)
9. The server executes the contents of the "run" registry values.
10. The server runs the user's logon script(s). (See Chapter 6 for details.)
11. The server runs any programs in the Startup folder of the user's Start Menu.

The above steps take place each time a user logs on. If you're using Citrix MetaFrame, then you can add more steps to address local time zone estimation and load calculations.

Now that you've seen what happens (or could potentially happen) each time a user logs on, you can start to trace this process in your environment to pinpoint where the delay could be.

Here's the approach that most people take, beginning with the easy steps and progressing to the more difficult ones:

1. Isolate the problem.
2. Check the roaming profile.
3. Check for anything that runs, executes, or is loaded when users log on.
4. Check for any other actions that take place when users log on.
5. Trace the logon process with server debug logging options.

Step 1. Isolate the Problem

Before you can start troubleshooting the performance of the logon process, you should get a feel for the situations in which slow logons occur. To do this, collect as much information about the symptoms of the problem as you can. Some potential questions to ask include:

- Are logons slow for some users or all users?
- If you're using Citrix MetaFrame, does a user with a slow logon via ICA also experience a slow logon via RDP?
- What happens if a user with a slow logon logs in via the server console?
- Are logons slow at all times of the day, or just sometimes?
- Do users experience slow logons every time, or is it sporadic?
- Is there anything else that the slow logon users have in common? Are they all in the same domain group or OU? Are they all in the same building? Do they all have the same type of client device or desktop image? Are they all accountants?

Answering these questions will help you frame your investigation. For example, if you determine that slow logons only occur via ICA and not via RDP sessions, then you'll be able to focus your efforts on the components of the ICA session startup process that differ from the standard Terminal Server startup process.

Once you've isolated the symptoms of the problem, you can move to Step 2 with the information you need to make an intelligent diagnosis.

Step 2. Check the Roaming Profile

Although checking roaming profiles doesn't logically seem like the best place to start, roaming profiles are probably responsible for 95% of all slow logon issues in Terminal Server environments. The proper use and design of profiles in Terminal Server environments covered in Chapter 6. If you're not using roaming profiles, skip directly to Step 3.

If you are using roaming profiles, check to see how big your users' profiles are. In theory, Windows 2003 should not allow the master copies of your users' profiles to include space-wasting items such as temporary Internet files. In practice, however, roaming profiles can contain all sorts of garbage, including temp files, Internet cache, crash logs, and hundreds of files that start with "~."

Remember that in environments with roaming profiles, the entire roaming profile needs to be copied across the network to the Terminal Server each time a user logs on. (The only exception to this is if the user logs onto the same server they last logged out of and a cached copy of the roaming profile is locally stored on that server.)

If you do have huge roaming profiles, then you'll need to make them smaller. By using today's techniques of folder redirection, home drives, and profile folder exclusion (all covered in Chapter 6), it's possible to design an environment in which roaming profiles never grow to more than a few megabytes in size.

Step 3. Identify Anything that Runs when a User Logs On

If you determine that huge profiles are not causing slow logons, you should next identify everything that runs when a user logs on. In Terminal Server environments, you must check several places.

Check the Logon Script

Remember from Chapter 6 that users can get logon scripts from several locations. In addition to a script applied as part of the user account settings, you can also have scripts applied as part of GPOs. Finally, don't forget that the *usrlogon.cmd* file still exists (even in Windows Server 2003), and it's possible that some processes are being launched from there.

Check the Registry

There are several registry locations that can launch processes when a user logs on. On your Terminal Servers, check the following registry keys:

Key: HKLM\SOFTWARE\Microsoft\Windows NT\CurrentVersion \Winlogon\

Value: AppSetup
Type: REG_DWORD

Data: This is a comma-separated list of executables that run at session startup.

For most servers, this list will contain UsrLogon.Cmd. (Don't forget to check UsrLogon.cmd to see what it also might be adding to the logon process.) If you're using Citrix MetaFrame, this registry value will also include "cmstart.exe." This is the program that configures the post-logon Citrix environment, including drive mapping and printer redirection.

Key: HKCU\Software\Microsoft\Windows\CurrentVersion\Run

Value: The name of a program to run.

Type: REG_DWORD

Data: The path of the program to run.

Key: HKLM\SOFTWARE\Microsoft\Windows\CurrentVersion\Run

Value: The name of a program to run.

Type: REG_DWORD

Data: The path of the program to run.

These two "run" keys are often used by software vendors who want to launch something at startup without giving the user the option of canceling it. This is how most of those annoying icons appear in your system tray. Each of these keys might list several programs in your environment. Just be sure you know what each one is.

Check the Startup Folders

Many people don't think to check the standard Windows Start Menu's Startup folders (both the *user's* folder and the *all users* folder). However, you'd be surprised at how many users manage to download garbage that installs itself and automatically launches via these folders.

Technically speaking, the contents of the Startup folders are launched after logon, since the Windows shell must be up and running first. However, these applications can still significantly slow the perceived logon time for your users.

Dealing with Programs that Run at Logon Time

Now that you have a list of what runs when a user logs on, what should you do? First, see if you can figure out what everything is and whether any one item is taking a long time to run. Since this is a Terminal Server, this is easy to do. Log in as an administrator and launch Task Manager or the Performance Monitor MMC snap-in. Then, log in as a user and observe the process names that are running for that user.

What should you do if you identify something that's taking too long? Delete it. If the program is required, however, there are still some tricks you can use. The best is to let the program run in its own window that doesn't affect the window. In essence, you can turn any program into a background process.

For example, the cmstart.exe application from Citrix has been known to take a long time to start, especially if users have many printers and printer mapping is enabled. Since the cmstart.exe program is invoked each time a user logs on via the "*AppSetup*" registry key we discussed previously, the user's session cannot start until cmstart.exe successfully completes. To combat this, delete cmstart.exe from the "*AppSetup*" registry location and add it to a user's logon script. If you add it to the *usrlogon.cmd* script (which ironically is also invoked via the "*App-Setup*" registry key), it will run for each user that logs onto the server.

Instead of adding a line to the logon script that simply reads "*cmstart*," add the following line:

start cmstart.exe

The "start" command will launch this process in its own command Window, allowing the system to move on without waiting for it to finish. You can use "start" to launch any application from a logon script with the confidence that the application won't slow down your logon process.

The key here is that the "start" method of launching programs won't make them run any faster, but it will at least let them run in the background so that your users can start working sooner.

Step 4. Identify Other Activities that Take Place at Logon Time

If you can't find a program that's slowing things down by running at logon time, then you'll need to make a list of everything else that happens at logon time.

To do this, check the configuration of all your programs. Look at what's happening with the RDP virtual channels. Do you have drive mapping enabled? How about printer mapping or port redirection? All of these options must initialize themselves when a new session starts.

You're probably wondering how much this can really affect the performance of the system. Consider these facts: disabling Citrix MetaFrame's client time zone estimation at startup allowed one company to increase their server loads from 65 to 110 users per server. Another company was able to increase from 35 to 62 users per server simply by disabling the automatic printer mapping since printer redirection takes significant time at logon as new printers are detected and installed by the spooler service. (See Chapter 4 for details.) Disable that feature or check the box that allows users to logon without waiting for their printers and watch your logon times drop.

This is not meant to be an exhaustive list of everything you should try to disable. Rather, these examples should give you some ideas of what to look for and examples of the dramatic affects they can have on logon times.

When considering the activities that take place at logon time, don't forget about non-Terminal Server and applications. For example, antivirus software is notorious for slowing down the logon process of a Terminal Server as it scans every file of the user's profile as it's loaded. Running virus software on your master profile file server instead of your Terminal Servers has great potential to substantially decrease logon times.

Step 5. Trace the Debug Logs from the User Logon Process

If after these four steps you haven't determined why you're experiencing slow logons, it's time to get your hands dirty. In Windows Server 2003, an application called "userenv.dll" is responsible for creating the entire user environment at logon time. This includes loading user profiles and applying GPOs.

Fortunately, you can enable diagnostic trace logging on all actions that the userenv.dll file conducts. These trace logs are *extremely* detailed, describing down to the millisecond exactly what the server was doing. For example, in addition to being able to trace the high-level logon process outlined previously, you can also see the *userenv.dll* verifying the profile file list build, checking for disk space, verifying *ntuser.dat*, loading *ntuser.dat* into HKCU, and replacing system variables in the path with actual variables.

By viewing this log you will see if a particular file in the roaming profile is getting stuck, if the file copy process is taking too long, or if DNS or WINS name resolution is holding the server up. It also allows you to track the application of GPOs to see if one is taking an inordinate amount of time or if you simply have too many GPOs that are slowing things down.

This log file can help you pinpoint slow logon issues related to things you might not have thought of otherwise. For example, one environment was experiencing slow logons due to the domain controller. The IT staff had been focusing their attention on the path between the Terminal Server and the file server hosting the master copies of the user profiles. However, when they looked at the userenv.dll logs, they discovered that the domain controller was so busy that it was taking 30-45 seconds to respond when the Terminal Server queried it to see where the user's roaming profile was stored. A $3,000 hardware upgrade to the domain controller saved this company 45 seconds on every user logon across 20 Terminal Servers.

You can enable userenv.dll logging by adding the following registry entry to a Terminal Server:

Key: HKLM\Software\Microsoft\Windows NT\CurrentVersion\Winlogon

Value: UserEnvDebugLevel

Type: REG_DWORD

Data: 10002 (Hex)

The data value of 10002 will enable verbose logging to a file on the server. Once you set this value, reboot your server and check for a "*userenv.log*" file in the *%SystemRoot%\Debug\UserMode* folder. Remember to turn this off when you're done troubleshooting it, since each user logon can easily add 100KB to the size of this log file.

Let's look at a small example from a *userenv.log* file. This example has been severely trimmed, and shows only a few random lines to give you a feel for the type of information that is available in this log file. (The complete log for this single user's logon process would have filled 25 pages.)

Notice that the exact time down to the millisecond is listed for every line in this log. This allows you to see exactly what's happening and where the hold-up could be.

Figure 13.1 Selected sample lines from a userenv.dll log

```
09:25:30:606 UnloadUserProfile: Entering, hProfile =
<0x850>
09:25:30:606 UnloadUserProfile: In console winlogon
process
09:25:30:616 UnloadUserProfileP: Entering, hProfile =
<0x850>
09:25:30:616 CSyncManager::EnterLock <S-1-5-21-
2364083253-1420309831-852573094-500>
09:25:30:616 CSyncManager::EnterLock: No existing en-
try found
09:25:30:616 CSyncManager::EnterLock: New entry cre-
ated
09:25:30:616 CHashTable::HashAdd: S-1-5-21-2364083253-
1420309831-852573094-500 added in bucket 19
```

```
09:25:30:616 UnloadUserProfileP: Wait succeeded.  In
critical section.
09:25:30:872 MyRegUnLoadKey: Returning 1.
09:25:30:872 UnloadUserProfileP:  Succesfully unloaded
profile
is local, not setting preference key
09:27:39:975 CreateLocalProfileImage:  One way or an-
other we haven't got an existing local profile, try
and create one
09:27:39:975 CreateSecureDirectory: Entering with
<C:\Documents and Settings\brian>
09:27:40:052 CreateSecureDirectory: Created the direc-
tory <C:\Documents and Settings\brian>
09:27:40:052 ComputeLocalProfileName: generated the
profile directory <C:\Documents and
09:27:42:068 CopyProfileDirectory: Leaving with a re-
turn value of 1
09:27:42:106 MyRegLoadKey: Returning 00000000
09:27:42:106 IssueDefaultProfile:  Leaving success-
fully
09:27:42:115 RestoreUserProfile:  Successfully setup
the local default.
09:27:42:115 SetupNewHive:  Entering
09:27:42:115 SetDefaultUserHiveSecurity:  Entering
09:27:42:335 SecureUserKey:  Entering
09:27:42:335 SecureUserKey:  Leaving with a return
value of 1
09:27:42:335 SecureUserKey:  Entering
09:27:42:345 SecureUserKey:  Leaving with a return
value of 1
09:27:49:719 ProcessGPOs: ----------------------
09:27:49:719 ProcessGPOs: Processing extension Micro-
soft Disk Quota
09:27:49:719 CompareGPOLists:  The lists are the same.
09:27:49:719 ProcessGPOs: Extension Microsoft Disk
Quota skipped with flags 0x6.
09:27:49:719 ProcessGPOs: ----------------------
09:27:49:719 ProcessGPOs: Processing extension QoS
Packet Scheduler
09:27:49:719 CompareGPOLists:  The lists are the same.
09:27:49:719 ProcessGPOs: Extension QoS Packet Sched-
uler skipped with flags 0x6.
09:27:49:719 ProcessGPOs: ----------------------
09:27:49:729 ProcessGPOs: Processing extension Scripts
09:27:49:729 CompareGPOLists:  The lists are the same.
09:27:49:729 ProcessGPOs: Extension Scripts skipped
because both deleted and changed GPO lists are empty.
09:27:49:862 ProcessGPOs: User Group Policy has been
applied.
09:27:49:862 ProcessGPOs: Leaving with 1.
09:27:49:872 ApplyGroupPolicy: Leaving successfully.
```

```
09:27:51:763 IsSyncForegroundPolicyRefresh: Synchro-
nous, Reason: policy set to SYNC
09:27:52:700 LibMain: Process Name:
C:\WINDOWS\system32\userinit.exe
09:27:53:139 GPOThread:  Next refresh will happen in
109 minutes
09:27:57:926 LibMain: Process Name:
C:\WINDOWS\system32\ie4uinit.exe
09:28:40:507 LibMain: Process Name:
C:\WINDOWS\system32\msiexec.exe
09:28:47:967 LibMain: Process Name:
C:\WINDOWS\system32\userinit.exe
```

With these tools and techniques, you should be equipped to troubleshoot slow logons. Keep in mind that the logon process always takes time, and in reality 15 or 20 seconds is probably as fast as you'll ever get it. However, if your current users are waiting a minute or two, there are steps you can take to speed up the process.

Getting More Users on your Server

Just about everyone wants to figure out how to support more users on their Terminal Servers. While this is a noble endeavor, it's crucial to remember the opening paragraphs of this chapter where we discussed the limitations of server hardware.

In order to fit more users on your system, you need to look for bottlenecks. At some point, a bottleneck will always occur on every server. You just want to see if you can find it and if it's easily fixable. If it is, you can then look for the next bottleneck. Eventually you'll encounter a bottleneck that you can't work around, but hopefully by this point you'll have a lot more users on your server than you started with.

Even the largest datacenter-class servers have practical limits to the number of users they can support, especially if they are running 32-bit versions of Windows. Today's biggest 32-bit systems can support up to about 500 simultaneous users, although most servers are configured to support somewhere between 50 to 150 users.

In order to determine whether your servers can support more users, you'll need to break the server down into its technical components and analyze the techniques required to assess and optimize each one. Let's start by looking at the version of Microsoft Windows that runs on your Terminal Server.

Choosing your Version of Windows

Before you begin to troubleshoot and track down the performance issues of your Terminal Servers, you should understand that the version of Windows that you use on your servers can have a significant impact on its performance. Since you're reading this book, it's probably safe to assume that you are using or will shortly be using Windows 2003 for your Terminal Servers. If not, you should seriously consider using Windows Server 2003.

All things being equal, Microsoft Windows Server 2003 will support 25 to 80% more users than Windows 2000 Server (based on studies by Gartner, HP, Unisys, Microsoft, and the experience of the authors of this book). Most people are skeptical until they see it for themselves, but it's proven that you can fit a lot more users on a Windows 2003 Server than a Windows 2000 server with identical hardware.

The only footnote to this rule is that Windows 2003 supports more users than Windows 2000 only when the servers are not constrained by a hardware limitation. In other words, if a server is low on memory or underpowered, then Windows 2003 and Windows 2000 will experience equivalent performance. However, if you have a large server running Windows 2000 (let's say four processors and 4GB of memory), upgrading to Windows Server 2003 will enable you to run more users on that server.

The reasons for this are twofold. First, Windows 2003 performs much better than Windows 2000 across the board, not just with regards to Terminal Services. Secondly (and much less relevant although still interesting), you don't need to tweak and tune Windows 2003 as much as Windows 2000. Windows 2003 includes all the Terminal Server-related tweaks that have been "discovered" in the past three years with Windows 2000.

Memory

Memory is easily the most important hardware component of a Terminal Server. The amount of memory in a server completely affects the performance of other hardware components. For example, in addition to not being able to support as many users as you'd like to, not having enough memory can add an extra burden to the processor and disk since the page file would be more heavily used.

If you really want to fit more users onto your Terminal Servers, you'll need to investigate the physical memory. There are several steps to take to be successful at this:

- You need to understand how memory works in Terminal Server environments.
- You need to figure out whether you have enough memory to do what you want to do.
- If the system seems to get slower over time, you need to check for memory leaks.

Real-World Memory Estimation

Before you even begin to think about whether a server has enough memory to support the desired number of users, it's not a bad idea to do a quick mental calculation to determine whether the server's memory is anywhere near appropriate.

The amount of memory required per user depends on the applications they use and the operating system of your server. It is typically appropriate to estimate about 128MB for the base system.

For heavy workers who use Outlook, IE, Word, and Excel and who often switch back and forth between them, a good estimation is to allow about 15MB of memory for each user. For light, task-oriented data entry users who only use a single application without the Windows shell, you can count on about 7MB per user. If your Terminal Servers support complex client/server line-of-business applications, then there's no way to guess how much memory you need. It could easily be 20, 30, or even 50MB per user, depending on the application.

Of course these numbers are just starting points, and your mileage may vary. At first glance these numbers may seem far too low, but in reality they're fairly accurate. (Remember, we're talking about *physical* memory—not the total memory—required per user.) To understand this, let's first look at how Windows 2003 Terminal Servers use memory.

How Memory Usage works in Windows 2003 Terminal Server environments

Every user that runs an application on a Terminal Server will use the memory for that application just as if it were running it on a normal workstation. A quick check of the task manager shows that Microsoft Word requires about 10MB of memory to run. Each user of Word will need 10MB, and 20 simultaneous users will require 200MB of memory.

Of course, this is on top of the overhead required for each user to run a session, which is about 4MB. Twenty users running Word require a collective 280MB of memory on the Terminal Server.

To this you must add the memory required by the base operating system, which is usually around 128MB on a Terminal Server. If you add all of these together, you'll find that 20 users will require that a server have 408MB of memory.

Before you run out and start checking the memory usage of your applications, you should know the two reasons that any calculations you make based on these parameters will be totally useless:

- Applications require varying amounts of memory. Although task manager showed Microsoft Word to consume only 10MB of memory, memory consumption will vary greatly depending on the open documents. Download and open a 300-page graphics-laden Windows 2003 white paper, and you'll see that Word can consume much more than 10MB. Also watch out for supporting files, such as DLLs, which sometimes consume the largest amount of memory.
- Windows treats multiple instances of the same executable in a special way. If 20 users are all using Word at 10MB each, then you would assume that 200MB of memory is being consumed, right? In actuality, Windows is a bit smarter than that. Because all 20 users are using the same copy of winword.exe, the system figures that it doesn't need to physically load the same binary executable image into memory 20 times. Instead, it loads the executable only once and "points" the other sessions to that first instance. This is done discreetly. The components controlling each user's session think that they have a full copy of the executable loaded locally in their own memory space, when in fact all they have is a pointer to another memory space. If one session should need to modify the copy of the executable in memory, the server seamlessly (and quickly) makes a unique copy of the executable for that session.

What is particularly tricky here is the fact that if you look at the task manager, each user's session will report the full amount of memory being used. Only in the total memory usage statistics will you see that the numbers don't add up.

Most people use Task Manager to provide information as to whether a server has enough physical memory (Performance Tab | Physical Memory (K) | Available). The problem here is that the number reported by Task Manager is a bit misleading. While it does correctly show the amount of physical memory that's free, it doesn't really show *why* that memory is free. For example, if Task Manager shows that you're almost out of memory, you might think that you need more, when in fact adding more memory won't help at all. To appreciate why, you need to understand how Windows manages memory allocation.

In the Windows operating system, individual processes request memory from the system in chunks. Each chunk is called a "page" and is 4K in size. Any pages of memory that Windows grants to a process are called its "committed memory." A process's committed memory represents the total amount of memory that the system has given it, and this committed memory can be in physical memory or paged to disk (or some of both).

Windows watches how each process uses its committed memory. The pages of memory that a process uses often are stored in physical memory. These are called a process's "working set." Of all of a process's committed memory, the working set portion is stored in physical memory and the rest is stored in the page file on the hard disk.

When physical memory is plentiful (i.e. when overall system memory utilization is low), Windows doesn't pay much attention to how each process uses the memory it's been granted. In these cases, all of a process's committed bytes are stored in physical memory (meaning that each process's working set is the same size as its committed memory—even if it doesn't actively use all of it.)

However, when overall physical memory utilization gets a bit higher (80% overall by default), Windows starts to get nervous. It begins checking with all the processes to see how much of their working sets they are actively using. If a process isn't using all of its working set, the system will page some of it out to disk, allowing the system reclaim some physical memory for other processes. It's important to note that this is natural, and does *not* negatively affect performance, since only unused portions of a process's working set are paged to disk.

Remember that the system doesn't start reclaiming unused working set memory until overall memory utilization reaches 80%. In systems with plenty of memory, Windows doesn't bother paging out unused working set memory.

A "side effect" is that when memory is plentiful, looking at how much memory the system is using at any given point in time (by looking at the working set memory) will show a number that's much higher than it needs to be. This can lead you down the path of thinking that your server needs more memory than it actually does.

To summarize, the committed memory for a process is the amount of memory that Windows allocated it, and the working set is the subset of committed memory that's in the physical RAM. If a process doesn't actively use all of its working set, the system might take away some of the working set in order to better use the physical RAM somewhere else. This does not affect overall system performance since the process wasn't using that memory anyway.

In environments that start to run out of memory, the system will get desperate and start to page out portions of the working set that a process is currently using. At that point, operations will begin to slow down for your users, and you won't be able to add any more users. This is the circumstance you need to look for with Performance Monitor.

Determining whether you have Enough Physical Memory

Using the Performance MMC snap-in to track actual memory usage is difficult. Now that you understand (or have read, anyway) how Windows 2003 processes use memory, let's use a real-world analogy so that you can start to appreciate the complexity of the issues that you'll need to track. Refer to Figure 13.2 as you read through this short analogy.

Figure 13.2 Components of the Windows memory usage analogy

Windows Servers	The Analogy
Physical RAM	Your office building
Page file	Offsite Document Storage
A Process or Program	Employee
Section of memory used by a process	A Paper Document
The System	The boss

Imagine you work in an office building processing documents. If there are only a few people in your office, you'll probably have plenty of room to store all your papers. Everything—even papers you haven't touched for the past twenty years—are stored in your office since space is plentiful. Even though you're storing a lot of unused documents, it doesn't matter since there's so much space in your office.

If you get some new coworkers, they will take up some of your office space. To mitigate this, your boss might say, "Sort through your files and put anything you haven't touched in five years in offsite storage." That would free up space to allow more people to work in the office. Doing this probably wouldn't affect your productivity, since you hadn't touched those papers in five years anyway.

As your company continues to add employees, you need to provide space for them. To free up space, your boss might ask you to move documents that are only a year old to offsite storage. This is not a big problem, since you can always request your documents back from offsite storage. (Of course, this takes a few days and you'd have to send something else there in its place to make room for the newly-retrieved documents.)

If your company continues to add employees, you might be forced to store documents that are only six-months old, and then one-month old. Eventually there will be so many people in such a small office that the majority of your documents will be in offsite storage and no one will be very productive. The only solution is to get a bigger office or lay off some employees (or just convince your customers that this is how all companies work).

Supposing you are a business analyst called in to alleviate this company's document problem, how would you measure it? It's obvious that they need more space or fewer people, but what is reasonable? How can you track productivity as compared to the ratio of onsite to offsite document storage? It's difficult to create hard numbers for this. Who can decide what's acceptable and what's not?

This difficulty is why it's hard to use the Performance MMC to track *real* memory usage on a Terminal Server. It's also why people have not traditionally been good at estimating the actual memory requirements in the past.

The best way to use Performance Monitor in this case is to track trends. You'll need to watch several counters at once to see how they relate to each other when your system starts behaving poorly. Here are the counters that you should track:

Process | Working Set | _Total

The Working Set counter is actually a property of a process, not the system memory. Therefore, you'll need to select the process object. You'll see every running process listed, but selecting the "_Total" will give you the grand total, in bytes, of all the working sets of all processes on the system. When you check this, remember that this will not include the base memory, so you'll need to add another 128MB or so.

Memory | Pages Input/Sec

This counter tells you the number of times per second that a process needed to access a piece of memory that was not in its working set, meaning that the system had to retrieve it from the page file. From our analogy, this is comparable to when an employee needed to use a document that was at the offsite storage facility.

Memory | Pages Output/Sec

This counter is the opposite of the "Pages Input/Sec" counter. It tells you how many times per second the system decided to trim a process's working set by writing some memory to disk in order to free up physical memory for another process.

Memory | Available Bytes

This counter tracks the amount of bytes that are free in the physical memory. Free bytes are ready to be used by another process. When memory is plentiful, these free bytes are used with reckless abandon, which is why you can't track this counter alone to determine memory requirements.

Terminal Services | Active Sessions

You should also track the number of user sessions you have on the system in order to have a reference point for what was going on.

So what exactly are you looking for? Start adding some users to the system by following the server sizing test process outlined in Chapter 5. One of the first things you'll notice is that the working set will grow at a very high rate. (Remember that the system doesn't bother managing it until physical memory starts running low.) You'll also notice that the Available Bytes counter will initially take a nosedive since the system freely lets processes' working sets stay in memory. At this point you'll see some activity in both the Memory Pages counters as new users log on, but nothing to be concerned about. (Spikes may be in the 200 range, but overall fairly low.)

As you continue to add users, you'll eventually notice that the working set counter starts to drop. This occurs when the physical memory starts to run low and the system has started trimming the unused portions of processes' working sets. The Pages Output/Sec counter will start to spike high (several thousand per second even) as the system begins writing those pages to disk. As you continue adding users, the Pages Output/Sec *spikes* will decrease, although the general trend will be that Pages Output/Sec will increase. This is to be expected, and the performance of your system will not suffer because if it. (Don't buy more memory just yet!)

As you continue to add more users, the working set will continue to drop, and both of the memory pages counters will continue to steadily rise. Available Bytes is down around zero at this point.

What does all this mean? How do you know how many users you can add, and whether more memory will help you? If your server doesn't show the trends as described, then you have plenty of memory. The critical counter to watch is the Pages Output/Sec. Remember that it remains low for a while and then starts spiking dramatically. The spikes slowly become less and less pronounced until the counter begins rising overall. The point between spike's dying down and the counter's slow rise is the sweet spot for a Terminal Server. If your counter never starts to rise significantly after it's done spiking, then you have enough memory and your user base is limited by something else. If you server's Pages Output/Sec counter starts to steadily climb after it's done spiking, then you could probably benefit from more memory or other tuning techniques outlined later in this chapter.

Identifying Memory Leaks

Another problem relating to memory that can negatively impact the performance of a Terminal Server is a memory leak. A memory leak takes perfectly good memory away from the system. Most memory leaks are progressive and take up more and more memory as time goes on. Depending on the leak, this could be as slow as a few KB per hour and as fast as several MB per minute. In all cases, memory leaks are due to a problem with an application or driver, and most can be fixed with a patch (assuming the application vendor is competent enough to create one).

A memory leak is like a cancer, slowly eating away at the system. Left unchecked, it will cause the system to slow down until it becomes completely unresponsive and hangs. Memory leaks can also cause client connection and disconnection problems, excessive CPU utilization, and disk thrashing. Sometimes you can identify the offending application and kill it manually. Other times a system reboot is the only fix.

The good news about memory leaks (if there is any) is that they are very rare these days, occurring most often in "homegrown" or "really crappy" applications. It seems like they used occur all the time in Windows NT, but not so much anymore. If you ever run into a consultant who's quick to suggest that all Terminal Server performance problems are due to memory leaks, you will know that this is an "old school" person who hasn't updated his troubleshooting skills in five years.

Identifying a memory leak is usually pretty easy. (Figuring out what's causing it is the hard part.) To do this, you'll also need to use the Performance MMC snap-in. In technical terms, a memory leak occurs when the system allocates more memory to a process than the process gives back to the system. Any type of process can cause a memory leak. You can see that you're having a memory leak by monitoring the Paged Pool Bytes (Memory | Pool Paged Bytes) and Page File Usage (Paging File | %Usage | _Total) counters. If you see either (or both) of these counters steadily increasing even when you're not adding more users to the system, then you probably have a memory leak. You might also have a memory leak if you see a more intermittent increase (still without adding new users), since memory leaks can occur in processes that aren't always running.

As noted previously, identifying that you have a memory leak is easy. Figuring out which process is causing it is harder. You can use Performance Monitor to track the amount of memory that each process is using (Process | Private Bytes | pick a process). Of course on Terminal Servers, you'll have hundreds of processes running, so it's not like you'll want to track each one. Unfortunately, there isn't an easier way to find it. (This is why IT departments need interns.) You can chart all processes at once by selecting the "all instances" radio button on the "Add Counters" dialog box. Sometimes this works well, especially on idle servers. The hundreds of lines paint horizontal stripes across the chart, and any increase is immediately visible. When you see it, enable highlighting (Ctrl+H) and scroll through your list of processes until you find the one that's steadily increasing.

What should you do if you weren't able to isolate the memory leak with Performance Monitor? In this case the memory leak was most likely caused by something operating in kernel mode. Kernel mode memory leaks usually require the assistance of Microsoft Product Support to identify. They'll have you run a utility (poolmon.exe, located on the Windows CD in the "support" folder) that monitors the kernel mode memory pool and outputs contents to a command window.

If you do manage to figure out the cause, there's nothing you can really do about it other than to contact the vendor for a fix or to discontinue using whatever's causing it.

Page File Usage

The Windows page file is an interesting creature. A common misconception is that it's "merely" an extension of physical memory used on servers that don't have enough memory. Most people think that if they buy enough physical memory, they'll never have to worry about the page file. In Terminal Server environments, nothing could be further from the truth. While it's true that the page file is used more when physical memory is scarce, Windows also uses the page file in other ways.

Remember from the previous section that Windows is smart enough to only load a single copy of a binary executable into memory when multiple processes (or users) utilize an application. That's technically called "copy-on-write" optimization, since Windows will make an additional copy of a portion of the application in memory only when a process attempts to write to it.

In Windows environments, every executable and DLL is written to as it's used. (This doesn't mean that the EXE or DLL files on the disk are written to. It simply means that once they're loaded into memory, the versions in memory change as they are used.)

Therefore, a single DLL is loaded into memory and the system lets multiple processes share it. However, as soon as a process tries to write to a portion of that DLL, the system makes a quick copy of it (via the "copy-on-write" functionality) and lets the process write to the copy instead. Additionally, the system also backs up that section of that DLL to the page file for safekeeping. This means that there are effectively three copies of that portion of the DLL in memory—the original, the copy for the other process to write to, and the backup in the page file. This same phenomena occurs for every program that is shared by multiple processes (or users), including EXE and DLL files.

In regular Windows environments, backing up the copy-on-written section of an executable to the page file is no big deal. However, imagine how inefficient this is in Terminal Server environments!

Think about a Terminal Server hosting 30 users who are all using an application such as JD Edwards One World. This application is a standard client / server application, and launching the JD Edwards client software loads an executable and several DLLs into the memory space of each user's session. However, Windows only initially loads a single copy of the executables into physical memory.

As all 30 users utilize the application, Windows' copy-on-write optimization will create 29 "copies" in memory of large portions of each JD Edwards executable. (One for the first user and 29 copies for the 29 other users.) This means that Windows will have also placed an *additional* 29 copies of the original executables in the page file before the copies were made. The 30 JDE users will effectively cause 59 copies of the single executable to be loaded in memory. Now, imagine this multiplied by each of the many EXEs and DLLs that JD Edwards loads.

Unfortunately, this is all too common. These fat client/server applications were never designed for Terminal Server environments. Applications like JDE One-World, Cerner, Lotus Notes, Siebel, PeopleSoft, SAP, and others all load massive client environments when they're launched. (This usually includes the core EXE plus several DLLs.)

Understanding this behavior starts to give you an idea of just how important the page file is in Terminal Server environments, regardless of how much physical memory you have. To help mitigate this, there are really only two things that you can do for a page file:

- You can change the way Windows uses the page file.
- You can make the page file faster.

Changing the way Windows uses the Page File

Windows' copy-on-write "optimization" is part of the core Windows memory management components, and you can't just turn it off. "Unfortunately," as Kevin Goodman puts it, "it's not like there's a 'NoCopyOnWrite' registry flag that you can use to disable it."

However, you can use third party software products to change the way that Windows implements this copy-on-write functionality. This can be done with RTO Software's TScale product, which is also sold by Wyse under the Expedian brand.

TScale watches how applications use their working sets and how multiple instances of an application are affected by the Windows copy-on-write optimizations. It logs potential optimizations to an optimization map file on the server's hard drive. Then, the next time a user launches the application, the server reads the optimization map.

This optimization allows multiple instances of an application to share the backup copies in the page file. This dramatically cuts down on page file usage, which in turn frees up the processor to support more users. TScale also decreases the working set of each instance of the application, freeing up memory that can allow you to support more users. Each application on a Terminal Server is analyzed separately, and each has its own optimization map.

TScale really shines with the big client/server applications. In fact (and quite ironically), the only applications that TScale doesn't greatly affect (maybe 10% more users instead of 30% more) are applications from Microsoft, such as Office, Visio, and Project. (It's almost as if the folks writing these applications in Redmond know something about they way Windows works that no one else does.)

RTO Software offers a 30-day evaluation copy that you can download from www.rtosoft.com. You can see for yourself how much of a difference it would make in your environment.

Making the Page File Faster

Even after applying TScale or Expedian page file optimizations, your page file will still be used in a Terminal Server environment. Because of this, you need to ensure that your page file is as accessible as possible.

A heavily-used page file will overly tax the disk I/O. Therefore, refer to the "Disk Usage" section of this chapter for information about how to determine whether your hard disk I/O capacities are causing bottlenecks in your environment. If you determine that your page file is your bottleneck and you'd like to make it faster, there are a few things that you can do:

- Put the page file on its own drive on its own SCSI channel.
- Buy one of those flash RAM hard drives like a TiGiJet from `www.tigicorp.com`). These look like regular hard drives except that they are solid state. They have Flash RAM instead of disks and spindles. They're very fast, but also very expensive, costing several thousand dollars for a few gigabytes.

None of these solutions will make a dramatic difference, and you shouldn't even attempt them until after you've implemented a software page file optimization solution like TScale or Expedian.

Page File Sizing

The last aspect of the page file that has the ability to affect how many users you can fit on your server is the page file size. If your page file runs out of space, then you won't be able to fit any more users on your server. The "official" page file size recommendation for Terminal Server environments is 1.5 times the amount of physical memory. However, this does not need to be strictly followed. When determining your page file size, look at the types and numbers of applications that users will be using. Also consider the amount of total system memory. If you have a server with 512MB, then 1.5x page file is adequate. If you have 8GB of memory, you can probably get away with a smaller page file. Try a 4GB page file first and then increase from there if necessary.

You can check the percentage of page file usage via the following Performance counter:

Paging File | % Usage | _Total

Once you figure out the size that you want your page file to be, go ahead and configure your server so that the page file starts out at full size. To conserve disk space, Windows allows you to specify a minimum and maximum page file size. The system starts with the minimum and then grows from there. Unfortunately, this means that your system would need to spend resources extending the page file right when the resources are needed most. (After all, that's why the page file is being extended anyway.) Configuring the page file to start out at the maximum size (by entering the same values for the maximum and minimum sizes) will let you avoid this situation. Besides, disk space is usually plentiful on Terminal Servers.

Processor Usage

Fortunately, understanding the processor usage of a Terminal Server is much easier than understanding memory usage. There are a few simple steps that you can take to evaluate the processor and address any issues you might find.

- Understand how Terminal Servers make use of processors and how you can track there usage.
- Take steps to minimize the impact that applications have to the processor.
- If your server is running on Intel Xeon processors, understand how enabling or disabling Hyperthreading will affect performance.

Tracking Processor Usage

Tracking processor utilization is easy with the Performance MMC. Add the following two counters to your chart:

Processor | % Processor Time | _Total

This counter shows how busy the processors are. If it pegs at 100% then you need more of something. However, if the processor is too busy, don't automatically think that you need more processing power. The processor might be busy because you're running out of memory and it is spending unnecessary time writing to and reading from the page file.

System | Processor Queue Length

If you notice that the processor utilization is fairly high, you might want to track the Processor Queue Length counter as well. This counter shows how many requests are backed up while they wait for the processor to get freed up to service them. By tracking this, you can see if the processor is very busy or too busy. (Yes, there is a difference.) A processor that is very busy might show 100% utilization, but it will back down as soon as another request comes through. You can see this because the Processor Queue Length will be almost zero. A processor that is too busy might also show 100% utilization, except that because it's too busy it cannot service additional requests, resulting in the Processor Queue Length beginning to fill up.

You should always use the Performance MMC instead of the Task Manager to get a good understanding of the processor utilization of your system. Task Manager is only meant to be used as a general estimation of the system and can be off by 5% or more at times.

Minimizing the Processor Impact of Applications

If you determine that the processing power of your server is limiting the number of users you can host, there are several things that you can do. Your overall approach will be to identify unneeded activities that are using processor resources and eliminate them.

Many applications have "features" that are enabled by default and wreak havoc on the performance of Terminal Servers. For example, disabling Microsoft Word 2000's background grammar checking will allow you to *double* the number of users on a server. Even though grammar checking might not be too taxing on a single system, one hundred users with constant background checking can severely impact a Terminal Server.

The good news is that you now know what can cause unneeded processor utilization. The bad news is that these issues are impossible to detect with Performance Monitor. (With 120 users on a server, would you really know that disabling background grammar checking could take each user's average utilization from 0.82% to 0.46%?)

Another example of this is that disabling Internet Explorer's personalization settings will dramatically increase its loading speed and allow you to run more users.

The bottom line here is that you'll need to manually weed through each of your applications and disable all the neat "features" that could potentially consume resources. Some people feel that they shouldn't be forced to do this. Whether you do or don't depends on what you want out of your servers. Do you want to fit the most users you can on a server or do you want to have shadows under your mouse cursors? You decide.

If your users can live with 256 colors instead of 24-bit color, you might be able to fit 10% more users on your servers. Remember that each option you disable won't have enough impact its own, but multiplying its effect by several hundred users can easily produce some dramatic results.

How your users actually use their applications also affects processor utilization. If you build a Terminal Server that hosts only Microsoft Word, you'll fit a lot more 20 WPM typists than you will 65 WPM typists.

As you analyze your application usage, don't forget to consider the applications that run in the background on the server. A good example of this is antivirus software. Whether you should run antivirus software on your Terminal Servers is a debate that will continue for some time. However, understand that running antivirus software that offers "live" file system protection will severely limit the number of users you can fit on a server. Again, this is not something that you'll be able to track with the Performance MMC. If you can devise an alternate antivirus plan (such as antivirus protection at the perimeter and file server level), you may be able to add 20 to 50% more users to your Terminal Servers.

Hyperthreading with Intel Xeon Processors

If your Terminal Server systems are running Intel Xeon processors, then you have the added option of enabling Hyperthreading (via the BIOS). Hyperthreading is an Intel-proprietary technology that makes one processor look like two to the operating system (and two processors look like four, etc.). Xeon processors have two data pipelines going in and out of the core processing unit on the chip. The processor generally alternates between the two pipelines. The advantage of Hyperthreading is that by having two inputs, the CPU will always have something to execute. If one pipeline is not quite ready, then the CPU can pull code from the other pipeline. This happens billions of times per second.

Hyperthreading does have some general disadvantages. One major disadvantage (which doesn't affect performance) is that many applications that are licensed based on the number of processors are tricked into thinking the system has doubled the amount of processors it actually has.

Another potential problem with Hyperthreading (which does affect performance) is that in terms of instruction execution, Windows isn't smart enough to know that you have Hyperthreading. It can't tell the difference between a two-processor system with Hyperthreading enabled and a regular four-processor system. This can lead to performance problems since the system might split up complex process across two of the four processors for faster execution. In a Hyperthreaded system, this might mean that those two threads are both going to the same physical processor, while the other processor sits idle.

Another potential problem with Hyperthreading is that some drivers are not multithreaded and therefore not able to make use of both virtual processors. For example, a single-threaded network card driver can cause system-wide bottlenecks if all network traffic is processed by a single virtual processor.

Given all the potential complications of Hyperthreading, studies show that enabling Hyperthreading can increase the overall performance of a Windows 2003 Terminal Server. According a Tim Mangan of TMurgent, enabling Hyperthreading on Windows 2003 Terminal Servers seems to give a 10 to 20% performance boost, meaning that the CPU can support 10 to 20% more users.

The overall effect of enabling Hyperthreading varies depending on the hardware, applications, and server load. Therefore, there is no rock solid rule regarding Hyperthreading. You'll need to try it in your environment to see whether it helps or hurts you.

Disk Usage

In terms of performance, the hard drives of a Terminal Server are rarely the bottleneck. However, they have the potential to be and you should certainly check them with due diligence.

Before you investigate your hard drives, be sure to check the memory and page file usage, since not having enough memory can cause excessive paging and your hard drives to work harder than they have to.

In most environments, your Terminal Servers only need to contain the Windows operating system, the page file, and your software application files. User and application data is usually stored on other servers or a storage area network (SAN), so the local drives don't slow things down based on user file access.

In order to evaluate whether your hard drives are slowing down your server, check the following Performance counters:

Physical Disk | % Disk Time

This counter shows you how busy your server's hard drives are. A value of 100% would indicate that the disks are 100% busy, meaning that you might need faster disks, more memory, or fewer users.

Physical Disk | Current Disk Queue Length

As with the processor counters, if your % Disk Time counter is at or near 100, you might also want to monitor this counter. It will tell you how many disk requests are waiting because the disk is too busy. If you have multiple physical disks in your server (that are not mirrored), you should record a separate instance of this counter for each disk instead of one counter for all disks. This will allow you to determine whether your disks are being used evenly, or if one disk is overworked while another sits idle.

Addressing Disk Usage Bottlenecks

If you do determine that your server's hard drives are the bottleneck, there are a few approaches you can take. The first is to investigate your server's disk configuration. You can also opt to replace the current disks with faster ones, or perhaps even change your disk architecture altogether.

Server vendors have all sorts of tricks you can implement to increase the performance of your disks. A now infamous example is that Compaq's RAID cards and disks came with 64MB of cache that was all configured as read-cache. Changing the cache configuration (via a software utility) to 50% read and 50% write cache allowed people to almost double the number of users they could put on a system.

As a quick side note, you'll notice that many of these solutions allowed companies to "almost double" the number of users they can support. Keep in mind that this entire performance analysis is all about finding bottlenecks. In your case, implementing one change might only yield a 5% increase since it would then reveal a new bottleneck. You might have to work your way through several bottlenecks before you see substantial performance gains.

If software configuration alone won't alleviate your disk-related bottleneck, replacing your current disks with faster ones should allow you to (at least partially) release some of the pressure from the disks. Remember that when dealing with servers, you can buy faster disks (15k verses 10k RPMs), a faster interface, or both.

Finally, you might ultimately decide that changing the architecture of your disks is the best way to fix your disk problem. If you have a server with two mirrored drives, you might decide that breaking the mirror and placing the operating system on one disk and the paging file on the other is the best way to make use of your hardware.

Server Network Usage

Limitations of the physical network interfaces on Terminal Servers certainly have the ability to cause a bottleneck. What's interesting about this is that it's usually not the RDP user sessions that clog the network card. Rather, it's the interface between the Terminal Server and the network file servers that usually cause the blockage. These connections are responsible for users' roaming profiles, home drives, load-balancing, and all other back end data that's transferred in and out of a server. Hundreds of users on a single server can easily saturate this link. As with all hardware components, if your network link is your bottleneck, you'll be limited as to how many users you can fit on your server regardless of how much memory or processing power you have.

The easiest way to check your network utilization is via Performance Monitor. Of course you can also use Task Manager (Networking Tab) to do a quick check, but you can't save anything or get any quick details from there. Within the Performance MMC snap-in, load the following counters:

Network Interface | Bytes Total/sec | Select your card

Be sure to select a different instance of this counter for each network card in your server. When you look at the results, keep in mind that a 100 Mb/second network interface is 100 mega*bits*, and the performance counter tracks bytes. Since there are 8 bits in a byte, the performance counter would max out at 12.5M bytes. If you factor in physical network overhead, the actual maximum of a 100Mb network is about ten megabytes per second.

Network Interface | Output Queue Length | Select you card

Just like the other counters, you can determine whether you have a network bottleneck by looking at the output queue lengths of your cards. If you see a sustained value of more than two, then you need to take action if you want to get more users on your server. Of course, there's no input queue length counter for network cards.

Addressing Network Bottlenecks

Identifying network bottlenecks at your server is easy. Fixing them can be as simple as putting a faster NIC or implementing NIC teaming or full duplexing to double the interface to your server.

However, you might be able to relieve some pressure from your server's network interface by adjusting the overall architecture of your Terminal Server environment. For example, you might choose to build a private network connection between your Terminal Servers and your user's home drives. This would allow users' RDP sessions to flow over one interface while their data would flow over another.

If your environment involves long-haul networks or WAN links, it's possible that a delay in that area could cause adverse performance issues. That issue is not tied specifically to the user capacity of a server though, and is discussed later in this chapter in the "Overall Sluggishness" section.

Kernel Memory Usage

In some cases, the performance of your system might slow down (or you might hit user limits) when it appears that plenty of hardware resources are available. What should you do when you're experiencing a major performance limit in spite of testing the memory, processor, disks, and network interface, and determining that none of them shows evidence of being the bottleneck?

By running hundreds or even thousands of processes, you're pushing the architectural limits of Windows Server 2003, especially on larger servers. To understand why (and how to fix it), you need to understand how Windows works.

Understanding how the Kernel Uses Memory

Have you ever wondered what the "32" means in 32-bit Windows? If you thought it has to do with 32-bit processors from Intel, you're half-right. In fact, the 32-bit Windows name derives from the fact that Windows has a 32-bit memory address space. Windows can only address 2^{32} bytes (or 4GB) of memory, regardless of the amount of physical RAM installed in a system. Thinking back to your Windows training, you'll remember that this 4GB memory space is split in two, with 2GB for user-mode processes and 2GB for kernel-mode processes.

Every user-mode process has its own personal 2GB address space. This is called the process's "virtual memory," since it is always available to the process regardless of the amount of physical memory. (A common misconception is that "virtual memory" refers to memory that's been paged out to disk. This is simply not true when discussing the kernel.)

The kernel and other important system functions all share the same "other half" of the 4GB total memory space. This means that all kernel functions must share the same 2GB memory area.

As you can imagine, this 2GB "kernel-mode" memory space can get quite crowded since it must house all kernel-related information (memory, drivers, data structures, etc.). There is effectively a limit on the amount of data-structures and kernel-related information a system can use, regardless of the amount of physical memory.

On particularly busy Terminal Servers, certain components running in this 2GB kernel address space can run out of room, causing your server to slow to a crawl and preventing additional users from logging on. This can happen in environments with plenty of memory, processors, disk space, and network bandwidth.

The good news is that you can tweak the kernel memory usage of some of the kernel's key components, allowing you to fit more users on your server. The bad news is that since all of these components share the same 2GB memory area, giving more memory to one component means that you have to take it away from another.

You're looking for the right balance. Increase one area 5% and you might get ten more users on a server. Increase it 6% and you might get twenty fewer users on the server.

Since adjusting one component affects another, start out by looking at several components together. The kernel memory area is divided into several parts, with the two major parts (called "pools") being a nonpaged pool and a paged pool. The nonpaged pool is a section of memory that cannot, under any circumstances, be paged to disk. The paged pool is a section of memory that can be paged to disk. (Just being stored in the paged pool doesn't necessarily mean that something has been paged to disk. It just means that it has either been paged to disk or it could be paged to disk.)

Sandwiched directly between the nonpaged and paged pools (although technically part of the nonpaged pool) is a section of memory called the "System Page Table Entries," or "System PTEs."

To understand what a PTE is, (and its relevance to Terminal Server sizing), you have to think back to what you just read about how each process can use up to 2GB of memory.

In reality, most processes don't actually use anywhere near their 2GB of memory. However, since each process thinks it has a full 2GB, it references all its memory as if it were the only thing running. Since the system must track the *actual* memory usage of every single process, it must "translate" each process's memory utilization to physical memory or page file locations. To do this, the system creates a memory page table for each process.

This page table is simply an index that keeps track of the actual locations of a process's memory pages. Each entry in this table tracks a different memory page, and is called a "Page Table Entry." The 2GB of memory that the kernel uses also has a page table. Entries in that table are called "System PTEs."

Why does all this matter when you're troubleshooting the performance of a Terminal Server? Simply, the maximum number of System PTEs that a server can have is set when the server boots. In heavily-used Terminal Server environments, you can run out of system PTEs. You can use the registry to increase the number of system PTEs, but that encroaches into the paged pool area and increases the risk that you could run out of paged pool memory. Running out of either one is bad, and your goal is to tune your server so that you run out of both at the exact same time. This will indicate that you've tuned the kernel's memory usage as optimally as possible.

In Windows 2003, the system file cache is the part of memory where files that are currently open are stored. Like PTEs and the Paged Pool, the System File Cache needs space in the 2GB kernel memory area. If the Paged Pool starts to run out of space (when it's 80% full by default), the system will automatically take some memory away from the System File Cache and give it to the Paged Pool. This makes the System File Cache smaller. However, the system file cache is critical, and so it will never reach zero (which means yes, the Paged Pool can still run out of space). The system will make a trade-off and try to extend the Paged Pool as much as possible.

Evaluating your Server for Kernel Memory Usage Problems

Remember that these symptoms occur on systems that are heavily loaded and that do *not* show *any* other signs of hardware limitations. If your processor is pegged at 100%, don't you dare try to make any of the changes outlined in this section.

Fortunately, Windows Server 2003 does a really good job of managing kernel memory. It has twice as many System PTEs as Windows 2000, and other memory management enhancements cause Windows 2003 to generally use less of the system paged pool than Windows 2000. All this means that you should be able to get four or five hundred users on a system before having to think about kernel memory tuning.

This does not mean that you can easily get four or five hundred users on a system. It means that most likely, *this particular problem* will not be seen until you get somewhere like four or five hundred users. Of course all this is application dependent, and could happen with only two or three hundred users.

Your Windows 2003 server will automatically use the maximum number of PTEs, so long as you:

- Boot the server without the /3GB option. (More on this later.)
- Do not have the registry key set that allows for this RAM to be used as system cache since it will be used for System PTEs instead. (Start | Right-click on My Computer | Properties | Advanced tab | Performance Settings button | Advanced tab | Check the "Programs" option in the Memory usage section)
- Do not have registry keys set that make session space or system mapped views larger than the default size (48MB).

If you feel that you might be running out of PTEs or paged pool on a Windows Server 2003 Terminal Server, there's an easy test to do. Instead of using the Performance Monitor, you can get a much more accurate snapshot of kernel memory usage with a kernel debugger. Using a kernel debugger probably conjures up nightmares about host machines and serial cables and all sorts of things that developer-type people handle that you probably never ever thought you would have to. Fortunately, times have changed.

In Windows Server 2003, using the kernel debugger is easy. It's windows-based, and you can even use it to debug the computer that it's running on. The kernel debugger can tell you amazing things about the state of the Windows kernel, which is exactly why we're going to use it here.

The first thing you have to do is to download the Debugging Tools for Windows. They're available from: `http://www.microsoft.com/whdc/ddk/debugging/`.

Go ahead and install them on the Terminal Server that you're testing. Choosing the default options should be sufficient in this case. Then, fire up the Windows Debugger (Start | All Programs | Debugging Tools for Windows | WinDbg).

Next, you'll need to establish a kernel debugging session with the local computer.

1. Choose File | Kernel Debug
2. Click the "Local" tab
3. Click "OK"

Now, before you can effectively use the debugger, you need to tell it where your "symbol" files are. Symbol files are files with the .SDB extension that tell the debugger how to interpret all the information that it's getting from the system. Without symbol files, the debugger is useless.

Information about obtaining symbol files is available from the Microsoft Debugging Tools for Windows webpage referenced previously. At the time of this writing, there are two ways to use symbol files with the Windows Debugger.

- You can download the symbol files to your hard drive (or copy them from the Windows Server 2003 CD). Then, you configure the Debugger so that it knows where to look for them.
- You can use Microsoft's new "Symbol Server," which allows the Debugger to automatically and dynamically download the required symbol files from Microsoft's web site.

Using the symbol server is by far the easiest option and the one you should choose unless your Terminal Server does not have direct Internet access. Configuring your Windows Debugger to use Microsoft's symbol server is easy:

Choose File | Symbol Path File in the Debugger.

1. Enter the following statement into the box:
   `SRV*c:\debug*http://msdl.microsoft.com/download/symbols`
   ("*c:\debug*" can be changed to an appropriate local storage path for your environment.)
2. Check the "Reload" box.
3. Click "OK."

Now you're ready to begin debugging. Have your users log into the system. Then, when your system begins to slow down, enter the following command into the "*lkd>*" box at the bottom of the debugger screen:

```
!vm 1
```

This will display a snapshot of the kernel's virtual memory (its 2GB memory area) usage, which should look something like this:

```
lkd> !vm 1

*** Virtual Memory Usage ***
      Physical Memory:     130908   (  523632 Kb)
      Page File: \??\C:\pagefile.sys
         Current:    786432Kb Free Space:    767788Kb
         Minimum:    786432Kb Maximum:      1572864Kb
      Available Pages:      45979   (  183916 Kb)
      ResAvail Pages:       93692   (  374768 Kb)
      Locked IO Pages:         95   (     380 Kb)
      Free System PTEs:    245121   (  980484 Kb)
      Free NP PTEs:         28495   (  113980 Kb)
      Free Special NP:          0   (       0 Kb)
      Modified Pages:         135   (     540 Kb)
      Modified PF Pages:      134   (     536 Kb)
      NonPagedPool Usage:    2309   (    9236 Kb)
      NonPagedPool Max:     32768   (  131072 Kb)
      PagedPool 0 Usage:     4172   (   16688 Kb)
      PagedPool 1 Usage:     1663   (    6652 Kb)
      PagedPool 2 Usage:     1609   (    6436 Kb)
      PagedPool Usage:       7444   (   29776 Kb)
      PagedPool Maximum:    43008   (  172032 Kb)
      Shared Commit:         1150   (    4600 Kb)
```

```
Special Pool:               0    (        0 Kb)
Shared Process:          2939    (    11756 Kb)
PagedPool Commit:        7444    (    29776 Kb)
Driver Commit:           2219    (     8876 Kb)
Committed pages:        63588    (   254352 Kb)
Commit limit:          320147    (  1280588 Kb)
```

Your output may be a bit different from this sample. (For example, multiprocessor systems will have five paged pools instead of the three shown here.) Out of all this stuff on the screen, only three lines really matter in this case:

- Free System PTEs
- Paged Pool Usage
- Paged Pool Maximum

If your PTEs are really low, then you'll need to try to increase them. If your paged pool usage is almost at the paged pool maximum, then you'll need to increase it. If neither of these is true, then you're not experiencing a kernel memory-related bottleneck.

Implementing Kernel Memory Usage Changes

The default paged pool and system PTE levels are configured via the registry. Let's look at the system PTE entries first:

```
HKLM\System\CurrentControlSet\Control\Session Man-
ager\Memory Management\SystemPages
```

This registry value allows you to (somewhat) control the number of system PTEs that Windows creates at boot time. A value of zero lets the system create however many it needs to, and a value of FFFFFFFF (Hex) tells the system that you want it to create the absolute maximum number of PTEs that it can. (However, with Terminal Services enabled in application mode, the system will always create as many as it can anyway.) Values anywhere between these two will cause the system to create the specified number of PTEs, although the system does reserve the right to do whatever it wants if the numbers you specify are too extreme.

Each PTE is 4K in size. For every PTE that you can afford to lose, you can add 4K to the size of your paged pool. If you have 10,000 free system PTEs, you can probably afford to lose 7000 (leaving you with 3000). If you have 14,000 free, you can afford to give up 11,000.

Take however many PTEs you can afford to give up and multiply that number by 4. Then, add that number to the size of your PagedPool Maximum as shown in the debugger. (Be sure to add it to the Kb value to the far right.) That number will be the size that you should set your paged pool to be. Open up your registry editor and set your value in the following location:

```
HKLM\System\CurrentControlSet\Control\Session Man-
ager\Memory Management\PagedPoolSize
```

This registry location stores the value in bytes, not kilobytes. Therefore, multiply your calculated value by 1024 to get the number that you should enter here. When you enter the value, be sure to enter it in decimal format. The registry editor will automatically convert it to Hex format.

A value of zero will allow Windows to automatically choose the optimum size, and a value of FFFFFFFF (Hex) will tell Windows to maximize the size of the paged pool (at the expense of the ability to expand other areas, including system PTEs). A hex value anywhere in between gives Windows an idea of what size you'd like the paged pool to be, although (as with the PTEs) Windows reserves the right to ignore your setting. If you limit the paged pool to 192MB or smaller (0C000000 Hex), Windows will be able to use the extra space for other things (such as system PTEs). Most systems will never let the paged pool get bigger than about 500MB.

There's one more registry value that you should understand here:

```
HKLM\System\CurrentControlSet\Control\Session Man-
ager\Memory Management\PagedPoolMax
```

The *PagedPoolMax* value specifies the maximum percentage of the paged pool that you want to be full before the system starts stealing space from the system file cache. The default value of zero will cause the system to reclaim space from the system file cache only when the paged pool is 80% full. If you want the system to wait until the paged pool is 90% full, then set this registry value to 90 (decimal). If you want the system to steal file system cache space when the paged pool is only 40% full, set this value to 40 (decimal).

The first thing you should do when tuning your kernel is to look at the values for these three registry keys. If any of these three values is not set to "0," then you should reset them all to zero, reboot the system, and run your test again.

If you have fewer than 3000 free system PTEs at this point then forget it, there's really nothing more you can do. If you have more than 3000 free system PTEs, you could try maxing out the paged pool size by changing the *PagedPoolSize* registry value to FFFFFFFF (Hex). Reboot your server and run your test again to see if your changes made a difference for the better.

The risk you run here is that your optimal system PTE and paged pool sizes might be somewhere in the middle of maxing out one or the other. The only way to avoid this is to use a kernel debugger to view the actual size of the paged pool.

At this point you can reboot your server and rerun your test to see if it made a difference. Keep in mind that Windows will override your manual setting if it doesn't like it, so it's possible that your registry editing won't change anything at all.

Understanding BOOT.INI Kernel Memory Usage Switches

While we're still on the topic of kernel memory usage, we should take a second to address the various boot.ini file switches that can be used in Terminal Server environments. If you do an Internet search on performance of Terminal Servers, you'll come across different theories about how these switches should be used. Let's debunk the theories and look at how these switches really work.

There are two boot.ini switches you should know about: */3GB* and */PAE*.

The /3GB Switch

As you recall, 32-bit Windows systems can address 4GB of memory, and that memory is split into two 2GB chunks, one for the kernel and one for each process. Quite simply, adding the "/3GB" switch to a boot.ini entry changes the way the server allocates the 4GB memory space. Instead of two, 2GB sections, using the "*/3GB*" switch changes the partition so that the kernel gets 1GB and each process gets 3GB.

This is useful for memory-hungry applications such as Microsoft Exchange or SQL Server. As you know, however, Terminal Servers have trouble with the Windows kernel due to the fact that it's by default limited to 2GB, and as you can imagine, limiting the kernel to only 1GB of virtual memory would have disastrous consequences in a Terminal Server environment. Besides, in order to use the full 3GB, an application has to be compiled in a special way, so it's not like adding the "*/3GB*" switch would affect "regular" applications anyway.

If your Terminal Server is booting up via a boot.ini entry with the /3GB switch, remove it immediately.

The /PAE Switch

The "Physical Address Extensions" (PAE) boot.ini switch is used when 32-bit Windows Terminal Servers have more than 4GB of physical memory. Since the 32-bit Windows operating system can only address 4GB of virtual memory, systems with more than 4GB have to perform some fancy tricks to be able to use the physical memory above 4GB. These "fancy tricks" are enabled by adding the "*/PAE*" switch to the entry in the boot.ini file. If you're using a server with more than 4GB of RAM, then be sure that you have the "*/PAE*" switch in your boot.ini file. (In order to use more than 4GB of physical memory, you'll have to use Windows Server 2003 Enterprise or Datacenter Edition.)

Registry Usage

In Windows 2000, busy Terminal Servers would often be limited as to the amount of users they could support when the registry ran out of space. Even though you could adjust the maximum size of the registry, you were still limited by the fact that the entire registry was loaded into the kernel's paged pool.

Fortunately, the architectural changes introduced in Windows Server 2003 (well, technically they were introduced in Windows XP) affect the way that Windows loads the registry into memory. In Windows Server 2003 environments, the registry is not stored in the paged pool, meaning that there is effectively no size limit to the registry. The registry only consumes 4MB of the paged pool space regardless of how large it actually is. (There is also no registry size limit setting in Windows 2003.)

Troubleshooting Erratic Spikes, Pauses and Hangs

The erratic freezes and pauses that sometimes occur on Terminal Servers are probably the most annoying and difficult performance problems to troubleshoot. The good news (and the bad news) about these kinds of problems is that they are almost never your fault. The resolution usually points back to a device driver, service pack, or hotfix of some sort.

Erratic issues usually fall into two categories:

- An application or process pegs the processor at 100% utilization for a short time and then returns to normal. During this time, users' sessions are usually unresponsive.

- The server just freaks out for a few seconds. Every so often everything freezes, including the Performance Monitor MMC snap-in. Then after a few (or even 20 or 30) seconds, the performance chart jumps ahead in time to the current position. However, the "blackout" period causes a blank, with all performance counters showing zeros or no data.

The best attack plan for these types of problems is as follows:

- Check the web for your specific problem.
- Update service packs, apply hotfixes, and/or update device drivers.
- Use the Performance MMC snap-in to check for anomalies.

Step 1. Search the Web for your Problem

Solutions to the erratic problems are almost never intuitive, so it's worth it to spend ten or fifteen minutes on the web to gain an understanding of your problem before you try to do anything on the server.

For example, Windows Server 2003 was released in April 2003. In July, Microsoft KB article 821467 was published with a title "Windows Server 2003 Terminal Server Stops Responding." This article indicated that the problem only happens with Windows 2003 Servers, and that a fix is available from Microsoft. Why bother troubleshooting on your own when someone else might have done it already?

Here are the most useful websites for searching for these types of problems. They're presented in the order that most people search for them.

1. Google groups (`groups.google.com`). You're best luck usually comes from the Microsoft news groups. Often the Microsoft MVPs keep these lists up to date with hotfixes, and they're usually faster than Microsoft KB articles.
2. Microsoft Knowledge Base (`www.microsoft.com/support`).
3. The THIN.net archives (`www.thethin.net`). The archive searching tool on the THIN's main website is sometimes awkward to use, so you might try searching the archives via their listserv provider. (`www.freelists.org/archives/thin`)
4. Citrix Support Knowledge Base (`support.citrix.com/kb`). The search engine never seems to find what you're looking for, but this site is a requirement for locating Citrix hot fixes.

Step 2. Update Service Packs, Hotfixes, and Drivers

Most of the erratic problems have already been fixed at some point. Do a quick search on the Microsoft Knowledge Base for "server stops responding" and you'll see that 90% of the solutions say "obtain the latest service pack or hotfix."

For example, Service Pack 2 for Windows 2000 fixes a problem with the registry cache locking. This problem usually occurs on busy Terminal Servers and causes the whole system to pause if any registry writes need to be made while the registry is being backed up (which Windows does periodically). Applying Service Pack 2 or newer completely eradicates the problem.

However, you also need to be careful about updating production servers. When Service Pack 4 for Windows 2000 first came out in August 2003, it broke many people's Terminal Server environments. Check the web resources listed in Step 1 to make sure that whatever patch you're applying is safe. Also, apply the patch to a test server before putting it on a production server. Roy Tokeshi's Thin Client Support community at `www.tokeshi.com` is a great reference site for all the latest Terminal Server support, hotfix, and service pack information.

While you're at it, you should also update the hardware device drivers and firmware. There have been countless cases in which hard drive firmware or driver updates have "magically" fixed the occasional hiccup. Keep in mind that the users in a Terminal Server environment really push a server to its limits, and your hardware (and the drivers) are definitely getting their exercise.

Step 3. Launch the Performance Monitor MMC Snap-In

If web searching and server patching didn't fix your erratic problems, you'll have to continue the investigation yourself. Chances are that you've already fired up Performance Monitor. If you're still having the problem, you'll need to have it active during one of the glitches.

Add counters for your processors (Processor | % Processor Time). It's best to add one counter for each processor instead of the "_Total," since that will allow you to more easily see whether a single process pegs the CPU.

If your problem is extremely intermittent, don't forget that you can configure an alert to watch for it. Then, you can configure that alert to automatically start a performance data log. The only problem with this is that you'll need to configure your alert to check at a frequent interval—maybe every few seconds. Be careful that you don't create a Catch-22 situation where your complex monitoring, logging, and alerting schemes actually tax the system more. The ideal situation is for you to be able to view the problem live. (You could also configure Performance Monitor on a remote computer to track your Terminal Server.)

Look for applications that are taking up 100% of the processor

Look at what exactly is happening when your system slows down. Does the CPU spike? If so, there are a few different approaches you can take. First, try to determine what's causing the spike. Is someone's roaming profile loading? Did a bunch of users just log on? In some cases, you may encounter an application or process that takes up too much CPU utilization.

Dealing with Overzealous Applications

The easiest solution in these cases (especially in Terminal Server environments) is to add CPU throttling software to your server. This software monitors all running processes and clamps down on anything that hits a predefined limit. This is helpful for applications that aren't really Terminal Server-friendly but that your users insist on using.

There are many vendors that make products to help ensure that CPU resources are available when they need to be. Here are some of the more popular tools:

- Appsense Optimizer (`www.appsense.com`)
- Aurema ARMTech (`www.aurema.com`)
- RES PowerFuse CPUShield (`www.respowerfuse.com`)
- RTO Software TScale 3.0 (`www.rtosoft.com`)
- TAME (`www.tamedos.com`)
- TMuLimit (`www.tmurgent.com/TMuLimit.htm`)
- ThreadMaster (`threadmaster.tripod.com`)

Each of these tools approaches CPU over-utilization in a different way, so you should investigate all of them. There are situations in which one of these tools will fail to control a process while another tool works. If you don't get the results you need with one tool, it's worth trying another.

Look for Periods when Everything Goes to Zero

Hopefully searching the web, patching your server, and updating your drivers and firmware will alleviate any sporadic problems that you were having. If you're still experiencing performance issues, there are a few things left to try.

In some cases, you'll notice that all Performance Monitor counters will just disappear for a few seconds and everything pauses. When the system comes back,

Performance Monitor has jumped ahead, with nothing but zeros left in the twilight zone.

In other less extreme cases, you might not notice anything strange in Performance Monitor. In fact, everything might look normal even as your system takes a performance hit. In these cases, you'll need to continue stepping through this document.

As with the previous problems, you'll also need to consider everything that's happening on your server. One company's Terminal Servers would max out at 25 users, even though Performance Monitor showed no problems. It was later discovered that this was due to the fact that they were redirecting the users' "Application Data" folder to a remote home drive location. By redirecting this critical profile folder, the server would slow to a crawl each time a user needed to access data from that folder (a very frequent event). Stepping through the performance troubleshooting steps caused them to consider everything that was happening on their server, and ultimately led them to experiment by turning off folder redirection. Thus they were able to isolate their problem.

Overall Sluggishness & Lack of Responsiveness

This chapter has previously focused on the idea that overall sluggishness of your Terminal Servers could be related to having too many users on a server. However, it's often the case that only some of your users will experience sluggish sessions while others will not. In these cases the issue can usually be traced back to poor network performance. Before we explore the details of how you can tune your network, it's important to review some basics of network performance.

Understanding Factors that Affect Network Performance

When considering network performance, you need to understand the difference between "latency" and "bandwidth." Both are used to describe the speed of a network. Bandwidth describes how much data can pass through the network in a given period of time, such as 10 megabits per second, or 256 kilobits per second. Latency describes the length of time, usually expressed in milliseconds (there are 1000 milliseconds in one second), that it takes for data to get from point A to point B. Bandwidth and latency are independent of each other.

The fact that bandwidth and latency are different from each other is an important concept to understand in Terminal Server environments. (This is so important that it calls for another analogy.)

Imagine that each packet of data is an automobile, and the network is a highway. In order for the data to get from point A to point B, an automobile would have to travel from one end of the highway to the other. In high-bandwidth environments, the highway has many lanes, and hundreds of automobiles can be on it at the same time. In low bandwidth environments, the highway is a narrow country road, and only a few automobiles can fit on it at the same time. The width of the highway is like the bandwidth of the network. Since latency affects how long it takes data to traverse the network, the speed of the automobiles on the highway represents the latency. Even on narrow highways (low bandwidth), there might be people who drive really fast and travel the road quickly (low latency). Conversely, even if you have a large number of automobiles on a wide highway (high bandwidth), the drivers may choose to drive slowly (high latency).

Bandwidth and latency are independent of each other because the width of the highway does not directly affect how fast you drive on it. However, as you've probably guessed by now, it's possible that bandwidth *can* affect latency.

Now imagine a low-bandwidth environment that also has low latency (a narrow highway where the people drive really fast). If there are only a few automobiles on the road, they can go fast without a problem. However, imagine that the highway begins to fill up with more and more autos. Even though the people want to drive fast, they can't because the highway is too crowded. The effect is that it will take longer for automobiles to get from one end of the highway to the other. In a sense, the latency has increased from low latency to high latency simply because there are too many vehicles on the highway.

There are several solutions to the overcrowded highway problem. You could:

- Widen the highway.
- Remove some of the vehicles.
- Force people to drive smaller vehicles.
- Install traffic signals and lane control devices to manage the traffic.
- Just tell people to "get used to it."

As you'll see, the potential solutions to the overcrowded highway problem are also the potential solutions to overcrowded networks in Terminal Server environments.

A network connection's bandwidth and latency each affect Microsoft RDP session traffic in different ways:

Bandwidth affects how much data the session can contain. Higher resolution sessions require more bandwidth than lower resolution sessions. Sessions with sound, printing, and client drive mapping all require more bandwidth than sessions without. If a particular session only has 15Kbps of bandwidth available, that session can still have decent performance so long as the resolution, color depth, and other virtual channel options are tuned appropriately.

Latency is usually more critical in Terminal Server environments. Since latency affects the amount of time it takes for communication to pass between the client and the server, environments with high latency can seem like they have a "delay" from the user's perception.

For example, imagine an environment in which a user was using Microsoft Word via a remote RDP session. When they press a key on their client device, the key code is sent across the network to the Terminal Server. The server processes the keystroke and prepares to display the proper character on the screen.

Because this is a Terminal Server, the screen information is redirected back across the network where it is displayed on the local client device. In order for a character to appear on the screen, data must travel from the client to the server and then from the server back to the client again.

In this situation, if the latency of the network is 10ms, the network delay will only add 20ms (because the data crosses the network twice) to the time between the key press and the character appearing on the user's screen. Since 20ms is only 0.02 seconds, the delay will not be noticeable. However, if the latency was 200ms, the total delay to the user would be 400ms, or almost one-half of a second. This length of delay would be noticeable to the user and would probably be unacceptable.

An easy way to get an approximation of the latency in your environment is to perform a TCP/IP ping. You can ping the server from the client or the client from the server, it doesn't matter which way. For example, if your server is called "server01," you would execute the following command from a client workstation:

ping server01

(Be sure that you execute the ping command locally on the workstation, not via an RDP session on the server.) The results will look something like this:

```
Pinging server01 [10.1.1.42] with 32 bytes of data:
Reply from 10.1.1.42: bytes=32 time=378ms TTL=118
```

```
Reply from 10.1.1.42: bytes=32 time=370ms TTL=118
Reply from 10.1.1.42: bytes=32 time=360ms TTL=118
Reply from 10.1.1.42: bytes=32 time=351ms TTL=118
Ping statistics for 10.1.1.42:
Packets: Sent = 4, Received = 4, Lost = 0
Approximate round trip times in milli-seconds:
Minimum = 351ms, Maximum = 378ms, Average = 364ms
```

Notice that the "time=" section of each line shows you the approximate latency. This time is the time that the "pinger" waited for a response from the "pingee," meaning that the time shown represents the entire round-trip. The above scenario with the 364ms latency could have occurred in a dial-up environment with a bandwidth of 28kbps or a frame-relay environment with 512kbps. In either situation, the performance would not be as good as in an environment with less latency.

Resolving Network Bandwidth Issues

Once you've determined whether your network performance issues are bandwidth-related or latency-related, you can begin to address them. If your network suffers from a lack of bandwidth:

- Install a hardware device to monitor and control applications and bandwidth. This is like adding a traffic cop and traffic signals in our highway example.
- See what type of traffic you can remove from the network. This is like removing extra automobiles in our highway example.
- Make the RDP sessions as "small" as possible. This is like convincing everyone to drive smaller cars.

Let's take a look at how you could implement each one of these three solutions.

Hardware Network Bandwidth Shapers

The most popular types of bandwidth management devices in Terminal Server environments are Packeteer's PacketShaper (`www.packeteer.com`), Sitara's QoSWorks (`www.sitaranetworks.com`), and Allot Communications' NetEnforcer (`www.allot.com`). Both are physical hardware devices that sit between your network and the WAN router as shown in Figure 13.3.

Figure 13.3 Bandwidth shaping hardware

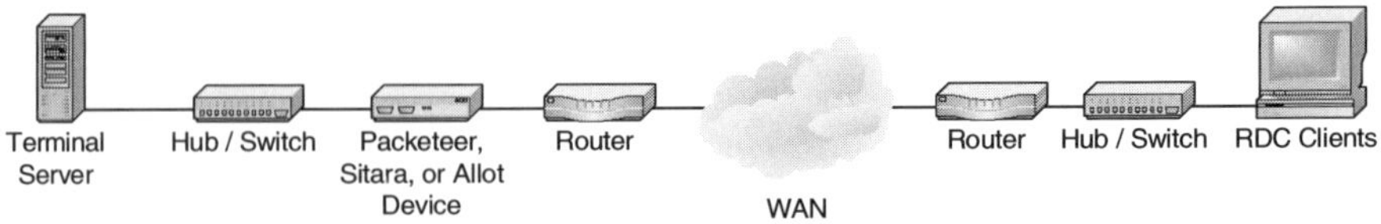

These devices allow you to analyze and capture current traffic usage (which is when you'll discover that 75% of your WAN traffic is web surfing). You can then give Microsoft RDP traffic priority over other types of traffic. You can even configure these devices to give different priorities to different IP addresses. You can also guarantee certain amounts of bandwidth to RDP (or any protocol).

These third-party devices are similar to Cisco Quality of Service (QoS) devices, except that the Sitara and Packeteer devices are "Layer 7" routers and can differentiate RDP traffic from other types of traffic.

Removing Traffic

One of the easiest things you can do to free up bandwidth for your RDP sessions is to remove as much non-Terminal Server traffic as possible. Are you backing up data across the network? Are your users downloading MP3s? All of this takes bandwidth away from RDP sessions.

Squeezing RDP

Once you've removed any unnecessary traffic from your network, you can start to think about squeezing the RDP protocol down as small as possible. There are several steps that you can take to do this:

- First, turn off as much desktop "glitz" as possible. This means disabling wallpapers, menu animations, and desktop themes.
- Next, disable any RDP virtual channels that you're not using, such as printing or local drive access.
- You should also configure the users' sessions so that they're using the minimally required settings, such as the lowest resolution and color depth needed.
- If you haven't done so yet, be sure that your Terminal Servers are running the most recent versions of service packs and hotfixes.

CHAPTER 14

Terminal Services Deployment in the Enterprise

You've designed your Terminal Server environment. You know which applications will be available and how your users will connect. Now it's time to deploy your Terminal Servers. This chapter does not focus on IT deployment methodologies or how to run a pilot project. Instead, this chapter focuses on the pure technical decisions you must make and the steps you must take to move your Terminal Server environment from the design stage to the production stage.

Fundamentally, there are only two steps to this process:

1. Deploy your Terminal Servers.
2. Deploy your applications to your Terminal Servers.

Let's begin by planning for the deployment of your Terminal Servers.

Deploying Terminal Servers

If your Terminal Server environment will consist of more than a few servers, you'll probably want to consider some method of automating their deployment to avoid having to manually install and configure each one.

There are two different methods that you can use to deploy Terminal Servers:

- Server drive imaging.
- Unattended or scripted installations.

Server Drive Imaging

As the name implies, server imaging involves creating a server image (or "clone") that will be used as the base image for target servers, then copying that image to other servers. To do this, you must use third party drive imaging software such as Norton Ghost (`www.symantec.com`) or StorageSoft ImageCast (`www.storagesoft.com`).

You can also create hardware-based images. Drive images can be created with an imaging machine that copies a source hard disk to one or more target disks. Alternately, you can configure your source server with two hard drives configured for RAID 1 and then break the mirror and use one of the drives in your target server.

Server imaging works well if all of your servers are going to be identical—both in terms or hardware and software. In order to use imaging to deploy your Terminal Servers, create a source server with a generic configuration. After that server's image has been deployed to your target servers, perform some minor configuration tasks on them to ready them for production use. (These minor tasks include changing the server name and IP address.)

Even though imaging requires that you spend some time configuring the clone and then finalizing each server that has been imaged, you can usually save quite a bit of time overall, even with only a handful of servers. The more servers that you have to deploy, the more time you can save.

Advantages of Server Imaging

- No need to install the base operating system on target servers before you image them.
- Applications can be imaged in addition to the operating system.

Disadvantages of Server Imaging

- Target servers must be "cleaned up" after they are imaged.
- All server hardware must be more or less identical.
- You must take the time to create a source server that is good enough to image.

Imaging a Terminal Server involves three steps:

1. Create the source server that will be imaged.
2. Create the image and deploy it to your target servers.
3. Finalize the target servers by making any post-image modifications.

Step 1. Preparing the Source Server

The source server should be your own version of "gold code." This server should be created from your lessons learned during the pilot and user acceptance testing phases (fully outlined in Chapter 15). A base install of the server may suffice, but if you've modified the server configurations during one of these phases, your changes should also be incorporated into the source server to limit the amount of post-configuration modifications that will need to be done. Items that may be included in your source server are:

- Registry tuning or configuration modifications
- Windows and service configurations
- Custom logoff or logon scripts
- Installed applications or monitoring software

- A modified default profile or mandatory profile

Once all of the required changes have been made, you're ready to prepare the server for imaging following these steps:

1. Install the base operating system but do not add the server to a domain.
2. Install any hotfixes or service packs required.
3. Make any service or server configuration changes.
4. Add any registry modifications required.
5. Install all of your required applications.
6. If you have teamed the network cards, un-team them.
7. If you have configured this server in a load balanced cluster, remove it from the cluster.

With these steps complete, your server should look like a production server short of being a member of the domain. You now must decide whether you will use a Microsoft tool or a third party tool for changing the computer's SID. (Remember from your old NT training classes that a SID, or Windows Security Identifier, is a unique identifier for a Windows computer. No two computers should have the same SID, so if you're imaging your servers, you'll need a way to change the SID after you image your server.)

Microsoft supplies a tool with the Windows resource kit called Sysprep. This utility allows you to strip the machine-specific configuration from the machine prior to imaging. When the target servers are booted after the imaging process, they begin the GUI portion of the Windows setup routine. This will requires you to enter any machine-specific information in the setup screen just as if it was a newly installed system. Since the server is imaged, all of your configurations, changes and applications are already installed.

If you do not wish to use Sysprep, there are several third party tools on the market that can be found as freeware or with the imaging product you have purchased. *NewSid.exe* from `www.sysinternals.com` can be run after the new target server is up and allows you to rename the server from a command line. Another classic SID changer is Ghost Walker from Symantec, which is included with almost every version of Ghost. Having decided on how the SID will be changed, you can then move on to deploying the image.

Step 2. Copy and Deploy the Image

Once you've prepared your server, perform the imaging process and deploy the image to your new target server or servers.

Step 3. Clean up the Newly-Imaged Target Server

The following steps will need to be performed on each newly-cloned Terminal Server before it can be used:

1. If you did not use Sysprep to prep the image, ensure that the server is off the network prior to turning it on.
2. Give the server a new SID since it has the same one as the source server. Technically, when you add the server to the domain, it will receive a new domain SID, but you should also use a tool to create a new local SID for the server. If you used Sysprep to prepare the image, a new local SID is created the first time the server is booted.
3. Configure the server with its permanent IP address.
4. Configure the server with its new computer name.
5. Turn off the server.
6. Plug in the network cable.
7. Turn on the server.
8. Add the server to the domain and reboot.
9. Re-team the NICs if necessary.
10. Configure load balancing if necessary.

Once you've completed these steps, your new server is ready to go. You can configure it just like any server.

Unattended Installations

Rather than imaging your Terminal Servers, you can perform unattended installations of the operating system and enable Terminal Services during that installation process. When you perform an unattended installation of Terminal Server, the standard installation file is executed on the server. However, an answer file to the installation prompts is supplied and the installation can complete without user interaction.

Advantages of Unattended Installations

- Unattended installations can be sent to many different types of hardware.

Disadvantages of Unattended Installations

- You must manually install the applications or distribute them via package.
- You must create the unattended installation script.

Unattended installations work well for Windows 2003 servers. However, do your homework before beginning to create your attended installation script.

Unattended installation (technically called "Unattended Setup") uses an answer file to automate the answers to the questions that the Windows setup process normally presents to the user during the installation. This answer file can also contain instructions for configuring operating systems and installing applications. You can distribute this answer file using a network share or by storing it on a custom created installation CD. Most people bundle their answer files together with any custom device drivers that are required for the installation.

The topic of unattended installs could fill an entire book in itself. For the sake of maintaining our focus on Terminal Services, we'll only discuss the modifications required in an unattended answer file to enable Terminal Services.

```
[Components]
ApplicationServer=ON
```

This configuration determines whether the Application Server (the official name for Terminal Server in application mode) is installed. The default is "*Off*."

```
[TerminalServices]
AllowConnections=1
```

This configuration determines whether Terminal Services connections are allowed. The default setting is "*1*" which allows connections.

```
PermissionsSetting=0
```

This configuration determines the permissions mode for Terminal Services. A value of "1" causes Terminal Services to be installed in the relaxed security mode, and a value of "0" forces Terminal Services to the new full security mode.

Deploying Applications

One of the primary advantages of Terminal Server is that you can significantly decrease your software deployment timeframe since you need to install applications only once on a server instead of dozens of times on client devices. However, as your Terminal Server environment grows, it quickly becomes apparent that you need a solution for your servers. With a large environment you must install applications onto dozens of servers. Although installing applications on dozens of servers is less work then installing them on hundreds of workstations, it is still a significant task that can be automated.

Fortunately, Terminal Servers are the perfect candidates for using automated software distribution tools to install and update your applications on multiple servers. Before examining the details and design components of these tools, let's look at how automated software distribution works in general.

An Overview of Automated Software Distribution

Automated software distribution is conceptually the same anywhere it is used, regardless of platform or tools. ZENWorks, SMS, Tivoli, Unicenter, and IntelliMirror all work in exactly the same way.

Fundamentally, no software distribution tool has the ability to "push" software applications to target computers. These distribution tools simply evaluate a set of conditions on a target computer. If these conditions indicate that software should be deployed, the distribution tool causes the target computer to execute a command that launches the automatic software installation.

Software distribution environments are made up of three components. These components apply to all software distribution programs listed previously.

- *Software Package.* This is a collection of files (the software application's source installation files) that are to be installed on the target computer.
- *Installation Command.* This is the command used to launch the installation of the software.
- *Software Distribution Agent.* This term describes the program that decides whether the software should be deployed. If so, it executes the installation command on the target computer.

Imagine that you want to install Notepad onto some computers. You create a software package that contains your source files—`notepad.exe` in this case. Then, you specify the command to be used to install the software. In this case, that command is *not* `notepad.exe`. To understand this, let's look at what happens on the target computer.

When the time came for the package to be installed, your software distribution agent would connect to the network location where your package was stored and run the installation command line. In this case, if you specified the installation executable as `notepad.exe`, when the software installation was scheduled to begin, the Notepad application would be launched (because you specified `notepad.exe`). The user would be confused, wondering why Notepad opened all by itself. He would close it and continue working. In this case the software distribution program did exactly what you wanted it to—it connected to the network share and ran `notepad.exe`. In fact, the software distribution program would report that there was a successful installation, because `notepad.exe` ran and exited successfully. In this scenario, the software distribution utility did its job. However, the administrator that configured it did not.

In order to successfully deploy Notepad with a software distribution utility, you must create an installation procedure. In this simple case, that is most easily done with a batch file. Let's create a batch file called *install.bat* made up of the following line:

```
copy \\networkserver\share\notepad.exe %system-
root%\system32\
```

As you can see, this "installation program" will copy notepad from the network share to the target computer's local hard drive. It's important to note here that the *%systemroot%* variable is used to specify the location on the target computer. That way, your program will work no matter how the target computer's drives are configured.

Once this installation program is complete, update your software package. Your new package will contain two source files—*notepad.exe* and *install.bat*. You must also update your installation procedure. Instead of running notepad.exe, your package is now launched by running *install.bat*.

Now, when the software distribution agent needs to install your package, it will work whether or not a user is logged on and will not interrupt them while he's working. As you have seen, this improvement step had nothing to do with a bug in the software distribution utility. It had everything to do with the skill of the people creating the package.

Let's take a look at another example. Imagine that you want to deploy Microsoft Office 2003 to 100 computers. Ordinarily, you would go to each computer and execute *setup.exe*. That setup program prompts you for several options, configurations, and information. When it has all the information it needs, the actual installation begins.

When using automated software distribution utilities, this process is no different. If the software distribution utility decides that a computer needs to have an application installed, then the software distribution utility instructs the computer to run the application's installation program.

If you simply copy the contents of the Microsoft Office 2003 CD to a network share and then instruct the target computers to run the command setup.exe to install Office 2003, each target computer would run the full GUI version of *setup.exe*. This GUI version requires user input along the way to enter the options, installation path, and CD key. Imagine what would happen in the real world if the executable for an Office 2003 distribution was *setup.exe*:

- Some computers would have no one logged on so the software distribution would fail, because Office 2003's *setup.exe* requires a user to be logged onto the computer in interactive mode.
- Other users would see the box pop up that said "Microsoft Office 2003 Setup." They would think to themselves, "Why is this happening? I didn't run this!" Then, they would immediately cancel the installation.
- Still other users would continue through the installation. In these cases, each user would probably choose different options, meaning that the Office 2003 installation is different on each computer.

If you want to deploy Microsoft Office 2003 to a large group of servers, you must create a software installation package for it.

In your package, specify the location of the source files and the command line needed to kick off the installation. Instead of specifying *setup.exe* to launch the installation, it is possible to create a "silent" installation of Microsoft Office 2003. Silent installation involves creating a configuration file that specifies all of the options that you want, and then running setup.exe with special command-line parameters that instruct it to read settings from the custom configuration file. This is done with the same methods used to specify "silent" installs of the RDP client software in Chapter 10.

To summarize, when using any software distribution environment you must first create the "silent" installation routine for your application before you can distribute it to any target computers (or target Terminal Servers in this case).

Automated Software Distribution Considerations

If you're thinking that using automated software distribution is too much work, consider this: Would you rather spend some time up front building packages for and testing your applications, or would you rather install your application over and over and over until it is on all your servers?

The decision of whether to use automated software distribution can be a difficult one to make. Fundamentally, everyone wants to use automated software distribution because on the surface, it simplifies the management of software and software updates. However, in the real world, it's not always that easy. To help you decide whether or not to use automated software distribution for your applications, ask yourself the following questions:

- How difficult is it to package your applications?
- How often are your applications updated?
- How long do these updates take to deploy?

How difficult is it to package your applications?

For each application, consider whether it comes to you ready to go in Windows Installer package or whether you need to manually create the application package. If you have an MSI file, then your application package is ready to go without much effort on your part. But if you must manually create an application package, you must do some testing to figure out how long it will take you to create that package.

Too often people spend four days trying to create a software installation package that they could have manually deployed to their servers in two days.

How often are your applications updated?

If you have an application that will need to be updated frequently, it may be worth your time to create an application package. Once you figure out the tricks you should be able to package new versions of the application quickly. On the other hand, if your application is only updated every 18 months, it might not be worth it.

How long do these updates take to deploy?

If the application updates only take ten minutes each and you have ten servers, then you can manually deploy all of your updates to all of the servers in less than two hours. Most likely, it will take longer than that to create an application package. But if you have 100 servers, it could take two full days to deploy all of the updates. If you can make an application package in one afternoon, then it's worth it.

Factors that May Lead to Automated Software Deployment

- Many Terminal Servers.
- Frequent application updates.
- Applications are easy to package, such as MSI applications.
- Good test lab environment.

Factors that May Prevent Automated Software Deployment

- Small number of Terminal Servers.
- Infrequent application updates.
- Complex applications that require significant effort to package.
- No test lab environment.

CHAPTER 15

Server Management and Maintenance

Once your Terminal Server environment is designed and implemented, you'll need to manage it on a day-to-day basis. In this chapter, we'll focus on the tasks involved in the management of your servers and the tools that you can leverage.

This chapter is laid out in the following order:

- Monitoring your servers
- Routine maintenance tasks
- Backup strategies
- The basics of change management
- A change management policy

Monitoring your Terminal Servers

Day-to-day monitoring can be one of the most important things an administrator does in his Terminal Server environment. We're not talking about performance monitoring per se, as was covered extensively back in Chapter 13, but rather, we're referring to two types of monitoring:

- Real time monitoring of servers.
- Historical data collection for reporting and trend analysis.

Real time monitoring software allows you to view the status of different components of your Terminal Servers. *Quality* real time monitoring software will also alert you to problems currently happening in the environment and possibly take "self-medicating" measures to correct them.

Collecting historical data from your servers allows you to go back in time and observe server performance over a set of points in the past. This technique is most useful when you are trying to determine either when a problem started or if an unusually high counter is really that unusual. Collecting historical data should help prevent the following conversation:

Your Pager: <beep beep beep>

You: Uh-oh. The helpdesk is saying that Server A is really slow.

Other Administrator: Really?

You: Yep. I see here that the context switches are really high—over 40,000 per second.

Other Administrator: Really?

You: Yeah, they've been that way for over two minutes now.

Other Administrator: Really?

You: Yeah, really.

Other Administrator: Is that bad?

You: ?

Other Administrator: ?

You: Well, it seems high. I think.

Other Administrator: So that's bad?

You: ?

The point of this dialogue is that unless you monitor your servers on a regular basis, you won't know what thresholds to set for alerts and whether a counter is high or low when it comes time to troubleshoot a problem. Considering the scenario above, the context switches might have been just fine. There may be no problem at all, or another issue altogether may be the problem, but the administrators have no idea where to start since they don't know how their servers normally run.

Most people collect *detailed* metrics when building their servers, but fail to collect metrics after they've been in use for several months. When a problem occurs, they have no idea which (if any) performance counters are out of line.

There are several tools you can use to monitor your servers. The old reliable method is the Performance Monitor MMC snap-in that comes built in to Windows. While this tool is useful, it's not as feature-rich as third party software monitoring tools like Citrix's Resource Manager, Lakeside Software's SysTrack, or NetIQ's AppManager. Of course, any third party tool also comes with a price tag, while the Performance MMC is free.

Let's take a look at the power of the Performance Monitor MMC snap-in before we turn to third-party tools.

Performance Monitor

The Performance Monitor MMC snap-in (still called "Perfmon" by many administrators) is an example of a simple monitoring tool that's built in and automatically installed onto every windows server. When used properly, Perfmon acts as a basic real-time monitoring tool and can be configured to send alerts when problems occur. It can also be used to automatically create log files of your server's performance.

Before we jump into the details of configuring Perfmon for sending alerts, we should first determine which counters you should monitor and what types of thresholds you should set for each counter. If you haven't yet done so, read Chapter 13 detailing how to conduct a performance load test of your Terminal Servers. That chapter also explains more about the Perfmon counters you'll be using here.

Objects and Counters

After baselining your servers, you should have some ideas about where your counters will read in production. You can choose to monitor any performance counter, but you'll usually end up configuring monitoring rules for different counters than you monitored when tuning the performance of your servers.

- *Processor | % Processor Time | _Total* An alert here can be used to notify you if some process has spun out of control or if you simply need to add faster processors. You don't always have to set this alert for 100%. If your Terminal Servers never show more than 60% processor utilization, then you should probably set this alert for something like 70 or 75%. That way, you'll know when something out of the ordinary takes place.
- *Memory | Available Mbytes* It's easy to run out of memory on a Terminal Server, and this counter can give you an advanced warning of that. Let all of these alerts, watch your server to establish a baseline, and then set your alert accordingly.
- *Physical Disk | % Disk Time* When configuring this alert, make a separate one for each physical disk.
- *Terminal Services | Active Sessions* This alert will let you know if one of your servers is getting overloaded. An overloaded server could indicate a load-balancing related problem.

No matter what alert you're configuring, know beforehand your server's true limitations. If you baselined your servers and determined that maximum load to be 50 users after which performance goes downhill, set your threshold just below that. That way, you'll be notified *before* the user load overwhelms your servers.

Configuring your Alerts

Now that you've decided which counters you want to monitor and at which levels you want to be notified, let's see what involved to actually configure the notification process.

1. Open Performance Monitor (Start | Administrative Tools | Performance) or (Run "Perfmon" from a command prompt).
2. Expand "Performance Logs and Alerts" and right-click the Alerts icon. Select "New Alert Settings."
3. Name the Alert Settings you are configuring.
4. In the Properties window of the new alert, add the counters you want to monitor. For example, for CPU monitoring, click the "Add" button and highlight the "Processor Object | % of total Processor" counter.
5. Click the "Add" button. It will seem like nothing happened, but really the counter was added to your alert. This lets you add many different counters at once. When you've added all the counters you need, click "Close."
6. For this counter (a counter that goes up as utilization increases) select the "Alert when value is over" option and set the limit to what you need. (A limit of 94 will alert you when CPU utilization reaches 95% or higher.)
7. Change the sample data interval to 30 seconds.
8. Just configuring an alert doesn't do any good until you give it an action via the "Action" tab.
   - *Log an entry into the application event log:* This logs a simple event into the event log that can be viewed using event viewer. This is nice tool since one of your daily tasks should be to check the event logs (see the routine maintenance tasks section later in this chapter).
   - *Send a network message to:* This allows you to send a message to a specific computer name or IP address on the network. In order to use this, the messenger service will have to be running on the computer slated to receive the message. This wasn't always an issue, although now that spammers have learned how to use the messenger service, most companies keep it turned off.
   - *Start performance data log:* This allows you to specify a saved performance counter log to start when the alert is kicked off. The log is useful when you are only monitoring a subset of counters all day but want more detailed information when a problem starts.
   - *Start this program:* This allows you to start a program when the alert is raised. The program is usually a script that performs some action such as sending an email.

9. Finally, the "Schedule" tab allows you to start or stop the alert counter manually or set up prescheduled times for the monitors to run, generally during working hours so that they monitor the servers when they're heavily utilized.

Performance Logs

Performance Monitor can be used to save historical performance data. Most people use such logs to generate simple comma-separated CSV files that can be imported into Excel in order to create charts and graphs in a readable format for future use and for your management staff. On the other hand, store the performance data in binary format only if you feel like viewing it in the Performance Monitor MMC.

Either way, CSV files enable you to collect the data that you'll eventually sort through, compare, and present.

Configuring the Performance Log

Set up for Performance logs is similar to that of alerts.

1. Launch the Performance MMC snap-in and expand the "Performance Logs and Alerts" icon.
2. Right-click on the "Counter Logs" icon and select "New log settings." Give it a descriptive name and click "OK."
3. Add your performance objects or counters. You have the option to look at all the counters in an object by simply adding the entire object. Alternately, you can select only specific counters to log.
4. Select the sampling interval for the Log. Since this log will run continuously, you probably should set it to 30 seconds or 1 minute intervals. Less time will yield too much data for long-term samples.
5. On the "Log Files" tab, configure your log file as a comma delimited file. You can also click the configure button and select its location, filename, and a size limit.
6. At this point you can configure your log to run on a schedule (as with the alerts) or you can choose to launch it manually.

CSV files can be opened directly into an Excel worksheet and used in data analysis. Open the file with Excel, highlight a column for one of the counters (their names are in the first row of each column), and select "Insert | Chart." It's helpful to highlight the counter you're interested in along with the active sessions (or total sessions) counters. That way you can compare your specific counter against the number of active users on the system and begin to see how the resource utilization goes up as the user load increases.

If you run a log like this once a week and save the file, you'll have data from which to create charts for processor usage (or any other counter) and compare the utilization from one week to the next or even one month to the next.

Third Party Monitoring Tools

Performance Monitor is free and useful for simple monitoring in small environments. Unfortunately, it soon becomes inadequate once your Terminal Server farm starts to grow. At that point, you'll need to implement a third party product.

Components

All third-party tools are made up of the same basic four components.

- Agents
- Data storage
- Analysis and monitoring tools
- Reporting tools

Agents

Most third party tools work by installing an agent on each of your Terminal Servers. These agents then collect performance information from the server and write it to a central storage location (usually a database). In addition to being able to collect information from the standard Windows performance counters, agents usually offer their own application-specific counters for certain environments (such as when Terminal Servers are used).

More recently, companies have begun to build agents that use WMI to gather information for performance monitoring. WMI capabilities are built into Windows 2003, and this is definitely the direction in which all monitoring is moving. When WMI is used, these reporting tools often work without requiring agent software.

Data Storage

Naturally, you need a place to store all this data flowing in from agents. Most software packages support multiple database platforms for storing server performance information. In most cases, the agents store the collected information locally on the server being monitored. Then, at predefined times, they push that data to a central database. The best of these tools allow you to create a tree structure with monitored servers pushing to upstream databases. This data can then be pushed even farther upstream to create an entire monitoring organization.

Analysis and Monitoring Tools

The third-party tools come with a console or monitoring tool for viewing your servers' performance. Most of these tools are available in web-based and Win32 applications. Either way, the tools allow you to configure the agents, monitor the servers, and send alerts. Some packages also come with scaled down versions of the same tools to be deployed to helpdesk technicians doing basic server monitoring.

Reporting Tools

Finally, the third party tools can be used to create reports based on server or application performance. Often theses packages have the ability to integrate with other report-creation tools such as Crystal Reports.

Popular Third Party Monitoring Tools

There are several great tools available, too many to mention here. However, here's a rundown of some of the more popular ones that work well in Terminal Server environments. An up-to-date list is always available at `www.brianmadden.com`.

NetIQ AppManager Suite

AppManager is an inclusive package that some people think is becoming the industry standard for monitoring applications and application servers in Windows. AppManager has specific connectors for Terminal Server and add-in products like Citrix MetaFrame.

AppManager allows you to monitor specific applications and application metrics on the servers. When using Terminal Services and network load balancing, the tool has a module that monitors windows load balancing for changes or problems, and even checks event logs for load balancing events. More information about AppManager can be found at `www.netiq.com`.

Lakeside Software SysTrack

Lakeside Software's SysTrack is one of the original monitoring tools used in Terminal Services environments. It has specific components for Terminal Servers but can also be used to monitor all of the servers in your environment. It supports all popular databases mentioned and is flexible and easy to configure. Many people use this tool to record usage of Terminal Servers and to automatically create invoices for users or departments. Details about SysTrack are available at `www.lakesidesoftware.com`.

Microsoft Operations Manager

Microsoft's Operations Manager (MOM) can be used to monitor Terminal Servers. Like many other products, it offers Terminal Server-specific "Management Packs." MOM also has the ability to aggregate event log information from your Terminal Servers. `Visit` `www.microsoft.com/mom` for more information.

Citrix Resource Manager

If you're using Citrix MetaFrame XP on your Terminal Server, discussion of other monitoring tools is probably not necessary. Resource Manager comes with MetaFrame XPe and is specifically made for monitoring Terminal Servers and their applications. Reports can be generated or customized with Crystal Reports and real time alerts can send messages via e-mail or SNMP. For more information on Resource Manager, visit `www.citrix.com` or `www.brianmadden.com`.

Routine Maintenance Tasks

In this section we'll outline several routine tasks that you will need to perform when administering your Terminal Servers. First we will look at tasks that should be done on a regular schedule, and then we'll examine those that can be performed on an as-needed basis.

Scheduled Tasks

These tasks outline a simple maintenance plan that will allow you to keep your Terminal Servers in a stable and known state, predict performance problems, and allow you to do some trend analysis on our servers. No maintenance plan in a book can be completely comprehensive for any specific environment, so we're just attempting to impart some of the industry standards that are used in other Terminal Server environments.

Daily Maintenance Tasks

These are routine tasks that should be performed on a daily basis. For the most part they amount to simple monitoring, but this monitoring keeps you on top of your environment.

- Verify that you can connect to each server in your Terminal Server cluster. This ensures that the servers are up and responding to client requests.
- Check the server event logs. Checking the event logs on a daily basis lets you determine if there are system or application problems on a

server prior to it being reported by the user. Often a problem is reported and a check of the event logs reveals that the problem has been happening for some time. You can also automate the process of event log checking with something as simple as TNT Software's Event Log Monitor or a higher-end solution from BMC orNetIQ. With even basic scripting skills, you can also these log files out on a scheduled basis and then view them from a single location instead of logging into each server or selecting the servers in Event Viewer.

- Check the help desk tickets for the day to see if any new problems are arising. If you have a large help desk using help desk management software, see if they are able to denote any problems with the Terminal Servers and send a report to you. This way you can identify problems with your server prior to them affecting everyone in the organization.
- Clear out any hung or disconnected sessions to keep them from eating up valuable CPU and Memory on your server. If you have short timeouts on these settings, this could be changed to a weekly task.

Weekly Maintenance Tasks

The following tasks should be completed on a weekly basis. These tasks generally fall into the "monitoring and trend analysis" set of tasks, but should be done to ensure that the servers are running properly and not seeing a huge increase in utilization.

- Based on the monitoring tools you've set up (see the previous section on Server Monitoring), gather a weekly report that shows the utilization for the week. It should include daily averages and a weekly average that can be compared against the previous weeks' reports.
- If you don't have an automated system for it, update your antivirus definitions. Most companies offer new updates once a week unless a severe virus is detected that requires an immediate update to the definitions. Your best bet is to ensure that your Terminal Servers are updated at least once a week. As always, remember that you should test new updates to be sure there is no ill effect on the Terminal Servers.
- Like it or not, you'll still need to reboot your Terminal Servers about once a week. Remember that these are not servers at all, but really workstations. Can you imagine not rebooting a user workstation for months on end? Now take that idea and multiply it by the number of users that use each server. Rebooting a Terminal Server flushes the system, keeps memory leaks at bay, unlocks "hung" profiles, and kills errant software processes. This ensures that a server doesn't "seem" to run fine for months only to blue screen one day because it is out of

memory. In clustered environments, it's a good idea to stagger these reboots within the cluster. This allows the servers to be pulled out of the cluster one or two at a time and still lets users to connect to the remaining servers. To reboot a server, you'll probably have to disable logons several hours before the reboot takes place to ensure that no users will be affected.

- Immediately after a reboot is a perfect time to "clean up" the server. Generally what is done to the server at this point will depend on the applications you're running. Clean up tasks can be scripted and hooked directly into the reboot. It is impossible to say which tasks you will need to perform or which directories will need to be cleaned up, but a few industry standards are to clean out the spool folder, delete any unused profiles, and clean out any temp folders.

Monthly Maintenance Tasks

Check for any new hotfixes, security updates, print driver changes or other system updates that are required once a month or so.

- If you're still not using third-party printer software, install any new print drivers into the cluster. Once a month take that list of print drivers people have been asking for and test them, then add them to they cluster. Doing this once a month ensures that the number of drivers added simultaneously won't overwhelm your driver replication scheme.
- Check the current hotfixes and service packs that are available from Microsoft. Finding the new security fixes and "critical updates" can be done using Windows Update. Most people let Windows Update run on a test server so that they're constantly informed, and then they manually download and install them to the Terminal Servers. (Remember to test them in your lab first!)
- Schedule applications updates or changes. A common problem in Terminal Server environments is that changes are not scheduled, but instead applications and changes are just installed "whenever." This leads makes it hard to backtrack to the offending update when new issues are found. See the section in this chapter about Change Management for more information.

Quarterly Maintenance Tasks

Every few months you should take a look at the overall utilization of the environment and perform cleanup on the servers themselves.

- Perform some trend analysis. This is where all those weekly reports come in handy. Once a quarter is the time to sit down and look at the utilization on your servers. Compare your servers' usage from last quarter to determine if utilization is up and if you need to expand. These reports will also show you if certain servers are being underutilized and if there are inconsistencies in utilization across the cluster.
- Do some "spring cleaning" on the servers. A practice that is becoming more and more common in the industry is to completely rebuild or re-image your servers once a quarter. Just like workstations, a good re-build helps to keep things running smooth. If feel that this is extreme, at least make sure that you have an up-to-date base image for the cluster to ensure that the image is up to date and ready to use for the deployment or recovery of servers.

Replacing a Terminal Server in a Cluster

Every so often it will become necessary to replace a Terminal Server in your cluster because a server had a hardware failure or because a server is being upgraded to a more powerful server.

The deployment method you choose for deploying your Terminal Servers (discussed in Chapter 14) will ultimately decide how easy it is to replace a Terminal Server. If you image your servers and you're replacing an existing server with a new piece of hardware, you may have to create a new image. If your server builds are completely scripted, you may have nothing to do other than simply to start the unattended installation process on new hardware. If you're hand-building your servers, you'll need to ensure that the new server is configured identically to the other servers in the cluster (at least from the end users' perspective) so that they do not notice the change when load balancing routes them to the new server.

In any case, the following steps can be applied to bringing the new server into the cluster:

1. Build the new server and install all required applications (this can be hand built, scripted, or imaged). It may be a good idea at this point to build the server outside of its production OU if you're using policies to manage its Terminal Server settings.
2. Ensure the server accepts RDP connections and the applications are configured properly.
3. Ensure required print drivers are installed if they are not configured in the base image.

4. Bring the new server into its Terminal Server cluster by configuring the load balancing settings (as discussed in Chapter 7).
5. Configure the connection listener port settings, session directory settings, and license server settings (if these are not configured automatically via a GPO).
6. Move the server into its production OU to apply the GPOs.
7. Verify the server accepts connections via the cluster name.

Your environment might require more specific steps, but these basics shouldn't be missed. You wouldn't believe how often people add new servers to clusters only to find out weeks later that a slight misconfiguration meant that the server never started accepting user connections.

Terminal Server Backup Strategies

By focusing on high availability, your environment will be able to survive the small day-to-day events that occur. However, you'll still need to have a solid backup strategy that kicks in when there is a major disaster or component failure.

Focus your back ups on the unique data. Since there should be no user data stored on a Terminal Server, you shouldn't need to back up the Terminal Servers the way you do normal servers. You do need to back up:

- User profiles.
- User home drives.
- Application data.
- Terminal Services Licensing Service Database.
- One Terminal Server from each load balanced group (if you do not use server imaging to deploy new servers).

If you don't use server imaging, backup a single server that you can use as a master to restore a failed server. Since Terminal Servers should not contain any unique data, you should be able to restore any server image to any target server within the same silo. (See Chapter 5 for more information about silos.) This allows you to have a quick recovery in the event of a Terminal Server failure. Store the server images on the SAN or the network. Then, if one should fail, kick off an automated process to restore it.

Make a bootable DOS floppy disk with an *autoexec.bat* file that connects to the SAN and kicks off the server imaging process. You can configure it so that a server is imaged with a generic name and IP address and then a lookup file is accessed based on the server's MAC address and the proper server name and IP address are automatically set after the imaging process is complete.

Many companies print step-by-step restore instructions and put them and the bootable floppy disk in a safe location. That way, they are always available in the event of an emergency. You might use a red-colored floppy disk and place it behind glass, for an "in case of emergency, break glass" effect.

Alternately, many of the new blade servers have auto-provisioning software available that can automatically detect a failed server and initiate the rebuilding process. Some environments that use this have less than a one hour turnaround time from the instant a server fails until it is rebuilt and ready to go.

Backing Up the License Database

Fortunately, it's easy to back up most of the components of Terminal Server environments that require it. However, backing up the license database is not intuitive. If you ever lose the server that is hosting the Terminal Services Licensing Service, you're officially supposed to contact the Microsoft license clearinghouse to get your licenses restored.

This is generally acceptable, because if you have a disaster you can easily build and activate new a TS Licensing Server. (Remember that for good redundancy you should already have an "extra" licensing server ready to go.) As soon as you do this it will immediately start handing out 90-day temporary TS CALs, meaning that you essentially have 90 days to get everything straightened out before your environment would stop working.

However, it is possible to back up the TS licensing database by backing up the "*LServer*" directory on the license server. This directory is in the location that you specified during the installation of the TS Licensing setup, *%systemroot%\System32\LServer* by default. The TS licensing database is similar to a Microsoft Exchange database. The *LServer* directory contains a couple of *.edb* files, a few *.log* files, and a *.chk* file.

If you ever need to restore a TS licensing server, rebuild the server with the same name as the old server; install the TS licensing service; stop the service; copy the contents of your backed-up *LServer* directory into the new *LServer* directory; and start the service.

Change Management

In this final section, we'll discuss some best practices regarding change control in your environment. A good change control policy can prevent that late night call from a panicked IT manager. This is generally the call you get after the application guy had an immediate update he just *had* to put on the Terminal Servers ASAP. (Of course, he tested it on his laptop but not in a real test environment.)

If you're looking for a single golden nugget from the 50 bucks you spent on this book, here it is: it is crucial that your Terminal Servers be managed as tightly as possible.

When using Terminal Services, a simple change that causes a problem could affect hundreds or thousands of users depending on the size of the farm. So, regardless of whether you have two Terminal Servers or fifty, strict change control is a must. In this chapter we will discuss the following:

- Change management strategies
- Change management policy
- Change management processes

Unfortunately, your servers and the applications that reside on them are constantly in flux. Application developers and owners want upgrades to applications, security fixes need to be installed, service packs get released, hotfixes are a constant battle, and of course user requests for changes are de rigueur in every environment, requiring a strict change control policy.

The saying, "An ounce of prevention is worth a pound of cure" contains great truth concerning change control. Does the following situation sound familiar?

Admin1: There's a problem on Server 12 with IE.

Admin2: What's the problem?

Admin1: It crashes whenever you run it.

Admin2: Well what happened?

Admin1: I don't know, I figured I would ask you.

Admin2: Well I didn't change anything.

Admin1: Neither did I.

Admin2: Well someone sure did, 'cause now we have 100 helpdesk calls about IE not working and all those users have been on Server 12.

Of course, if these two administrators were the only ones with access to the servers (and if they were truthful with each other), then this dialogue might not occur. Often, even with just two administrators, verbal change control is not enough. A simple update to an application or the operating system could cause downtime on a mission-critical application.

The Basics of Change Management

Managing changes in your environment, from the initial build through deployment and future upgrades, does not have to be a complex task. Change management is really about testing changes, documenting changes, and having a way to back out of unsuccessful changes. If you can accomplish those three now then you have a basic change control plan.

Let's examine some specifics of change control for Terminal Server environments.

The Initial Build

The change control process begins with the initial build of your servers. You should create documentation showing how each server (or the server image) was built and any late additions or modifications made to the build.

It's rare for your server's first build to be the one that is put into production. In most cases, issues will crop up during testing that will cause changes to your server build process. Each of these changes should be documented and logged as additions to the base build document. In this manner you create a repeatable process for building an identical server, and you have the ability to backtrack and back out changes as they are made.

If you're using imaging for server deployment, it's generally a good idea to store checkpoint images along the way. Read through the following procedure to understand how a "check point" imaging process works.

1. Install the operating system.
2. Install any service packs.
3. Install any hot fixes.
4. Prepare the operating system for imaging (using sysprep, etc.).
5. Take image of server. (This will be Image 1.)

6. Update the operating system application components needed (i.e. MDAC, Oracle client, etc.).
7. Install third-party software for Terminal Server (such as Citrix MetaFrame or Tarantella Canaveral iQ).
8. Tweak the operating system performance settings.
9. Prepare the operating system and third-party software for imaging.
10. Take an image (Image 2)
11. If you're planning to deploy your servers with all applications installed, install your applications.
12. Verify that all applications function properly.
13. Prepare the server for imaging.
14. Take an image (Image 3).

This process affords you three server images, and the option to revert back to a prior image should problems arise. Each image serves a specific purpose:

- *Image 1* gives you a base operating system (fully updated and patched) for any purpose. This image acts as a checkpoint prior to the installation of any third-party software and can be used as a base build if the third-party software is updated. If you don't have this image, you'll have to build a new image from scratch next time there is a software update.
- *Image 2* gives you a base image that can be used across all your servers, clusters and silos. While this image has no applications on it, it's ready for production. If you deploy your applications via script or some other automated process, then this image will be your base server build. If not, then this image gives you a clean build with no applications for use in creating different cluster images without having to hand-build each one.
- *Image 3* is your production image used to deploy servers into your cluster.

Remember that you should be logging all the changes that are made to any of the builds. This change log should be created whenever a new build is created or a new cluster is deployed. It can be as simple as a spreadsheet with the changes entered linearly or as complex as a dedicated change management database. Either way, the end result is that everything in the image and every single change has been documented for the entire life of the server.

Post Rollout

In many ways, a good change management system really starts to shine after your servers are deployed. Ideally, you'll be able to log changes to production servers and tie these changes back to your build process so that it incorporates the most recent changes. Figure 15.1 shows the typical lifecycle of a change control process.

Figure 15.1 The change management lifecycle

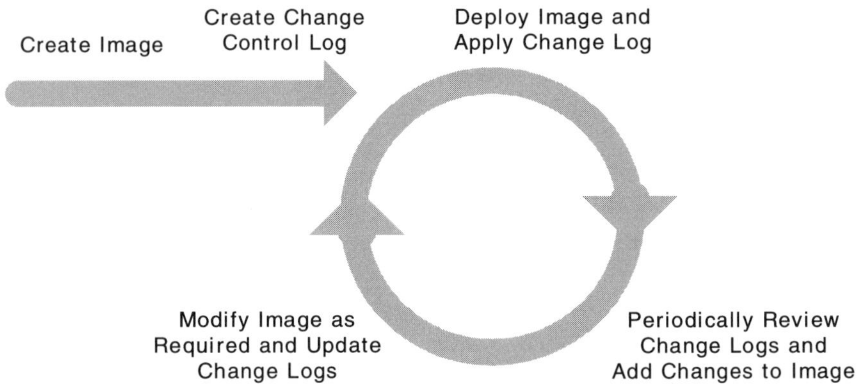

After the initial deployment, changes to the servers will be constant. The trick is to ensure that all servers are managed as one. When a change is made on one server in the group, all servers should receive the same change. Every change applied to production servers should be documented in the change log so you could build a new server identical to your production servers.

Periodically review your change logs and add all of the changes into your image to keep the number of changes required post build to a minimum and make it simpler to build a server.

A Change Management Policy

In addition to creating your change log and change control process, you should create a change management policy documenting the procedures around any change that might occur in your Terminal Server environment.

Implement the policy with all changes—be they as "insignificant" as updating a single DLL or INI file, or as major as a service pack or operating system update.

The policy should provide for the following:

- Definitions of development, testing, and production environments.
- Lists of who has access to each environment.
- Definition of the standard change control cycle.
- Procedures for requesting a change.
- Service Level Agreements (SLAs) for different types of changes.
- Identification of those individuals who can sign off on a change in each environment.
- Procedures for emergency changes.
- Procedures for logging changes as they progress through the cycle.

These items describe a general change control policy. Your specific applications or hardware might demand a more specific policy. Let's focus on each component of the change management policy.

Development, Testing, and Production Environments

If you're serious about building a stable Terminal Server environment, you'll ideally create three identical, yet separate, environments:

- A development environment to be used for initial testing of changes.
- A user acceptance testing environment, to be used for final testing before moving into production.
- A production environment that incorporates the changes that have successfully moved through the other environments. These are the servers that users will access on a daily basis.

In some small deployments, building three environments is simply not possible due to the cost of extra servers and licensing. If this describes your situation, you should still build two environments (development and production). If necessary, a workstation-class machine for your development environment is better than nothing.

Development Environment

In the development environment your team is able to test new changes, determine the affects of these on the servers, and test and decide on a deployment strategy for the change. This environment can also be used for simple baselining of new applications and applications upgrades, testing new service packs and hotfixes, and testing new scripts.

In larger environments, developers can also be given access to the development environment in order to develop and test any application upgrades or changes.

As anyone with experience in the industry knows, developers have a nasty habit of "writing and flying," throwing some code out on production servers then going on vacation for three weeks while you troubleshoot problems. (To be fair, developers feel that we systems engineers do nothing but hamper their creativity with all our pesky change management.) By giving the developers an environment in which to run tests, and by limiting their access rights to other areas, you can (theoretically) protect yourself from the "write and fly" problem.

It's good practice to design the development environment to be completely independent from the production servers. The idea is that this "dev" environment is an exact replica of the production environment (only smaller). Any change made in the development environment *should* affect the development servers in the same way that it would affect the production servers. The servers from both environments should be built using the same image and have the same updates and changes performed on them. The result is a real test environment that can accurately demonstrate how changes will affect production users before promoting them into the production environment.

Proposed changes are generally approved by the necessary people before being promoted into the next change control phase—the user acceptance and testing environment.

User Acceptance Testing Environment

In the user acceptance testing (UAT) environment, real end users test the functionality of the applications. These testers should be diverse in their job functions to achieve a good representation of how the applications will used in the production environment. Think of this as an ongoing pilot.

By monitoring the changes in this testing environment, you can find problems that were missed in the cursory testing of the development environment.

Production Environment

As its name implies, the production environment contains the servers that are used for the day-to-day operations of your Terminal Server systems. You should be *extremely* protective about any changes to this environment. Once a system is running smoothly in the production environment, the last thing you want is to be forced to pull an all-nighter rebuilding servers from some botched application upgrade.

Even if your production environment is home to many applications and configurations, each server is only part of one silo and therefore only has one image that applies to it. Remember that even if you don't use automated imaging software to deploy your servers, all servers that are in the same silo should have the same "image" in the sense that they are all identical. Any change made to one server should be made to all servers. (Of course, any change made to these production servers previously endured exhaustive testing as outlined in this change management process.)

Who has access to each of these Environments?

As innocent as the question may sound, deciding who has access to each of the three change management environments is critical. A more accurate phrasing of this question is, "Who *needs* access to each environment and what level of access do they need?"

For the sake of simplicity, let's divide access to a Terminal Server into two groups: administrator-level access and user-level access. Individuals with administrative-level access can install applications, make configuration changes, and essentially do whatever they want to a server. Those with user-level access have the ability to connect to and run applications on Terminal Servers but cannot install applications or modify permissions.

Figure 15.2 illustrates how companies typically allocate access to their employees.

Figure 15.2 Typical users and their permissions

Environment	Administrative Access	User Access
Development	Administrators, Application Developers, Application packagers	Test Users
User Acceptance Testing	Administrators	Production Users, Application Developers, Application packagers
Production	Administrators	Production Users, Application Developers, Application packagers

This security configuration protects your environment while allowing you to truly replicate the production servers. When a change leaves the development environment, it should be ready to work in production. If not, the change should be rolled back into development for further development. By isolating the developers and packagers in the testing environment, you discourage the "little tweaks" made by the coders that fail to replicate the true change.

The Change Control Cycle

Your change control policy will ultimately provide a cycle that repeats as changes are required to your Terminal Servers. Although the exact cycle will vary from company to company, Figure 15.3 outlines the basic flow of the steps.

Figure 15.3 The complete change control cycle

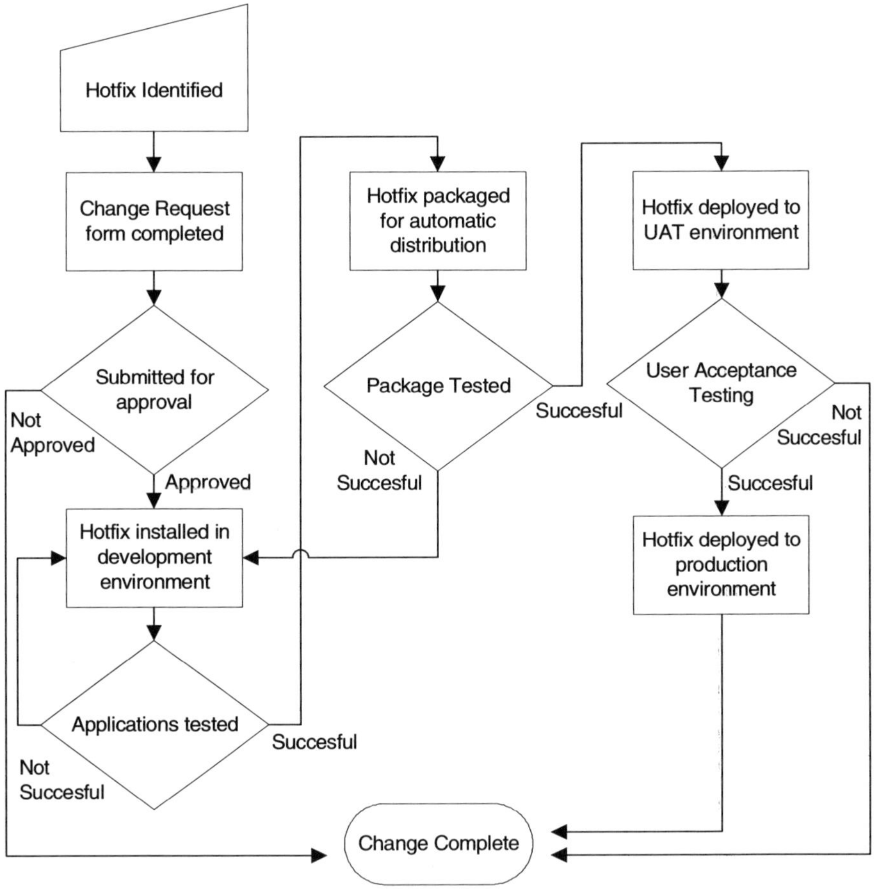

As the flow chart depicts, success points throughout the process ensure that the overall process will be successful. Any problems introduced by the change can be rolled back into development for further testing. Trying to fix a problem in the production environment does nothing more than introduce changes to the system that might not be necessary.

Procedures for Requesting a Change

As a Terminal Server administrator, requests for change most likely come to you every day. (Of course, most of these are not official requests and therefore do not get treated as such.)

In an ideal environment, each change request should be documented, providing an audit trail for why each change was made, when it was requested, who requested it, and its impact on the business.

In general, changes will come from application owners or managers within the business, but there will also be change requests from within the IT staff (such as a new service pack or hotfix). In either case, the change should follow the official change management cycle.

As an administrator, it's in your best interest to see only change requests that are based upon legitimate business purposes. (You can't always control this, but that doesn't mean that it's not in your best interest.)

The Change Request

For the most part, completing a change request is a split effort between the IT staff and the person requesting the change. The requestor specifies some basic information about the change and the IT staff fills in the rest of the blanks. (A sample change request is on the following page.)

In this change request (like many), only the basic information about what needs to be changed and why is supplied by the requester. It is up to the IT staff to elaborate about how the change will be implemented and tested. This information can then be given to the IT manager or business managers for approval.

Service Level Agreements for Change

A simple service level agreement (SLA) addressing change requests is required in all environments. An SLA will define the minimum or maximum amount of time it will take a change to be tested and deployed into the production environment. The SLA definition will usually not include the process of requesting or approving the change, rather, it will identify how long it should take to get the change into production. The timeframe associated with a change is usually dependent on the priority level of the change request.

The necessity of defining a change request SLA is appreciated by those who have ever encountered the following scenario:

CHANGE REQUEST

To: Terminal Server Admin Team

From: Susie Doe (Office Application Owner)

Date: November 26, 2003

Subject: Tier I – Office XP service pack update

Level of Request: Level II

Request Number: 119

Description

Service Pack 1 for Office XP has been released and is currently being rolled out to the desktops. The current version of Office on the Terminal Server farm needs to be updated to this new service pack in keeping with our Office standards.

Potential Impact on Environment

The Service Pack could cause problems with other applications dependent on Office. A back-out plan for this upgrade should be designed. Existing applications that have Office dependencies may not support this upgrade. Vendors should be contacted and applications should be retested prior in the test environment prior to deployment.

Approach

The IT staff will complete integration testing for the service pack on one Tier1 server in the test environment. The Packaging team will then test the automated distribution of the package to the Dev and UAT servers. Once the change has been validated and no problems exist in Dev and UAT, the change will be deployed to production. The IT staff will continue to monitor the environment to ensure that no problems arise after this service pack has been applied.

Estimated Effort

This change will take approximately one week to complete testing and deployment. Required resources to facilitate this effort are one engineer to test and deploy the update.

Test Plan

1. Review all available technical documentation for the update.
2. Plan and architect integration of the update into the existing environment.
3. Document installation procedures. Modify when necessary to stay within best practices for the server farm and supported application environment.
4. Apply the upgrade to the dev environment on one test Tier 1 server.
5. Test for connectivity and usability, making sure to re-test existing applications in the environment.
6. Document all processes.
7. Coordinate user acceptance testing to functionally test the update in the UAT environment to ensure that no issues exist. Obtain user signoff once complete.
8. Install update to the production environment during the weekend so as to ensure no user disruption. To ensure redundancy while this is taking place, install the update on one server at a time.
9. Coordinate a final production signoff to ensure that all functionality still operates properly. Obtain user signoff once complete.

Turnover Process

The turnover date for production is estimated for December 2, 2003. Turn over SOP information and documentation to Operations Staff.

Friday 2:45pm: "Hey, Joe. I need you to drop this update on the servers today... Yeah, I promised the staff I would have it updated by this weekend but it has taken me longer to put it together than I thought. We REALLY have to have this. Have a good weekend!"

Of course most peoples' first inclination is to help the guy out. The problem arises when you realize that since this is Friday afternoon, no real testing of the change won't happen before the weekend. Slapping this untested change on the servers could cause you and your users a lot of grief on Monday morning if something else is broken by the change.

To prevent this, having a documented SLA in place could allow you to fall back on it and say, "Sorry, our change control SLA states five days minimum for testing. We can't do anything until we run it all through the process." Saying this might not win you any friends, but at least you won't be working over the weekend.

Change Control Cycle Approval

Each environment serves a different purpose and is used by different people. In order for a change to move between the development, testing, and production environments, someone has to verify that testing was successful in the previous environment before the change is rolled into the next.

If we look at a simple scheme of what goes on in each environment, we can easily correlate who should determine at each stage whether the change was successful and caused no other problems.

Development Approval

The development environment is generally used for testing new code and other changes. Applications are reviewed for functionality and are regression tested. The change is also tested to determine if it will have an effect on performance.

In this environment, it is generally the administration team or an IT manager that signs off on the change. They review the testing results, then authorize that the application be promoted into UAT.

User Acceptance Testing Approval

In the UAT environment, current applications and builds are combined with new changes to simulate the production environment. More IT staff testing may happen here, but the idea is that actual users use the system as they would on a daily basis.

Users will report any problems in this testing environment. Their sessions should be monitored closely for both performance-related issues that could negatively impact the production environment and for any problems caused in other applications. Once the users find there are no problems with the system, the change request can be handed-off to the IT manager (or other approver).

Production Approval

Once the change has been implemented in the production environment, it should still be monitored for any problems not found in the first two environments. In theory, proper testing and movement through the change control cycle should prevent a "bad" change from getting into production, however, it does happen and should be something that you're prepared for. (The most frequent cause of bad changes making it into production is when non-identical hardware is used in the production and testing environments.)

Emergency Changes

In the real world there are always emergencies. Your change control policy and SLAs will have to allow for emergency changes to be implemented. Consider the following two scenarios:

- A new Microsoft security bulletin was just issued. It describes a vulnerability of Terminal Servers to denial of service attacks. You realize that you have ten Terminal Servers accessible by the Internet and need to apply this fix right away.
- You have been experiencing a consistent blue screen of death on two of your servers. You finally receive the information from Microsoft on what is causing it and how to fix it. This fix requires a driver update in the form of a hotfix which needs to be applied to get your users working again.

In both of these cases the changes need to be implemented as soon as possible. Your users (and management) cannot sit around for a week or two while you test the change. In situations like this, most companies opt to apply the change to the production environment after receiving sign off on the development environment—completely bypassing the testing environment.

Sign off for the implementation of the emergency change usually comes from someone higher up in the company than would be required for a standard change. In most cases, the IT staff requiring the change submits an emergency change control request. The person signing off on the request generally reviews the facts, the possible impact of the change, and the existing problem, and then determines whether an emergency change is best for the business. In some cases, the approver may reject the "emergency" status of the change, instead opting for the standard change control process.

When facing an emergency change, the testing process is usually shortened. Emergency changes are (at minimum) tested in the development environment to ensure that the change installs properly and causes no immediate issues. Then, the "back out" plan is tested (i.e. performing an uninstall of a hotfix). Once these two tests are completed successfully, the testing team can obtain sign off and implement the change in the production environment.

The reality that an emergency change could become necessary at any time underscores the importance maintaining a development environment that is identical to your production environment, both in terms of hardware and software.

Though emergency changes follow their own shortened change process, it's still important that they are documented properly order to maintain an identical build across all three environments and modify your image for future server deployments.

The Change Log

A change log should be created that documents all change requests, technical information about a change, and dates and times that changes were deployed to various servers. It should contain enough information about each change and how it was implemented so that a change can be reversed or replicated in the future.

While there are some very nice change control applications for Windows, a simple spreadsheet will also suffice in most cases.

The log sheet is useful in that you can reference changes quickly. Such sheets can be created per server, per-cluster, or for the entire environment. The larger the environment, the more granular the change logs should be.

In Figure 15.4 (next page) you'll notice that each entry has a "Change Document" reference. This slot should be used to reference external documents pertaining to the change, including the change request with signoffs and the detailed technical procedure that was used to implement the change.

Figure 15.4 A sample change control log entries

Date: Dec 12, 2003

Requestor: Brian Madden

Signed Off By: Holli Madden

Change Description: Install Windows SP4 on all servers

Affected Servers: ALL

Affected Users: ALL

Change Document: DOC ID 1247

Date: Dec 14, 2003

Requestor: Ron Oglesby

Signed Off By: Ron Oglesby

Change Description: Disable auto-created Client printers since AA users are confused by number of printers they are seeing. This was done at the connection level.

Affected Servers: chictx01 – chictx05

Affected Users: AA users

Change Document: DOC ID 1252

Terminal Server 2003 is a robust platform on which to deploy applications. However, as with many Microsoft products, there are situations in which you might want to extend the base capabilities. Several third party vendors offer middleware components and utilities for Terminal Server that help increase the reach of the product.

Two companies offer end-to-end server-based computing solutions: Citrix and Tarantella. Citrix MetaFrame and Tarantella New Moon Canaveral iQ are products that install on top of Terminal Server and offer advanced load-management, security, client options, and administrative tools. While this book won't go into the details of these two products, we will provide you with a solid foundation of knowledge that you can use to determine if your environment's requirements can be met with pure Terminal Services or if a third-party solution is required. A comparison of third party products and Terminal Server can be found in the appendix.)

Furthermore, there are dozens and dozens of specialty software products designed specifically for server-based computing environments. From security to printing to performance enhancement to management, these products can simplify your life as a Terminal Server administrator. Rather than focusing on all these products at once, this book mentions relevant third-party products as they are relevant, and includes a full list of third-party products and vendor websites in the appendix. (You may always refer to `www.brianmadden.com` for a current list of third party products and vendors.)

Appendixes & Index

Server Based Computing Software Product Comparison

Terminal Server 2003 Big Feature Chart

Links Mentioned in this Book

Index

A. Third Party Server-Based Computing Product Comparison

We mentioned several third party server-based computing products in this book, and we alluded to some of their advanced features. In this section, we'll look at the "add-on" products that extend the Terminal Services functionality of Windows Server 2003.

Since the vendors' products and capabilities tend to change, you can download an up-to-date version of this section from `www.brianmadden.com`.

The Contenders

This section compares the following products:

- Microsoft Windows Server 2003 Terminal Services
- Citrix MetaFrame XP Presentation Server 1.0 with Feature Release 3
- Jetro CockpIT / BoostIT 3.0
- Tarantella New Moon Canaveral iQ 2.0
- DAT Panther Server 2002

Before we get into the side-by-side comparison of all the products, let's take a quick look at an overview of each one.

Terminal Services for Microsoft Windows Server 2003

What's interesting about Terminal Server (in this case) is that it's an absolute requirement if you want to use any of these third party products. Your real decision is whether you want to use Terminal Server by itself or whether you want to use a third-party product in addition to Terminal Server.

Terminal Server has come a long way since Microsoft released the first version of it in 1998. From a pure protocol standpoint, Terminal Server's RDP protocol is just as good as Citrix's ICA protocol. They both support virtually any client platform, and they both support access to all local client resources (ports, printers, audio, and the clipboard). Additionally, the new version of RDP supports 24-bit color and very high resolutions.

This protocol equality does not mean that there is no longer a need for third-party products, however. It just means that there are other things you must look for when deciding which products are best for your server-based computing solution.

For example, Terminal Server still has some major weaknesses, including:

- Load-balancing is limited to 32-nodes. Furthermore, the load-balancing algorithm is based on network traffic--not user or processor load.
- Applications cannot be accessed "seamlessly." This is not a problem if you only plan to run full remote desktops, but the integration of local and remote applications is not that great.
- Users must access a server to access an application. For example, third-party software allows a user to request an application by name (i.e. "Excel"). Terminal Server requires that an administrator manually set up shortcuts to each application. Again, this is less of a problem if the server is to be used exclusively for remote desktop access instead of remote application access.

The bottom line with Terminal Server is that it can stand on its own in smaller environments where users will be accessing full remote desktops, but it cries out for third-party tools in larger and more complex environments.

Citrix MetaFrame

Citrix is the company that essentially invented modern day Microsoft Windows server-based computing. MetaFrame XP offers dozens of features, including the all-important application load-balancing, application publishing with seamless windows, and a web interface user portal.

In addition to the core features of MetaFrame, the license fee includes rights to use applications such as "Citrix Secure Gateway" (CSG). CSG lets you funnel all of your users, completely encrypted, through a single port on a single IP address. Think about it. With Citrix, you can provide secure remote access to thousands of remote users over a single IP address/port combination.

While not included with the core product, Citrix also offers a number additional products that further extend MetaFrame's capabilities. Example include MetaFrame Conferencing Manager (a product that enables real-time application sharing and collaboration between users anywhere in the world) and MetaFrame Secure Access Manager (which provides secure and personalized information via a web portal).

The downside to Citrix is their price. While Citrix MetaFrame clearly offers the most features and capabilities, it is also the most expensive, with per-user MSRP prices starting at almost $100 more than the next most-expensive competitor.

Jetro CockpIT / BoostIT

Jetro Platforms' current server-based computing product is CockpIT 3.0. Jetro does not view themselves as a direct competitor to Citrix, Microsoft, or Tarantella. Instead, they focus on creating a "management platform" that allows you to manage your existing environments whether they're Terminal Servers, Citrix MetaFrame servers, or a combination of both.

Jetro uses its own client software that contacts a Jetro server which maintains application lists, server load, user policies, and permissions. Once it determines which server a user should connect to, the Jetro client passes the connection information to the user's standard RDP or ICA client, and the session is launched.

Jetro sells two products: CockpIT and BoostIT. These products are technically 100% identical, with the only difference being how they are licensed. CockpIT adds all of Jetro's capabilities to Terminal Server and RDP environments. BoostIT supports ICA sessions in addition to RDP. Now, here's where it gets interesting. BoostIT is much cheaper than CockpIT. That's right. The product that supports RDP and ICA is much cheaper ($40 per user) than the product that supports RDP only ($160 per user). Jetro's reasoning behind this is that if you need the ICA version, you've already spent enough money on thin client computing licenses, so they give you a break. (Think of it as a "competitive upgrade.") The catch, of course, is that you have to have previously bought a Citrix ICA license for each BoostIT license that you buy, and they require proof of this upon ordering.

Jetro adds some impressive features onto native Terminal Server. In addition to the now "standard" third-party offerings of seamless windows, application publishing, a slick web interface for application access, and application level load-balancing, Jetro's products also allow you to seamlessly publish and manage applications to users regardless of whether they access them via ICA or RDP.

Tarantella New Moon Canaveral iQ

Canaveral iQ 2.0 is the latest iteration of the Canaveral iQ server series from Tarantella / New Moon. Tarantella's focus is to bring to the market a less expensive alternative to MetaFrame. Canaveral iQ maintains about 80% of the functionality of MetaFrame for about 40% of the price.

Canaveral iQ can run on Windows Terminal Server 4.0, Windows 2000, or Windows 2003. Canaveral has all the "major" features of a third-party application server, including application publishing, seamless windows, a web interface, and application-level load-balancing.

Load balancing is accomplished independent of Windows through the use of the Canaveral Load Balancer. This operates in much the same way as the Citrix Load Manager to achieve a load-balanced environment. This fact alone can save a company several thousand dollars in a farm with several servers when compared to using pure Terminal Server since Canaveral load-balancing doesn't require the Enterprise Edition of Windows 2003.

One of the features of Canaveral iQ that sets it apart from the rest of the pack is the ability to publish applications to specific terminals or groups of terminals, rather than simply to users and groups. This is very beneficial in a kiosk or shop floor environment, where terminals have one, dedicated purpose.

Tarantella is one of the few companies that officially licensed Microsoft's RDP technology, and therefore they provide their own version of Microsoft's Terminal Services Advanced Client (TSAC). While using the RDP protocol at its core, the Canaveral client also provides access to additional services like seamless windows and the web interface. Tarantella offers Canaveral clients for 32-bit Windows and Windows CE, and a Java client is in currently in beta testing for use on Linux and Macintosh platforms.

The feature set of Canaveral iQ, albeit less robust than MetaFrame, is significantly more robust than Windows Terminal Services. Tarantella has succeeded in adding the most used features of Citrix MetaFrame to Windows Terminal Services and has made their product available at a fraction of the cost of MetaFrame.

DAT Panther Server

The DAT Group is a large UK-based Microsoft partner that is primarily known for their customized mobile applications. DAT Panther Server 2002 adds some basic functionality on top of Terminal Server. Leveraging the RDP protocol, Panther adds seamless windows, application publishing, and application-level load balancing to Terminal Server environments.

While it lacks a web application interface and some of the other features of the competing software packages, DAT Panther adds basic functionality to Terminal Server for a reasonable cost.

Server-Based Computing Software Feature Comparison

In addition the basic information about each vendor's offerings, this chart provides a side-by-side comparison of the features and capabilities of each product.

Key

- ● The full circle indicates that the feature is explicitly part of this product.
- ○ The empty circle is for the products that run on top of Terminal Server that inherit this functionality from Terminal Server.

Basic Product Information	TS2003	Citrix	Jetro	New Moon	DAT
min. Terminal Server version required	n/a	2000	2000	NT4	2000
Remote Session Protocol	RDP	ICA	Both	RDP	RDP
Cost per user (US$)(3)	Base	$250-350	$40-160	$199 or 103	$150
Maintenance cost per user / per year		$40-50	1yr Free $16 after	1yr Free 5% after	Free/ $25
License Type (concurrent or named user)	Either	Conc.	Conc.	Either	Conc.
Major Features	**TS2003**	**Citrix**	**Jetro**	**New Moon**	**DAT**
Application Publishing		●	●	●	●
Seamless Windows		●	●	●	●
Application Load Balancing		XPa	●	●	●
Web Application Interface		●	●	●	
Other Features					
Content Publishing		●	●	●	●
Content Redirection		●	●	●	
Publish applications to specific workstations				●	
Connect to single application (instead of a full desktop)	●	●	●	●	●
Print driver mapping	●	●	○	○	○
Print driver replication	●	●	○	○	○
Universal Printing		●	●	●	
Server load-balancing	●	XPa	●	●	●
Server availability scheduling		●	●		
Session Shadowing	●	●	●	○	○
Client Features	**TS2003**	**Citrix**	**Jetro**	**New Moon**	**DAT**
Web-based client install	●	●	●	●	
Auto client update (7)		●	●	●	
Local Drive Access	●	●	○	○	○
Local Printer Access	●	●	○	○	○
Local / Remote Clipboard	●	●	○	○	○

Mapping					
Local COM/LPT Port Access	●	●	○	○	○
Audio Mapping	●	●	○	○	○
Client Desktop Integration		●	●	●	●
Has it's own client	●	●	●	●	●
24-bit color, high resolution	●	●	○	○	○
Client multi-monitor support		●	●		
Client Platforms	**TS2003**	**Citrix**	**Jetro**	**New Moon**	**DAT**
32-bit Windows	●	●	●	●	●
16-bit Windows	●	●			
DOS	●	●			
Macintosh	●	●			
Linux/Unix	●	●			
Java	●	●			
Windows CE / PocketPC	●	●	●	●	●
Security Features	**TS2003**	**Citrix**	**Jetro**	**New Moon**	**DAT**
SSL Encryption	●	●		●	
TLS Encryption	●	●	○	●	○
Proxy Support	●	●	○	○	○
SSL Gateway Support		●		●	
Pass-through authentication		●		●	
Protocols (TCP/IP, IPX/SPX, NetBEUI)	TCP/IP	All	TCP/IP	TCP/IP	TCP/IP
Management Features	**TS2003**	**Citrix**	**Jetro**	**New Moon**	**DAT**
Delegated administration	●	●	●	●	○
Remotely push server install			●	●	
User policies	●	●	●	○	○
Centralized Mgmt Console		●			
Clone Server				●	●
System Monitoring	●	XPe			
Detailed Usage Reporting		XPe	●	●	●
Application packaging & delivery		XPe			
Full Active Directory Integration	●		●	●	○

B. Big Feature Chart

Several of Terminal Server 2003's features can be configured in multiple locations. This chart shows which features can be configured at which levels.

	User Account	GPO (Computer)	GPO (User)	Client	Connection	Server
Profile Path	●	●				
Home Folder	●	●				
Allow Login to Termina Server	●					
Enable Remote Control	●	●	●		●	
Remote Control Levels	●	●	●		●	
Start Program at Logon	●	●	●	●	●	
Connect Drives	●	●		●	●	
Connect Printers	●	●		●	●	
Default to Main Printer	●	●			●	
End a Disconnected Session	●	●	●		●	
Active Session Limit	●	●	●		●	
Idle Session Limit	●	●	●		●	
Session Limit Action Taken	●	●	●		●	
Allow from any client	●	●	●		●	
Keep Alive Connections		●				
Automatic Reconnection		●				●
Restrict Users to Single Session		●				●
Enforce Removal of Wallpaper		●		●		
Deny Console Admin Logoff		●				
Number of Connections		●			●	
Limit Color Depth		●		●	●	
Resolution		●		●		

	User Account	GPO (Computer)	GPO (User)	Client	Connection	Server
Enable TS		●				
Local admins may customize permissions		●				
Remove Windows Security from Menu		●				
Time Zone		●				
Clipboard		●			●	
Smart Card		●				
Audio		●		●	●	
COM		●		●	●	
LPT		●			●	
Windows Key Combinations				●		
Always prompt for password		●			●	
RDP Encryption level		●			●	
Authentication type					●	
Generic Logon					●	
Licensing Server Security Group		●				
Prevent License Upgrade		●				
"Per session" temp folders		●				●
Delete temp folders on exit		●				●
Session Directory		●				●
IP Address Redirection		●				●
SD Server		●				●
SD Cluster Name		●				●
SD IP Address						●
Show contents while dragging				●		
Menu and Windows animation				●		
Themes				●		
Cache Bitmaps				●		
Licensing Mode						●
Disable Active Desktop						●
Permission Compatibility						●

C. Links Mentioned in this Book

Resource Websites
www.brianmadden.com
ron.oglesby.com
thethin.net
www.dabcc.com
www.printingsupport.com
www.tokeshi.com

RDP Client Software
www.rdesktop.org
www.terminal-services.net
www.hobsoft.com
www.ddhsoftware.com

Performance Utilities
www.microsoft.com/whdc/ddk/ debugging
www.appsense.com
www.aurema.com
www.respowerfuse.com
www.rtosoft.com
www.tamedos.com
www.tmurgent.com/TMuLimit.htm
threadmaster.tripod.com

Printing Software
www.thinprint.com
www.tricerat.com
www.uniprint.net
www.go-eol.com

Security Software
www.securecomputing.com
www.rsa.com
www.saflink.com

Utilities
www.oneapp.co.uk
www.symantec.com
www.storagesoft.com
www.sysinternals.com
www.netiq.com
www.lakesidesoftware.com
www.hiddensoft.com/AutoIt
www.winbatch.com
www.wintask.com
www.scapatech.com
www.mercuryinteractive.com
www.logincosultants.nl
www.kixtart.org
www.microsoft.com/licensing
www.softricity.com

Bandwidth Shaping Hardware
www.packeteer.com
www.sitaranetworks.com
www.allot.com

Index